Emma Ruth Grenville Gee

Corfu

Cain

CW00850598

Ovid's Causes

Ovid's Causes

Cosmogony and Aetiology in the *Metamorphoses*

K. Sara Myers

Ann Arbor

THE UNIVERSITY OF MICHIGAN PRESS

Copyright © by the University of Michigan 1994
All rights reserved
Published in the United States of America by
The University of Michigan Press
Manufactured in the United States of America
♾ Printed on acid-free paper

1997   1996   1995   1994   4   3   2   1

A CIP catalogue record for this book is available from the British Library.

Library of Congress Cataloging-in-Publication Data

Myers, K. Sara, 1961–
    Ovid's causes : cosmogony and aetiology in the Metamorphoses / K.
Sara Myers.
        p.   cm.
    Includes bibliographical references (p.   ) and index.
    ISBN 0-472-10459-4 (acid-free paper)
    1. Ovid, 43 B.C.–17 or 18 A.D. Metamorphoses. 2. Mythology,
Classical, in literature. 3. Cosmology, Ancient, in literature.
4. Metamorphosis in literature. 5. Cosmogony in literature.
6. Causation in literature. I. Title.
PA6519.M9M94   1994
871′.01—dc20   94-18866
                                                                  CIP

For my parents and John

Preface

volet haec sub luce videri

—Hor. *Ars Poetica* 363

Ovid's proclaimed theme in the proem of the *Metamorphoses* is meta-morphosis: *mutatas . . . formas* (1.2).[1] His intention is to write a sort of universal history, a chronological survey of the metamorphosis theme from the origins of the world to the present: *primaque ab origine mundi / ad mea . . . tempora* (1.3–4). Although the chronological sequence will frequently be disrupted, Ovid suggests that the history of the world can be told through this theme; the way in which he accomplishes this is through the aetiological focus of his many mythological stories, which provide explanations for how things in the physical world have come about. While the aetiological character of many of Ovid's stories has long been recognized,[2] because the actual metamorphoses in the poem have largely been considered unimportant, the ramifications of Ovid's explanatory approach to myth have not been fully explored. The aetiological focus of the *Metamorphoses* is an essential feature of Ovid's narrative structure and discourse; more than simply a conceit, it shapes the way

---

1. The title of *Metamorphoses* attested for this poem: Seneca *Apo.* 9.5; Quintilian *I.O.* 4.1.77.

2. See G. Lafaye, *Les Métamorphoses d'Ovide et leurs modèles grecques* (Paris, 1904), 105, 188; M. de Cola, *Callimaco e Ovidio* (Palermo, 1937), 31; S. Jannacone, *La Letteratura Greco-Latina delle Metamorfosi* (Messina and Florence, 1953), 23; L.P. Wilkinson, *Ovid Recalled* (Cambridge, 1955), 154; L. Castiglioni, *Studi Intorno Alle Fonti e Alle Composizione delle Metamorfosi di Ovidio* (Rome, 1906), 10ff.; P. Brunel, *Le Mythe de la Métamorphose* (Paris, 1974), 55; E.J. Kenney, Introduction and Notes to *Ovid's Metamorphoses,* trans. A.D. Melville (Oxford, 1987), xxii; E.J. Bernbeck, *Beobachtungen zur Darstellungsart in Ovids Metamorphosen* (Munich, 1967), 105–6; J.F. Miller, "Callimachus and the Augustan Aetiological Elegy," *ANRW* 2.30.1 (1982): 396 n.103; P.E. Knox, *Ovid's Metamorphoses and the Traditions of Augustan Poetry* (Cambridge, 1986), 65–83; G.O. Hutchinson, *Hellenistic Poetry* (Oxford, 1988), 340, 342; G. Tissol, "Narrative Style in Ovid's *Metamorphoses* and the Influence of Callimachus," Ph. D. diss., (University of California at Berkeley, 1988).

Ovid treats much of his mythical material and constitutes an important aspect of his generic and thematic aims in the poem.[3]

Many of the stories in the *Metamorphoses* are aetiological in focus in that they purport to explain the origin of some natural or cultural object. Most, but not all, of these *aetia* are embodied in a metamorphosis. For the most part Ovid's Greek myths in the poem do not provide the traditional explanations for religious and social institutions, but instead explain natural phenomena. Fritz Graf has usefully labeled this new aetiology "métamorphose physique."[4] These metamorphoses will form the subject of chapter 1, where we will look closely at the way in which Ovid's language in his aetiological descriptions of metamorphosis connects his mythical stories with natural philosophical themes. We can divide the *aetia* in the *Metamorphoses* into roughly two categories, natural and cultural. Among these we can further distinguish six types: in the first category, animal, phenomenological, and geographical (although this final type can sometimes also be placed under cultural); in the second category, religious, foundation legends (historical), and mythological. Natural *aetia* include the numerous transformations of people into animals that explain the creation and characteristics of various species, as well as natural phenomena such as dew (13.621), thunder, lightning, and earthquakes (6.690–99). Mythological *aetia* include explanations for the origin of Pan's pipe (1.705–12), Athena's aegis (4.802–3), the Sirens (5.551–63), and the Cornucopia (9.1–88). Mythical foundations of cities include Caunus in Caria (9.633–34), Miletus (9.443–49), and Croton (15.1ff.). Throughout the *Metamorphoses* there is a good deal of religious aetiology, the topic of Ovid's other large work, the *Fasti;* this includes the brief reference to the Pythian games (1.446–47), the Io-Isis identification (1.747), Libyan Ammon (5.325–28), the references to the Hyacinthia and Adonia which frame Orpheus' song in Book 10, and the numerous Roman religious themes in Books 14 and 15. In chapters 2 and 3 we will look at the way in which Ovid seems to highlight the Callimachean nature and antecedents of these cultural *aetia* by constructing narrative situations strikingly similar to Callimachus' own aetiological frame narratives. Under the category of geographical *aetia* are included the numerous transformations of humans into rocks that form geographical landmarks (e.g., Battus [2.676–707], Niobe [6.146–312], Scylla [14.70–74]), the origins of many streams and fountains (e.g., Hippocrene [5.256–63], Cyane [5.409–37],

---

3. For a description of aetiological myth see G.S. Kirk, "Aetiology, Ritual, Charter: Three Equivocal Terms in the Study of Myths," *YCS* 22 (1972): 83–102.

4. F. Graf, "Ovide, Les Métamorphoses et la Véracité du Mythe," in *Métamorphoses du Mythe en Grèce Antique,* ed. C. Calame (Geneva, 1988), 62.

Arethusa [5.572–641]), the mountains of Aetna (5.346) and Atlas (4.657), the Echinades islands (8.573–610), and the origins of the names of various places (Pithecusae [14.90], Icaria [8.234–35], Ardea [14.579–80]), as well as natural thaumasia (the golden stream of Pactolus [11.141–45], the Salmacis fountain [4.285–388]).

The aetiological treatment of myth exploits the inherent explanatory capability of mythology and becomes, as T.M. Klein has argued, "the literary equivalent for a scientific principle."[5] A recognition of Ovid's humorously "scientific" treatment of his mythical material is important both in considering the generic affiliations of this notoriously ambiguous epic and in evaluating Ovid's narrative persona in the poem. To take the latter point first, the aetiological treatment of myth is one of the ways in which Ovid's highly self-conscious narrative persona in the *Metamorphoses* insists on bringing to our attention issues of fiction and authentication in epic poetry. In terms of the genre, the *aetia* suggest that the poem should be read simultaneously as a cosmogonic epic in the tradition of the lofty "scientific" or cosmological epics of Hesiod and Lucretius and as learned Alexandrian poetry in the tradition of Callimachus' *Aetia*. Ultimately, I believe that this dual reading of the aetiological focus of the *Metamorphoses* may assist in making less blunt the dichotomies traditionally drawn, but increasingly challenged, between the reception of these two literary traditions in Rome.

The organization of this book takes its cue from the structure of the poem itself. In the first and last chapters, we will consider the way in which Ovid establishes a "scientific" framework for his mythical metamorphoses and the implications this has for understanding the poem as a response to the epic tradition of cosmological narrative. In chapters 2 and 3 we will consider the second tradition with which Ovid's aetiological myths share an affiliation: Callimachean and neoteric narrative. In these central chapters attention will be given to the way in which Ovid's narrative structures and techniques are especially indebted to these aetiological models. In the final chapter, as in *Metamorphoses* 15, the two traditions of *causae* are juxtaposed and the concerns and tensions of the poem as a whole are recapitulated, even if the poem ultimately does not allow them to be resolved.

---

5. T.M. Klein, "The Role of Callimachus in the Development of the Concept of the Countergenre," *Latomus* 33 (1974): 227.

Acknowledgments

I have benefited from the support of many people in the writing of this book. First of all, I want to thank Stephen Hinds. At every stage in the writing of this work he has offered me his penetrating criticism and unfailing encouragement. I also owe a great debt to Ted Courtney, teacher and advisor, who directed an earlier version of this study as a dissertation at Stanford University. It is a pleasure also to thank the many people who have read and improved this work at various stages: Gregson Davis, J.C. McKeown, Elaine Fantham, and David Potter. I am also grateful to J.F. Miller for his advice and his permission to quote from an earlier article in *CJ*. Friends, colleagues, and teachers at Oberlin College, Stanford University, and the University of Michigan offered and continue to offer support, advice, and diversion (thanks Martha, Kathy, Livia, Cliff, Amy, Mary, Jeri). I wish especially to thank James Rives and Cynthia Damon, unfailing friends, critics, and editors. I owe them more than I can say. The readers for the University of Michigan Press and my editor, Ellen Bauerle, have been extremely helpful and offered detailed comments that greatly improved this work. For the deficiencies which remain, I am fully responsible. My greatest debt is to my family, especially my parents and my husband, John Dillery. I cannot begin to express my thanks to them for their unstinting encouragement. Without their generous emotional support and their stimulating and inspiring company I could neither have begun nor completed this task. I dedicate this work to them with all my love and gratitude.

Contents

Abbreviations and Texts

Abbreviations of the names of classical authors and works follow or are more explicit than *The Oxford Classical Dictionary*. Titles of periodicals are abbreviated according to the system of *L'Année philologique*. Works of modern scholarship are cited by the author's name and abbreviated title when they are included in the bibliography. I quote for the most part from G.P. Goold's Loeb of *Ovid's Metamorphoses* (Cambridge, MA, 1977–84), and note every significant variation from W.S. Anderson's *Ovidius, Metamorphoses* (Leipzig, 1977). All quotations from the *Fasti* are from E.H. Alton, D.E.W. Wormell, and E. Courtney, eds., *Ovidius, Fasti* (Leipzig, 1978). The following abbreviations may be noted:

ANRW	H. Temporini. *Aufstieg und Niedergang der römischen Welt*. Berlin, 1972–.
Bömer, *Fast.*	F. Bömer, ed. *P. Ovidius Naso, Die Fasten*. 2 Vols. Wissenschaftliche Kommentare zu lateinischen und griechischen Schriftstellern. Heidelberg, 1957–58.
Bömer, *Met.*	———. *P. Ovidius Naso, Metamorphosen*. 7 Vols. Wissenschaftliche Kommentare zu lateinischen und griechischen Schriftstellern. Heidelberg, 1969–86.
Buechner	C. Buechner. *Fragmenta Poetarum Latinorum*. Leipzig, 1982.
Chantraine	P. Chantraine. *Dictionnaire étymologique de la langue grecque, histoire des mots*. Paris, 1968–80.
CIL	*Corpus Inscriptionum Latinarum*. Berlin, 1863–.

Degrassi	A. Degrassi. *Inscriptiones Italiae XIII.ii Fasti Anni Numani et Iuliani.* Rome, 1963.
Ernout-Meillet	A. Ernout and A. Meillet. *Dictionnaire étymologique de la langue latine, histoire des mots.* 4th ed. Paris, 1959.
FGrHist	F. Jacoby. *Die Fragmente der griechischen Historiker.* Berlin and Leiden, 1923–58.
FHG	C. Müller. *Fragmenta Historicorum Graecorum.* Berlin, 1841–70.
GRF	G. Funaioli. *Grammaticae Romanae Fragmenta.* Stuttgart, 1969.
Haupt-Ehwald	M. Haupt, R. Ehwald, and M. von Albrecht, eds. *P. Ovidius Naso, Metamorphosen.* Vol. 1, 10th ed. Vol. 2, 5th ed. Zurich and Dublin, 1966.
HRR	H. Peter. *Historicorum Romanorum Reliquiae.* 2 Vols. Stuttgart, 1967.
LSJ	H.J. Liddell and R. Scott, rev. H. Stuart Jones, eds. *A Greek-English Lexicon.* 9th ed. Oxford, 1925–40.
M-W	R. Merkelbach and M.L. West. *Fragmenta Hesiodea.* Oxford, 1967.
Morel	W. Morel. *Fragmenta Poetarum Latinorum.* Leipzig, 1927.
OCD[2]	*Oxford Classical Dictionary.* 2d ed. Oxford, 1970.
OLD	*Oxford Latin Dictionary.* Oxford, 1968–82.
Platner-Ashby	S.B. Platner, rev. T. Ashby. *A Topographical Dictionary of Ancient Rome.* Oxford, 1929.
Powell	J.U. Powell. *Collectanea Alexandrina.* Oxford, 1925.
RE	*Real-Encyclopädie der classischen Altertumswissenschaft.* Stuttgart, 1893–1978.
Roscher	W.H. Roscher. *Ausführliches Lexicon der griechischen und römischen Mythologie.* Leipzig, 1884–1937.
SH	H. Lloyd-Jones and P.J. Parsons, eds. *Supplementum Hellenisticum.* Berlin and New York, 1983.
TLL	*Thesaurus Linguae Latinae.* Leipzig, 1900–.
Westermann	A. Westermann. *Paradoxographoi Graeci.* Braunswieg, 1839. Reprint. Amsterdam, 1963.

The Generic Question: Cosmogonic and Callimachean Aetiology

Est autem heroicum quod constat
ex divinis humanisque personis
continens vera cum fictis.

—Servius *ad Aen.* 1.11

The opening lines of the *Metamorphoses* govern the reader's expectations as to the scope and nature of this unique epic. In this notoriously short proem, Ovid announces his new theme and meter in four compact and extremely complex lines:

In nova fert animus mutatas dicere formas
corpora; di, coeptis (nam vos mutastis et illa)[1]
adspirate meis primaque ab origine mundi
ad mea perpetuum deducite tempora carmen.

(1.1–4)

[My spirit leads me to tell of shapes changed into new
bodies; gods, breathe favorably on my beginnings
(for you have changed even them) and bring down
my poem uninterrupted from the first origin of the
world to my own times.]

---

1. The manuscripts have *illas.* R.J. Tarrant, "Editing Ovid's *Metamorphoses:* Problems and Possibilities," *CP* 77 (1982): 350–51, points out, however, that *illa* is not a modern conjecture (Anderson attributes it to Lejay), but a medieval variant, appearing in e and U[3]. Tarrant (351 n.35) also draws attention to "the fact that the words *nam vos mutastis et illa* coming at the end of the second line, mark the point at which the meter reveals itself as hexameters rather than elegiacs." E.J. Kenney, "*Ovidius Prooemians,*" *PCPS* 22 (1976): 46–53, provides a convincing defense of *illa.* See now also Knox, *Traditions of Augustan Poetry,* 9; D. Kovacs, "Ovid *Metamorphoses* 1.2," *CQ* n.s. 37 (1988): 458–65.

As Gian Biagio Conte has commented, "The opening is the place where all the signals point to the originality of the work or to its position within literary production. . . . It classifies the genre so that the new text enters the literary system as a literary work, as though by hereditary right."[2] The generic signals in this brief opening have been understood as being far from straightforward. What would a contemporary reader of the poem have expected from these opening lines? At issue are both Ovid's choice of programmatic words and the generic associations of his declared themes of metamorphosis and universal history. Discussion about the generic affiliations of the *Metamorphoses* has preoccupied Ovidian scholarship for many years and has been revitalized in two of the most recent works on the poem, those of S.E. Hinds and P.E. Knox. Their works represent the two major strands of the debate. Knox suggests that the stylistic diversity of the poem, associated with Kroll's famous theory of generic mixing, "Kreuzung der Gattungen," defies generic classification,[3] while Hinds restates the importance of generic epic norms.[4] The question is far more than a literary-historical one in so far as the interpretation of the text extends beyond literary or generic concerns. Genre conveys meaning. Ultimately the generic concerns of the poem are deeply implicated in determining both Ovid's aims in writing the poem and in its reception. In light of recent reinterpretations of the epic tradition at Rome, specifically regarding Vergil, we need to reconsider Ovid's claims.

When Ovid calls his poem a *carmen perpetuum* (1.4) it is commonly recognized that he is translating Callimachus' ἓν ἄεισμα διηνεκές at *Aet.* 1 fr. 1.3, the sort of poem which, as Callimachus tells us in his much-quoted Prologue to

---

2. G.B. Conte, *The Rhetoric of Imitation*, ed. C.P. Segal (Ithaca, 1986), 76, 82. E.J. Kenney, "Ovid," in *The Cambridge History of Classical Literature*, vol. 2, ed. E.J. Kenney and W.V. Clausen (Cambridge, 1982), 433, suggests that with the emphatic *nova* in the first line, Ovid proclaims "the novelty of his literary undertaking," and also remarks on the fact that the first four words of the poem, *in nova fert animus*, can be read autonomously.

3. W. Kroll, *Studien zum Verständnis der römischen Literatur* (Stuttgart, 1924), 202–24; Knox, *Traditions of Augustan Poetry*, esp. 1–26; cf. J. Farrell, "Dialogue of Genres in Ovid's Lovesong of Polyphemus (*Met.* 13.719–897)," *AJP* 113 (1992): 235–68; D.A. Little, "Richard Heinze: Ovids elegische Erzählung," in *Ovids Ars Amatoria und Remedia Amoris: Untersuchungen zum Aufbau*, ed. E. Zinn (Stuttgart, 1970), 64–105; G.K. Galinsky, *Ovid's Metamorphoses: An Introduction to the Basic Aspects* (Berkeley and Los Angeles, 1975), viii; J.E.G. Zetzel, "Recreating the Canon: Augustan Poetry and the Alexandrian Past," *Critical Inquiry* 10 (1983): 100–101.

4. S.E. Hinds, *The Metamorphosis of Persephone: Ovid and the Self-conscious Muse* (Cambridge, 1987), esp. 99–134 (developing R. Heinze, *Ovids elegische Erzählung* [Leipzig, 1919]); cf. on the importance of generic classification, Conte, *Rhetoric of Imitation*, and *idem*, "Love without Elegy: The *Remedia amoris* and the Logic of a Genre," *Poetics Today* 10.3 (1989) 441–69.

the *Aetia,* he was criticized for not having written.[5] What Callimachus may have meant by this term is increasingly debated and perhaps irrecoverable,[6] and in any case probably different from how it was understood and used by the Roman poets. Generally, when Callimachus' words are considered in connection with other key passages from his surviving work, he is understood to be defending his choice to avoid writing lengthy heroic epic in the Homeric tradition and instead to compose either non-epic poems in which heroic themes are treated in a nontraditional manner (*Aetia*), or new sorts of shorter epic poems featuring nonheroic themes (*Hymns, Hecale*).[7] What seems at stake is the redefinition of thematic and stylistic criteria in tune with contemporary norms: epic grandeur, not the epic genre, is to be rejected. Epic poetry is renewed on the dual, and not antithetical, models of Homer (for language, themes, and poetic authority), and Hesiod (for alternative themes and a new style of narrative self-consciousness); generic norms, however, are still respected. Theocritus and Apollonius are equally involved in this reinvention of epic poetry.[8]

The Roman poets interpreted Callimachus' remarks in ways that were most useful to their own purposes, most often as an already-sanctioned polemic for the rejection of tradition[9] or as a declaration of aesthetic refinement. The

5. On *carmen perpetuum* as a technical term see Pfeiffer, *ad Aet.* 1 fr. 1.3; W. Wimmel, *Kallimachos in Rom* (Wiesbaden, 1960), 76 n.1, 331 n.1; Nisbet and Hubbard, *ad Hor. Odes* 1.7.6; Lafaye, *Métamorphoses d'Ovide,* 77 n.1; H. Herter, "Ovid's Kunstprinzip in den Metamorphosen," in *Ovid,* ed. M. von Albrecht and E. Zinn (Darmstadt, 1968), 351–61.

6. A. Cameron, "Genre and Style in Callimachus," *TAPA* 122 (1992): 305–12, has recently challenged the traditional view that Callimachus was discussing the viability of epic at all, and argues that the proem to the *Aetia* is concerned only with different ways of writing elegy. Cf. Knox, *Traditions of Augustan Poetry,* 10. For a restatement of epic concerns see the reviews of Knox by S.E. Hinds, *CP* 84 (1989): 270–71, and W.S. Anderson, *AJP* 109 (1988): 457–61.

7. See N. Hopkinson, ed., *A Hellenistic Anthology* (Cambridge, 1988), 85–101; S. Koster, *Antike Epostheorien* (Wiesbaden, 1970), 119f. (it would, in fact, be useful to be able to use the German distinction between "Großepos" and "Kleinepos"); J.K. Newman, *The Classical Epic Tradition* (Madison, 1986), 16–32, 53–54. Other relevant Callimachean passages include *Ep.* 27, 28 Pf., frr. 398, 465, *Hy.* 2.105–12.

8. For illuminating discussions of Theocritus' bucolic genre see S. Goldhill, *The Poet's Voice* (Cambridge, 1991), 223–83; B. Effe, "Die Destruktion der Tradition: Theocrits mythologische Gedichte," *RhM* 121 (1978): 48–77; D. Halperin, *Before Pastoral: Theocritus and the Ancient Tradition of Bucolic Poetry* (New Haven, 1983); for Apollonius' epic see most recently Goldhill, *The Poet's Voice,* 284–333; D. C. Feeney, *The Gods in Epic* (Oxford, 1991), 57–98; Newman, *Classical Epic Tradition,* 73–103.

9. Conte, *Rhetoric of Imitation,* 92. On the neoteric simplification of Alexandrian ideologies in their polemic see Newman, *Classical Epic Tradition,* 115, 126, 156; see Wimmel, *Kallimachos in Rom,* 128f. and throughout, for the most thorough discussion of the Roman adaptation of Callimachean poetics.

neoteric poets in their search for poetic freedom and new forms of more personal expression avoided the larger forms of epic, which from the beginning at Rome had been historical and encomiastic. Because of the close link between Latin epic and nationalist ideology, it is always difficult at Rome to distinguish between aesthetic and Augustan politics. Callimachean anti-epic polemic can function, as in all likelihood it also did in the Alexandria of the Ptolemies, as much as a rhetorical tool for the choice or avoidance of political themes as it does as a statement of a stylistic ideology.[10] The need for a form of "apology," the *recusatio,* which developed perhaps in response to new political pressure exerted under Augustus, led to the heightening of the polemic qualities of Callimachean poetics.[11] The love poets, through references to Callimachus' Prologue in the *recusationes* of elegy and lyric, defend their choice to write in the lesser genres by a polemical contrast with traditional lofty epic and on the basis of Callimachean aesthetic ideology. Ovid by using this term suggests that his poem will indeed conform to traditional Homeric epic standards of magnitude, chronological continuity (*ab origine . . . ad mea tempora*), and thematic grandeur, but in no other sense can the *Metamorphoses* be considered a conventional *epos.*[12]

When Ovid simultaneously asserts that he will also remain true to Callimachean aesthetic principles, this seems to be somewhat of a tease. *Deducite* in the fourth line of the *Metamorphoses* has recently been understood as activating a reference to the *carmen deductum,* representing Callimachus' chosen Μοῦσαν λεπταλέην (*Aet.* 1 fr. 1.24),[13] a symbol of the vast importance

---

10. Cf. W.V. Clausen, "Callimachus and Latin Poetry," *TAPA* 99 (1968): 193; Nisbet and Hubbard *ad* Hor. *Odes* 1.6; Conte, *Rhetoric of Imitation,* 74 n.43, chap. 5; Hopkinson, *Hellenistic Anthology,* 98; and esp. Wimmel, *Kallimachos in Rom.* Note the persistent rejection of specifically martial themes in Roman *recusationes:* e.g., Prop. 2.1, 2.10, 3.1.7, 3.3.41–42; *Ecl.* 6.3; Hor. *Odes* 1.6, 2.12, 4.15; Ov. *Am.* 1.1.

11. Wimmel, *Kallimachos in Rom,* Introduction 1–12, *passim.*

12. When Callimachus was understood as vehemently anti-epic, Ovid was perforce understood by his use of this term to be declaring himself opposed to Callimachean poetics. See Zetzel, "Recreating the Canon," 89 (on Callimachus); B. Otis, *Ovid as an Epic Poet* (Cambridge, 1970), 45–46; M. von Albrecht, "Zum Metamorphosen-Proem Ovids," *RhM* 104 (1961): 269–78.

13. This force of *deducite* was pointed out independently by O.S. Due, *Changing Forms* (Copenhagen, 1974), 95; C.D. Gilbert, "Ovid *Met.* 1.4," *CQ* 26 (1976): 111–12; Kenney, "*Ovidius Prooemians,*" 51–52. See further H. Hofmann, "Ovid's *Metamorphoses: Carmen Perpetuum, Carmen Deductum,*" *PLLS* 5 (1985): 223–41; Knox, *Traditions of Augustan Poetry,* 10–11; Hinds, *Metamorphosis of Persephone,* 18–21, 121; Feeney, *Gods in Epic,* 188–90; J.B. Hainsworth, *The Idea of Epic* (Berkeley and Los Angeles, 1991), 116–17. Hutchinson, *Hellenistic Poetry,* 334 n.115, rejects this interpretation, as does Kovacs, "Ovid *Metamorphoses* 1.2." For discussion of *carmen deductum* as a Callimachean term see Wimmel, *Kallimachos in Rom, passim;* E. Reitzenstein, "Zur Stiltheorie des Kallimachos," in *Festschrift Richard Reitzenstein,* (Leipzig and Berlin, 1931), 25–40; W. Eisenhut, "*Deducere Carmen.* Ein Beitrag zum Problem der literarischen

placed by Callimachus on poetic artistry and refinement. The announcement of the theme of metamorphosis also would have suggested to the Roman reader a connection with Hellenistic poetry. By Ovid's day the notion of an epic written in a Callimachean manner was by no means novel; Callimachus himself had initiated the endeavor to apply new aesthetic standards to the epic genre. Yet because of the way in which Ovid so blatantly flirts with non-epic and especially elegiac themes, styles, and even narrative structures after having so loudly declared his lofty epic goals at the commencement of his poem, he clearly intends to make an issue of the generic associations of his poem. ←
Without underestimating the complexity of the Alexandrian and Augustan poetic ideologies and without ignoring the anti-epic polemic rhetorically exploited by the writers of non-epic, we must formulate a view of Roman epic that makes room for the influences of both Callimacheanism and the tradition of heroic or Homeric grand epic.

I suggest that by identifying the aetiological nature of Ovid's metamorphosis stories, we can better understand how Ovid attempted and accomplished the feat of writing a continuous narrative epic of cosmic scope in a Callimachean manner. We must recognize that the tradition of aetiological mythology extends from the weighty epic themes of Hesiodic and "scientific" cosmogony to the erudite and erotic mythical tales popular with the Alexandrians, who themselves acknowledged their debt to the earlier Hesiodic tradition. It is the twofold nature of the aetiological tradition of mythology that may provide a key to the dual affiliations of the poem as a *carmen perpetuum* and *deductum*. For the Romans, cosmology or scientific poetry was precisely a ground on which Callimacheanism and grand epic could meet. Although for the purposes of organization I have here divided these two approaches to aetiology, one natural historical (Cosmogonic) and the other historical or cultural (Callimachean), I will argue that the two in fact are closely related. In the course of the *Metamorphoses* Ovid makes it abundantly clear that he is a poet qualified to sing of *causae* of both kinds.

Cosmogonic Aetiology

The announcement of the thematic material of the *Metamorphoses* in its opening line as *mutatas . . . formas* (1.1) distinguishes Ovid's proem from those of Homer or Vergil announcing heroic themes; it is instead reminiscent of the

Beziehung zwischen Horaz und Properz," in *Gedenkschrift für Georg Rohde, Aparchai* 4 (Tübingen, 1961), 91–104; D.O. Ross, *Backgrounds to Augustan Poetry: Gallus, Elegy and Rome* (Cambridge, 1975), 26–27, 65–66, 134–35. Cf. Macrob. *Sat.* 6.4.12 *deductum pro tenui et subtili eleganter positum est.*

proems to the didactic poems of Hesiod (*Th.* 105 γένος), Aratus (*Phaen.* 17 ἀστέρας), and Nicander (*Ther.* 1 μορφάς τε σίνη τε).[14] Ovid's design of a collection of metamorphoses is obviously indebted to didactic models.[15] The echo from Lucretius *De Rerum Natura* 5.548 (*prima concepta ab origine mundi*) at *Met.* 1.3, which announces the cosmogony occupying the first lines of the poem, makes it clear that Ovid has in mind Lucretius' natural-philosophic epic. In the same way that Vergil has been shown to be deeply concerned with confronting Lucretius' natural philosophic claims in his *Georgics* and *Aeneid,*[16] references to Lucretius throughout the *Metamorphoses* suggest that Ovid is similarly engaged in an intertextual dialogue with Lucretius' poem that involves charting the similarities and differences in their themes and aims—often to humorous purpose. The way in which Ovid's *Metamorphoses* continues the cosmogonic themes announced in the opening is precisely through the aetiological focus of his myths, which explain the origins of numerous natural and cultural phenomena. The cosmogony at the beginning of the poem is echoed at the end of the poem in the Speech of Pythagoras, in Book 15. This eclectic natural-philosophical framework of the poem does not encode a philosophical justification for or explanation of the metamorphosis theme, but rather constitutes an important literary statement of the poem's epic affiliations.[17] The cosmogony initially places the *Metamorphoses* within the tradition of "scientific" cosmogonic epic and mythological universal history that reaches back to Hesiod's *Theogony.*[18] Although the epic tone as well as the

---

14. J. Latacz, "Ovids *Metamorphosen* als Spiel mit der Tradition," *WJA* 5 (1979): 137ff. Cf. Ovid *Fasti* 1.1–2, *Ars* 1.33. It is worth considering that the introduction of the poem with a preposition, *in nova,* is paralleled most importantly by ἐκ Διὸς at Aratus *Phaen.* 1 and Theocr. *Id.* 17, an opening imitated by Ovid's Orpheus in his cosmogonic proem at *Met.* 10.148 *ab Iove;* cf. Cicero *Aratea* fr. 1; *in nova:* Manilius 3.1, *Aetna* 7; ἀμφὶ *Hymn. Hom. VII, XIX, XXII, XXXIII*). It may be a component of the continual generic interplay between the *Fasti* and *Metamorphoses* that the Proem to the *Fasti* has a distinctly epic ring; see J.F. Miller, *Ovid's Elegiac Festivals: Studies in the Fasti* (Frankfurt am Main, 1991), 9.

15. Otis, *Ovid as an Epic Poet,* 3.

16. Most recently P.R. Hardie, *Vergil's Aeneid: Cosmos and Imperium* (Oxford, 1986), J. Farrell, *Vergil's Georgics and the Traditions of Ancient Epic* (New York, 1991), C.G. Perkell, *The Poet's Truth: A Study of the Poet in Virgil's Georgics* (Berkeley and Los Angeles, 1989).

17. Otis, *Ovid as an Epic Poet,* 91–93; L. Alfonsi, "L'Inquadramento Filosofico delle Metamorfosi," in *Ovidiana,* ed. N.I. Herescu (Paris, 1958), 265–72; Due, *Changing Forms,* 120; Hinds, review of Knox, *Traditions of Augustan Poetry,* 269. See also Hardie, *Cosmos and Imperium,* 22–25 and *passim,* on the connections between cosmology and epic in ancient poetry.

18. So Kenney, "Ovid," 432; Otis, *Ovid as an Epic Poet,* 48, 318; W. Ludwig, *Struktur und Einheit der Metamorphosen Ovids* (Berlin, 1965), 83–86. We should remember that the ancients considered that the mythological series of love stories of the *Eoiai* was a continuation of the *Theogony;* see M.L. West, ed., *Hesiod, Theogony* (Oxford, 1966), 48–50, *The Hesiodic Catalogue of Women* (Oxford, 1985), 127f. Hardie, *Cosmos and Imperium,* 67, has best articulated the

chronological sequence will be frequently abandoned in the course of the series of erotic stories that constitute the bulk of the *Metamorphoses,* the epic criterion established in the opening lines of the poem remains relevant.[19]

In this opening, Ovid suggests that the *Metamorphoses* is the type of mythological cosmogonic history that Apollonius Rhodius and Vergil had attributed to mythical bards in their poems: Orpheus (*Argon.* 1.492–511), Clymene (*Geo.* 4.345–47), Silenus (*Ecl.* 6), and Iopas (*Aen.* 1.740–46). These much-discussed passages seem to represent as ideal the poet who understands and controls nature, and have been made the bases for mapping out much of the poetic terrain of both the Alexandrian and the Latin literary traditions.[20] The ideal represented by these ecphrases has been understood as primarily a reference to the Alexandrian tradition, based on its veneration of the Hesiodic model of poetry as scientific, self-reflective, mythological, nonheroic, aetiological, and in catalog form.[21] The original Hesiod as a model of didactic and grand cosmogonic *epic* is largely ignored, and consequently an overly one-sided view of Roman poetics has developed that underplays the influence of the epic tradition.[22] Thus it has been argued that the theme of cosmogony has "no intrinsic connection with the central concerns of epic,"[23] a claim based mainly on the frequently observed similarity of the *Metamorphoses* to the structure of the Song of Silenus in Vergil's sixth *Eclogue,* a self-confessed Callimachean *carmen deductum* (6.5).[24] Yet we ought to consider whether Silenus' narrative,

cosmogonic aspect of the Hesiodic tradition: "Translated into philosophical claims, the temporal Hesiodic sequence becomes the historical component of a description of the universe, reaching from cosmogony, through zoogony, and anthropogony, to history proper."

19. As Hinds, *Metamorphosis of Persephone,* 121, has emphasized: "even if only as a point of reference for generic conflict." See also Conte, *Rhetoric of Imitation,* 81: "Reference to the norm obviously does not mean submission to the norm; rather it delimits the common space within which the new poetry can both emulate tradition and speak with a fresh voice." Cf. T. Todorov, "The Origin of Genres," *NLH* 8 (1976 / 77): 160.

20. See especially Ross, *Backgrounds to Augustan Poetry,* 28–31, on the notion of the "scientific poet." For Hardie, *Cosmos and Imperium,* 16, this is the ideal of the *vates.*

21. Ross, *Backgrounds to Augustan Poetry,* 36–37; R.F. Thomas, *Vergil's Georgics* (Cambridge, 1988), *ad Geo.* 4.347 (Clymene), also *ad* 2.76 on *Ascraeum carmen.* For the importance of Hesiod for the formulation of Alexandrian poetics see Wimmel, *Kallimachos in Rom,* 238–41; A. Kambylis, *Die Dichterweihe und ihre Symbolik* (Heidelberg, 1965), 31–68; Reitzenstein, "Zur Stiltheorie des Kallimachos," 41–59; H. Rheinsch-Werner, *Callimachus Hesiodicus* (Berlin, 1976). On the Hesiodic "Kataloggedicht" and "Kollektivgedicht" see E. Martini, *Einleitung Zu Ovid* (Darmstadt, 1970), 105–34.

22. See Fantham's protestations in her review of *Virgil: Georgics,* ed. R.F. Thomas, *CP* 86 (1991): 164, against the "absolute privileging of the Hellenistic and neoteric"; cf. Newman, *Classical Epic Tradition,* 113.

23. Knox, *Traditions of Augustan Poetry,* 12.

24. Knox, *Traditions of Augustan Poetry,* 10–26; Otis, *Ovid as an Epic Poet,* 48–49.

which also begins with a cosmogony and proceeds to metamorphic, erotic, and aetiological themes, and the contemporary figure of Gallus, does not also explore themes associated with grand epic.

At the beginning of the sixth *Eclogue,* Vergil borrows directly from Callimachus' Prologue to the *Aetia* to defend his refusal to write on the heroic epic themes of *reges et proelia* (6.3); more precisely, he seems to be rejecting a historical-panegyric form of epic praising Varus' martial accomplishments. Vergil contrasts this form of grand epic with his own Theocritean *deductum carmen* (6.5). In what follows, it is not Vergil, however, but Silenus as secondary internal narrator to whom the song is attributed, and this fact deserves consideration. Although the content of Silenus' song is extremely complex and diverse, the metamorphic, aetiological, and erotic themes are all markedly neoteric in nature and seem to be offered as Alexandrian epic alternatives to the heroic epic themes rejected at the opening of the poem.[25] The cosmogonic opening of the song also clearly places it in the Hesiodic tradition of scientific *epos* (cf. lines 69–70) and has thus also been classified as purely Alexandrian. If we recall, however, that Hesiod's poetry offered two quite different models: the *Works and Days,* which the Alexandrians embraced as offering alternative themes to heroic epic, and the *Theogony,* an aetiological poem dealing with the loftiest of epic themes, Titanomachy and Theogony,[26] then we realize that Vergil is doing more than evoking Callimachus through Hesiod. The numerous echoes of Lucretius combine to suggest as well that this is a meditation on the boundaries between Alexandrian *epos* and loftier epic forms and themes. The fact that Silenus is *inflatus* (6.15) is perhaps a hint that the content of his song will explore as well grander forms of epic than that in which it is placed.[27] Vergil's choice of an internal narrator in this poem, as in all his other poems, to sing a cosmogonic song, signals a narrative self-consciousness of his juxtaposition of different kinds of epos.[28] M. Hubbard alerts us that Silenus is a narrator from whom Vergil's contemporaries could expect a natural philosoph-

---

25. E. Courtney, "Vergil's Sixth *Eclogue," Quaderni Urbinati* 34 (1990): 112; Farrell, *Traditions of Ancient Epic,* 293. See also the discussions of the poem by Z. Stewart, "The Song of Silenus," *HSCP* 64 (1959): 179–205; Ross, *Backgrounds to Augustan Poetry,* 18–38; J.P. Elder, "*Non iniussa cano:* Virgil's Sixth *Eclogue," HSCP* 65 (1961): 109–25; O. Skutsch, "Zu Vergils Eklogen," *RhM* 99 (1956): 193–201.

26. Hardie, *Cosmos and Imperium,* 7.

27. Wimmel, *Kallimachos in Rom,* 143–44; R.B. Rutherford, "Virgil's Poetic Ambitions in *Eclogue* 6," *GR* 36 (1989): 46; Farrell, *Traditions of Ancient Epic,* 309.

28. On the importance for bucolic poetry of definition by juxtaposition, see Halperin, *Before Pastoral.* Cf. the similar loftier tone in *Ecl.* 4, and see Conte, *Rhetoric of Imitation,* 100–129, on the tenth *Eclogue* as a display of the differences between bucolic and the 'lesser' genre of elegy.

ical discourse.[29] His framed narrative is more than a statement of poetic affiliation or literary criticism—it is a meditation on the truth value of poetry by a poet who expresses an interest in philosophy in all of his work. The ideal that this type of natural philosophical poetry represents will be that to which both the *Georgics* and the *Aeneid* aspire, and it is one that is now seen to be associated not only with the Hesiodic/Callimachean tradition, but also with traditional grand epic.

Consequently, reference to Hesiod by the Roman poets is not necessarily always to be understood merely as an emblem for Callimachean or Alexandrian aesthetic ideals, but also as an invocation of the *Theogony* as a model for the grandest form of epic poetry.[30] In other words, we should perhaps reevaluate currently prevalent, but increasingly challenged, views about a clear-cut dichotomy in the ancient epic tradition between "Homeric" epic and nonheroic, discontinuous, and scientific epic, "Hesiodic"—as represented by the Alexandrians and "Neoterics." One of the ways that the Roman reception of these two traditions of epic poetry is now being recast is through reference to the ancient exegetical tradition of physical allegory, which interpreted Homer as a cosmological poet. The allegorical interpretation of Homer developed already in the sixth and fifth centuries in response to philosophic attacks on the authority and validity of poetry, and it was further developed in the Hellenistic period, especially by the Stoics.[31] The myths and divinities of Homer and Hesiod were understood to contain disguised philosophic truths about the nature of the physical world. (The ancients had to hand at least one explicit cosmology attributed to Homer in the Homeric *Hymn to Hermes,* 423ff.) This mode of exegesis allowed the genealogy of the scientific epic to be seen as a continuous line to be traced back to Homer, as well as Hesiod.

---

29. M. Hubbard, "The Capture of Silenus," *PCPS* 21 (1975): 60; cf. J. Notopoulos, "Silenus the Scientist," *CJ* 62 (1967): 308–9.

30. Farrell, *Traditions of Ancient Epic,* 317.

31. In the rapidly expanding bibliography on allegory, see, for the development of allegorical interpretations of Homer, F. Buffière, *Les Mythes d'Homère et la Pensée Grecque* (Paris, 1956), 79–248; R. Pfeiffer, *A History of Classical Scholarship* (Oxford, 1968), 8–11; N.J. Richardson, "Homeric Professors in the Age of the Sophists," *PCPS* 21 (1975): 65–81; Feeney, *Gods in Epic,* 8–10, 32–33, 36–37; M. Murrin, *The Allegorical Epic: Essays in its Rise and Decline* (Chicago, 1980); J. Whitman, *Allegory: The Dynamics of an Ancient and Medieval Technique* (Oxford, 1987), 21ff.; R. Lamberton, *Homer the Theologian: Neoplatonist Allegorical Reading and the Growth of the Epic Tradition* (Berkeley, 1986), 15f.; D. Dawson, *Allegorical Readers and Cultural Revision in Ancient Alexandria* (Berkeley and Los Angeles, 1992), 12f. For important reassessments of Stoic allegoresis see A.A. Long, "Stoic Readings of Homer," in *Homer's Ancient Readers,* ed. R. Lamberton and J.J. Keaney (Princeton, 1992), 41–66, and G.W. Most, "Cornutus and Stoic Allegoresis: A Preliminary Report," *ANRW* 2.36.3 (1989): 2014–65.

The Hellenistic period saw a flowering of interest in scientific literature and was marked by a great increase in the popularity of didactic poetry. The allegorical approach to Homer seems, however, to have been largely rejected by the Alexandrian scholars and poets, who preferred a more philological approach to the Homeric texts, with the exception of the Stoic poets Cleanthes and Aratus.[32] Although the evidence is again scant, scientific themes seem to have been identified primarily with Hesiod, the model for didactic and personal poetry (cf. Call. *Ep.* 27 Pf. on Aratus), as distinguished from the model of grand heroic epic represented by Homer. The cosmogony of Apollonius' Orpheus at *Argon.* 1.492–511 presents an appropriately abbreviated form of cosmological poetry that nevertheless suggests an awareness of the allegorization of Demodocus' song of Ares and Aphrodite at *Od.* 8.266ff. as a form of Empedoclean physics.[33] Scientific themes appear frequently in Alexandrian prose and poetic works, although natural science in Callimachus, Theocritus, and Apollonius is sparse.[34] The best known Hellenistic works combining science and poetry include Eratosthenes' *Hermes,* Cleanthes' *Hymn to Zeus,* Aratus' *Phaenomena,* and Nicander's numerous didactic works; they were all written in hexameters.

The interpretation of Homer as crypto-natural philosopher was available to the Romans as well, and P.R. Hardie has recently suggested that Ennius first combined the two traditions of heroic and Callimachean epic by adapting in the *Annales* the allegorical tradition of interpreting Homer as a scientific poet.[35] The Latin epic tradition can thus be unified by tracing the connection between cosmogony and epic from Ennius through Lucretius to Vergil. From its beginnings Roman epic not only dealt with Roman history, but also made cosmic claims. This suggests that the frequently repeated connection between scientific poetry and Alexandrianism at Rome is a claim that now needs to be qualified. Cosmological themes in the Roman poets should not be understood as exclusively associated with Alexandrianism, nor need they be anti-Homeric.

Lucretius' *De Rerum Natura* represents the next important interpretation of the epic and cosmological tradition after Ennius', and it is increasingly being

32. Pfeiffer, *History of Classical Scholarship* I, 140; Feeney, *Gods in Epic,* 37–38 (with further bibliography). On Aratus' *Phaenomena* as Stoic didactic see especially B. Effe, *Dichtung und Lehre* (Munich, 1977), 40–56, with Kenney's review in *CR* 29 (1979): 71–73.

33. See Buffière, *Les Mythes d'Homère,* 168–72.

34. Callimachus' *Coma Berenices* and *Hecale* contain astronomy, and Apollonius includes a number of *aetia* for natural phenomena in his *Argonautica,* which we will look more closely at in the following chapter; all three poets reveal an interest in medical science. See Pfeiffer, *History of Classical Scholarship,* 152f.

35. Hardie, *Cosmos and Imperium,* 76–83. See chap. 4 for further discussion of this aspect of the *Annales*.

given its due attention in the consideration of the development of Augustan epic. Clearly, Lucretius' philosophic poem cannot be allied easily with either a purely Alexandrian or a purely Homeric epic tradition. While his debt to his Hellenistic didactic predecessors is evident, as well as his awareness of the requirements of Alexandrian *doctrina* associated with Callimachus, Lucretius invokes as his literary models and predecessors such diverse poetic models as Empedocles, Homer, and Ennius.[36] In Latin literature earlier than and contemporary with Lucretius we find a sustained interest in scientific, cosmological, and especially astronomical themes, in all likelihood inspired by Hellenistic works. Although the evidence is meager, these topics seem to have been quite popular with the earliest Roman poets as well as with the later neoterics. We know of scientific poetry, much in hexameters, by—among others—Lucilius (e.g., *Sat.* 1308 Marx), Ennius (*Epicharmus,* trochaic), Egnatius (*De Rerum Natura*), Cicero (*Aratea*), Cinna (fr. 11, p. 89 Morel; p. 116 Buechner), Varro Atacinus (*Chorographia* and *Ephemeris*), and Catullus in his translation of Callimachus' *Coma,* poem 66.[37] It is impossible to know whether the neoterics associated their scientific poetry exclusively with Hellenistic poetry, but the following generation had as models for scientific poetry the two epic traditions represented by Hellenistic didactic and Homeric grand cosmological epic, both combined to some extent in the works of Ennius and Lucretius. Thus, for the Augustan poets there existed this dual tradition of cosmological poetry.

In the next generation cosmogonic and natural philosophic themes appear prominently in the *recusationes* of the Augustan poets, and this reveals their association with the loftiest form of epic.[38] Vergil is clearly the central figure in this debate, as the recent studies concerned with his poetry reveal. P.R. Hardie's *Cosmos and Imperium* now convincingly argues the importance of recognizing the cosmological aspects of the *Aeneid* and Vergil's indebtedness to the physical allegorical interpretation of Homer in much of his poetry. J. Farrell has

---

36. For discussion of Lucretius' diverse literary models, see, e.g., E. Ackermann, *Lukrez und der Mythos* (Wiesbaden, 1979), 31; Hardie, *Cosmos and Imperium,* 193–219; C. Murley, "Lucretius *De Rerum Natura* Viewed as Epic," *TAPA* 78 (1947): 336–46; R. Mayer, "The Epic of Lucretius," *PLLS* 6 (1990): 35–43; R.D. Brown, "Lucretius and Callimachus," *ICS* 7 (1982): 77–97; E.J. Kenney, "*Doctus Lucretius,*" *Mnemosyne* 23 (1970): 366–92.

37. J. Granarolo, "L'époque néotérique ou la poésie romaine d'avant garde au dernier siècle de la République (Catulle excepté)," *ANRW* 1.3 (1973): 280, stresses the continuity between the poetry and poetics of Ennius and the neoterics; also H. Bardon, *La Littérature Latine Inconnue I* (Paris, 1952), 335. See A. Traglia, *Poetae Novi* (Rome, 1962), 84–93, 145–49, on Varro Atacinus.

38. Prop. 2.1.19f., 2.34.27f., 51–54, 3.5.25; Hor. *Epist.* 1.12.14–20; Verg. *Geo.* 2.475f. (on which see more below); *Ciris* 21–41. For the connection between Titanomachy and Cosmogony, see Hardie, *Cosmos and Imperium, passim,* and D.C. Innes, "Gigantomachy and Natural Philosophy," *CQ* 29 (1979): 165–71. Cf. Orpheus at *Met.* 10.150–54, *Fasti* 1.295–310.

further elaborated the way in which physical allegory informs Vergil's imitation of Homer in the *Georgics* as well.[39] The association of natural philosophical and nationalistic themes in Vergil's *recusatio* at *Georgics* 2.458–3.48 suggests again they both represent modes of grand epic.[40] The cosmogonic songs of Iopas, Clymene, and even Silenus can now be seen as more probably based upon an ideal representing the cosmogonic epic poet in a dual Homeric and Hesiodic tradition, one which is simultaneously grand epic and Callimachean.[41] An important difference between the associations of scientific poetry in Alexandria and Rome, then, is that it is only at Rome that cosmological epic came to be seen as an alternative form of grand heroic epic. In Alexandria, on the other hand, scientific poetry associated with Hesiod provided an alternative form of a "humbler" and more personal poetry as opposed to the heroic tradition of "Großepos." This interpretation of cosmological poetry offers a way to understand how the Roman writers of epic seem to conceive of themselves as writing simultaneously within the Callimachean, Hesiodic, and Homeric traditions; it also reinforces the view that the poetic tradition in Rome should not be seen as one that was wholly factionalized by on one side Callimachean neoterics, who abhorred traditional epic, and on the other the "Roman" tradition of grand epic as represented by Ennius and Lucretius.

While the presence of elements of almost all poetic genres in the *Metamorphoses* has been taken as a sign of the irrelevance of generic criteria to the poem, it is rather an indication of the *inclusiveness* and universality of the epic tradition. The same generic polyphony has been perceived in the *Aeneid.* The two poems are no less "epic" for their admixture of elements from effectively all other genres, for epic is the one genre that can accommodate and indeed even aims for such diversity.[42] It is the lesser genres of poetry that more closely

---

39. Farrell, *Traditions of Ancient Epic,* chap. 6, 207–72, esp. 257f. Other allegorical interpretations of Vergil include R. Heinze, *Virgil's Epische Technik* (Stuttgart, 1957), 304–10; G. N. Knauer, *Die Aeneis und Homer.* Studien zur poetischen Technik Vergils mit Listen der Homerzitate in der Aeneis. Hypomnemata 7 (Göttingen, 1964), 168; Murrin, *The Allegorical Epic,* 3; Whitman, *Allegory,* 50f.; A. Wlosok, "Gemina Doctrina: On Allegorical Interpretation," *PLLS* 5 (1985): 75–84.

40. Wimmel, *Kallimachos in Rom,* 143; Hardie, *Cosmos and Imperium,* 33–51.

41. Knauer, *Die Aeneis und Homer,* 168 n.2; *Cosmos and Imperium,* 52–67, 83–84; Farrell, *Traditions of Ancient Epic,* 259–61, 270–71.

42. Hardie, *Cosmos and Imperium,* 67, observes that "the use of a cosmic setting may be prompted by a variety of motives. Most simply it may spring from a desire for completeness, what might be called an encyclopaedic drive." Cf. *idem, The Epic Successors of Virgil: A study in the dynamics of a tradition* (Cambridge, 1993), 71, and Zetzel, "Recreating the Canon," on the generic diversity of the *Aeneid.*

watch their thematic boundaries and define themselves by contrast with the claims of the most elevated forms of epic. Thus cosmogonic passages in such poetry as Vergil's *Eclogue* 6 and *Georgics* 4 are given to internal narrators; hence the elegists use the *recusatio* to contrast and simultaneously extend their generic range in relation to the grandest epic themes. In both of his elegiac didactic poems Ovid includes a cosmogony as a gesture of mock-epic cosmological pretension (*Fasti* 1.103–14 and *Ars Amatoria* 2.467–80), and in both poems the inclusion of this epic theme is seen to place a strain on the lighter genre.[43]

Epic registers no such generic strains. Ovid modulates his style and themes in the *Metamorphoses* among the ranges of Alexandrian and neoteric elegy and heroic epic, and much that comes between, but measures them all against the always theoretical—but all important—norms of epic.[44] Generic crossing does not constitute the deconstruction of generic categories, merely a reconstruction or redefinition through "the exploration of the boundaries of a poetic genre."[45] Ovid's *Metamorphoses* must be placed within this tradition of Roman cosmological epic, whether as exemplified by the didactic epics of Lu-

---

43. In the *Fasti* it is again not Ovid but Janus as narrator who tells of cosmogony, and in the *Ars* the cosmogony is interrupted by the appearance of Apollo at line 493 (*haec ego cum canerem, subito manifestus Apollo*), in a line reminiscent of Vergil's *recusatio* at *Ecl.* 6 (cf. J.F. Miller, "Callimachus and the *Ars Amatoria*," *CP* 78 [1983]: 32). On the generic strains of the nationalistic subject matter of the *Fasti*, see S.E. Hinds, "*Arma* in Ovid's *Fasti* Part 1: Genre and Mannerism," *Arethusa* 25 (1992): 81–112, "*Arma* in Ovid's *Fasti* Part 2: Genre, Romulean Rome and Augustan Ideology," *Arethusa* 25 (1992): 113–53; J.C. McKeown, "*Fabula proposito nulla tegenda meo:* Ovid's *Fasti* and Augustan Politics," in *Poetry and Politics in the Age of Augustus*, ed. A.J. Woodman and D.A. West (Cambridge, 1984), 183–84; Miller, *Ovid's Elegiac Festivals*, 16–17.

44. See Hinds, review of *Traditions of Augustan Poetry*, by P.E. Knox, 269, and Conte, *Rhetoric of Imitation*, 69–96, esp. 91–96, on the importance of the generic norm. See Cameron, "Genre and Style in Callimachus," 312, for a restatement of Callimachus' concern with the essential forms and styles appropriate to the different genres, in opposition to much recent criticism arguing for generic "contamination," e.g., D.L. Clayman, *Callimachus' Iambi*, Mnemosyne Supplement 59 (Leiden, 1980), 51; L.E. Rossi, "I generi letterari e le loro leggi scritte nelle letterature classiche," *BICS* 18 (1971): 83–86; Zetzel, "Recreating the Canon"; M. Fantuzzi, "La Contaminazione dei generi letterari nella letturatura greca ellenistica: rifiuto del sistema o evoluzione di un sistema?" *Lingua e Stile* 15 (1980): 433–50.

45. Conte, *Rhetoric of Imitation*, 126. Contrast Farrell's suggestion, "Dialogue of Genres," 267, that the *Metamorphoses* cannot be defined in purely formal terms and instead "draws upon a variety of constituent genres without belonging to any of them." R.F. Thomas, review of *The Metamorphosis of Persephone*, by S.E. Hinds, *CP* 85 (1990): 80, concludes that the generic question of the *Metamorphoses* may be "partly a matter of perspective, of whether the generic cup is half-full or half-empty," while D.F. Kennedy, in his review of Hinds and Knox, *JRS* 79 (1989): 210, contrasts a "dynamic" with a "static" concept of genre. Similarly T.G. Rosenmeyer's article, "Ancient Literary Genres: A Mirage?" *Yearbook of Comparative and General Literature* 34 (1985): 82, suggests that we adopt a view of ancient literature that allows for more modulation and freedom within generic categories throughout the tradition.

cretius and Vergil's *Georgics* or by the heroic epics of Ennius and Vergil's *Aeneid,*[46]—the differences will of course be in tone and intent. When Ovid poses as a *vates* he invariably plays with his own pretensions.[47] Traditional epic of both the mythological and philosophical type presents a valorized picture of the past that accounts for the present through a heroic past "of beginnings" and "peaktimes," "of fathers and founders, firsts and bests."[48] Ovid, on the other hand, while accepting the challenge of the tradition of epic causality, consistently refuses to assume an authoritative voice and presents instead the origins of the first flowers, bats, and lizards.

Even if at some point cosmology becomes associated with all genres of poetry, insofar as it signifies poetry that has the power both to understand and to express cosmic and human truths, it remains generically bound up with the "loftiest" of the genres, epic, precisely because Homer and Hesiod are seen as the primary models.[49] Therefore, when Ovid begins his epic with such themes, he clearly wishes it to be understood in these generic terms. Yet the addition of *deductum* serves to reveal an understanding on Ovid's part that this tradition of "scientific poetry" has reached him through a number of different interpretations of this tradition, most notably those of Callimachus and Vergil. It also serves as a reminder that Ovid's poem will, despite its length and themes, remain true to the high standards of Callimachean learning and artistry— indeed the large scale offers an even grander scope for such display.

In the *Metamorphoses,* as in his other poetic works, Ovid presents his chosen genre, here epic, writ large. We see him exploring and exploding the traditions of epic poetry, its themes, narrative strategies, and authoritative claims, from Hesiod and Homer to Lucretius and Vergil. He lays bare with his usual straight-faced explicitness the cosmological framework that has now been uncovered in the *Aeneid.*[50] Having chosen a quintessential Hellenistic

---

46. Hardie, *Cosmos and Imperium,* 380. On the cosmogonic aspects of later epic as well, see *ibid.,* 380–83. For discussion of the growth in popularity of universal history in the later Republic (e.g., Cornelius Nepos' *Chronica* [from the reign of Saturn], Varro's *De Gente Populi Romani* [origins of man], Polybius, Diodorus Siculus) see Hardie, *Cosmos and Imperium,* 378; T.P. Wiseman, *Clio's Cosmetics* (Leicester, 1979), 154ff.; Ludwig, *Struktur und Einheit,* 74ff.

47. E.J. Kenney, *"Nequitiae Poeta,"* in *Ovidiana,* ed. N.I. Herescu (Paris, 1958), 201.

48. M.M. Bakhtin, *The Dialogic Imagination,* trans. C. Emerson and M. Holquist (Austin, 1981), 13, in his definition of the valorized world of epic.

49. Innes, "Gigantomachy and Natural Philosophy," 169, has also shown that "we are . . . justified in arguing from rhetorical theory not only that natural philosophy might as a literary theme claim great grandeur, more so than moral philosophy, but that its preeminent theme will be the nature of the universe and its creation."

 50. Cf. Hardie, *Cosmos and Imperium,* 379–80, on the *Metamorphoses* as a universal epic in imitation of Virgil.

theme of the most fabulous nature, Ovid treats it in an aetiological manner that pretends to be "scientific" in its close attention to detail and the explication of natural phenomena and submits it to epic expansion. Cosmogony is reimagined and reconfigured in a wholly original way, which incorporates the two traditions of both the *carmen perpetuum* and the *carmen deductum* while revealing a deep understanding of their affinities.

Callimachean Aetiology

We should have no problem fitting the many elegiac and neoteric aspects of the *Metamorphoses* within the concept of epic as it had been represented from Apollonius and Aratus to Lucretius and Vergil. All of these writers evidently saw themselves as participating in a tradition of epic poetry attempting to align itself with Callimachean aesthetic norms and poetic ideals, although the accommodation of grander epic themes to Callimachus' precepts was felt and signaled as problematic. Ovid's debt to Callimachus and the neoteric followers of the Alexandrians has been well documented.[51] While Ovid's *Fasti* is more obviously similar to the *Aetia,* scholars have noted the similar composition of the *Metamorphoses* and *Aetia*—both consist of a large number of diverse episodes linked by a common theme.[52] Even closer to Ovid's composition perhaps are other Hellenistic catalog poems similarly erotic in content, such as Hermesianax's Λεόντιον Book 3 (frr. 7–8 Powell, pp. 98–106), Nicaenetus of Samos' Γυναικῶν Κατάλογος (fr. 2 Powell, p. 2), or Phanocles' Ἔρωτες ἢ Καλοὶ (frr. 1–7 Powell, pp. 106–9), all in the tradition of the "Hesiodic" Ἠοῖαι. In addition, Ovid's display of recherché mythological learning, his novel versions of traditional stories, his modernizing treatment of myth, his ironic distance, and his very frustration of narrative and generic expectations place him in the Alexandrian tradition. Even more prominently Callimachean are Ovid's aetiological metamorphoses, especially those explaining the origins of geographical, mythical, religious, and cultural phenomena.[53] Moreover, in the *Metamorphoses* many of the stories that treat these aetiological themes are embedded in narrative frames similar to those Callimachus employs for aetiological conversations in the first two books of the *Aetia.* While these

51. Lafaye, *Les Métamorphoses d'Ovide,* 105; Martini, *Einleitung zu Ovid,* 125–30; Wilkinson, *Ovid Recalled,* 152–55; Kenney, Introduction and Notes to Ovid's *Metamorphoses,* xxi–xxiii; Knox, *Traditions of Augustan Poetry,* 10–11, 65–83; Hopkinson, *Hellenistic Anthology,* 85. See also Garth Tissol's Ph. D. dissertation (Univ. of California at Berkeley, 1988), *Narrative Style in Ovid's Metamorphoses and the Influence of Callimachus.*

52. Kenney, "Ovid," 432; also Hutchinson, *Hellenistic Poetry,* 329.

53. As Lafaye, *Les Métamorphoses d'Ovide,* 105, long ago suggested; cf. Bernbeck, *Beobachtungen zur Darstellungsart,* 105.

aetiological stories are spread throughout the poem, it has been noticed that as the *Metamorphoses* approaches the Italian mythological territory of the *Fasti* Ovid's treatment of his themes in the two poems becomes increasingly similar.[54]

While the aetiological treatment of myth is a feature found in prose and poetry from the beginning of the Greek and Roman literary traditions,[55] after Callimachus, who included *aetia* not only in his famous poem of that name, but in almost all of his work, aetiology became an essential part of the learned poet's treatment of his mythical material from Apollonius Rhodius through Vergil's *Aeneid,* and was associated with Callimachus' poetic ideals and the influence of Hesiod.[56] In the first poem of his fourth book of elegies, probably the first collection of Roman aetiological elegy, Propertius repeats his earlier claims (e.g., 3.1, 3.3) to be the *Romanus Callimachus* (4.1.64) and he thereby places Roman aetiological elegy squarely in the Callimachean tradition.[57] The popularity of aetiological themes in the poetry of the Alexandrians and especially Callimachus has elicited much discussion and merits closer attention.

The Hellenistic preoccupation with aetiology can be set down in part to the fundamental scholarly inclinations of the period and the manifest delight of the antiquarian writers in researching the obscure details of myth. The logographers and local historians were mined by the Alexandrian poets for their information about the origins of cities, cult practices, and geographical features. Callimachus in his *Aetia* presents a series of explanations of, among other things, the origins of various cult rituals and festivals, and occasionally

---

54. Cf. Lafaye, *Les Métamorphoses d'Ovide,* 234–35; Knox, *Traditions of Augustan Poetry,* 65–83, chap. 5: "The Roman Callimachus" on Book 15; Graf, "Les Métamorphoses et la Véracité du Mythe."

55. For a survey of the early appearances of aetiology in the lyric poets and tragedians, see the useful article by G. Codrignani, "L'Aition nella poesia greca prima di Callimaco," *Convivium* 26 (1958): 527–45. Wiseman, *Clio's Cosmetics,* 151, reminds us that the antiquarian and aetiological impulses, frequently seen as uniquely Hellenistic, are found widely in earlier poets and historians. For discussion of the pervasiveness of the aetiological approach in pre-Hellenistic Greek historiography, see L. Pearson, "Apollonius of Rhodes and the Old Geographers," *AJP* 59 (1938): 443–59; O. Murray, "Herodotus and Hellenistic Culture," *CQ* 22 (1972): 200–213.

56. P.M. Fraser, *Ptolemaic Alexandria* (Oxford, 1972), 514. The *Hecale* explains the foundation by Theseus of the deme of Hecale and the cult of Zeus Hecaleius (see A.S. Hollis, ed., *Callimachus Hecale* [Oxford, 1990], 8); the aetiological *Iambi* are 7 (fr. 197), 8 (fr. 198), 9 (fr. 199), 10 (fr. 200), 11 (fr. 201); the *Hymns* are aetiological throughout. We also have evidence for works about foundation stories (*Suda;* Pfeiffer, *Callimachus,* 339), rivers (frr. 457–59), winds (fr. 404), nymphs (fr. 413), barbarian customs (fr. 405).

57. It is likely, though by no means undisputed, that it was Gallus who first (except for Catullus 66) wrote aetiological elegy (*Ecl.* 6.64–73). See especially Ross, *Backgrounds to Augustan Poetry,* 31–38; Miller, "Callimachus and the Augustan Aetiological Elegy," 378–80. For further discussion of Roman aetiological poetry see chap. 3.

cites his historical sources.[58] Apollonius Rhodius, who also wrote on founda-
tion legends (frs. 4–12 Powell, pp. 5–8), includes in the *Argonautica* many
aetia for religious rites, strange customs, and geographical features.[59] Al-
though aetiology establishes important links between the past and present by
accounting for the present through past events and by simultaneously confirm-
ing these events through contemporary evidence,[60] the *aetia* of Callimachus,
Apollonius, Aratus, or Nicander for the most part do not have the sort of
cultural and political implications that we find later in Vergil's *Aeneid.* The
festivals, most of them very strange, are frequently no longer practiced (e.g.,
human sacrifices at *Aetia* frr. 44–47, frr. 91–92 [Dieg. III 10–11; *SH* 275], frr.
98–99 [Dieg. IV 12ff.]) and the *aetia* at times are humorously trivial, such as
Callimachus' story of the origin of the mousetrap (*Aetia inc. lib.*, fr. 177 Pf. =
Aetia 3 [*SH* 259]) or Apollonius' explanation of the fleshlike color of the
pebbles on Aethalia (*Argon.* 4.654–58). The Alexandrian poets seem less
interested in the *aetia* themselves than in how they function narratologically.
Rather than accounting for aetiology in the Alexandrian poets as simply a
scholarly conceit or a symptom of cultural nostalgia,[61] we can more fruitfully

---

58. At *Aetia* 3 fr. 75.53–55 (Acontius and Cydippe), he mentions Xenomedes of Ceos as his
source; Pfeiffer *ad loc.* suggests that another historian was mentioned at the end of *Aet.* 4 fr. 91–92
(Melicertes). The Schol. Flor. 35ff. *ad Aet.* 1 frr. 3–7.14 (the Graces) suggest that Callimachus may
have mentioned that his source was the history of Agias and Dercylus of Argos (*FGrHist* 305 F8).
The same two may have been noted as a source elsewhere in the *Aetia,* as the Diegeseis suggest *ad
Aet.* 1 fr. 26–31a (Linus and Coroebus); Pfeiffer notes that *Aet.* fr. 65–66 (Springs of Argos)
probably came from the same source. For more on Callimachus' use of local historians see
Hutchinson, *Hellenistic Poetry,* 41; Fraser, *Ptolemaic Alexandria,* 721–32.

59. There are over forty-five *aetia* in the *Argonautica,* most in Book 4. See Fraser, *Ptolemaic
Alexandria,* 626–38; Hutchinson, *Hellenistic Poetry,* 93–95; R.L. Hunter, ed., *Apollonius of
Rhodes Argonautica Book 3* (Cambridge, 1989), 12–38; M. Fusillo, *Il tempo delle Argonautiche*
(Rome, 1985), 116–58; D.N. Levin, *Apollonius' Argonautica Reexamined: The Neglected First
and Second Books,* Mnemosyne Supplement 13 (Leiden, 1971); Goldhill, *The Poet's Voice,* 321ff.;
Hopkinson, *Hellenistic Anthology,* 182. For a discussion of the vexed question of Apollonius'
possible debt to Callimachus in his treatment of Argonautic *aetia,* see Pfeiffer, *ad Aetia* fr. 7.19–21
(= *Argon.* 4.1694ff.), *ad Aetia* 4 fr. 108–9 (= *Argon.* 1.953ff.), and *Callimachus* vol. 2, xli–xlii;
U. von Wilamowitz-Moellendorff, *Hellenistische Dichtung in der Zeit des Kallimachos* (Berlin,
1924), 168–83.

60. See G.S. Kirk, *Myth: Its Meaning and Functions in Ancient and Other Cultures* (Berkeley
and Los Angeles, 1970), 258, on the function of aetiological myth in "binding the volatile present
to the traditionally and divinely sanctioned regularity of the past."

61. For the frequently voiced idea that the popularity of aetiology in the Hellenistic period was
mainly due to a sense of temporal and cultural discontinuity, see Fraser, *Ptolemaic Alexandria,*
761; P. Bing, *The Well-Read Muse: Present and Past in Callimachus and the Hellenistic Poets*
(Göttingen, 1988), 71. Against this view see Hutchinson, *Hellenistic Poetry,* 41–42, and cf. C.W.
Fornara, *The Nature of History in Ancient Greece and Rome* (Berkeley and Los Angeles, 1983),
16–23, on the development of local history.

view it as a strategy of narrative representation, a structurally dynamic feature of the discourse.[62]

Callimachus' aetiological focus must be understood in the light of both his narrative and generic concerns. The aetiological themes of Callimachus' *Aetia* allowed him to compose a large-scale work that simultaneously presented him with completely novel poetic material and at the same time allowed him to treat epic themes, ἥρωας (*Aet.* 1 fr. 1.5), such as Hercules (*Aet.* frr. 22–25, *SH* 254–69) or the Argonauts (*Aet* fr. 7.19–21, frr. 108–9), in a non-epic, noncontinuous narrative manner associated with Hesiod.[63] By the same token, the aetiological approach allows for a sidestepping of overtly encomiastic and contemporary themes by a retreat to the mythical past. Apollonius, Vergil, Propertius, and most importantly Ovid, in both his *Fasti* and the *Metamorphoses*, exploit this narrative technique as one of the methods by which they adapt epic (and Augustan) themes to fit with their Callimachean ideals. At the root of the aetiological interest, however, lies its ability to produce explanations for phenomena, whether natural or cultural, and in this way aetiology is intimately bound up with the pervasive Alexandrian self-conscious preoccupation narrative authority. While the Alexandrian scholars rejected allegorical exegesis of Homer that saw his mythology as disguised scientific theory, their interest in the aetiological function of myth similarly exploited myth's power to explain problematic features of the world, now more cultural than physical phenomena. The pseudo-scientific handling of myth which aetiology represents provided Callimachus and Apollonius with a voice of scholarly authority and the credentials of the traditional cosmological poet. Ovid understood this, and in his own *Metamorphoses* and *Fasti* he combines aetiological and "scientific" approaches in his own exploration of the creation of narrative credibility and of the "vatic" voice.

The presentation of aetiological material entails a narrative voice far more prominent than that of the traditional epic narrator.[64] Callimachus' scholarly persona in the *Aetia* actively controls and participates in the presentation of his material. The overtly authoritative narrative voice of the aetiological narrator

62. Goldhill, *The Poet's Voice*, 323; cf. G. Binder, "Aitiologische Erzählung und Augusteisches Programm in Vergils *Aeneis*," in *Saeculum Augustum II*, ed. G. Binder, (Darmstadt, 1988), 262.

63. Heinze, *Virgil's Epische Technik*, 373; see W. Wimmel, '*Hirtenkrieg' und arkadisches Rom, Reduktionsmedien in Vergils Aeneis* (Munich, 1972), 104, on "die verweisende Charakter des Aition." See also Klein, "Concept of the Countergenre," on aetiology as an inner disruptive force in epic narrative and, similarly, Fusillo, *Il tempo delle Argonautiche*, 116–58.

64. Using the terminology of narratological theory, as outlined by, among others, S. Chatman, *Story and Discourse: Narrative Structure in Fiction and Film* (Ithaca, 1978), 5, we can speak of "degrees of audibility of the narrator," and of overt and covert narrators.

has frequently been compared to that of the didactic narrator and we will find that certain features of Ovid's narrative style in the *Metamorphoses* are quite close to formulations found in the more obviously didactic *Fasti*.[65] By including an *aetion* the author interjects his own authoritative position, because an *aetion* corresponds to contemporary actuality and is meant to be "true." In other words, the authoritative scholarly narrator validates the truth of his narrative through these external referents.[66] Frequent appeals to the Muses, tradition, and sources in Alexandrian poetry are further features of this concern with narrative authority and fictionality. Yet as we have seen with Callimachus, and as becomes even clearer in Apollonius and Ovid, this ostensibly critical and objective method is applied to myth of the most fantastic character. We sense that these poets are concerned far less with being "believed" than with making an issue of the relationship between truth, or reality, and fictionality. Simon Goldhill has detected in Apollonius an "ironic and varied treatment of the power and scope of aetiological explanations,"[67] which seems very relevant to an understanding of Ovid's treatment of myth and his tone in the *Metamorphoses*.

In both the *Argonautica* and the *Metamorphoses* we can see aetiology creating an ironic contrast between the authoritative "scientific" voice of the aetiological narrator and the fantastic mythical material of his poetry.[68] Ovid perhaps exploited this paradox beyond all earlier poets. Although one often reads that it is part of Ovid's poetic "agenda" to point out the fictitious nature of

---

65. Klein, "Concept of the Countergenre," 219, has argued that aetiological poetry represents "a sophistication of the didactic." While the *Aetia* acknowledges a debt to Hesiod, it is not helpful to label it didactic, as has been the tendency recently (e.g., Clausen, "Callimachus and Latin Poetry," 184). Miller, "Callimachus and the Augustan Aetiological Elegy," 405, rightly suggests that the similarities of the *Aetia* with didactic poetry are limited to the learned subject matter of the poem and the basically explanatory nature of the *aetion*. We should reserve the title of didactic for poems written in hexameters, while recognizing that poets such as Callimachus and Ovid explore in their elegiac works (e.g., *Aetia, Ars Amatoria*) affinities with the didactic tradition and transform it. See Effe, *Dichtung und Lehre,* E. Pöhlmann, "Charakteristika des Römischen Lehrgedichts," *ANRW* 1.3 (1973): 813–901, for definitions of didactic. For more on the similarities of diction between the *Fasti* and the *Metamorphoses* see chap. 2.

66. Feeney, *Gods in Epic,* 93; G. Zanker, *Realism in Alexandrian Poetry: A Literature and Its Audience* (London and Sydney, 1987), 113, 123; Binder, "Aitiologische Erzählung und Augusteisches Programm," 263; cf. R. Barthes, *S/Z,* trans. R. Miller (New York, 1974): 18–20, G. Genette, *Narrative Discourse Revisited,* trans. J.E. Lewin (Ithaca, 1988), 46, on the creation of "mimetic illusion" through detail.

67. Goldhill, *The Poet's Voice,* 326; see also Feeney, *Gods in Epic,* 93–94.

68. Goldhill, *The Poet's Voice,* 326, describes this phenomenon as "part of the Alexandrian discourse of knowledge that combines divina comedia and natural history as analytic modes." Feeney, *Gods in Epic,* 93, similarly discusses the interplay between fantasy and reality in the *Argonautica*.

mythology,[69] we should rather understand that Ovid reveals "a keen awareness of the suspension of disbelief and belief which constitutes fiction."[70] Seymour Chatman describes the self-conscious narrator as one who in his (or her) writing emphasizes "the absolute arbitrariness of invention."[71] Ovid as such a narrator continually calls attention to his authorial control over the fabrication of his narrative and to the way in which fiction creates its own reality.[72] Ovid's frequent use of framed narratives, a feature indebted to Alexandrian techniques, is another indicator of this narrative self-reflexivity. Like the Alexandrian poets, Ovid uses scholarly aetiological and etymological detail to play with suggestions of veracity and credibility, while eschewing an authoritative epic posture.

This is very different from the way in which Vergil uses *aetia* in the *Aeneid*, where they serve as genuine authenticating devices and forge important connections between the Augustan Rome of the present, its institutions, landmarks, and values, and its Greek and Italian past.[73] When Ovid embarks on Italian aetiological themes the tension between Roman reality and his fictions becomes more uncomfortable.[74] Like the Alexandrian poets before him, and earlier Roman poets as well, Ovid in the *Metamorphoses* is exploring the

---

69. E.g., J.B. Solodow, *The World of Ovid's Metamorphoses* (Chapel Hill, 1988), 64–79; Galinsky, *Ovid's Metamorphoses*, 16, 173–79. Slightly differently, M. von Albrecht, *Die Parenthese in Ovids Metamorphosen und ihre dichterische Funktion* (Hildesheim, 1964), 213–14. This view is based on Ovid's other statements about myth in his poetry. The usual citations include *Tr.* 2.63–64, where Ovid's words about the content of the *Metamorphoses: in non credendos corpora versa modos* (64) should not be understood literally as "bodies transformed in ways that are not to be believed" (Hutchinson, *Hellenistic Poetry*, 334), but rather as "bodies transformed in amazing ways." Likewise, the other commonly cited passages need to be considered with respect to their rhetorical functions in context: *Tr.* 3.8.1–12; *Am.* 3.6.13–18, 3.12.21–42; *Ars* 1.637; for these types of expressions see T.C.W. Stinton, "'*Si credere dignum est*': Some Expressions of Disbelief in Euripides and Others," *PCPS* 202 n.s. 22 (1976): 60–89.

70. Feeney, *Gods in Epic*, 229; Feeney discusses the whole issue of fictionality and contemporary critical attitudes to the levels of verisimilitude expected in epic at pp. 5–56; on Ovid, see esp. pp. 224–32.

71. Chatman, *Story and Discourse*, 250.

72. See R. Alter, *Partial Magic: The Novel as a Self-conscious Genre* (Berkeley, 1975), x, on narrative that "probes into the problematic relationship between real-seeming artifice and reality." This is almost precisely the approach to the *Metamorphoses* explored by G. Rosati in his illuminating *Narciso e Pigmalione: Illusione e spettacolo nelle Metamorfosi di Ovidio* (Florence, 1983).

73. So E.V. George, *Aeneid VIII and the Aitia of Callimachus*, Mnemosyne Suppl. 27 (Leiden, 1974), 88. Cf. R.D. Williams, ed., *P. Vergili Maronis Aenidos Liber Quintus* (Oxford, 1960), *ad Aen.* 5.117; R.G. Austin, ed., *P. Vergilius Maronis: Aeneidos Liber Sextus* (Oxford, 1977), *ad Aen.* 6.235; Kenney, "Ovid," 434; Feeney, *Gods in Epic*, 185–86; Binder, "Aitiologische Erzählung und Augusteisches Programm," 284; N. Horsfall, "Virgil and the Poetry of Explanations," *GR* 38 (1991): 203–11.

74. Graf, "Les Métamorphoses et la Véracité du Mythe," 68.

validity of alternate modes of explanation of the world: epic and philosophical, scientific and mythological. His narratological polyphony suggests that Ovid is more interested in playing with *how* authority is created and in drawing our attention to the stratagems of narrative authentication, than in maintaining a consistent and authoritative epic voice. The humor of the disjunction between Ovid's assumptions of the authoritative narrative pose of the universal epic poet and his fantastic mythical content is further highlighted by the didactic speech of Pythagoras in Book 15, where a natural philosopher is depicted as discussing physics in the manner of a poet. In antiquity natural philosophy, as well as aetiology, frequently slid into paradoxography, and Ovid charts these affinities with his metamorphic themes.

Hellenistic Collections of Metamorphoses

It is likely that the metamorphosis theme also would have suggested to the Roman reader a connection with Alexandrian aetiological literature. While metamorphosis formed an important part of much of Greek myth and appears in Greek literature from Homer onwards,[75] it is in the Hellenistic period that a collection of metamorphoses first appears. Moreover, the extant Hellenistic collections are of a primarily explanatory or didactic nature and in them metamorphosis is clearly aetiological in function.[76] We can see how collections of this sort were a natural product of the Alexandrians' obsession with cataloging, as well as their mythological, aetiological, and natural-scientific interests. Not only would the theme of metamorphosis have appealed to the Hellenistic taste for the bizarre, but it would have been an inherent part of many of the myths they found in the logographers and paradoxographers.[77] What was sought above all was the remarkable and unusual. Fraser has argued that the interest in paradoxography—the collection of the fantastic in nature, culture,

---

75. See now P.M.C. Forbes Irving, *Metamorphosis in Greek Myths* (Oxford, 1990), for a survey of the metamorphosis theme, and also Lafaye, *Les Métamorphoses d'Ovide*, 1–65. While little is known of the metamorphosis theme in the period between Hesiod and the Alexandrians, we know that it was popular in tragedy. Note that Horace at *A.P.* 185–87 mentions that transformations, like murders, should not take place upon the stage: *ne . . . coram populo/ . . . / aut in avem Procne vertatur, Cadmus in anguem.*

76. Forbes Irving, *Metamorphosis in Greek Myths,* 20.

77. Callimachus included the transformation of Diomedes' men to birds (a story narrated at *Met.* 14.464–511) in his thaumastic collection, explaining the birds' wondrously strange friendliness towards the Greeks (fr. 407.XLIII). His sources are said to be Lycus (*FGrHist* 570 F 6) and Timaeus. See Pfeiffer *ad loc.* For more on this metamorphosis see chap. 3 below, pp. 102–3.

mythology, and history—is the hallmark of all third-century literary production.[78]

We have, however, little evidence of the metamorphosis theme in Callimachus' work. The *Aetia* may have contained the metamorphoses of Ciris (cf. *Met.* 8.1–151) and Hippolytus (cf. *Met.* 15.492–546).[79] The *Suda* also attributes to Callimachus a Γλαῦκος, which may or may not have dealt with the mythical Glaucus of Anthedon, whose story was also treated by Alexander Aetolus (fr. 1 Powell, pp. 121–22), and was later popular among the neoterics. Ovid tells his story at *Met.* 13.906ff. (cf. p. 101 below). Considering Apollonius Rhodius' obvious enjoyment of the fantastic, there are surprisingly few metamorphoses in the *Argonautica;* they include Zeus' transformation into a horse upon being caught *in flagrante delicto* (2.1236–37), the catasterism of Ariadne's crown (3.1002–4), and the transformation of the Hesperides (4.1423–30). Apollonius Rhodius also treated the metamorphosis of Byblis (*Met.* 9.454–605) in the mythical story of the *Foundation of Kaunos* (fr. 5 Powell, p. 5) and that of Pompilus into a fish in the *Foundation of Naucratis* (fr. 7–9 Powell, p. 6). Catasterisms, a related form of mythological explanation for natural phenomena, were the subject of Eratosthenes' *Catasterismoi,* and appear also in his aetiological elegy, the *Erigone* (frr. 22–27 Powell, pp. 64–65). Catasterisms are also among the mythological digressions found in Aratus' extremely influential *Phaenomena* (the most detailed being the story of Orion at 637–47, cf. 197–204 Andromeda, 216–224 Helicon). Phanocles in his Ἔρωτες ἢ Καλοί (frr. 1–7 Powell, pp. 106–9) may have exploited the pathetic aspect of metamorphosis; he probably included the metamorphosis of Cycnus (fr. 6 Powell, pp. 108–9).[80] Moschus' "epyllion" *Europa* involves two bovine metamorphoses, those of Zeus and Io.

---

78. Fraser, *Ptolemaic Alexandria,* 454. Fraser notes that paradoxography and aetiology closely approximate one another, since the cults and customs that required elucidation might frequently "themselves be regarded as historical paradox" (773). See below, chap. 4, pp. 147ff., on paradoxography in the Speech of Pythagoras in *Met.* 15.

79. Pfeiffer *ad loc.* hesitantly suggests that fr. 113 may relate the story of Ciris' transformation (her name and οἰωνός must be restored) and may have been included in Book 1 of the *Aetia.* Cf. also A.S. Hollis, ed., *Ovid Metamorphoses VIII* (Oxford, 1970), 32, and R.O.A.M. Lyne, ed., *Ciris: A Poem Attributed to Vergil* (Cambridge, 1978), 7. On Hippolytus *(Aet.* fr. 190 = Serv. Verg. *Aen.* 7.778) see pp. 127–29 below. Fr. 632 *(Inc. Sedis)* may have dealt with the story of Callisto (cf. *Met.* 2.401–530); fr. 90 Hollis mentions Scylla, but we have no way of knowing whether a metamorphosis was narrated. The "Coma" at the end of the *Aetia* 4 fr.110 has a catasterism. Callimachus also seems to have written a work on birds (frr. 414–28), on which see Pfeiffer *ad* fr. 428: *nullum certum exemplum fabulae metamorphosis.*

80. Hopkinson, *Hellenistic Anthology,* 178, also notes that "the αἴτιον-theme was clearly prominent in Phanocles' poem."

The first collection of metamorphoses we know of is Nicander of Colophon's lost Ἑτεροιούμενα, dating probably from the mid-second century, a hexameter poem containing at least four books.[81] This same author also wrote two other poems of a didactic nature, the *Theriaca* and the *Alexipharmaca*, both based on treatises of the third century. It is interesting to see in these two poems the combination of the "scientific" and the mythological. We rely on the summaries of Antoninus Liberalis, a mythographer of the early centuries C.E., for an idea of Nicander's Ἑτεροιούμενα.[82] Based on these we can conjecture that most of Nicander's stories were aetiological in focus and explained the origins of surviving cults and local cult practices, as well as a few geographical landmarks and features, very much like Callimachus' *Aetia*.[83] Another author cited as a source in Antoninus Liberalis is a Boios, to whom is attributed a poem called the Ὀρνιθογονία.[84] His metamorphoses seem to have explained each bird's most notable habits and why certain birds are of good or bad omen. Other Hellenistic authors of collections of metamorphoses are for the most part merely names: Theodorus (*SH* 749 [+750?]), Didymarchus (Μεταμορφώσεις *SH* 378 A), Antigonus (Ἀλλοιώσεις *SH* 50).

At Rome the themes of metamorphosis and aetiology seem to have been especially associated with Alexandrian literature. Cicero in his youth translated Aratus and wrote a *Glaucus,* and an *Alcyones,* containing among the first

81. For Nicander's fragments see A.S.F. Gow and A.F. Scholfield, eds., *Nicander, the Poems and Poetical Fragments* (Cambridge, 1953), and now also *SH* 562?–563A?. Gow and Scholfield, 8, give the date, but A.W. Bulloch, "Hellenistic Poetry," in *The Cambridge History of Classical Literature,* vol. 1, ed. P.E. Easterling and B.M.W. Knox (Cambridge, 1985), 602, more cautiously claims that Nicander cannot be dated with any security. The *Suda* mentions five books, but Antoninus Liberalis cites only from four. Gow and Scholfield, 206, think that the *Suda* must be mistaken.

82. I refer throughout to the edition of M. Papathomopoulos, *Antoninus Liberalis: Les Métamorphoses* (Paris, 1968). I believe that we are justified in reconstructing something of the character of Nicander's and Boios' poems from Antoninus Liberalis, since certain recurrent features seem to be displayed in the attributions; cf. Forbes Irving, *Metamorphosis in Greek Myths,* 20–24. The date and reliability of the attributions of sources included in these headings is uncertain. Papathomopoulos cautiously dates them to the fourth century and later (xix). Gow and Scholfield, *Nicander, the Poems and Poetical Fragments,* 206, agree that although the headings probably do not proceed from the authors, "it seems safe to assume that the stories to which [Nicander's] name is attached were in fact handled by him."

83. A.L. 1, 4, 13, 17, 25, 26, 27, 29, 32, [40, 41] are all cult *aetia.* There is, in fact, no evidence to support Otis' claims, *Ovid as an Epic Poet,* 48, that Nicander's poem "seems to have been rather bold didactic . . . with the metamorphoses geographically arranged."

84. For the (vexed) name of this author and the title of the work see Athen. 9.393e; Jacoby, *ad FGrHist* 28 F 214; Forbes Irving, *Metamorphosis in Greek Myths,* 33. See A.L. 3, 5, 7, 11, 15, 16, 18, 19, 20, 21. In A.L. 20 Boios is cited along with Simmias of Rhodes. His fragments are also included in Powell, *Coll. Alex.,* pp. 24–25.

metamorphoses in Latin literature and prefiguring later epyllia.[85] Valerius Cato
perhaps also wrote Alexandrian erotic and aetiological poetry.[86] But it was the
late Republic that saw a flowering of mythological narrative, especially epyllia,
inspired by the Alexandrian and especially Callimachean tradition. Parthenius,
considered to be the crucial impetus for the so-called neoteric school of po-
etry,[87] wrote a *Metamorphoses*—another of the lost ancient texts whose
discovery would presumably illuminate much for us.[88] The only story at-
tributed to this collection is that of Scylla (*SH* 637). There is also an intriguing
unplaced five-line elegiac fragment attributed to Parthenius (*SH* 640), which
tells of the metamorphosis into a spring of a maiden in love with a Cydus. In his
collection of short prose summaries of tragic love stories, Περὶ Ἐρωτικῶν
Παθημάτων, which was preserved in the same manuscript as Antoninus Liber-
alis[89] and was written for Cornelius Gallus as a handbook of themes to use in
the composition of ἔπη καὶ ἐλεγείας (Pref. 2), Parthenius included three
metamorphoses (11 Byblis, 13 Harpalyce, 15 Daphne), two of which are also
treated by Ovid, and numerous *aetia* (7, 11, 15, 26, 30, 32, 34). Parthenius'
erotic themes were conspicuous in the epyllia of Catullus and his contempo-
raries. We know of Cinna's *Smyrna* (frr. 6–7, pp. 88–89 Morel; p. 115
Buechner), Calvus' *Io* (frr. 9–14, pp. 85–86 Morel; p. 111 Buechner), and
Cornificius' *Glaucus* (fr. 2, p. 90 Morel; p. 117 Buechner), all of which seem to

---

85. *Aratea N.D.* 2.104 (*a te admodum adulescentulo*), *Div.* 2,14, *Leg.* 2.7, *Att.* 2.1.11;
Glaucus: Plut. *Cic.* 2.3 (ἔτι παιδός); *Alcyones* fr. 1, p. 66 Morel; pp. 80–81 Buechner. See also E.
Courtney, *The Fragmentary Latin Poets* (Oxford, 1993), 149–53.

86. We hear of a *Lydia* (subject unknown), and a *Dictynna* (mentioned with approval by Cinna
fr. 14, p. 90 Morel; p. 116 Buechner), which may have dealt with the aetiology of Diana's name
Dictynna, from the nymph Britomartis, a story Callimachus narrated in *Hymn* 3.189–203.
R.O.A.M. Lyne, "The Neoteric Poets," *CQ* 28 (1978): 173, and T.P. Wiseman, *Cinna the Poet*
(Leicester, 1974), 55, both think it likely that the *Dictynna* was an aetiological epyllion.

87. See especially Clausen, "Callimachus and Latin Poetry," and N.B. Crowther, "Parthenius
and Roman Poetry," *Mnemosyne* 29 (1976): 65–71; also Lyne, "The Neoteric Poets." On Par-
thenius' dates see, differently, Wiseman, *Cinna the Poet*, 48, and E. Rawson, *Intellectual Life in
the Late Roman Republic* (Baltimore, 1985), 70 n.18. On the problems involved in using the term
"epyllion," see W. Allen, Jr., "The Epyllion: A Chapter in the History of Literary Criticism," *TAPA*
71 (1940): 1–26.

88. All of the poetic fragments of Parthenius are now conveniently collected in *SH* 605–66.
We do not know whether the *Metamorphoses* was in verse or prose. See the discussion of Lyne,
Ciris, 13–14, who concludes: "I see no clinching evidence against the idea that the *Metamorphoses*
was a mythographical source-book like the ἐρωτικὰ παθήματα." There is no support for Otis'
suggestion, *Ovid as an Epic Poet,* 48, that it was "a kind of *Aetia* specializing in metamorphoses."

89. For the text of Parthenius see S. Gaselee's Loeb translation, with Longus *Daphnis and
Chloe,* trans. G. Thornley, rev. J.M. Edmunds (Cambridge, Mass., 1935); P. Sakolowski and E.
Martini, eds., *Mythographi Graeci* II.i (Leipzig, 1896).

have incorporated metamorphosis as well as aetiology. Catullus translated Callimachus' *Coma* (C. 66), and wrote an Alexandrian epyllion (C. 64). Aemilius Macer translated Boios' work into Latin in a poem of the same title (frr. 1–6, pp. 107–08, Morel; pp. 138–39 Buechner). In the next generation, we have, of course, Vergil's sixth *Eclogue,* which contains references to all of the topics most prominent in the neoteric poets: tragic and bizarre mythological love stories, epyllia, aetiology, and metamorphosis. But by the time of the publication of the *Georgics,* some ten years later, the mood of the time had largely changed, *omnia iam vulgata (Geo.*3.4),[90] and it was for the most part left to Ovid to revive in his poetry the Greek mythological stories most popular with the earlier Roman Alexandrians.[91]

Ultimately the question of the generic affiliation of the *Metamorphoses* is bound up with Ovid's claims and intentions in his epic. A purely ludic or programmatic reading of this poem ignores the multiplicity of meanings and the deep psychological insights that Ovid's mythical stories convey.[92] Although the *Metamorphoses* has been denied epic status precisely because of a perceived lack of aim,[93] if Ovid is given full credit as a poet of ability (as he is increasingly), we should assume that he understood the tradition within which he was writing and attempted to contribute something to the ongoing dialogue about poetic authority and the viability of epic. By presenting his epic poem as cosmogonic in scale Ovid placed himself, however ironically, within the tradition of poets and philosophers who have claimed the power of explaining nature through an understanding of *causae.* His inclusion of the narrative of Pythagoras further juxtaposes and conflates these two modes of explanation, poetry and philosophy. The worldview that the *Metamorphoses* presents is one profoundly defined and destabilized by constant mutability; the landscape created is a human one formed from violence and pain. Ovid does not in the end wish to cast doubt on the believability of metamorphosis, but rather on the power of any poet to explain and perhaps even survive in a universe in which power is ultimately arbitrary and beyond the control of any poets or philoso-

---

90. There are, however, metamorphoses in the *Aeneid,* including Picus, 7.189–91; Virbius, 7.761–82; ships to nymphs, 9.117–22; Cycnus, 10.189–93; Diomedes' men, 11.271–78; see on these chap. 3, pp. 98ff.

91. Cf. Kenney, "Ovid," 421; Martini, *Einleitung zu Ovid,* 130. On the evidently increasing popularity of amatory themes in epic poetry of Ovid's day, see *Pont.* 4.16 and L. Duret, Dans l'ombre des plus grands," *ANRW* 2.30.3 (1983): 1490.

92. See Hinds, "Generalizing about Ovid," against reductive interpretations of Ovid's poetry.

93. Hainsworth, *Idea of Epic,* 120.

phers, since it rests in the hands of the powers in the heavens and on the Palatine.[94]

Political
destabilization

---

94. See Feeney, *Gods in Epic*, 223, on the overlap in attitude in the Roman world towards the underlying arbitrariness of the power of the Princeps and the gods. Much of the most interesting recent work on Ovid has been done precisely in the area of the possible political ramifications of Ovid's depictions of poetry and power; cf., e.g., Hinds, "*Arma* in Ovid's *Fasti:* Genre and Mannerism"; U. Schmitzer, *Zeitgeschichte in Ovids Metamorphosen* (Stuttgart, 1990); E.W. Leach, "Ekphrasis and the Theme of Artistic Failure in Ovid's *Metamorphoses,*" *Ramus* 3 (1974): 102–42.

Chapter 1

Cosmogonic Metamorphosis and Natural Philosophy in the *Metamorphoses*

Omnia enim stolidi magis admirantur amantque
inversis quae sub verbis latitantia cernunt
—Lucretius 1.641–42

The cosmogonic themes with which Ovid's epic begins and ends are not abandoned in the central portions of the poem. Throughout the *Metamorphoses* many of Ovid's marvelous metamorphic tales account for and explain the origins of various existing natural and geographical phenomena and thus, like Pythagoras in Book 15 who teaches *rerum causas* (*Met.* 15.68), they continue in a manner the natural-philosophical themes that introduce the poem. The Cosmogony at the opening of the poem and the concluding "philosophical" discourse of Pythagoras in Book 15 establish a sort of "scientific" field of reference in which Ovid suggests we may read his mythical stories. These stories, moreover, as Ovid reminds us, have been understood through physical allegory and aetiology to perform the explanatory function of myth that was taken over by philosophical speculation. Resonances of the scientific, and especially elemental, language contained in these framing passages are heard throughout the epic. In Book 1 Ovid presents, as we shall see, not merely one cosmogony, but a series, suggesting that the cosmogonic process is one that will continue throughout the poem: *ad mea . . . tempora.* Ovid is not to be understood as conceiving of his metamorphoses as following some coherent scientific or philosophic principle; rather he is exploiting the incongruity of applying to these fantastic mythical stories language borrowed from natural-philosophical poetry, especially that of Lucretius, while simultaneously engaging in the debate over authority between physics and poetry in which his predecessors had been involved. Ovid's cosmogonic passages owe much to Lucretius, and should alert us to the possibility of further intertextual engagement with *De Rerum Natura,* in which Lucretius set out precisely to challenge the validity of mythological explanation. What is involved in this intertextual relationship between these two poems is an exciting dialogue culminating in *Metamorphoses* 15, about the very nature of the world and the ability adequately to explain it. This chapter will investigate the range of Ovid's play with the language and themes of cosmogony and natural science throughout the *Metamorphoses*.

There are many types of metamorphosis in the *Metamorphoses;* like the poem as a whole, the term defies generalization.[1] These transformations are not simply perfunctory addenda at the end of his stories, tacked on in order to conform to the stated theme of the poem,[2] but rather an important part of the narrative and of Ovid's intentions in his epic. Metamorphoses include sex-changes (Tiresias, 3.316–38, Iphis, 9.666–797, Caeneus, 12.169–209), the petrifaction caused by Medusa's head (5.177–249), Pygmalion's statue (10.243–97), Midas and his golden touch (11.85–193), and numerous apotheoses and catasterisms. There are also self-transformers, such as Mestra, Thetis, Proteus, Periclymenus, and Vertumnus, not to mention the numerous gods who take on temporary disguises. We will be examining here stories in which a human being is metamorphosed permanently into some sort of natural phenomenon, either an animal, or a plant, or a geographical feature. In most cases some aspect of the character or merely appearance of the person involved serves as an explanation for the primary characteristics of the particular animal or plant into which s/he has been metamorphosed. Ovid's aetiological tales frequently provide the same sort of generally zoologically accurate, or at least detailed, descriptions of the primary physical features and habits of various species as we find later in Pliny's *Natural History.*

The connection of the theme of mythological metamorphosis with natural science might initially seem strange, but in fact it may be seen in poetry beginning with Hesiod and Homer, and much later reaches perhaps its most profound expression in the Middle Ages, during which Ovid's *Metamorphoses* was an important source for medieval scientific literature.[3] This connection lies

1. H. Herter, "Verwandlung und Persönlichkeit in Ovids *Metamorphosen,*" in *Kulturwissenschaften: Festgabe für Wilhelm Perpeet zum 65. Geburtstag* (Bonn, 1980), 185–228; H. Haege, *Terminologie und Typologie der Verwandlungsvorgangs in den Metamorphosen Ovids* (Göppingen, 1976), 2; Forbes Irving, *Metamorphosis in Greek Myths,* 36. See Lafaye's Appendix A, *Les Métamorphoses d'Ovide,* 245–55, in which he classifies all the metamorphoses in the poem. W.S. Anderson, "Multiple Change in the *Metamorphoses,*" *TAPA* 94 (1963): 1–27, shows that Ovid extends the language of metamorphosis to the workings of emotions, especially love.
2. Typical are Otis, *Ovid as an Epic Poet,* 81, and Galinsky, *Ovid's Metamorphoses,* 49. For a different view of the centrality of metamorphosis see Solodow, *World of Ovid's Metamorphoses.*
3. See S. Viarre, *La Survie d'Ovide dans la Littérature Scientifique des XIIe et XIIIe Siècles* (Poitiers, 1966), and L. Barkan, *The Gods Made Flesh: Metamorphosis and the Pursuit of Paganism* (New Haven, 1986), 94–136, esp. 11–17.

Lucretius = natural-scientific aetiology

essentially in the aetiological origins of many of these myths that explain
natural phenomena. Already in Homer, along with other types of meta-
morphoses,[4] we find the metamorphoses of Niobe (*Il.* 24.614–17)[5] and of the
Phaeacians' ship (*Od.* 13.154–78) to geographically located stone formations.
These are, as Fauth in his study of Homeric metamorphosis suggests, types of
religious "Lokalätiologie."[6] *The Hesiodic Catalogue of Women* contains many
aetiological metamorphoses, among which seem to have been the transforma-
tions of Battos into a rock (fr. 256 M-W, cf. *Met.* 2.676–707), the story of
Coronis and the crow's change of color (fr. 60 M-W, cf. *Met.* 2.531–632), and
Callisto's transformation into a bear/star (fr. 163 M-W, cf. *Met.* 2.401–530).[7]

Are star-aetiologies - different?

We have seen that in the Hellenistic period the metamorphosis theme ap-
pears prominently in literature and is intimately connected with the widespread
interest in aetiology. Aristotelian natural scientific investigation inspired much
of the cataloguing work of the Alexandrians, and ironically, the scientific
works of Aristotle and Theophrastus on natural subjects became mines for
later, and far different, paradoxographical and pseudoscientific writers on
nature.[8] It is clear that there must have been conflict, as we see in later scien-
tific literature,[9] between those who were approaching nature mythologi-
cally and those who were proceeding scientifically. In his *Theriaca* and the
Alexipharmica, Nicander combined the "scientific" and the mythological
seemingly with complete unembarassment.[10] In the *Theriaca* he included

---

4. Such as the ability of self-transformation (*Il.* 7.58–59, Athena and Apollo; *Od.* 4.417ff.,
Proteus) or the ability to transform others (*Od.* 10.237–43, 388–99, Circe). At *Od.* 19.518–23, the
nightingale is called the daughter of Pandareos, suggesting Procne's transformation.

5. This metamorphosis was, evidently, a famous point of dispute among ancient critics. F.
Williams explains in his commentary to Callimachus' *Hymn to Apollo* (Oxford, 1978), 32–33, that
the lines describing Niobe's metamorphosis were athetized by Aristophanes and Aristarchus, and
thus by including Niobe's metamorphosis in lines 22–24, "Callimachus is defending the vexed
lines against criticism, both textual and philosophical" (33).

6. W. Fauth, "Zur Typologie Mythischen Metamorphosen in der Homerischen Dichtung,"
Poetica 7 (1975): 261.

7. Other metamorphoses include the self-transformers Periclymenus (fr. 33a–b M-W) and
Mestra (frr. 43–44 M-W); also Actaeon (fr. 346 M-W *Dubia*).

8. Fraser, *Ptolemaic Alexandria,* 770–73; Pfeiffer, *Scholarship,* 152. See also A. Giannini,
"Studi Sulla Paradossografia Greca I. Da Omero a Callimaco: Motivi e Forme del Meraviglioso,"
Ist. Lomb. 97 (1963): 258–65; Westermann, *Paradoxographoi Graeci,* xi–xii; Lafaye, *Les Méta-
morphoses d'Ovide,* 12–13.

9. See Galen's Preface to his *De Simplicium Medicamentorum Temperamentis ac Facultatibus*
(V.XI, p. 792f. Kühn), where he complains that Pamphilus had included ληρώδεις μεταμορ-
φώσεις in his botanical work (*Περὶ Βοτανῶν*). Agatharchides (*GGM* 1.117.8 [Müller]) also
launches an attack on the use of mythology in supposedly scientific inquiries.

10. Gow and Scholfield, *Nicander, the Poems and Poetical Fragments,* 18, argue that the
mythological ornaments are probably Nicander's own. Hopkinson, *Hellenistic Anthology,* 143,

Nicander

mythological aetiologies (and some of these include metamorphosis) for spiders (Titan's blood 8–12), the exfoliation of snakes (343–58), the lizard (483–87), and the hyacinth (902–6), among others. His poetic collection of metamorphoses most likely fit into this strange category of mythological-scientific didactic epic.

Natural Metamorphoses in the *Metamorphoses*

In constructing his stories of natural metamorphosis, Ovid seems to have shown a greater interest in the actual process of metamorphosis than his predecessors. One reason for this was to give his physical metamorphoses a sort of humorously "scientific" coloring by providing detailed explanations for the prominent traits of the natural phenomena that result from the transformations. We should get a sense that part of the pleasure of reading the *Metamorphoses* is in observing Ovid's ability to incorporate into his dramatic stories these detailed metamorphoses, which function as explanations for the most prominent characteristics of the animal or plant into which his characters are transformed. Jean-Marc Frécaut has nicely described Ovid's technique as a sort of "esprit de logique."[11] He locates the humor precisely in the methodically rigorous and pseudo-scientific sounding nature of Ovid's minutely detailed descriptions of the fantastic acts of metamorphosis. There are over sixty metamorphoses of humans to animals or plants in the *Metamorphoses,* and most of these occur in Books 1 through 11 in the sections dealing with Greek mythology, while the metamorphoses in the final books of the poem are primarily concerned with religious aetiology.

A fascination with the physical details of metamorphosis is often said to be a characteristic of the Alexandrian period, the *locus classicus* being Jason's sowing of the dragon's teeth in Apollonius' *Argonautica* (3.1381–98).[12] Yet this description and the few others that we actually have, such as Horace *Odes* 2.20 and *Ciris* 493–519, both commonly considered to be based on Hellenistic

---

observes on the *Theriaca* that "this contrast between subject-matter and presentation, 'science' and poetry, is the driving force behind the poem."

11. J.-M. Frécaut, *L'Esprit et l'Humeur chez Ovide* (Grenoble, 1972), 261–62. Barkan, *The Gods Made Flesh,* 21ff., writes of the "the emotional logic" of Ovid's metamorphoses.

12. So Hollis, *Ovid Metamorphoses VIII,* xvi–xvii. He points out early evidence of this interest in the plays of Euripides (fr. 930 N²) and Sophocles (*Inachus*). Wilkinson, *Ovid Recalled,* 160, generalizes that "a taste for the grotesque was characteristic of the jaded palate of Hellenistic decadence." As proof, he lists a number of wall paintings at Pompeii showing the process of transformation. Actual Hellenistic examples are few, and we should note Moschus' very brief description of Zeus' transformation into a bull in the *Europa:* κρύψε θεὸν καὶ τρέψε δέμας καὶ γείνετο ταῦρος (79).

models,[13] do not reveal the same aetiological intention in the narration of the metamorphosis as we see in Ovid, but instead a taste for bizarre realism. Although Ovid was no doubt motivated by the same inclination and frequently indulges in the grotesque in his narrative, what we suspect is new in Ovid's metamorphoses is the aetiological focus of his descriptions, which serves to account for natural features.

Comparison of Ovid's metamorphoses with earlier treatments is almost impossible because of the lack of surviving texts. Our most extensive evidence of the treatment of the metamorphosis theme in this period comes from the text of the later mythographer Antoninus Liberalis in his summaries of the works of Nicander and Boios, which, as we have seen, evidently represent the first poetic collections of metamorphoses. In these summaries the metamorphoses for the most part are aetiological, but, as far as we can tell, there seems to be little interest in describing in detail the actual process of transformation. In the only probable fragment from Nicander's *Heteroioumena* of any length to survive independently from Antoninus, the transformation of Hecuba is presented briefly and with no elaboration (fr. 62 Gow-Scholfield). Ovid includes in the *Metamorphoses* versions of all but four of the stories Antoninus Liberalis attributes to Nicander's *Heteroioumena,* but, as we shall see, Ovid's metamorphoses are very different.[14] Ovid also seems to have been aware of Boios' Ὀρνιθογονία (cf. Aeropus at *Met.* 7.390, A.L. 18) and, as we shall see, to have made use of it in a very original manner. As the title implies, Boios' work dealt with the transformations of humans into birds. Most of the characters metamorphosed have the same name as the bird they become, or Boios provides an explanation for how the bird got its name. Some of the transformations also provide explanations for why certain birds are of good or bad omen (A.L. 11, 15, 19, 21). In their aetiological intent Boios' metamorphoses seem closer to those of Ovid, yet his stories do not seem to have incorporated the same degree of sophistication and detail as Ovid's. We know that Ovid was familiar (*Tr.* 4.10.43–44) with Aemilius Macer's first-century B.C.E. translation of Boios' work into Latin (frr. 1–6, pp. 107–8 Morel; pp. 138–39 Buechner). What

---

13. See Lyne's suggestion, *Ciris, ad* 497, that direct Ovidian influence may be detected in the description of the transformation.

14. It is probably not necessary to pause at any length over the vexed question of the extent of Ovid's debt to Nicander, since Ovid's use of his sources is so independent. See W. Kroll, *RE* 17.1 (1936): 250–65, who challenges the tendency of earlier scholars such as E. Bethe, "Ovid und Nikander," *Hermes* 39 (1904): 1–14, and C.W. Vollgraf, *Nikander und Ovid* (Groningen, 1900), to find in Nicander a primary source for Ovid. See also Hinds, *Metamorphosis of Persephone,* 14–15, 54–55, 139 n.39, 166–67 n.40, for a detailed discussion of Ovid's relationship to Nicander in *Metamorphoses* 5 (with much helpful background material).

little evidence we have suggests that Aemilius Macer's treatment of meta-morphosis in his *Ornithogonia* may have been similarly aetiological.[15] By way of taking a closer look at Ovid's natural or physical metamorphoses, let us compare Ovid's version of the story of Galanthis in Book 9 with the similar story preserved by Antoninus Liberalis under Nicander's name (A.L. 29). This will highlight the different aetiological focus of Ovid's version of this meta-morphosis, which explains in this case the reasons for most notable natural characteristics of the animal instead of the origins of a cult.[16]

In Nicander's story Galinthias, a companion of Alcmene, is punished for her trickery against Hera by being transformed into a weasel. Her transformation is merely stated by Nicander's epitomizer Antoninus: ὅτι θνητὴ τοὺς θεοὺς ἐξηπάτησεν, καὶ αὐτὴν ἐποίησαν δολερὰν γαλῆν (A.L. 29.3). He adds that as a weasel she will be fertilized through her ears and give birth through her mouth. The story ends with a cult *aetion* for the worship of Galinthias in connection with Heracles, and this is clearly Nicander's main interest, ταῦτα νῦν ἔτι τὰ ἱερὰ Θηβαῖοι φυλάττουσι (4). Ovid, on the other hand, mentions nothing about her cult worship or statue, and we should note that since Alc-mene is telling this story, she could hardly know of later cultic institutions.[17] He is interested, instead, in elaborating her metamorphosis into a weasel. The story is made vivid by the first-hand narration of Alcmene herself, who describes Galanthis:

> "una ministrarum, media de plebe, Galanthis,
> flava comas aderat, faciendis strenua iussis
> officiis dilecta suis. . . ."

(9.306–8)

---

15. See J.-P. Néraudau, "Aemilius Macer, ou la gloire du second rang," *ANRW* 2.30.3 (1983): 1730, and H. Dahlmann, *Über Aemilius Macer* (Wiesbaden, 1981), 7. In his monograph, Dahlmann has reviewed the fragments attributed to the *Ornithogonia* in Morel and argues (6ff.) that only frr. 1–4 belong to the work; frr. 5–6 are more likely to belong in the *Theriaca*. E.J. Kenney, in a brief review of Dahlmann in *CR* 32 (1982): 277, is inclined to accept his conclusions, as is Courtney, *Fragmentary Latin Poets,* 293–94. We are thus left with only the story of Picus (fr. 1 Morel) and that of Cycnus (fr. 4 Morel), a fragment that supports the idea of the importance of augury to Macer: *Cycnus in auspiciis semper laetissimus ales.*

16. We rely, of course, on the faithfulness of Antoninus Liberalis to his original (in this case Nicander is the only stated source). See Forbes Irving, *Metamorphosis in Greek Myths,* 20–24, for a discussion and defense of Antoninus' reliability, and 29–32 on Nicander's metamorphoses and Ovid; also Papathomopoulos *ad* A.L. 29 n.5. For a different emphasis, on "preservation or clarification through metamorphosis," see Solodow, *World of Ovid's Metamorphoses,* 193.

17. So also the story Iole in turn narrates about the transformation of her sister Dryope into a Lotus tree (9.325–93) contains no trace of Nicander's version (A.L. 32), in which Dryope is made a nymph and has a sanctuary and rites consecrated in her honor, to which no women are allowed.

In this short description, Ovid has prepared the ground for his aetiological metamorphosis. Galanthis tricks the goddess Lucina, thus allowing Hercules to be born, as in Nicander (who employs the Fates, instead of Lucina), and then to underline her impiety she laughs at the goddess. Galanthis is promptly punished for her action and in the ensuing description of her metamorphosis each aspect of her new animal form is explained by her previous character, behavior, appearance, and circumstances:

> strenuitas antiqua manet; nec terga colorem
> amisere suum: forma est diversa priori.
> quae quia mendaci parientem iuverat ore,
> ore parit nostrasque domos, ut et ante, frequentat.
>
> (9.320–23)

Ovid has explained not only why the punishment fits the crime, but why the weasel has reddish hair (*flava comas*), why she is so energetic (*faciendis strenua iussis*), why she gives birth through her mouth and lives in houses.[18] The punishment exacted by Juno captures and embodies both Galanthis' crimes and the main theme of the story, as L. Barkan remarks, "by uniting the organs of speech and parturition."[19] This disturbing conjunction was evidently based on ancient belief, caused probably by seeing the weasel carry its children about in its mouth (Pliny *Nat.* 29.60). Galanthis' name is also the *aetion* for the Greek name of the weasel, γαλέη.

The scholarly and etymological conclusion of this story and others has been targeted as one of the techniques whereby Ovid distances his reader emotionally from the moral and ethical content of his stories.[20] Instead these aetiological endings often serve to underline the moral implicit in the tale and even, as here, heighten the revulsion increasingly evoked in the course of the poem by the long series of unjust metamorphoses brought about by offended deities. Galanthis' minutely particularized transformation elicits horror from readers as we watch the positive features of this industrious, clever, and helpful woman become perverted into natural and animal functions. The human power of speech, by which she overcame the goddess, is replaced with the function of parturition—which is both human and animal. The aetiological ending contributes to the emotional impact of the story, rather than robbing it of meaning.

18. Pliny *Nat.* 29.60 writes that there are two types of weasels: *Mustelarum duo genera . . . haec autem quae in domibus nostris oberrat.* See further Celoria, *Metamorphoses of Antoninus Liberalis,* 191–93.

19. Barkan, *The Gods Made Flesh,* 67.

20. Galinsky, *Ovid's Metamorphoses,* 13, 62; Solodow, *World of Ovid's Metamorphoses,* 157, 168–72; Hutchinson, *Hellenistic Poetry,* 340; Due, *Changing Forms,* 157.

[handwritten margin note: The stars are the intrusion of metamorphosis into the Fasti. Πάντα ῥεῖ - could also be Lucr. V]

Other parallels with Nicander's metamorphoses bring out the same differences. In most cases Ovid reveals his concern with an explanation of the origins of the natural features and habits of particular species of animals or birds, as opposed to Nicander, who seems to have been interested mainly in cultural and religious *aetia* and consequently, we suspect, was not interested in describing the transformations themselves or in investing his stories with this sort of logical dramatic or psychological continuity.[21] We are, of course, at the mercy of Antoninus' summaries, but we should consider that in six of the stories attributed to Nicander characters simply disappear instead of being transformed (A.L. 1, 13, 25 and [40]) or turn into nymphs (A.L. 30, 32). We may, for example, compare Nicander's account of the metamorphosis of the Emathides (Pierides, A.L. 9) with that of Ovid in Book 5, lines 669–78. In Nicander the Emathides are transformed into nine different, apparently arbitrary, birds, whereas Ovid focuses his story by having them all change into magpies (*picae*), birds which, he explains, retain their vociferousness: *nunc quoque in alitibus facundia prisca remansit / raucaque garrulitas studiumque immane loquendi* (5.677–78). Again, the Minyeides are in Nicander (A.L. 10) transformed into bats and owls with the remark Ἔφυγον δὲ αἱ τρεῖς τὴν αὐγὴν τοῦ ἡλίου (A.L. 10.4). In the *Metamorphoses,* however, all three sisters become bats (4.389–415), and Ovid's clever narrative here dramatically explains the most prominent traits of bats—their nocturnal habits, their love of dark corners and houses, as well as their name (*tenent a vespere nomen* [4.415], that is, in Latin *vespertilio,* νυκτερίς in Greek)—as the result of the sisters' fright at the sudden light with which Dionysus fills their house (*ignes ac lumina vitant* 4.406). The small, shrill voices of bats are also explained as a punishment for the Minyeides' improper choice of telling stories when they should have been worshiping Dionysus (4.31–35). We suspect that even if Nicander did include more description, the dramatic and psychological development of these stories may be attributed to Ovid's unique genius.

Among the metamorphoses attributed to the writer Boios we find natural aetiological explanations closer to those of Ovid. It has been suggested that the metamorphosis of Perdix recounted in *Metamorphoses* 8 is possibly drawn from Boios' Ὀρνιθογονία, "For regular features of the Greek poem, paralleled here, were the intervention of a particular god to transform a human being into a bird of the same name, and the explanation of the bird's most notable habits as due to a character trait, or accident which befell it, when still in human

---

21. Similarly Forbes Irving, *Metamorphosis in Greek Myths,* 27. *[handwritten: Stars]*

[handwritten margin note: arrow]

form."[22] Ovid first of all announces that Perdix's metamorphosis does indeed herald the creation of a new species of bird: *unica tunc volucris nec visa prioribus annis, / factaque nuper avis longum tibi, Daedale, crimen* (8.239–40). We then learn that Perdix was himself the inventor of the saw and the compass (8.244–49, note *primus* 247).[23] Daedalus traditionally cast his nephew Perdix off the Acropolis out of jealousy at these inventions, and for this reason he was forced to flee from Athens to Crete.[24] In Ovid's version, Pallas out of pity and respect for Perdix's ingenuity saves him from death by turning him into a bird in mid-fall (8.250–53). In the description of his metamorphosis Ovid explains why partridges do not fly and instead, relying on their nimble feet and wings, stay safely on the ground:

> sed vigor ingenii quondam velocis in alas
> inque pedes abiit; nomen quod et ante, remansit.
> non tamen haec alte volucris sua corpora tollit,
> nec facit in ramis altoque cacumine nidos:
> propter humum volitat ponitque in saepibus ova
> antiquique memor metuit sublimia casus.
>
> (8.254–59)

Hollis suggests that Ovid in line 255 echoes Boios' language as exemplified in a typical paraphrase in Antoninus Liberalis (7.7): γενομένους ὄρνιθας τῷ αὐτῷ ἐποίησαν ὀνόματι καλεῖσθαι καθὰ καὶ πρὶν ἢ μεταβαλεῖν αὐτοὺς ὠνομάζοντο. Whether or not the metamorphosis of Perdix is original to Ovid, we can see here how Ovid in the retelling of this traditional Greek myth has neatly managed to incorporate into his story an explanation for both the name and behavior of the partridge. The effect of the precision of Ovid's explanation here, as elsewhere, is not without humor. Yet at the same time the *aetion* also serves as a significant parallel and contrast to the fate of Daedalus' son Icarus.

22. Hollis, *Ovid Metamorphoses VIII, ad* 236–59. The metamorphosis is found in no earlier sources.
23. Hollis, *Ovid Metamorphoses VIII, ad loc.:* "The style is probably that of a Hellenistic treatise." The attribution of these inventions to Perdix is traditional. In Diod. 4.76.5 Perdix (Talos) is said to have invented the potter's wheel and other things as well.
24. Versions of the story may be found in Hygin. *Fab.* 39; Apollod. 3.15.6; Diod. 4.76 (in these two sources Daedalus' nephew is named Calos or Talos and his sister is called Perdix). We do not know whether the name Perdix (first attested in Sophocles' *Camici* fr. 323 Pearson) was associated with the bird in mythology. For the name of the partridge see Chantraine: "on a dérivé de πέρδομαι etymologie qui remonte à l'antiquité. Il peut s'agir du bruit fait par l'oiseau en s'envolant." Cf. Bömer's discussion, *Met., ad* 8.236–59.

He too experiences a *casus,* but, although dressed in the guise of a bird by his father, Icarus is significantly not "saved" from death by being metamorphosed into a real bird as he falls into the sea (8.227–30).

Two other ornithological metamorphoses, those of Daedalion and Aesacus, both in *Metamorphoses* 11, share similar aetiological features with that of Perdix.[25] In all three stories metamorphosis transpires in mid-air, after the character has attempted to leap off a cliff (or been pushed off, as in Perdix's case), and is the result of divine intervention motivated by pity,[26] and in all three an explanation is provided for the name and characteristic behavior of the bird into which the character is transformed. The metamorphoses of Daedalion and Aesacus frame the episode of Ceyx and Alcyone in Book 11, which produces a series of three consecutive ornithological metamorphoses. It may be that Ovid has included by means of this trio an acknowledgment of the aetiological metamorphoses of his predecessor Boios.[27]

At the very beginning of his description of his brother Daedalion's metamorphosis, Ceyx, Ovid's internal narrator, underlines the continuity of the character of Daedalion into his transformed state—a falcon:[28]

"vir fuit (et—tanta est animi constantia—iam tum
acer erat belloque ferox ad vimque paratus)
nomine Daedalion. . . ."

(11.293–95)

When Daedalion had tried to kill himself by hurling himself off Mount Parnassus, Apollo out of pity had transformed him into a bird, one which now takes out its own suffering on other species of birds: "*et nunc accipiter, nullis satis aequus, in omnes / saevit aves aliisque dolens fit causa dolendi*" (11.344–45). Commentators note that A.L. 3, attributed to Boios, presents a similar story.[29] It tells of a man called Hierax who was changed by Poseidon out of pity and to save his life into a bird that took his name ('Ιέραξ is a hawk or falcon), which explains the bird's fierce behavior towards other birds (cf. Boios A.L.

---

25. Both of these stories first appear here. Daedalion is later found in Hyg. *Fab.* 200: "unter Einfluss Ovids,"(Bömer, *Met., ad* 11.291–345). Aesacus appears in Apollod. 3.147.

26. The motivation of pity in causing metamorphosis is not uncommon in the poem as a whole; see also, e.g. 4.531 (Ino), 11.741–44 (Ceyx and Alcyone), 15.547–51 (Egeria).

27. G.M.H. Murphy, ed., *Ovid's Metamorphoses XI* (Bristol, 1979), *ad* 291–345; Bömer, *Met., ad* 11.749–95 (p. 430).

28. A further parallel between the stories of Daedalion and Aesacus is that both are narrated by internal narrators. An unnamed old man narrates the story of Aesacus' metamorphosis (11.749–51).

29. Bömer, *Met., ad loc.,* and Papathomopoulos *ad* A.L. 3.

3.4: πλείστους . . . ὀρνίθων ἀποκτεῖναι). We might expect an explanation for the name of the bird in Ovid as well and perhaps he has in fact deftly provided an etymology for the Latin name of the bird, *accipiter,* in his story. Ernout-Meillet explain the etymology of *accipiter* in the following way: "le mot est parallèle à *acupedius, acu-pedius* rapelle gr. ὠκύ-πους, *accipiter* rapelle gr. ὠκύ-πτερος."[30] Now, it has often been remarked that Daedalion's metamorphosis is uniquely anticipated in Ceyx's description of his brother's race to Parnassus (11.332–39) and it seems that these lines may contain a hint at the etymology of *accipiter: "iam tum mihi currere visus / plus homine est,* alasque pedes *sumpsisse putares / effugit ergo omnes* velox*que cupidine leti"* (336–38). As we will see elsewhere in the poem, Ovid enjoys this grafting of a Latin etymology onto a tale of Greek origin.

On the other hand, Aesacus' character does not, in fact, continue into his transformed state, but rather his final action of leaping provides an explanation for his new bird name (*mergus;* the Greek name for this bird, probably a grebe, κολυμβίς, has the same etymology, from κολυμβάω—to plunge headlong; cf. Varro *L.L.* 5.78: *mergus quod mergendo in aquam captat escam*) and for this bird's most characteristic behavior, an element we find in Boios as well (A.L. 7).[31] In anger at having been thwarted in his suicide, Aesacus continues in bird-form to seek his death under water:

"fecit amor maciem: longa internodia crurum,
longa manet cervix, caput est a corpore longe;
aequor amat nomenque tenet, quia *mergitur* illo."

(11.793–95)

In all three of these ornithological metamorphosis stories, we can discern Ovid's aetiological and etymological intent. We can also see how Ovid has evidently developed the literal and matter-of-fact aetiological metamorphoses of his predecessor Boios into complex and dramatically satisfying narratives.

In many of these stories involving natural metamorphosis, we have seen that the name of the character is identical to that of the animal or plant into which s/he is transformed. Not surprisingly, most of these are Greek. The names reflect the aetiological affiliations of many of these myths; for example Daphne, Cycnus, Nyctimene, Narcissus, Crocus, Smilax, Lyncus, Arachne, the

---

30. Ernout-Meillet, s.v. *accipiter. OLD accipiter* prob. *acu-peter "swift-flying" (for acu, cf. perh. acupedius; for peter, cf. skt. patram "bird" . . .).

31. See Bömer, *Met., ad* 11.749–95, 791–92.

Meleagrides, Lotis, Cyparissus, Hyacinthus, Myrrha, and Alcyone[32] all name animals and plants. Throughout the *Metamorphoses* Ovid displays an evident interest in foregrounding the etymological intent of many of his stories, an occupation intimately connected with both his cosmological and scholarly interests. Frequently he will alert us to the aetiological import of these significant character names, sometimes noting the preservation of a character's name in an aetiological footnote at the end of the transformation. A good example comes at 10.501–2, in the story of Myrrha—*est honor et lacrimis, stillataque robore murra / nomen erile tenet nulloque tacebitur aevo*—or again at 14.396, in the tale of Picus and Canens—*nec quicquam antiquum Pico nisi nomina restant* (also 8.255, 9.348, 12.145). At other times Ovid will take pains to explain the etymology of a name of the new animal or plant if it differs from the character's name. For example, when Ovid describes the appearance of the poisonous plant aconite as arising from the foam from Cerberus' lips, he notes that a common etymology for the name (*agrestes aconita vocant* 7.419) derives from the plant's habit of growing on rocks, without soil (ἀκονιτί, cf. Pliny *Nat.* 27.10.1). Here he is perhaps slyly suggesting with *agrestes* that an alternate derivation of *aconitum* from ἀκόνη (*caute*) is in fact the more accurate etymology.[33] The name of the ciris bird into which Scylla is transformed will again be explicitly etymologized: *in avem mutata vocatur / Ciris et a tonso est hoc nomen adepta capillo* (8.150–51).[34]

There are also a number of interesting instances in which Ovid goes out of his way to explain the specifically Latin name for an animal. This parallels Varro's preference for deriving, if possible, Latin words from Latin sources.[35] For example, the metamorphosis of Arne (*Met.* 7.465–68), who betrayed Paros for gold, is mentioned only briefly and her character is emphasized in her transformation: *mutata est in avem, quae nunc quoque diligit aurum, / nigra pedes, nigris velata monedula pennis* (7.467–68). The story and her name do not seem to have appeared elsewhere, although the tale does bear a notable

---

32. Bömer remarks *ad loc.* on the "naturwissenschaftliche Züge" of Alcyone's transformation at *Met.* 11.742ff.

33. On this etymology see J.C. McKeown, ed., *Ovid: Amores Vol. I. Text and Prolegomena* (Liverpool, 1987), 59–60.

34. See Hollis, *Ovid Metamorphoses VIII, ad loc.* Greek etymologies implied, but not explicitly explained, include the bilingual wordplay on the name for the *aeropus*, pointed out by Kenney, Introduction and Notes to *Ovid's Metamorphoses, ad* 7.390, and that for the name of the anemone at 10.738–39, as noted by Haupt-Ehwald *ad* 10.735ff.

35. On animal names see *L.L.* 5.75–79, 95–101. Note how Varro supplies false Latin antecedents for the name Proserpina (5.68), but elsewhere mistakenly gives Greek etymologies for native words (e.g., 5.96–97 *sus, ovis, vitulus*).

resemblance to that of Tarpeia.[36] Indeed, it seems certain that Ovid's etymology cannot be Greek in origin, for the Greek name for the jackdaw is κολοιός. The etymology of *monedula* is debated; Ernout-Meillet conjecture that the word is formed from the two words *moneta-edula* (on the pattern of *ficedula*).[37] Whether the word for jackdaw was or was not truly derived from the stem of *moneta,* it seems likely that Ovid is exploiting this obvious wordplay with the Latin name of the bird and its love of bright objects at *Met.* 7.467 (cf. Cicero *Flac.* 76: *non plus aurum tibi quam monedulae committebant;* Pliny *Nat.* 10.10.41). We should note that *nunc quoque* underlines the *aetion.* Elsewhere the Latin names are explained for the lizard or gecko, *stellio* (Greek ἀσκάλαβος / ἀσκαλαβώτης: *nomen habet variis stellatus corpora guttis* 5.461),[38] bats (4.415), and the grebe (11.795). The Latin names for the woodpecker, *picus* (Greek: κελεός: 14.320–436), and the heron, *ardea* (14.578–80, Greek ἐρωδιός) result directly from character names. Ovid's technique reflects that of contemporary and earlier attempts on the part of Roman antiquarians to find an etymological significance for Latin names on the basis of Greek etymological theory. As a number of scholars remind us, etymology in antiquity was not only a branch of linguistics, but also of science and philosophy, since many names were considered to be related intimately to the nature of the objects they named.[39] In Ovid the suggestion made by these Latin aetiological stories, however tongue-in-cheek, is that the Roman language also has a basis in the natural world.

Ovid's primary interest in his metamorphoses of the type considered above seems to have been to construct a narrative that is at the same time both psychologically compelling and explanatory, leading naturally, and often humorously, to an aetiological metamorphosis that explains a prominent feature of the animal or plant into which the person is transformed.[40] The appearance

36. As W.S. Anderson, ed., *Ovid's Metamorphoses Books 6–10* (Oklahoma, 1972), *ad loc.* notes; cf. R.M. Ogilvie, ed., *A Commentary on Livy Books I–V* (Oxford, 1970), *ad* Liv. 1.11.5–9, on the Tarpeia legend and similar versions. Forbes Irving, *Metamorphosis in Greek Myths,* 226, suggests that Aemilius Macer may have first related the story in his *Ornithogonia.*

37. Ernout-Meillet, s.v. *monedula.* Also *OLD* [dub.; cf. *ficedula*]. Bömer, *Met.,* *ad* 7.468 disagrees. The word is first attested in Plautus' *Capt.* 1002 as a term of endearment.

38. See further on this etymology, K.S. Myers, "The Lizard and the Owl: An Etymological Pair in Ovid, *Metamorphoses,* Book 5," *AJP* 113 (1992): 63–68.

39. See F. Cairns, *Tibullus: A Hellenistic Poet at Rome* (Cambridge, 1979), 90.

40. The idea that Ovid's metamorphoses are intended to express the "essential or deep-seated character" of the person transformed seems difficult to uphold, especially in light of the great variations in the transformations; for a statement of this position see esp. Solodow, *World of Ovid's Metamorphoses,* 176ff., Galinsky, *Ovid's Metamorphoses,* 47–48, and H. Dörrie, "Wandlung und Dauer: Ovid's Metamorphosen und Poseidonius' Lehre von der Substanz," *AU* 4.2 (1959): 95–116.

of the forms of the adjective *novus* or the word *nuper* does not always guarantee the aetiological status of a story. When Ovid tells us that Cycnus (2.377), the Pierides (5.300–301, 674), and Picus (14.390–91) all become "new" birds, it is unclear whether this newness refers to the species as a whole or to these individuals,[41] especially since he gives us three versions of swan metamorphosis (*Met.* 2.367–80, 7.371–72, 12.144–45) and two hyacinth *aetia* at 10.207 and 13.396. This lack of certainty does not weaken the aetiological focus of Ovid's metamorphoses; if the transformations are only of individuals, they nevertheless function emblematically, as the identical names suggest. Even if they are not the first of their species, the descriptions of the metamorphoses of, for example, Arachne into a spider or the Lycian peasants into frogs, all incorporate dramatically logical explanations for certain characteristics of the animals into which these characters are transformed, while they simultaneously reveal psychological insights and involve real moral issues. As Kenney has suggested, the whole poem offers a sort of "ethopoeia" of nature.[42] Ovid's genius consists precisely in his ability to combine the psychological and aetiological in his narrative, reminding his reader of his role set out in the proem as a narrator of both cosmogonical and dramatic epic narrative. The *Metamorphoses* is a poem that accommodates and invites interpretation on any number of levels.

Ovid's Elements

Ovid's anthropomorphized or anthropogonic depiction of the creation of the natural world through these aetiological mythical stories implies a profound connection between humans and the physical world. Human as microcosm is not merely subject to the same physical influences as the larger macrocosm, but itself forms and becomes a part of the whole. The implied parallels between the natural and human world are underpinned by Ovid's use of the scientific terminology of his opening and concluding cosmogonic passages in many of his descriptions of the process of metamorphosis. Ovid suggests that it is through a recognition of the fluid nature of the world of the elements, as set out in *Metamorphoses* 1 and 15, that we can understand the processes, the

---

41. So also *novae . . . ranae* (6.381), and *flosque novus* (10.206), *nova . . . arbor* (10.310). Words associated with newness are extremely common in all of Ovid's descriptions of metamorphosis.

42. E.J. Kenney, "*Discordia Semina Rerum,*" review of *L'image et la Pensée dans les Métamorphoses d'Ovide,* by S. Viarre, *CR* 17 (1967): 52. See now E.A. Schmidt, *Ovids Poetische Menschenwelt: Die Metamorphosen als Metapher und Symphonie* (Heidelberg, 1991).

"physics," of the transformations that take place throughout the poem. Ovid hereby further associates his fantastic mythological stories of supernatural metamorphosis with the natural-philosophical framework of his epic by lending them a scientific color borrowed from a narrative mode essentially foreign to mythical poetry. The deliberate disparity between the large-scale cosmogonic plan of the poem and the local content of the metamorphic tales generates a tension and humor peculiar to this epic. Specifically, in the language Ovid uses to describe metamorphosis there are a number of references to the theory of the four elements that is first set out in the Cosmogony of Book 1.[43] We will first consider these echoes and then turn to an examination of the effect produced by the conjunction of philosophical and mythological narrative modes.

Ovid's Cosmogony at *Metamorphoses* 1.5–75 comprises an eclectic combination of various philosophical theories.[44] In many of its features it is similar to the poetic cosmogonies of Apollonius in the *Argonautica* (1.492–511) and Vergil in his *Eclogues* (6.31–40).[45] The appearance in these opening lines of Titan (*Met.* 1.10), Phoebe (11), and Amphitrite (14), in metonymy for the sun, moon, and sea, infuses the scene with an initial poetic hue that soon gives way to the technical scientific language of natural philosophical didacticism, *physica*.[46] The metonymies serve, however, to remind us, along with the translation at *Met.* 1.7 of Hesiod's Χάος (*Th.* 116), that Cosmogony was originally Theogony.[47] Clearly central to these accounts, and repeated as well in the Speech of Pythagoras at *Met.* 15.237–51, is the physical theory of the four elements

43. Similarly F. Norwood, "Unity in the Diversity of Ovid's *Metamorphoses*," *CJ* 59 (1964): 171, and Haege, *Terminologie und Typologie der Verwandlungsvorgangs*, 268–71; cf. S. Viarre's long list of the appearances of earth, air, fire, and water in metamorphosis, in *L'Image et la Pensée dans les Métamorphoses d'Ovide* (Paris, 1964), 309–48.

44. For the enormous range of bibliography on this passage see Bömer, *Met., ad loc.;* also G. Maurach, "Ovids Kosmogonie: Quellenbenutzung und Traditionsstiftung," *Gymnasium* 86 (1979): 131–48; F. Lämmli, *Vom Chaos Zum Cosmos: Zur Geschichte einer Idee* (Basel, 1962), 1–28; Wilkinson, *Ovid Recalled,* 213–14; P. DeLacy, "Philosophical Doctrine and Poetic Technique in Ovid," *CJ* 43 (1947): 155–61; F.E. Roberts, "The Creation Story in Ovid's *Metamorphoses* 1," *CP* (1913): 401–14; W.C. Stephens, "The Function of Religious and Philosophical Ideas in Ovid's *Metamorphoses*" (Ph.D. diss., Princeton University, 1957), 44–77; L. Alfonsi, "L'Inquadramento Filosofico delle Metamorfosi," in *Ovidiana,* ed. N.I. Herescu (Paris, 1958), 265–72. Cf. Ovid's similar cosmogonies at *Fasti* 1.103ff., 5.11ff.; *Ars* 2.45ff.

45. See Knox, *Traditions of Augustan Poetry,* 10–26, W. Spoerri, *Späthellenistische Berichte über Welt, Kultur und Götter* (Basel, 1959), 43–52.

46. Due, *Changing Forms,* 97–99, is excellent on this passage. He suggests that *tellus* at *Met.* 1.12 should perhaps be seen as a fourth metonymy (97).

47. See Lämmli, *Vom Chaos Zum Cosmos: Zur Geschichte einer Idee,* 3 n.9.

associated with Empedocles: fire, air, water, and earth, which serve as the primary components of all other things.[48] Although Ovid describes these in Lucretian atomistic terms as *semina rerum* (1.9), Lucretius had, of course, attacked Empedocles' theory that the elements were the actual primary matter (*DRN* 1.705–829).[49] These four elements, forming as they do pairs of opposites, were initially at war (*discordia Met.* 1.9, *litem* 21, cf. *discors concordia* 433) with each other: *frigida pugnabant calidis, umentia siccis, / mollia cum duris, sine pondere habentia pondus* (*Met.* 1.19–20).[50]

The universe is created when the elements have been separated off from each other into their proper spheres, (*diremit* 21, *abscidit* 22, *secrevit* 23, etc.), determined by the relative weight and density of their properties (1.21–31):

> ignea convexi vis et sine pondere caeli
> emicuit summaque locum sibi fecit in arce;
> proximus est aer illi levitate locoque;
> densior his tellus elementaque grandia traxit
> et pressa est gravitate sua; circumfluus umor
> ultima possedit solidumque coercuit orbem.

(1.26–31)

Thus the four elements are established as the basic constituents from which all things are formed and accordingly are interrelated, by means of sort of "metamorphic geochemistry."[51] In this context too we ought to recall that ancient medical scientists used these elemental categories in postulating the physiological theory of the four humors as the grounds of human health.[52] Human

---

48. Arist. *Met.* 985a29–985b4 (DK 31 A37). See G.E.R. Lloyd, "The Hot and the Cold, the Dry and the Wet in Greek Philosophy," *JHS* 84 (1964): 92–106, for a discussion of the origins of these opposites in Greek philosophy. For the possible influence on Ovid of Sallustius' *Empedoclea*, see F. della Corte, "Gli Empedoclea e Ovidio," *Maia* 37 (1985): 3–12. Cf. for the four elements Cic. *N.D.* 2.84, *Tusc.* 1.17.40; Diod. 1.7.1–2; Vitruv. 1.4.5–6, 8 Praef.; Manil. 1.137ff.; Sen. *N.Q.* 7.27.4, *Dial.* 4.19.1; Diog. Laer. 7.142 (Posidonius, Chrysippus, Cleanthes, Antipater).

49. For Lucretius the four elements are instead the *maxima mundi / . . . membra* (*DRN* 5.243–44, 380–81), of which the mortal physical world is composed: *e quibus haec rerum consistere summa videtur* (5.237).

50. Again Ovid is using Lucretian language largely derived from the cosmogony at *DRN* 5.416–95. Lucretius speaks similarly of an original indistinct mass (*moles* 436, cf. *Met.* 1.7 *moles*) and of the war between the beginnings of things (*discordia* 437, cf. 5.380–83, 1.759–62). The notion of strife is associated with Empedocles, cf. Ap. Rhod. *Argon.* 1.498 (νεῖκος); Hor. *Epist.* 1.12.19–20: *rerum concordia discors, / Empedocles;* Manil. 1.42.

51. The phrase is Barkan's, from *The Gods Made Flesh*, 30.

52. See I.M. Lonie, *The Hippocratic Treatises* (Berlin, New York, 1981), 54–62, on the theory of the four constituent humors; also E.D. Phillips, *Greek Medicine* (London, 1973), 48–58, and J. Scarborough, *Roman Medicine* (Ithaca, 1969), 52ff. on Varro, Celsus, and Vitruvius.

physiognomy and the cosmos are intimately related because of their identical constituents. This close relationship may suggest why in the *Metamorphoses* the transitions between human, animal, and natural phenomena seem to be so frighteningly fluid and easy.

The agent of this separation and arrangement of the original primal chaos is referred to as *deus et melior. . . natura* (*Met.* 1.21; cf. 1.32, 48, 57, 79), usually taken to reflect Stoic thought.[53] The creation of plant, animal, and human life on earth is also brought about by this divine agency (1.32–88). At *Metamorphoses* 1.76–88 Ovid presents in the typical manner of a didactic narrator two alternative theories for the origin of man. He suggests that if humankind was not created *divino semine* (1.78), then it arose from a combination of all four elements:

sive recens *tellus* seductaque nuper ab alto
aethere cognati retinebat semina *caeli.*
quam satus Iapeto, mixtam pluvialibus *undis,*
finxit in effigiem moderantum cuncta deorum.

(1.80–83)

The Golden Age (1.89f.) was the product of this divinely well-ordered universe (*concordi pace* 1.25), and it did not last long. After the gods' destruction of the first human race, a punishment provoked by the Gigantomachy (1.151–62), Ovid describes the second anthropogony (1.156–62). This short-lived race is produced from the intermingling of warm blood (*calidum cruorem* 158) with the earth. It is Lycaon's impiety which causes the destruction of this generation. The earth is then deluged by a flood and is plunged once again into a disorder similar to the original chaos described at the beginning of the book (1.260ff, esp. 291–92.).[54] Amusingly, Jupiter's idea for this punishment seems to result from his recollection of Stoic philosophic theories about the destruction of the world by fire (1.256–59).[55] After this disaster, anthropogony and zoogony are again repeated (1.395–437). The creation of animal life at *Met.*

53. Diog. Laer. 7.1.135ff.; Sen. *Ep.* 65.23; see Spoerri, *Späthellenistische Berichte über Welt, Kultur und Götter,* 43–45; Lämmli, *Vom Chaos Zum Cosmos,* 5–6; Stephens, *Function of Religious and Philosophical Ideas,* 53–54; Bömer, *Met.,* and Haupt-Ehwald *ad* 1.21.

54. C.C. Rhorer, "Ideology, Tripartition, and Ovid's *Metamorphoses,*" *Arethusa* 13 (1980): 305; R.D. Brown, "The Palace of the Sun in Ovid's *Metamorphoses,*" in *Homo Viator: Classical Essays for John Bramble,* ed. M. Whitby, P. Hardie, and M. Whitby (Oak Park, Ill., 1987), 216.

55. Due, *Changing Forms,* 72. F. Ahl, *Metaformations* (Ithaca, 1985), 53–54, suggests that Ovid's etymological wordplay in this passage (*fulmen-flumen-flamen*) provides an example of his general tendency to make his language illustrative of the instability and shifting of the material elements.

1.416–37, as many commentators have seen, is very close to ancient physical theories involving the generation of life from the interaction of the elements of heat and water in the earth.[56] Lucretius mentions the same theory, as does Diodorus Siculus, both in terms quite similar to those of Ovid.[57] This process Ovid explains to us with didactic precision and technical scientific language, expanding on the briefer reference to these theories in the earlier second anthropogony (1.156–62):

quippe ubi temperiem sumpsere umorque calorque,
concipiunt, et ab his oriuntur cuncta duobus,
cumque sit ignis aquae pugnax, vapor umidus omnes
res creat, et discors concordia fetibus apta est.

(1.430–33)

In both of these new creation scenes, the divine element of the initial creation is now significantly missing in the composition of humankind.

After the third anthropogony we begin to suspect that the harmony of the elements depicted in the divinely ordered universe of the opening cosmogony has permanently broken down and that, because of the basic instability of the elements, the processes of destruction and creation are doomed to be repeated. Cosmogony continues in the following book. Soon after the flood in Book 1 of the *Metamorphoses* the ecpyrosis caused by Phaethon's tragic ride in Book 2 causes yet another universal disorder and prompts the earth herself to complain: "*si freta, si terrae pereunt, si regia caeli, / in chaos antiquum confundimur!*" (2.298–99). R. Brown has recently argued that the cosmogonic themes of Book 2 are introduced already at the beginning of the book in the description of the doors of the Palace of the Sun (2.1–18). He points out that the ecphrasis presents a parallel scene of the cosmic order of the elements, which contains many echoes of the opening cosmogony in the first book of the *Metamorphoses,* and that "despite the initial creation from chaos to cosmos, the overall tendency of both books is from cosmos to chaos, or at least disorder."[58]

56. Bömer, *Met., ad* 1.416–51.

57. See Spoerri, *Späthellenistische Berichte über Welt, Kultur und Götter,* 34–38, 117–19, on the numerous connections between Ovid's passage and Diodorus 1.7.3f. (including the example of the Nile flood, Diod. 1.10.1ff.; cf. Pliny *Nat.* 9.179) and their common sources. Numerous parallels with Lucretius' description of the same process at *DRN* 5.795ff. appear in Ovid's version as well. Even the progression from the creation of living beings to the creation of the serpent Python at *Met.* 1.438f. is prepared for in Lucretius where the earth creates *portenta* (*DRN* 5.837f.); see C. Bailey, ed., *Lucretius De Rerum Natura* (Oxford, 1947), *ad DRN* 5.783–820.

58. Brown, "The Palace of the Sun," 216, also M. Lausberg,"'Ἀρχέτυπον τῆς ἰδίας ποιήσεως: Zur Bildbeschreibung bei Ovid," *Boreas* 5 (1982): 120–22.

The physical world of the poem after the initial cosmogony of Book 1 becomes a place closer to the description of the constant presence of change which Ovid's internal narrator Pythagoras depicts in Book 15: *cuncta fluunt* (15.178).[59] Here we find a world composed of permanently unstable elements involved in an eternal process of separation and reunion (15.237–51): *omnia fiunt / ex ipsis et in ipsa cadunt* (15.244–45). The process seems to repeat endlessly the cosmogonic flux among the elements described in *Met.* 1.5–31. This elemental instability has implications for the mythological metamorphosis stories that form the bulk of the poem. Barkan suggests that "this cosmology of layers is the precondition for a metamorphic universe because it establishes the orders among which the flow of transformations will take place."[60] Ovid's stories take place in a world in which new animal and plant life is still being created, and in which the transition of human bodies into water, rocks, and birds is frequently merely a matter of liquefaction, rarefaction, or solidification.[61] Humans are influenced by the elements both externally and internally. The importance of the harmony of the elements in the physical world is paralleled in ancient medical theory in its description of health as the proper mixture or equilibrium of the humors in the body. As Vitruvius explains: *e principiis animalium corpora composita sensu percipimus et exsuperationibus aut defectionibus ea laborare dissolvique iudicamus* (1.4.8).[62]

The fourth anthropogony in the poem, that of humans from the stones cast by Deucalion and Pyrrha after the flood (1.395–415), provides a sort of paradigm in reverse for the process of metamorphosis most common in the poem, the transformation from human form into natural elements. The stones are seen to soften (400–404), flesh forms from the wet and earthy elements (*ex illis aliquo pars umida suco / et terrena* 407–8), and bones and veins come from the properties of the stone itself (409–10).[63] This race owes to its origins its hardy nature, *genus durum sumus* (414),[64] unlike the second race of man, which, having been created from warm blood (1.158), exhibited according to contem-

59. Brown, "The Palace of the Sun," 217.

60. Barkan, *The Gods Made Flesh*, 28.

61. Lucretius' discussion of the dissolution of all elements to like elements is perhaps interesting in this context: *corpora distribuuntur et ad sua saecla recedunt, / umor ad umorem, terreno corpore terra / crescit, et ignem ignes procudunt aetheraque aether* (*DRN* 2.1113–15).

62. See Lonie, *The Hippocratic Treatises*, 55. Cf. Varro *L.L.* 5.61: *omne corpus, ubi nimius ardor aut humor, aut interit aut, si manet, sterile.*

63. Cf. Lucr. 3.786: *nec cruor in lignis neque saxis sucus inesse.*

64. Cf. Verg. *Geo.* 1.61–63, Lucr. 5.925–26; on the implied etymology, see McKeown, *Ovid: Amores Vol. I*, 47.

porary medical theories a passionate nature: *scires e sanguine natos* (1.162).[65] Variations of these processes will continue, as the contrasts of cold and hot, wet and dry, soft and hard, light and heavy, set out above at *Metamorphoses* 1.15–20, recur in Ovid's descriptions of metamorphosis.

Bones will in the course of the poem revert to their original substance as numerous humans harden and dry into stone. Thus when Echo loses all of the moisture from her body, she becomes petrified: *ossa ferunt lapidis traxisse figuram* (3.399, cf. 4.660).[66] Aglaurus' petrifaction is similarly described in terms of a loss of blood: *amisso sanguine* (2.824) and heat. Like a disease, *immedicabile cancer*, the hardening encompasses her whole body and she sinks under the weight of the heaviest of the elements: *gravitate, riget, frigus, duruerant* (2.819–32, cf. 1.29–30). Alternately in the poem humans may soften and melt into water, following the rule articulated by the "philosopher" Pythagoras in Book 15: *resolutaque tellus / in liquidas rarescit aquas* (*Met.* 15.245–46). Thus Cyane dissolves in her grief: *lacrimisque absumitur omnis / et, quarum fuerat magnum modo numen, in illas / extenuatur aquas: molliri membra videres* (5.427–29).[67] The learned internal narrator of this story, Calliope, explains in a scholarly parenthesis how this process commences: *nam brevis in gelidas membris exilibus undas / transitus est* (5.433–34). If thinned even farther, humans may melt into the air, as in the metamorphosis of Canens: *tenues liquefacta medullas / tabuit inque leves paulatim evanuit auras* (14.431–32; cf. 15.246: *tenuatus in auras*). Fire symbolizes the last of the four regions or elements and appropriately is involved in the deifications of Hercules (*radiantibus intulit astris* 9.272), Caesar (15.843–51), and Ovid (15.875–79).[68]

The earth does not lose the power to create human life after Book 1. At 7.121–30 Jason sows a field of armed men, and the image of the pregnant earth, familiar from *Met.* 1.420–21, Lucr. 5.795ff., and Diod. 1.7.3, is again

---

65. On the hot quality of blood see, e.g., the Hippocratic treatise *The Nature of Man*, ch.7; on the connection between heat and anger see Lucr. 3.288ff., and 307–9: *quamvis doctrina politos / constituat pariter quosdam, tamen illa relinquit / naturae cuiusque animi vestigia prima.*

66. Cf. Vitruv. 8. *Praef.* 3: *animalia vero si fuerint sine umoris potestate, exsanguinata et exsucata a principiorum liquore interarescent.*

67. See von Albrecht, *Die Parenthese*, 52. Other liquid metamorphoses include Arethusa 5.621–42, Hyrie 7.380–81, Egeria 15.547–51.

68. G. Davis, "The Problem of Closure in a *Carmen Perpetuum:* Aspects of Thematic Recapitulation in Ovid's *Metamorphoses* 15," *Grazer Beiträge* 9 (1980): 126, notes that "the successive apotheoses of the heroes Hercules, Aeneas and Romulus reveal an Ovidian 'game of the elements' in which the separation of the soul occurs in different elemental media: Hercules' soul separates into fire, Aeneas' into water, Romulus' into *aer* and Caesar's into *aether*." So also Barkan, *The Gods Made Flesh*, 84.

evoked—*gravidae telluris imago* (7.128). The reference to scientific theory is underscored by the use of language that recalls medical terminology (7.125–29).[69] The first crop of men had arisen at 3.101–14, and at the end of the poem in Book 15 Tages, the Etruscan prophet, springs out from a clod of dirt (553–59, hence the etymology of his name: Schol. Lucan 1.636, ἀπὸ τῆς γῆς). Snakes are created from Medusa's blood (4.619–20), and the anemone from that of Adonis at 10.731–39, where in the very brief description of the transformation, we see Ovid using scientific theory with jolting incongruity:[70]

> sic fata cruorem
> nectare odorato sparsit, qui tactus ab illo
> intumuit sic, ut fulvo perlucida caeno[71]
> surgere bulla solet . . .
>
> (10.731–34)

Elsewhere in the *Metamorphoses* we should not fail to note the physics joke in Jupiter's additional miniature zoogony in Book 1, where, in his rather feeble attempt to mislead Juno, he explains that the cow into which he has transformed Io is a result of spontaneous generation: *Iuppiter e terra genitam mentitur* (1.615).[72]

In addition to references to elemental theory, a number of Ovid's aetiological metamorphoses acquire a pseudo-scientific coloring through echoes and adumbrations of Lucretius' natural philosophical speculation in *De Rerum Natura*.[73] Critics have long noted the Lucretian echoes in Aeacus' graphic description of the plague at Aegina in *Met.* 7.501–613, as well as in certain physical or technological similes used to describe metamorphoses. The most remarkable of these is Ovid's description of Lichas' metamorphosis into a rock formation at *Met.* 9.211–29.[74] Hercules angrily whirls Lichas, who was unlucky enough to have been the deliverer of Deianira's poison, into the air, and his action is compared to a slingshot (*tormento fortius* 218). Anderson explains

69. W. Burkert, *Lore and Science in Ancient Pythagoreanism*, trans. E.L. Minar, Jr. (Cambridge, Mass., 1972), 266 n.131, connects Ovid's passage with theories of birth in the Hippocratic treatise *On Generation* 2.7.484L.

70. Spoerri, *Späthellenistische Berichte über Welt, Kultur und Götter*, 123 n.4, compares this passage with Arist. *Gen. An.* 762a23f. and Diod. 1.7.3.

71. Anderson at 10.733 alone prints *caelo* for *caeno*, following Merkel. See Bömer, *Met., ad loc.,* for a defense of *caeno*.

72. M. Boillat, *Les Métamorphoses d'Ovide: Themes majeurs et problemes de composition* (Berne and Frankfurt, 1976), 27.

73. For a partial list of Lucretian imitations, see A. Zingerle, *Ovidius und sein Verhältnis zu den Vorgängern und gleichzeitigen römischen Dichtern 2* (Innsbruck, 1871), 12–47.

74. Due, *Changing Forms*, 29–33; Galinsky, *Ovid's Metamorphoses*, 114–26.

that Ovid is playing games here with Lucretian theory, for "the conventional expansion of such a simile would have put emphasis upon the *heating* of the shot, not its freezing and hardening."[75] Ovid does in fact twice in the *Metamorphoses* (2.726–29, 14.825–26, cf. Vergil *Aen.* 9.588–89) use the "scientific" simile of a heated projectile (*plumbea*) as described by Lucretius at *DRN* 6.177ff. and 306ff. Lichas' petrifaction is, however, explained as a meteorological phenomenon, according to Lucretius' description of the atomistic origins of precipitation at 6.495ff., and 527ff.:

> ille per aerias pendens induruit auras:
> utque ferunt imbres gelidis concrescere ventis,
> inde nives fieri, nivibus quoque molle rotatis
> adstringi et spissa glomerari grandine corpus,
> sic illum validis iactum per inane lacertis
> exsanguemque metu nec quicquam umoris habentem
> in rigidos versum silices prior edidit aetas.

(Met. 9.219–25)

Ovid's repeated avowals of the authority of tradition (*ferunt, prior edidit aetas*) seem to "footnote" his source.[76] Words such as *auras, spissa, glomerari*, and *umoris* evoke the scientific context of the opening cosmogony, and suggest that Lichas' metamorphosis represents a sort of reversal of the original anthropogony from stone.

At *Metamorphoses* 13.600–619 we sense again that Ovid is hinting at scientific terminology in his description of the creation of a new type of bird (*memnonides*, ruffs) from the smoke and ashes of Memnon's funeral pyre.[77] Commentators note that Ovid's passage contains several echoes of Lucretius' explanation in his cosmogony of the formation of the sky (*aether*) from the lighter particles of fire and air at *De Rerum Natura* 5.449–70.[78] Both Ovid and Lucretius use a simile describing fog to illustrate their narratives: *veluti cum*

75. Anderson, *Ovid's Metamorphoses Books 6–10, ad loc.* See also Barkan, *The Gods Made Flesh,* 20; H. Bardon, "Ovide et la métamorphose," *Latomus* 20 (1961): 492.

76. Haupt-Ehwald *ad* 220. Other versions that relate only Lichas' death include Sen. *Herc. O.* 815ff., Diod. 4.38.2, Apollod. 2.7.7; the metamorphosis is mentioned by Hyg. *Fab.* 36.4, and *Myth. Vat.* 1.58, (2.165 *Thetis vertit*).

77. The metamorphosis story occurs first here (later Quint. Smyrn. 2.642, Serv. auct. Vergil *Aen.* 1.751), but the birds and their strange behavior are mentioned by Pliny *Nat.* 10.74, Paus. 10.31.6, Aelian 1.751.

78. Bömer, *Met., ad* 13.602–3, refers to *DRN* 5.461f., Haupt-Ehwald *ad* 13.602 note the verbal echoes from the similar description of fog at *DRN* 6.476–82. The allusion to Lucretius' passage is perhaps underlined by the *aetion* for dew that follows this transformation in the *Metamorphoses* (13.621–22), for Lucretius had also included a description of the morning dew (5.460–64).

flumina natas / exhalant nebulas (*Met.* 13.602–3, *DRN* 5.463 *exhalantque lacus nebulam*).[79] The language of condensation (*glomerata* 604, *densetur* 605), heat (*calorem* 605),[80] and fire (601–2, 606) all suggest cosmogony as well.[81] We may similarly be tempted to associate Arethusa's strange, sweaty liquefaction with the Lucretian passage describing the formation of the sea from the sweat of the earth (*DRN* 5.487–88) and the passage that likewise by means of the example of sweating proves the porous nature of all things (*DRN* 6.936–45). Ovid's lines describing Arethusa's metamorphosis, *cadunt toto de corpore guttae / quaque pedem movi, manat lacus* (*Met.* 5.633–34), seem to contain elements of Lucretius' text at *DRN* 6.943–44: *sudent umore et guttis manantibus stillent. / manat item nobis e toto corpore sudor.*[82] Ovid is pointedly having fun at Lucretius' expense by recontextualizing his scientific theory in this mythological scene.

Through references to scientific theories involving the four primary elements, Ovid destabilizes the physical world of the poem after the flood of Book 1. This instability of matter establishes a context for the processes of metamorphosis in the mythological stories, in which humans are transformed with a disturbing facility into related natural beings or objects.[83] Ovid thus continues his pose as a cosmogonic epic narrator, fulfilling humorously and perversely the expectations set up by his lofty cosmological opening. There is of course considerable irony in Ovid's pseudo-scientific posture. By exploiting the language of physics to describe myths of the most fabulous nature, Ovid creates a humorous incongruity between this authoritative posture and the fictional content of his mythological epic narrative, while simultaneously challenging the cosmological claims of his epic predecessors, Ennius, Lucretius, and Vergil.

Poetry and Physics

The basis of Ovid's irony lies in the essential dichotomy between the nature of mythological poetry, which at a very early stage was granted autonomy by both

79. Cf. *Met.* 4.434, 11.595–96, for similar formulations.

80. Anderson reads *colorem* (codd. pler.), while Bömer, *Met., ad loc.,* defends *calorem* (W[1]p. edd. pler.).

81. Bömer compares *alto . . . igne* at *Met.* 13.600–601 with the discussion of the elements at *Met.* 15.243 and rejects the idea that Ovid's *animam ex igni* at 13.606 refers to the monistic theory of fire attributed by Lucretius to Heraclitus at *DRN* 1.635ff.

82. Note also Varro's etymological connections between *humus, humor, udor, and sudor* (*L.L.* 5.23–24).

83. The fluidity of the Ovidian cosmos shares features with M.M. Bakhtin's description of the grotesque body, or "open body," which "is not separated from the world by clearly defined boundaries; it is blended with the world, with animals, with objects"; *Rabelais and His World*, trans. H. Iswolsky (Indiana, 1984), 26–27.

critics and poets alike, and scientific or philosophical endeavors in natural physics, which perforce were meant to correspond faithfully to reality. When the mythology of the poets came under attack, it was precisely from the philosophers, who objected primarily to the harmful effects of the anthropomorphism of the gods,[84] or from historians and rationalists, who criticized myths on the basis of historical improbability.[85] As far as we can reconstruct the ancient critical tradition about the nature of poetry, and we are now helped in this by the illuminating study by D.C. Feeney, poetry was largely granted "its own rules of meaning and effect."[86] There existed no expectation of "veracity"; poets knowingly and willingly "lied" and this was expected of them: *poetis mentiri licet* (Plin. *Ep.* 6.21.6).[87] Plutarch in his *Quomodo aud. poet.* explained that poets intentionally "lie" for the purpose of pleasing the reader: πρὸς ἡδονὴν ἀκοῆς καὶ χάριν, ἣν οἱ πλεῖστοι διώκουσιν (*Mor.* 16.2 A). The fantastic was expected and desired in poetry for the effect it produced, for, as Aristotle remarks, τὸ δὲ θαυμαστὸν ἡδύ (*Poet.* 1460a17, cf. 1460b8). Aristotle further argued that epic as a genre was particularly suited to the inclusion of the marvelous because of its essentially nonmimetic character (*Poet.* 1460a15). In the Hellenistic and Roman triad of literary forms, arranged according to their assumed degree of verisimilitude, poetry came under the heading of *fabula* or *falsum* (μῦθος), distinguished from *fictum* or *argumentum*

---

84. Cic. *N.D.* 1.42–43 (Pease *ad loc.* provides an extensive list of philosophical critiques of poetry), 2.70; Pliny *Nat.* 2.14–27. See also Feeney, *Gods in Epic*, 6ff.; B. Cardauns, ed., *M. Terentius Varro Antiquitates Rerum Divinarum* (Wiesbaden, 1976), *ad* fr. 7. Varro displays the philosophic tendency to reject all stories of poets that attribute *incongrua* to the gods: *Et tamen Marcus Varro non vult fabulosis adversus deos fidem adhibere figmentis, ne de maiestatis eorum dignitate indignum aliquid sentiat* (Varro fr. 8P *De Gente Populi Romani* [= August. *C.D.* 18.10]). But fr. 17P records that Varro told of the metamorphoses of Diomedes' men into birds, and Augustine (18.16) complains of Varro's inclusion of metamorphosis myths. Varro was able to include mythology in his work by dividing history into three periods: (fr. 3P) the beginnings (*adelon*), *mythicon* (or *fabulosa*), and *historicon*.

85. Diod. 4.77.5–7 and Paus. 9.11.4–5 on Daedalus; Polyb. 2.16.13–15 against the Phaethon myth. For further discussion of the critique of myth see Koster, *Antike Eposttheorien*, 10–15, and pp. 144–46 below.

86. Feeney, *Gods in Epic*, 29; see esp. chap. 1, "The Critics," 5–56.

87. See Aristotle's famous statement about Homer (*Poet.* 1460a18): δεδίδαχεν δὲ μάλιστα Ὅμηρος καὶ τοὺς ἄλλους ψευδῆ λέγειν ὡς δεῖ. On the importance of Aristotle's development of the granting of autonomy to poetry see Feeney, *Gods in Epic*, 25–29, 40; S. Halliwell, *Aristotle's Poetics* (London and Chapel Hill, 1986), 3–4, 132–33, 265–66; W. Rösler, "Die Entdeckung der Fiktionalität in der Antike," *Poetica* 12 (1980): 309–14. Agatharcides (*GGM* 1.117.8) also admits that he does not object to mythology in the poets, and he forgives Aeschylus for frequently lying, because the goal of poetry is pleasure. For similar arguments see McKeown, "Ovid's *Fasti* and Augustan Politics," 182–83.

(πλάσμα) and *verum* (ἱστορία).[88] Quintilian formulates a definition of *fabula* as *quae versatur in tragoediis atque carminibus, non a veritate modo sed etiam a forma veritatis remota* (*Inst.* 2.4.2). The examples he then lists all involve metamorphosis, which, like divine interventions and actions, were events least likely to conform to any constraints of plausibility.[89] The acceptance of the freedom of poetry from irrelevant criteria of veracity led to the claim that the aim of poetry was not to portray external truths, but to provide pleasure.[90] Scientific didactic poetry, on the other hand, was by nature meant to be both true and convincing, and therefore frequently included imprecations against the myths of the poets, a feature we shall consider in greater depth when we look at Pythagoras' discourse in Book 15.[91]

For Ovid to import into his mythological and unnaturalistic poem aspects of natural physics is simultaneously to exploit the ironic contrast between the different truth claims of scientific and mythological poetry and to blur the boundaries between the two narrative modes. For, by the early exegetical tradition of physical allegory that had developed already in the sixth century, poetry, or rather the mythology in poetry,[92] had also been credited with the power to express scientific truths about the physical universe. In antiquity the dichotomy between science and poetry, between their conflicting claims to express essential truths about the world and humankind, was less an established fact than an active issue of debate. In the sixth century, when philosophy was first developing and "still looking wistfully over her shoulder towards her origins in the world of myths and poetry," there existed no firm boundaries

---

88. See C.O. Brink, ed., *Horace on Poetry: The 'Ars Poetica'* (Cambridge, 1971), *ad A.P.* 338ff.; Feeney, *Gods in Epic*, 31, 42–44; R. Häussler, *Das Historische Epos der Griechen und Römer bis Vergil* (Heidelberg, 1976): 212–31. For the three types of narrative defined by ancient rhetorical theory see further Sextus Empiricus *Adv. Gramm.* 1.252 (Asclepiades of Myrleia), 1.263f.; Cic. *Inv.* 1.27; *Rhet. Her.* 1.13; Strabo 1.2.17 (C25).

89. Cf. Palaephatus' rationalizing attacks on the implausibility of metamorphosis in N. Festa, *Mythographi Graeci*, vol. 3.2 (Leipzig, 1902), 1–72 (cf., e.g., 15, 17.9, 11.4), with Feeney, *Gods in Epic*, 31, 232.

90. Quint. 10.1.28: *genus . . . quod solam petit voluptatem eamque etiam fingendo non falsa modo sed etiam quaedam incredibilia sectatur.* See Brink *ad* Hor. *A.P.* 338ff.; also Koster, *Antike Epostheorien*, 143–51; Feeney, *Gods in Epic*, 40, on poetic *licentia*.

91. For the importance of the claim of truth for didactic poetry see the remarks of Pöhlmann, "Charakteristika des Römischen Lehrgedichts," 854 n.253, and Effe, *Dichtung und Lehre*, 242. Cf. Lucr. (e.g., 2.1023), *Ars Amatoria* (*vera canam* 1.30), *Fasti* (e.g., 6.3 *facta canam*), Manil. 3.36–37, *Aetna* 91–92.

92. This distinction is the main thrust of A.A. Long's important study "Stoic Readings of Homer," in *Homer's Ancient Readers*, ed. R. Lamberton, and J. J. Keaney (Princeton, 1992), 41–66.

between mythical/poetic and philosophical thought.[93] Philosophers borrowed the forms of poetry and myth to express their new truths in a more accessible manner.[94] Poetry, in order to maintain its privileged position, had to be measured and defended against the new philosophical discourse of knowledge developing in the sixth century, while the newly developing philosophy strove to annex the traditional authority that had belonged to poetry. Pre-Socratic philosophers such as Xenophanes, Parmenides, and Empedocles wrote philosophical poetry in hexameter, thus placing themselves in the tradition of Homer and Hesiod, and thereby borrowing the poets' prestige, while simultaneously attacking their impious depictions of the divine. In terms of content, the two modes of discourse throughout the ancient literary tradition cannot always easily be separated.

The development of the physical allegorical tradition, which, as we have seen, interpreted with an apologetic aim the mythology in Homer and Hesiod as natural philosophy, alongside that of philosophy in the sixth century guaranteed that the competition between the two narrative modes would be a generating principle behind much of ancient poetry. The *causae* of the universe, which the pre-Socratics were busy investigating, were discovered by apologists in the poetry of Homer and Hesiod. The underlying basis for the physical interpretation of myths through physical allegory was the theory of the four elements, fire, air, earth, and water.[95] The combination of mythological and cosmological speculation is seen at the earliest period of Greek literature and continued throughout its history.[96] The truth claims of philosophy and poetry continued be interrelated and this is at the heart of the poetic dialogue at Rome between the writers of epic, beginning with Ennius and culminating in Lucretius and Vergil, to whom we must understand Ovid to be responding.

 Stoic etymology

At Rome, as we have seen, the development of the epic tradition from Ennius' *Annales*—which began with a reference to the physical allegorical interpretation of Homer as a natural philosopher (2–11 Sk.) and included scientific theory elsewhere as well—guaranteed that Latin epic poetry would

---

93. Richardson, "Homeric Professors," 81; cf. H. Fränkel, *Early Greek Poetry and Philosophy*, trans. M. Hadas and J. Willis (Oxford, 1975), esp. 187, 285–86, 321–24, 422–29, 481–508; Whitman, *Allegory*, 22.

94. Long, "Early Greek Philosophy," 246.

95. Buffière, *Les Mythes d'Homère*, 101–22.

96. See Fränkel, *Early Greek Poetry and Philosophy, passim*, on philosophical speculation and poetry, e.g., 26–68, on Solon; 471ff., 556ff. on Pindar; 163–65, 253ff. on Alcman; cf. C.P. Segal, "Archaic Choral Lyric," in *The Cambridge History of Classical Literature*, vol. 1, ed. P.E. Easterling and B.M.W. Knox (Cambridge, 1985), 179; M.L. West, "Three Presocratic Cosmologies," *CQ* 13 (1963): 154–76, and *idem, The Orphic Poems* (Oxford, 1983).

be connected with philosophic speculation, as well as Roman history. There is clear evidence in the fragments of the *Annales* that the theory of the elements, presented directly in the *Epicharmus* (*Var.* 47, 51–58 Vahlen),[97] was referred to and that Ennius incorporated philosophical themes elsewhere in the epic (*Ann.* 220–21, 555 Sk.).[98] The appearance of these scientific themes in Ennius' epic suggest that he made use of philosophic theory to support his claims that he was presenting an authoritative view of Roman history as well as to elevate generically his new type of Roman historical epic. The most important work to follow in the tradition of epic is of course Lucretius' philosophical *De Rerum Natura,* in which we discern a very real tension between the truth claims of Lucretius' philosophical precepts and his use of poetic forms and mythology.

Although Lucretius' mixture of mythological or poetic elements with serious scientific speculation has precedents in the poetry of the earlier philosopher-poets, such as Empedocles, Epicurus almost certainly seems to have disapproved of the use of either poetry or myth in the explication of philosophical principles.[99] Lucretius thus takes some pains to justify his employment of poetry as a medium and to explicate his use of myth. In his famous *apologia* for poetry at *DRN* 1.921–50 (cf. 4.1–25), Lucretius defends his use of poetry on the basis of its psychagogic function and his apparent belief that the obscure and difficult precepts of Epicurus could be better understood through the medium of poetry.[100] Through its charm, poetry holds the reader's attention (*DRN* 1.948 *animum tenere*), and through the convention of mythological illustration, the naturally hidden precepts of Epicurean atomism may be rendered more concrete and visible (1.143–45, 921–22, 933–34).[101] The danger of the use of poetry and myth, both inherently deceptive, is not glossed over,[102]

97. See also Courtney, *Fragmentary Latin Poets,* 33–36 (frr. 36–39).

98. O. Skutsch, ed., *The Annals of Q. Ennius* (Oxford, 1985), *ad locc.;* H.D. Jocelyn, "Romulus and the *di genitales* (Ennius, *Annales* 110–11 Sk.)," in *Studies in Latin Literature and its Tradition in Honour of C.O. Brink,* ed. J. Diggle, J.B. Hall, and H.D. Jocelyn (Cambridge, 1989), 54–55; Hardie, *Cosmos and Imperium,* 77–83 (with further bibliography); Feeney, *Gods in Epic,* 120–23. We will be looking more closely at Ennius' Homer and Pythagoreanism in chap. 4.

99. P. DeLacy, "Lucretius and the History of Epicureanism," *TAPA* 79 (1948): 19–23; C.J. Classen, "Poetry and Rhetoric in Lucretius," *TAPA* 99 (1968): 110–14; Ackermann, *Lukrez und der Mythos,* 6–10.

100. P.H. Schrijvers, *Horror ac Divina Voluptas: Études sur la poétique et la poésie de Lucrèce* (Amsterdam, 1970), 33–34, 37, points out the suggestive *figura etymologica* of *suavis / suadere.*

101. Ackermann, *Lukrez und der Mythos,* 55; Schrijvers, *Horror ac Divina Voluptas,* 38–42, 87–147, suggests this is related to the very insistence of Epicurean theory on the importance of attention and perception; cf. Hardie, *Cosmos and Imperium,* 219ff.

102. For more on Lucretius' philosophical attacks on myth, see chap. 4.

but the salutary protreptic end justifies the means (*per falsa ad vera*),[103] as long as critical distance is maintained: *deceptaque non capiatur* (1.941). In his apology for the use of myth at *DRN* 2.600–60, Lucretius employs both physical and moral allegorical strategies of exegesis to explain how, stripped of its religious dimension (*dum vera re tamen ipse / religione animum turpi contingere parcat* 2.659–60), myth can be rationalized (*significant* 641) and understood to provide pictorially vivid depictions of both physical and ethical truths.[104] Since he was writing consciously within a Roman epic tradition traceable back to Ennius (*DRN* 1.117ff. *Ennius . . . noster*), Lucretius' use of myth and metonymy has a generic dimension as well.[105]

We need to understand Ovid's use of pseudo-scientific terminology both as a response to Lucretius and in the light of similar techniques earlier exploited by Vergil in his response to Lucretius. P.R. Hardie has shown how a great deal of Lucretian scientific theory is incorporated into the poetry of the *Aeneid*.[106] Hardie emphasizes the "cosmic outlook" of both Lucretius and Vergil and their tendency to "universalize" their themes by creating a physical and "scientific" parallelism between different levels of reality.[107] D.O. Ross' emphasis of the importance of the physical theory of the four elements in Vergil's *Georgics* reminds us of the centrality of the elements to ancient ways of thinking.[108] We have seen that Ovid similarly appropriates the scientific terminology of the elements in order to "universalize" his metamorphosis theme into a form of cosmology. Like Vergil, Ovid reacts against Lucretius' purely materialistic explanation of natural phenomena, and by incorporating physics into his unrelentingly unnaturalistic and supernatural metamorphoses he consciously "remythologizes"[109] Lucretius' rationalist allegorizations of myth. The aetiologi-

---

103. Bailey *ad loc.;* Schrijvers, *Horror ac Divina Voluptas,* 40f.; Ackermann, *Lukrez und der Mythos,* 20, 217; J.H. Waszink, *Lucretius and Poetry* (Amsterdam, 1954), 10–15.

104. See Schrijvers, *Horror ac Divina Voluptas,* 50–60; Ackermann, *Lukrez und der Mythos,* 81–94; Hardie, *Cosmos and Imperium,* 186.

105. West, *Imagery and Poetry;* Hardie, *Cosmos and Imperium,* 193–219.

106. Hardie, *Cosmos and Imperium,* 176ff.

107. Hardie, *Cosmos and Imperium,* 157–75; Whitman, *Allegory,* 49–54 (on Vergil).

108. D.O. Ross, *Virgil's Elements: Physics and Poetry in the Georgics* (Princeton, 1987), 31ff., 54–74, provides a helpful summary of the background of the scientific context of the four elements and humors. See also J. Pigeaud, "Virgile et la médecine: Quelques réflections sur l'utilisation de la pensée physiologique dans les Géorgiques," *Helmantica* 33 (1982): 539ff., and *idem,* "Die Medizin in der Lehrdichtung des Lucrez und des Vergil," in *Saeculum Augustum II,* ed. G. Binder (Darmstadt, 1988), 216–39. For the pervasiveness of elemental theory, note Varro *L.L.* 5.13: *Quare quod quattuor genera prima rerum, totidem verborum.*

109. To borrow the term used by Hardie, *Cosmos and Imperium,* 178, to describe Vergil's reworking of Lucretian themes, and later Ovid's technique in "Lucretius and the Delusions of Narcissus," *MD* 20–21 (1988): 71–89. See also Perkell, *The Poet's Truth,* 139–90, on Vergil's

cal focus of Ovid's mythological stories actively engages with and challenges the claims of Lucretius' cosmological epic to explain the world. Yet Ovid's poem represents in many ways a complete reversal of Lucretius' endeavors, and he quite intentionally targets specific passages in which Lucretius had rationalized or rejected myth in favor of materialist physics.

Ovid's Phaethon episode at *Met.* 1.750–2.400, for example, incorporates many echoes of Lucretius' passage at *DRN* 5.396–410, which is pointedly directed against just such mythological accounts.[110] Lucretius rationalizes stories of the flood and fire as mythological allegories of actual temporary victories of the elements water and fire over the other elements with which they are in constant battle (*DRN* 5.380–415). Although the allegorized myth serves as a sort of "illustration" of elemental warfare, it must be recognized as a false poetic depiction (*procul a vera nimis est ratione repulsum* 5.406) of events or natural phenomena, which the Epicureans have explained through *physica ratio* (5.407–15).[111] The episode is a clear example of the way in which Ovid remythologizes an event natural philosophy had demythologized, in its attempt to provide rational and scientific explanations for the causes which mythology had traditionally provided. Hardie has also shown how Ovid's Echo and Narcissus episode at *Met.* 3.339–510 represents a deliberate remythologizing of Lucretius' theories of vision and love in *De Rerum Natura* 4.29ff. He suggests that "Ovid's mythological narrative of Echo and Narcissus pointedly reverses the rationalism of Lucretius' materialist account of the world; this reversal, or inversion, of the model in itself represents a continuation of Lucretian imitative practice, but turned against Lucretius."[112] In other passages of the *Metamorphoses*, we can see Ovid reviving the mythical accounts that Lucretius had attempted to quell.

At *Metamorphoses* 6.693–97 we find Boreas giving a scientific account of the origin of lightning and thunder from clouds very similar to that of Lucretius' meteorological theory at *De Rerum Natura* 6.84–422. Boreas mentions as well that earthquakes are caused by underground wind tunnels (6.697–99), a scientific theory expounded by Lucretius (*DRN* 6.557ff.) and later by

explicit challenge to the power of scientific explanation in the *Georgics* in favor of the power of mythical or poetic expression to interpret experience.

110. Ovid's passage contains many echoes of Lucretius, as has been noted by Due, *Changing Forms*, 31–32; Bailey *ad* Lucr. 5.396–405; Bömer, *Met., ad* 15.111.

111. Ackermann, *Lukrez und der Mythos*, 94–98.

112. Hardie, "Lucretius and the Delusions of Narcissus," 72. Another Ovidian reversal of Lucretian rationalization may be seen in the story of the *cornix* in *Met.* 2.547–95, which provided the mythical explanation for why crows avoid the Acropolis. Lucretius attacks this mythical story (6.749–55) and asserts instead that there is a natural cause: *non iras Palladis acris / pervigili causa, Graium ut cecinere poetae, / sed natura loci opus efficit ipsa suapte* (6.753–55).

Ovid's "philosopher" Pythagoras in the *Metamorphoses* (15.346ff.). In Ovid's story, Boreas has not been successful in his pursuit of Orithyia, the sister of Procris, and in his anger he boasts of the power of his winds in a speech whose language conflates rape with scientific theory, *apta mihi vis est* (6.690). Ironic intent lies behind the combination of the mythical and amatory language with the scientific elements of the passage. As Anderson comments, "the difference between Boreas' egoistic assertion and Lucretius' objective description of the properties of *ventus* is crucial."[113] Lucretian scientific theory is re-mythologized and the equation of rape (*vis*, cf. *Met.* 6.525, 14.770) with a natural force (*venti vis*, cf. *DRN* 1.271) serves to emphasize the extent of divine power over humans in the world of Ovid's poem. This flies directly in the face of Lucretius' Epicurean beliefs about the nature of divinity.

Perhaps one of the most telling examples of Ovid's remythologization of Lucretius comes in his version of the invention of "song" at *Met.* 1.682–714, in the tale of Syrinx. Lucretius had treated the invention of song and music in his section on the civilization of primitive man as an empirical discovery based on careful observation of nature: *et zephyri, cava per calamorum, sibila primum / agrestis docuere cavas inflare cicutas* (5.1382–83). Echoes of Lucretius' account of the natural invention of the pipe are found in Ovid's aetiological and erotic story of the attempted assault on Syrinx by Pan and of the transformation of the nymph into a reed pipe.[114] In Ovid the invention of song is put back into divine hands and the power of mythological poetry is ironically emphasized by the strength of its desired soporific effect on the hundred-eyed Argus.[115]

Through the repeated use of language suggestive of natural philosophy Ovid subtly, and with full awareness of the incongruity, suggests that his fantastic metamorphoses are somehow part of a natural process. Yet these minutely particularized and scientifically colored descriptions of meta-morphosis ultimately do not render metamorphosis any more "natural" or plausible. Metamorphosis is profoundly unnatural, or rather supernatural, and Ovid's choice of metamorphosis as a topic is a strong statement of the autono-mous and nonmimetic character of his poetry.[116] Importantly, few of Ovid's transformations are presented as purely natural events; rather they appear as arbitrary acts of divine will. His depiction of causation is unrelentingly super-

113. Anderson, *Ovid's Metamorphoses Books 6–10, ad Met.* 6.695–96.
114. *Met.* 1.676 *ut pastor,* Lucr. 5.1387 *pastorum; Met.* 1.701 *per avia,* Lucr. 5.1386 *avia per nemora; Met.* 1 .704 *liquidas,* Lucr. 5.1379 *liquidas; Met.* 1.708 *querenti,* Lucr. 5.1384 *querelas; Met.* 1.709 *dulcedine,* Lucr. 5.1384 *dulcis.*
115. We can fruitfully compare this scene with Horace *Odes* 2.13.33–34, where the music of Alcaeus has a similar effect on the *belua centiceps* Cerberus; cf. Orpheus in *Odes* 3.11.15–20.
116. Cf. Rosati, *Narciso e Pigmalione,* 84.

natural. To play with details of science and veracity in the context of such tales is to test the interplay between the different narrative modes and truth claims of fiction (*fabula*) and philosophy, between fantasy and realism.[117] The scholarly "voice of science" conflicts with the voice of the poet.[118] By proclaiming his cosmogonic pretensions overtly at the beginning of his poem, and by baldly juxtaposing mythological and scientific ways of explaining things throughout his poem, Ovid lays bare the disjunction between the mythological layer and the underlying scientific "truth" which had been created by the hermeneutic practice of physical allegory. Through his greater explicitness, Ovid takes Vergil's remythologizing of Lucretius a step further. At the same time, Ovid robs myth of much of its symbolic content through his modernizing and deadpan manner of presentation, a technique he inherited from the Alexandrians, who were similarly intent on examining and exposing the truth claims of mythology and poetry.

Ovid explores the pretenses and claims of epic poetry to philosophic truth by revealing the supposed scientific underpinnings of myth. In doing so he both participates in the epic cosmological tradition and, by exposing it, undermines its authenticating power. This is more than traditional Ovidian *reductio ad absurdum* of the philosophic claims of epic poetry. Ovid's use of elemental language represents a literalization of the suggestions of physical allegory, which posited a scientific truth behind myth. Rather than participate in Lucretius' and Vergil's epic agendas of producing valorized depictions of either the universe or of a particular set of cultural values through a legitimizing "scientific" explication, Ovid's *aetia* uncover a "sedimented world"[119] created by arbitrary divine acts of anger. For Lucretius the homogeneity of existence at all levels guarantees the order of the universe; for Ovid this discloses its instability. Like Vergil, Ovid suggests that a purely naturalistic explanation of natural phenomena is inadequate, and, like Vergil, he stresses the human cost of history and the essential failure of human understanding in the face of nature and the divine, yet unlike Vergil, Ovid refuses to take a position of authority.

Ovid seems instead more interested in drawing our attention to the way in which the voice of science has been used in poetry as a stratagem to create authority and veracity. As G.-P. Rosati has shown, Ovid is preoccupied with the very process of the creation of the illusion of reality through artifice, not with

---

117. Feeney, *Gods in Epic,* 93.

118. See Barthes, *S/Z,* 205–6; on *aetia* as authenticating detail similar to Barthes' "referential code," see Feeney, *Gods in Epic,* 93, and Goldhill, *The Poet's Voice,* 326.

119. Goldhill, *The Poet's Voice,* 325–26. Cf. Dawson, *Allegorical Readers and Cultural Revision,* on interpretation and cultural values.

producing a faithful mimesis of external reality in a naturalistic form of narrative.[120] Numerous critics have argued that Ovid is preoccupied throughout the poem with proclaiming the freedom of the poet to create poetic illusion, and that to that end he frequently adds reminders of his work's fictional and non-mimetic status.[121] All of Ovid's poetry reveals a fully self-conscious desire to direct the reader's attention to his facility of invention and to his play with "the relationship between poetry as an autonomous reality and the literary process which constructs that reality."[122] His famous lines at the end of *Amores* 3.12 reflect a recognition of the autonomy granted to poetry by ancient rhetorical theory and an exultation in his imaginative license: *Exit in inmensum fecunda licentia vatum, / obligat historica nec sua verba fide* (41–42).[123]

Ovid's use of scientific terminology in his poetry has much in common with the Alexandrians, especially Callimachus and Apollonius, whose inclusion of science in their poems is related to their interest in exploring the explanatory function of myth and the concomitant concern with narrative authority entailed with making these claims for poetry of a mythological nature. In the Hellenistic period Aristotelian research into causation and natural science made an important impact on ways of thinking, and the scholarly poets were likely to be learned in scientific as well as literary matters. The popularity of didactic poetry, which exhibits a similar mixture of the scientific with the mythological, attests to this. Although the Alexandrian scholar-poets rejected allegorical interpretations of Homer and myth, as poets they were nevertheless deeply involved in the discourse about poetic authority and truth. This, as I have suggested earlier, is one of the bases for their interest in aetiology as a pseudo-scientific and authenticating approach to myth. The *causae* of aetiological myth merge with the *causae* of philosophical investigation of the physical world.[124] Although most of the aetiological themes in Callimachus and other major Alexandrian poets are cultural and religious, we have already seen

---

120. Rosati, *Narciso e Pigmalione, passim.*

121. Feeney, *Gods in Epic,* 229; Galinsky, *Ovid's Metamorphoses,* 173–79; E. Doblhofer, "*Ovidius Urbanus:* eine Studie zum Humor in Ovids Metamorphosen," *Philologus* 103–4 (1959–60): 223–27.

122. Conte, *Rhetoric of Imitation,* 63; cf. Rosati, *Narciso e Pigmalione,* 82–84, *passim.* See Chatman, *Story and Discourse,* 248–53, on the self-conscious narrator.

123. On the poem see G. Lieberg, "*Poeta Creator:* Some 'Religious' Aspects," *PLLS* 5 (1985): 23–32; J.C. McKeown, "Ovid *Amores* 3.12," *PLLS* 2 (1979): 172, who suggests that Ovid "is berating the audience for lack of literary critical ability."

124. Whitman, *Allegory,* 21, 51. On the importance of the investigation of causes in natural philosophy, see on Aristotle Diog. Laert. 5.32, and on Posidonius, see I.G. Kidd, "Philosophy and Science in Posidonius," *Antike und Abendland* 24 (1978): 7–15.

aetiology "applied on a large scale to the natural world" in Nicander.[125]
Aetiological metamorphoses in the *Argonautica* that explain natural phenomena include the origin of snakes from Medusa's blood (*Argon.* 4.1513–17, cf.
Met. 4.617–20), the fall of Phaethon into the Eridanus, and his transformed
sisters, the Heliades (*Argon.* 4.595–605, *Met.* 2.319–80).[126] Apollonius and
Callimachus also incorporate references to contemporary scientific and medical theories into their poetry. Callimachus has been shown to have included in
his poetry references to the recent medical discoveries of Herophilus and other
scientific theories,[127] and in the *Argonautica* numerous references to both
contemporary medicine and science have been detected.[128] These scientific
references integrated into supernatural mythological tales do more than advertise the erudition of these scholarly poets; like *aetia,* as markers of either
scientific or historical "truths," they participate in the creation of poetic authority, and at the same time as components of a work of fiction they "tease the
reader with the difficulty of securely determining the voice of fiction, the voice
of scholarly accuracy."[129] Perhaps the highest level of sophistication attained
in this ongoing discourse of authority and poetry was in the poetry of Eratosthenes, now sadly almost completely lost to us. A true scientist, he included
scientific and philosophical speculation in his poems such as the *Hermes* (frr.
1–16 Powell, pp. 58–63), but accompanied it in his criticism with the theoretical disclaimer that poetry did not aim at instruction, but rather pleasure (Strabo
1.2.3).[130]

Ovid's inclusion of the figure of Pythagoras at the end of the *Metamorphoses* will provide us with another overtly philosophical cosmogonic
narrative with which we may compare the rest of the poem. Between the two
philosophical passages that frame the poem and create, as I have suggested, a
sort of force field of scientific resonances, there are many stories that do not

125. Forbes Irving, *Metamorphosis in Greek Myths,* 20.

126. See Goldhill, *The Poet's Voice,* 325, on the *aetion* of the Etesian winds at *Argon.* 2.500–527.

127. G.W. Most, "Callimachus and Herophilus," *Hermes* 109 (1981): 188–96; Pfeiffer, *History of Classical Scholarship,* 152; Hollis, *Callimachus Hecale, ad* fr. 74.12, where he suggests Ovid may have adapted this "mixture of mythology with scientific speculation in *Am.* 1.13.29–30."

128. Hunter, *Apollonius of Rhodes Argonautica Book 3, ad* 296–98, 762–63; M.W. Dickie, "Talos Bewitched: Magic, Atomic Theory and Paradoxography in Apollonius *Argonautica* 4.1638–88," *PLLS* 6 (1990): 267–96 (listing *Argon.* 1.496ff., 643ff., 3.755ff., 4.259ff., 672ff., 1506–12).

129. Goldhill, *The Poet's Voice,* 329.

130. Pfeiffer, *History of Classical Scholarship,* 152–70; Bulloch, "Hellenistic Poetry," 604.

involve metamorphosis into animals or plants and are very far from having anything to do with natural-philosophic themes. Instead, they offer *aetia* of a religious or cultural nature that are closer in subject and manner to poetry traditionally associated with the Alexandrian and neoteric tradition. It is to these stories that we will now turn.

Chapter 2

Callimachean *Aetia* and Framed Aetiological Narratives in the *Metamorphoses*

> cetera de genere hoc monstra ac portenta loquuntur,
> ne loca deserta ab divis quoque forte putentur
> sola tenere. ideo iactant miracula dictis
> —Lucretius 4.590–92

In Book 1, after the "second" cosmogony following the flood (416–37), a shift in theme is abruptly signaled by the introduction of the story of Apollo and Daphne: *Primus amor* (1.452). This first amatory tale has received a great deal of attention: it has been seen to function programmatically in the *Meta-morphoses* in effecting a transition from the opening cosmogonic sequence of the poem to the amatory themes that occupy the bulk of the narrative. This erotic tale directly follows Apollo's slaying of the Python and thus serves to form a contrast with the emphatically epic tones of the preceding episode (the weight of which is underlined by Ovid's description of the Python as *tumidum* 460),[1] as well as with the earlier council of the gods and the storm in Book 1.163ff., two scenes indebted to the model of the *Aeneid*.[2] Apollo's transformation into an elegiac lover effected by Cupid replays and verbally echoes Ovid's own earlier scene of initiation in *Amores* 1.1. Here in a humorous version of a Callimachean scene of poetic initiation and admonition, Cupid prevents Ovid from writing Vergilian or Augustan epic by shortening the meter of his second line.[3] Both scenes mark the transition from heroic epic themes (*arma gravi*

---

1. The epic weight of this episode is also underlined by Propertius 4.6.35–36: *qualis flexos soluit Pythona per orbis / serpentem, imbelles quem timuere lyrae.*

2. See the excellent discussion by W.S.M. Nicoll, "Cupid, Apollo, and Daphne (Ovid, *Meta-morphoses* 1.452ff.)," CQ n.s. 30 (1980): 174–82. Note also Knox's arguments for the elegiac associations of the episode, *Traditions of Augustan Poetry*, 14–18, and further discussion by Schmitzer, *Zeitgeschichte in Ovids Metamorphosen*, 72–73, and A. Primmer, "Mythos and Natur in Ovids 'Apollo und Daphne,'" WS 10 (1976): 210–20.

3. Compare esp. *Met.* 1.456 and *Am.* 1.1.5, *Met.* 1.519–20 and *Am.* 1.1.25–6. See G.B. Conte's discussion of the two scenes, "Il genere tra empirismo e teoria," in *Generi e Lettori* (Milan, 1991), 149.

numero Am. 1.1.1, *fortibus armis Met.* 1.456) to erotic themes more closely associated with elegy. Although Vergilian reminiscences from the *Aeneid* (*primus* 452, *saeva Cupidinis ira* 453) humorously strike an epic tone at the beginning of the story, the episode amounts to a programmatic declaration of the amatory and neoteric content of much of the material following in the rest of the poem. This story also serves to establish an erotic pattern followed in much of the rest of the poem: unsuccessful pursuit and the equation of hunting and the refusal of love.[4] Although the story's aetiological focus is less often noticed,[5] it functions equally to introduce the many cultural aetiologies in the Alexandrian tradition that will follow.

The story commences with the mention of the founding of the Pythian games:

instituit sacros celebri certamine ludos,
Pythia de domitae serpentis nomine dictos.

(1.446–47)

Ovid points out that at these first games the winners received garlands of oak leaves, and explains: *nondum laurus erat* (1.450). He thus sets up the following story of Daphne as an explanation of how the laurel became associated with Apollo: "*at quoniam coniunx mea non potes esse, / arbor eris certe*" *dixit* "*mea*" (1.557–58). Apollo does not succeed in raping Daphne, but her aetiological transformation guarantees that he will nevertheless possess her.[6] There is no escape for Daphne, whose response in arboreal form to this appropriation is left unclear (*refugit tamen oscula lignum* 556, *adnuit utque caput visa est agitasse cacumen* 567). A natural-historical note is included to explain the nondeciduous nature of the laurel tree (1.564–65).[7] Numerous allusions to neoteric and Alexandrian literature have been detected within the episode, to Gallus, Propertius, and Callimachus.[8] By providing an *aetion* for the use of

---

4. On these motifs and on both the first and last amatory tales, see the important study by G. Davis, *The Death of Procris* (Rome, 1983); see also J. Heath, "Diana's Understanding of Ovid's *Metamorphoses*," CJ 86 (1991): 233–43.

5. See, however, F. Williams, "Augustus and Daphne: Ovid's *Met.* 1.560–63 and Phylarchus FGrH 81 F 32(b)," PLLS 3 (1981): 249.

6. W. Ginsberg, "Ovid's *Metamorphoses* and the Politics of Interpretation," CJ 84 (1989): 229–30.

7. Brunel, *Le Mythe de La Métamorphose,* 56.

8. See Nicoll, "Cupid, Apollo, and Daphne," and Knox, *Traditions of Augustan Poetry,* 14–17. Williams, "Augustus and Daphne: Ovid's *Met.* 1.560–63 and Phylarchus FGrH 81 F 32(b)," and J. Wills, "Callimachean Models for Ovid's Apollo–Daphne," MD 24 (1990): 143–56, convincingly enumerate many probable Callimachean allusions that may be found in this episode. A number of

laurel at Roman triumphs and to decorate Augustus' door, the episode also
looks forward to the reintroduction of Augustan themes at the end of the poem.
In this first love-story of the *Metamorphoses* Ovid combines amatory, natural-
metamorphic, and aetiological themes, thus foreshadowing his practice in
much of the rest of the poem. In contrast with the preceding cosmogonic and
epic stories, the episode also highlights the stylistic polyphony typical of the
poem as a whole. The following stories of Io and Syrinx reinforce the Alex-
andrian and erotic tone introduced by this episode, but this register will soon
give way to the epic slaying of Argus (1.713ff).

We have so far considered Ovid's stories in the *Metamorphoses* that involve
transformations of humans into natural phenomena such as animals and plants.
A different kind of cosmogony is suggested in Ovid's stories that provide
explanations for geographical, cultural, and religious features—in other
words, historical, rather than natural-historical, *aetia* of the sort closely associ-
ated with the aetiological writing of the Hellenistic period. There are a number
of ways in which Ovid makes it clear that his *carmen perpetuum* is also
deductum; indeed the whole spirit of Ovid's narrative persona or voice in the
Metamorphoses is one recognizably within the Alexandrian tradition. P.E.
Knox has delineated many neoteric features of Ovid's language and style that
serve to associate the narrative of his epic with the background of
Callimachean-neoteric elegy and epyllion.[9] In this chapter we will look at the
ways in which Ovid also makes use of linguistic and structural features typical
of the narrative of Alexandrian aetiological poetry to signal the aetiological
focus of his stories.

Aetiological Phraseology in the *Metamorphoses*

One of the most useful ways in which aspects of Ovid's language and phraseol-
ogy that draw attention to the aetiological character of stories in the *Meta-
morphoses* can be elucidated is to compare them with similar narrative conven-
tions he uses in the elegiac *Fasti*. This poem, which Ovid seems to have been
composing at the same time as he was working on his epic project,[10] is

---

critics observe that the conclusion of Apollo's speech with *finierat Paean* (1.566) may recall
Callimachus' *Hy.* 2.97–104, which explains the origin of the paean after the killing of the Python:
πρώτιστον ἐφύμνιον εὕρετο λαός. See Schmitzer, *Zeitgeschichte in Ovids Metamorphosen*, 66,
on the political implications of this motif in both Ovid and Callimachus.

9. Knox, *Traditions of Augustan Poetry*, esp. 27–47.

10. Most scholars agree that the two poems were composed between the years 1 and 8 C.E.
Those who have argued for simultaneity of composition include Heinze, *Ovids elegische
Erzählung*, 1; H. Fränkel, *Ovid: A Poet Between Two Worlds* (Berkeley, 1945), 143, 238 n.2;

commonly considered the most ambitious and extensive Latin realization of Callimachus' *Aetia*.[11] Ovid's other main poetic models for the *Fasti* were Aratus and the aetiological elegies of Propertius in Book 4, and he drew on the antiquarian researches on Roman themes undertaken by Varro, Verrius Flaccus, Hyginus, and Livy. The subject, like that announced by Propertius in the first poem of Book 4, *sacra diesque canam et cognomina prisca locorum* (4.1.69),[12] is the same as that of Callimachus' *Aetia:* religious rites and customs. Apollonius Rhodius exhibits in his epic *Argonautica* the same Alexandrian antiquarian and scholarly interests and includes many *aetia* of a similar kind.[13] These are the cultural aetiological themes and concerns also prominent in Vergil's *Aeneid*. By comparing Ovid's treatment of similar themes in the *Metamorphoses* with these Greek and Roman models, along with others, we can become more aware of the ways in which Ovid draws our attention to the aetiological focus of his epic.

The word in Latin that most closely translates the Greek αἴτιον is *causa;* clear evidence for this is Servius' comment at *Aen.* 1.408: CUR DEXTRAE IUNGERE DEXTRAM *maiorum enim haec fuerat salutatio, cuius rei* τὸ αἴτιον, *id est, causam Varro, Callimachum secutus, exposuit.* The first two lines of Ovid's *Fasti*, which announce his aetiological theme, also confirm this translation: *Tempora cum causis Latium digesta per annum / lapsaque sub terras ortaque signa canam.*[14] Throughout the *Fasti* the word *causa* is repeatedly used with

---

Wilkinson, *Ovid Recalled,* 241; Otis, *Ovid as an Epic Poet,* 21–22; W. Kraus, "Ovidius Naso," in *Ovid,* ed. M. von Albrecht and E. Zinn (Darmstadt, 1968), 72; D.E.W. Wormell, "Ovid and the *Fasti*," *Hermathena* 127 (1979): 40–41; E.J. Kenney in *OCD²*, 764; Hinds, *Metamorphosis of Persephone,* 10–11, 137 n.23. R. Syme, *History in Ovid* (Oxford, 1978), 21–36, argues for the priority of the *Fasti*. The most recent study of their relative chronology, F. Bömer, "Über das zeitliche Verhältnis zwischen den Fasten und den Metamorphosen Ovids," *Gymnasium* 95 (1988): 207–21, cautiously reexamines the parallel passages in the two works and offers no certain answer. It is interesting to consider that Ovid may have composed his *Phaenomena* around this time as well.

11. Miller, "Callimachus and the Augustan Aetiological Elegy," 413; McKeown, "Ovid's *Fasti* and Augustan politics," 178, 186.

12. Hanslik in his Teubner edition of Propertius' elegies prints *deosque,* following a suggestion by J.P. Sullivan, *Propertius* (Cambridge, 1976), 138. Cf. *Fasti* 2.7: *idem sacra cano signataque tempora fastis.*

13. E.g., 1.989–1077 (Cyzicene *aetia:* rites, path, stone, fountain of Cleite), 1.1138–39 (Magna Mater rites), 2.296–97 (Strophades), 2.498–528 (Etesian winds, cult of Zeus Icmaios in Ceos), etc.

14. So Bömer, *Fast., ad loc.: "causis:* Sie bezeichen das Genos der Gattung, die Aitia." Further uses of *causa* in aetiological contexts include Prop. 4.10.1 *Nunc Iovis incipiam causas aperire Feretri,* and line 45; Arnobius *adv. nat.* 5.18 *suis . . . in causalibus Butas;* Cicero *Acad. Post.* 1.3.9; Varro *L.L.* 6.37; Manilius 2.27. See Lafaye, *Les Métamorphoses d'Ovide,* 106; K. Gieseking, *Die Rahmenerzählung in Ovids Metamorphosen* (Diss., Tübingen, 1965), 30–31;

this meaning (e.g., 1.91, 115, 133, 166, 189, 233, 278, 319, 332, 392, etc.). In key passages in the *Metamorphoses* as well, Ovid uses *causa* to render *aetion* (e.g., 4.287, 794; 9.2). Another related word we will find marking aetiological passages in the *Metamorphoses* is *origo*,[15] as in Vergil's famous passage in his sixth *Eclogue: his tibi Grynei nemoris dicatur origo* (72). The word *auctor*[16] also signifies an originator or a first occurrence, as do other passages marked by *primus, tunc primum*,[17] and *novus*.[18] These words are characteristic of aetiological exposition, which is concerned with beginnings, and they serve to signal the aetiological focus of episodes in the *Metamorphoses*.

Ovid's interest in and attention to etymology in the *Metamorphoses* is an obviously Alexandrian trait he shares with almost all the Latin poets. We have already, for example, considered Propertius' programmatic intent at 4.1.69 to treat *cognomina prisca locorum*. In chapter 1 we observed that Ovid was frequently concerned to explain at the completion of a metamorphosis the origin of the name of the new animal or plant created. Even when the name of the character transformed is identical to the created species, Ovid frequently appends these etymological tags to the end of his stories.[19] Ovid's interest in names extends beyond these types of natural *aetia* for animal and plant species. In the *Metamorphoses* he gives us notes explaining the *nomina* for such diverse things as veins (1.410), hermaphrodite (4.291, 384), lakes, fountains, and

---

Miller, "Callimachus and the Augustan Aetiological Elegy," 372–73 n.4; S. Shechter, "The *Aition* and Virgil's *Georgics*," *TAPA* 105 (1975): 350.

15. *Met.* 1.3, (cosmogonical), 252 (new race of men), 415 (stones to men); 5.262 (Hippocrene, on which see Hinds, *Metamorphosis of Persephone*, 4–5); 7.654 (Myrmidons); 15.69 (lightning). In the *Fasti origo* is used at 1.611; 2.269; 3.433; 4.783, 807; 5.277, 445; 6.11; also *ratio, Fasti* 1.31; 3.847.

16. *TLL* 2.1205.31–48: *moris institutor, rei primus inventor et cognitor. Met.* 5.657; 13.617; 15.9, 103. In the *Fasti* 2.543; 3.733; 6.203, 569, 709. *Aen.* 8.269 (*primus auctor*).

17. Used in this way in the *Metamorphoses: primus* 1.452, 8.247, 13.930, 15.72, 73, 558; *tum primum* 1.119, 121, 123; 2.171, 10.45 (*tum primum*), 12.526, 13.960, 14.576. *Fasti: primus* 3.151, 731; 4.109, 559; 4.404 (*tunc primum*). On *Ars* 1.101 (*primus*) see A.S. Hollis, ed., *Ovid Ars Amatoria 1* (Oxford, 1977), *ad loc.:* "Ovid here parodies the ancient preoccupation with inventors." Cf. also *Aen.* 8.269ff.; Prop. 4.10.5 (*primae . . . palmae*); Tib. 2.1.39ff.; Manil. 1.30. See Shechter, "The *Aition* and Virgil's *Georgics*," 351. Greek parallels include the Hom. *Hy. Herm.* 25, 108–11; Hes. *Theog.* 113, 115, 116; Call. *Hy.* 2.58–64, 72, 97–104, *Hy.* 3.212–13; Ap. Rhod. *Argon.* 4.116; Nic. *Alex.* 449. For the ancient preoccupation with inventors and inventions see Pliny *Nat.* 7.19–215; A. Kleingünther, *Protos heuretes. Philologus* Suppl. 26.1 (Leipzig, 1933).

18. *Novus* signals an *aetion* at *Met.* 1.678, 709; 2.377; 5.256, 674; 6.381; 8.609; 10.206, 310; 14.390–91; 15.749

19. *Nomen, nomina,* or *nominat* appear in association with animal and plant *aetia* at 4.415; 5.461; 6.674; 8.151, 255; 9.348; 10.502, 739; 11.795; 12.145; 14.396, 579, most of which are discussed above at pp. 37–39. Related expressions include forms of *dicere, appellare,* and *vocare:* 1.447; 2.706, 840; 5.411, 7.473–74, 524; 8.150, 235, 591, 798; 9.229; 10.644; 13.648; 14.90, 338, 348, 851.

rivers (5.411, 6.400–401, 7.381, 9.665, 14.616), islands (8.235, 10.297, 14.90), cities (9.449, 15.57), and geographical landmarks (13.569–70).[20] A similar interest is displayed by Ovid's internal narrators; such as Venus, who in an unusually scholarly manner gives us the Greek etymology for her own name: *"aliqua et mihi gratia ponto est, / si tamen in medio quondam concreta profundo / spuma fui Graiumque manet mihi nomen ab illa"* (4.536–38).[21]

Ovid's use of *nunc quoque* at the conclusion of a metamorphosis was noted in chapter 1 as a conventional formula associated with *aetia,* and it has frequently been recognized as such, although often considered parodic.[22] It is the equivalent of the Greek εἰσέτι καὶ νῦν, ἔτι νῦν, and similar expressions, which stress the continuation of the custom or landmark being described up to the present time; these are found associated with *aetia* in Callimachus, Apollonius Rhodius, and at the end of almost every one of Nicander's and Boios' metamorphoses in Antoninus Liberalis.[23] In Latin literature we find similar phrases in Vergil, marking aetiological passages in the *Georgics* and the *Aeneid.* At *Aen.* 6.234–35 Vergil explains the origin of the name of Cape Misenum from the Trojan helmsman Misenus: *qui nunc Misenus ab illo / dicitur,*[24] and at *Aen.* 5.602 he relates the origins of the *lusus Troiae: Troiaque nunc pueri, Troianum dicitur agmen.* In Ovid's own poetry, we find the expression used frequently with *aetia,* as we would expect, in the *Fasti* (2.301, 671; 3.328; 4.494, 504, 710, 806; 5.128, 428; 6.106, 307, 533), and in the *Ars Amatoria* it is found at the end of Ovid's humorous send-up of the aetiological tale, the rape of the Sabine Women at *Ars* 1.101–34: *Scilicet ex illo sollemni more theatra / nunc*

---

20. Cf. *Met.* 1.447; 2.675; 7.654; 8.230; 10.223; 13.648–49, 699, 897; 14.157, 434, 626, 760–61. Interest in the origin of names is also pervasive in the *Fasti,* and similar etymological notes occur at *Fasti* 1.103f., 237–38, 319–36; 2.449, 475f., etc. Cf. Prop. 4.2.10–21, 3.93–94, 9.16–20, 10.45–48; Vergil *Aen.* 1.247–49, 5.116f., 6.212–35, 242, 381, 7.1–4, etc. Callimachus wrote a treatise on names, κτίσεις νήσων καὶ πόλεων καὶ μετονομασίαι (Pfeiffer, p. 339), and elsewhere displays the same interest, e.g., *Aet.* frr. 26–31, 94–95, *Hy.* 1.37–41, 42–44, 47–49, etc. Cf. *Argon.* 1.591, 1019–20, 624f., 989, 1067–69, etc.

21. Of the approximately fifty explicitly introduced and signaled etymologies in the *Metamorphoses,* almost half are spoken by internal narrators. See Ahl, *Metaformations,* for etymological word-play throughout the *Metamorphoses.*

22. Galinsky, *Ovid's Metamorphoses,* 178 n.35; Bernbeck, *Beobachtungen zur Darstellungsart,* 105. The phrase is found in the *Metamorphoses* associated with a metamorphosis at 1.235; 2.706; 4.602; 5.677; 6.374, 312 (*etiam nunc*); 7.467, 656; 11.743; 14.73; 9.664; associated with a clear *aetion* at 4.750, 802; 5.328; 9.226; 10.160; 11.144; 13.622, 715 (*nunc*).

23. Hom. *Hy. Herm.* 123–26; Call. *Hy.* 2.47, *Hy.* 3.77, 220, *Aet.* fr. 43.78–79; Ap. Rhod. *Argon.* 1.1061–62, 1075–77, 1354, 2.250–52, 717, 850, 4.480, 534–36, 599, 1153–55; Phanocles fr. 1.28 Powell, p. 107; Nicander (A.L.) 13.6, 17.6, 18.3, 29.4, 31.5, 32.5, 9.3 (καὶ ἔτι νῦν), 1.6 (ἄχρι νῦν), 2.7, 4.7, 23.6, 25.5, 26.5, 30.4, 35.4; Boios (A.L.) 3.4, 7.8, 16.3, 18.3.

24. See E. Norden's comment, *P. Vergilius Maro, Aeneis Buch VI,* 3d ed. (Leipzig and Berlin, 1926), *ad loc.:* "der Konventionel Stil der aetiologischen Poesie"; also *Aen.* 7.1–4 (*nunc*).

quoque formosis insidiosa manent (1.133–34).[25] The word *unde* is often found
signaling aetiologies either in conjunction with this formula or alone, as either
an introductory or concluding phrase, as at *Fasti* 3.265–66—*hic latet Hippo-
lytus loris direptus equorum, / unde nemus nullis illud aditur equis*[26]—or
3.327–28—*eliciunt caelo te, Iuppiter, unde minores / nunc quoque te
celebrant Eliciumque vocant.* [27] With these we can compare similar passages
in the *Metamorphoses,* as at 5.327–28—*unde recurvis / nunc quoque formatus
Libys est cum cornibus Ammon*—or 14.337–8—*rarior arte canendi, / unde
Canens dicta est.*[28] These expressions are obvious stylistic mannerisms that
Ovid's *Metamorphoses* shares with other aetiological poems. They draw atten-
tion to the aetiological focus of many stories in the *Metamorphoses.* Moreover,
the stories in which they appear frequently are placed in narrative structures
typical of aetiological poetry.

Aetiological Frame Narratives[29]

The most conspicuous narrative trait the *Metamorphoses* shares with the *Fasti*
is the frequent use of internal narrators.[30] It has often been noted that Ovid's
use of multiple interlocutors in the *Fasti* is indebted to Callimachus' narrative

25. Hollis, *Ovid Ars Amatoria 1, ad loc.;* Miller, "Callimachus and the Augustan Aetiological
Elegy," 397–98, and "Callimachus and the *Ars Amatoria*," 34. Cf. *Amores* 3.13.21, Ovid's
aetiological poem about the Argive origins of a festival to Juno celebrated in Falerii: *nunc quoque
per pueros iaculis incessitur index.* Other Latin examples where the expression is used in aetiologi-
cal contexts include Prop. 4.10.45, Manilius' *Astronomica* 1.341, 432, 749; 5.36, Aem. Macer (fr.
1, p. 107 Morel; p. 138 Buechner). Also in Varro *L.L.,* e.g., 5.41.
26. Vergil *Aen.* 7.778–80 relates the same *aetion: unde etiam templo Triviae lucisque sacratis
/ cornipedes arcentur equi* (778–79). Also *Aen.* 5.123, 568, *Geo.* 1.63.
27. Also *Fasti* 3.118, 408, 4.51, 5.445, 6.578. Cf. Prop. 4.1.26, 4.2.50. The Greek equivalents
are ἔνθεν (Call. *Hy.* 1.43, *Hy.* 4.253, 314; Ap. Rhod. *Argon.* 1.1061–62, 1075–77 (ἔνθ' ἔτι νῦν),
1138–39, 4.480, 1765–72); ὅθεν (Call. *Hy.* 3.197; Ap. Rhod. *Argon.* 4.116; Nic. *Ther.* 318); ἐκ τοῦ
(Hes. *Theog.* 556); ἐξότε (Nic. *Ther.* 355); ἐκ κείνου (Phanocles fr. 1.21 Powell, p. 107) etc.
28. Also *Met.* 4.285, 4.620, 5.552, 7.686, 10.223, 14.626, 15.69.
29. See M. Bal, *Introduction to the Theory of Narrative,* trans. C. van Boheeman (Toronto,
1985), 143, on "frame narratives" as "narrative texts in which at the second or third level a
complete story is told."
30. These are instances when a character in the text narrates a story in direct discourse. The
primary narrator narrates the primary text, which sets up the framework or situation for a charac-
ter's narration at the secondary level. We may call the character who narrates an "internal,
secondary, or character narrator" and the narrative s/he produces an "internal, inset, framed, or
embedded narrative/speech." The circumstance in which the story is told is "the narrating or
generating instance or situation." The terminology I have adopted from narratological theory is
derived mainly from Bal, *Introduction to the Theory of Narrative,* and I. de Jong, *Narrators and
Focalizers: The Presentation of the Story in the Iliad* (Amsterdam, 1987), both of whom have built
on the work of G. Genette, *Narrative Discourse,* trans. J.E. Lewin (Oxford, 1980); cf. also
Chatman, *Story and Discourse.*

framework in the first two books of his *Aetia,* in which the primary narrator (we may call him Callimachus, for convenience) asked questions of the Muses on a variety of antiquarian subjects and received their answers.[31] In the existing fragments of the *Aetia,* we have evidence of at least seven occasions on which a Muse, either Clio, Calliope, or Erato, responds to Callimachus' questions.[32] Near the beginning of the poem, for example, the *Scholia Florentina* (*ad Aet.* 1 frr. 3–7.14) reveal that Callimachus asked the Muses why the Parians sacrifice to the Graces without flutes and garlands (*Aet.* 1 fr. 3.1–2). Clio responded to his question with the story of Minos and the death of his son Androgeos (frr. 4–5), and after receiving this explanation, Callimachus asked her a second question, this time about the genealogy of the Graces (*Aet.* 1 frr. 6–7.14). Callimachus' use of this divine framework in the first two books of the *Aetia* is a humorous and explicit acknowledgement of the Hesiodic model of inspiration from the Muses.[33] The Muses, furthermore, provide the sort of authority for his narrative that Callimachus elsewhere supplies by citing his historical sources and on occasion other internal narrators.[34] At *Aet.* frr. 178–85 Callimachus interrogates a fellow diner at a banquet about his local cult practices and in *Aet.* fr. 114 a statue of Apollo discourses on its own attributes.[35] Callimachus' *Iambi* 7 (fr. 197) and 9 (fr. 199) also exhibit aetiological internal narrators, and his *Hecale* included an embedded aetiological narrative spoken by a crow (frr. 70–74 Hollis), which was imitated by Ovid at *Metamorphoses* 2.534–95.[36] It seems that the use of internal narrators for aetiological disquisi-

---

31. Pfeiffer *Call.* II, xxxv: *In universum Ovidius in Fastorum libris exemplum Aetiorum lib. I / II secutus esse videtur.* Cf. Heinze, *Ovids elegische Erzählung,* 96–97; Wilkinson, *Ovid Recalled,* 248; Miller, "Callimachus and the Augustan Aetiological Elegy," 402; D. Porte, *L'Étiologie Religieuse dans les Fastes d'Ovide* (Paris, 1985), 31.

32. *Aet.* 1 frr. 3–4 (Clio); fr. 7.22 (Calliope answers a question about sacrifices on Lindos and Anaphe); fr. 31b-e (the Diegeseis at 31b-e 1–2 seem to show that Callimachus asked both about the rites of Linus and Coroebus and about the statue of Diana at Leukas); fr. 43 *ad* 28ff. (Pfeiffer: *poeta quaesivisse videtur quare Zanclaei conditorem urbis non nomine appellent*), fr. 43. 56 (Clio answers: τὸ [δ]εύτερον ἤρ[χετο μ]ύθ[ου], and fr. 43.84ff. (Callimachus begins a second question); *SH* 238.8 (Erato answers an unknown question); fr. 759 (*Frag. Inc. Auc.*) (Calliope answers).

33. *Aet.* 1 fr. 2 (*Somnium*) with the Schol. Flor. *ad* fr. 2.16ff: ὡς κατ' ὄναρ σ(υμ)μείξας ταῖς Μούσ[αις ἐν 'Ε-/λι]κῶνι εἰλήφοι π(αρ' α)ὐτ(ῶν) τ(ὴν) τ(ῶν) αἰτίων [ἐξήγη-/σιν; cf. Hes. *Theog.* 22ff., *Erga* 662. See Bulloch, "Hellenistic Poetry," 554; Rheinsch-Werner, *Callimachus Hesiodicus,* 324ff.; Kambylis, *Die Dichterweihe und ihre Symbolik,* 89–98; Hutchinson, *Hellenistic Poetry,* 278 n.2.

34. Kambylis, *Die Dichterweihe und ihre Symbolik,* 97, thus qualifies the Muses as "Stufe der Legitimation"; cf. Rösler, "Entdeckung der Fiktionalität in der Antike," 292.

35. For more on both of these passages see below pp. 74f.

36. Four other fragments from the *Aetia* suggest possible internal narrators. At fr. 64 Simonides (or his tomb) may be speaking, at fr. 97 the Pelasgian walls, at fr.103 a stele seem to be speaking (τόδε κύρβις ἀείδει), and at fr. 110 the Lock of Berenice addresses the queen. These two

tions might have become associated with Callimachus' aetiological poetry. In general, Callimachus' narrative poetical pose as the consulter of authorities and the follower and innovator of tradition offered Roman poets a model relevant to their own problems of inspiration, authentication, and originality within a long-established poetic tradition.

In the *Fasti* Ovid adopts a structure very similar to that of Callimachus' numerous learned discussions with both divine and human interlocutors in the *Aetia*. Ovid presents himself in the *Fasti* as an investigator of antiquarian information[37] and asks a variety of informants for explanations for various aspects of the calendar and religious practices.[38] In Ovid's poem, as in that of Callimachus, the epiphanies serve the dual purpose of vouching for the poet's divine inspiration and for the authentication of the truth of his narrative—both important aspects of his pose in the *Fasti* as a *vates*. This concern with "veracity" also is an example of one of the ways in which Ovid as primary narrator in the *Fasti* displays features of the didactic persona.[39] J.F. Miller has drawn attention to Ovid's use in the *Fasti* of didactic language and mannerisms in both his primary narrative and secondary framed narratives. This language highlights the explanatory nature of Ovid's aetiological poem and again underscores Ovid's pose as a scholar "who dispenses antiquarian information to his reader."[40] It should not surprise any reader of Ovid, however, that the very traditions and conventions upon which this poem is based are ultimately problematized. Ovid's informants, both divine and human, frequently report conflicting and uncertain information.[41]

---

examples may be closer to the speaking-monument type of epigram, as in Callimachus *Ep.* 5 and 24.

37. Miller, "Callimachus and the Augustan Aetiological Elegy," 401. Cf. Hutchinson, *Hellenistic Poetry,* 45; C. Newlands, "Ovid's Narrator in the *Fasti,*" *Arethusa* 25 (1992): 33–54. Passages that especially exhibit this aspect of Callimachus' persona include *Aet.* 2 fr. 43.84–85 and *Aet.* fr. 178.21–22.

38. Janus 1.89–288; Muse 1.657–62; Mars 3.167–258; Vesta 3.697–710; Erato 4.181–372; "*quidam senior*" 4.377–86; "*hospes antiquus*" 4.679–712; flamen 4.905–42; Polyhymnia, Urania, Calliope 5.7–110; Flora 5.183–378; Tiber 5.635–62; Mercury 5.663–720; Juno, Juventas, Concordia 6.1–100; Sancus 6.213–18; *coniunx* 6.219–34; *anus* 6.395–416; Minerva 6.649–710; Clio 6.797–812. See J.F. Miller's valuable study "Ovid's Divine Interlocutors in the *Fasti,*" in *Studies in Latin Literature,* ed. C. Deroux (Brussels, 1983), 156–92.

39. Miller, "Callimachus and the Augustan Aetiological Elegy," 401–9. See also B. Harries, "Causation and the Authority of the Poet in Ovid's *Fasti,*" *CQ* n.s. 39 (1989): 164–85, who is unfortunately unaware of Miller's work.

40. Miller, "Callimachus and the Augustan Aetiological Elegy," 409. He points out that Propertius in Book 4 had also adopted features of didactic language (385), as at 4.10.1: *Nunc Iovis incipiam causas aperire Feretri.* See now also *idem,* "The *Fasti* and Hellenistic Didactic: Ovid's Variant Aetiologies," *Arethusa* 25 (1992): 11–31.

41. See Newlands, "Ovid's Narrator in the *Fasti.*"

Distinguish
2 ?
2 ,

   The affinity between the narrative strategies of didactic and aetiological
poetry is again an indication of the concern of Alexandrian and Roman poetry
with exploring the nature of authoritative claims for fiction; the *Meta-
morphoses* shares this concern. The use of frame narratives has itself been
shown to be "a reaction to the problematic status of writing poetry in the
Hellenistic era,"[42] as well as a powerful device for poetic self-reference. Inter-
nal narrators bring to the fore the issue of the reliability of the narrator, which
has implications for understanding Ovid's authorial posture in the poem as a
whole.[43] His embedded narratives provide repeated and contrasting paradigms
for the very nature of tale-telling and for audience-response.[44] The technique is
related to the general fondness in Alexandrian poetry for complex narrative
structures. The story within a story, embedded either in an artistic ecphrasis or
an inset narrative, and internal narrators are features common to nearly all
poems in this tradition, e.g., Theocritus' *Idylls* 1, 7, 11, Moschus' *Europa,*
Catullus 64, and Vergil *Geo.* 4.453–527 (the Song of Proteus). The prominence
of the theme of story-telling in the *Metamorphoses,* evinced largely by the
many inset narratives in the poem, has been the subject of much important
recent Ovidian criticism. The very fact that Ovid has chosen to set up an
instance of internal narration must provoke an interest in the nature of the story
receiving this framework.[45] We need to approach his internal narratives by
asking the questions that narratology has taught us to ask: namely, why Ovid
chose to have certain stories narrated by internal narrators, why he chose
particular characters to narrate these stories, what the motivations and circum-
stances of the narration are, who the internal audience is and what is their

Mercury

---

   42. S. Goldhill, "Framing and Polyphony: Readings in Hellenistic Poetry," *PCPS* 212 n.s. 32
(1986): 31, cf. *idem, The Poet's Voice,* 223–83; G.A. Seeck, "Dichterische Technik in Theokrits
Thalysien und das Theorie der Hirtendichtung," in *Dorema Hans Diller* (Athens, 1975), 195–209;
F.T. Griffiths, *Theocritus at Court* (Leiden, 1979), 80–82.
   43. H. Cooper in her article, "Chaucer and Ovid: A Question of Authority," in *Ovid Renewed,*
ed. C. Martindale (Cambridge, 1988), 71–81, offers a fascinating discussion of Chaucer's in-
debtedness to Ovid as a model for the use of embedded narratives for literary self-reflection.
   44. See Leach, "Ekphrasis and the Theme of Artistic Failure," 104–6; B.R. Fredericks
[Nagle], "Divine Wit vs. Divine Folly: Mercury and Apollo in *Met.* 1–2," *CJ* 72 (1977): 244;
eadem, "Ovid's *Metamorphoses:* A Narratological Catalogue," *Syllecta Classica* 1 (1989): 97; D.
Lateiner, "Mythic and Non-Mythic Artists in Ovid's *Metamorphoses,*" *Ramus* 13 (1984): 1–30;
A.M. Keith, *The Play of Fictions: Studies in Ovid's Metamorphoses Book 2* (Ann Arbor, 1992),
esp. 3–6. For discussion of the way in which embedded narratives in general offer self-reflective
"models of reading and interpretation," see J.J. Winkler, *Auctor and Actor: A Narratological
Reading of Apuleius' The Golden Ass* (Berkeley and Los Angeles, 1985).
   45. Bal, *Introduction to the Theory of Narrative,* 43, asserts that "the narrative act of the actor
which produces an embedded text is an important event in the fabula of the primary text."

reaction, and finally, what effect this framework has on an interpretation of the embedded narrative.

Other examples in Latin poetry support the suggestion that the use of framed internal narratives for aetiological narratives was specifically associated with Callimachus' aetiological poetry.[46] For example, W. Wimmel has suggested that Vergil's choice of an internal narrator, Silenus, in his sixth *Eclogue* is a further acknowledgment of the Alexandrian pedigree of this passage.[47] In Book 8 of the *Aeneid* Vergil makes extensive use of the motif of question and answer as Evander leads Aeneas over the site of ancient Rome and explains to him the origins of various well-known landmarks. E.V. George has discussed the similarity of this book of the *Aeneid* to the first two books of the *Aetia,* in the "rich succession of aitia told in conversation, in which speakers and listeners play prominent parts."[48] Aeneas to some extent reproduces the eager pose of investigator that Callimachus and Ovid exhibit in their aetiological poems: *Aeneas, capiturque locis et singula laetus / exquiritque auditque virum monimenta priorum (Aen.* 8.311–12). Similarly, Propertius in his fourth book of elegies includes internal narrators in every poem except for 4.10.[49] Most notably, in poem 4.2 a statue of the rustic deity Vertumnus gives an aetiological disquisition on its origins. We will be looking at this poem's close relationship to Callimachus' *Aet.* fr. 114 in the following chapter.[50] In 4.1, a poem dealing with topography of ancient Rome which exhibits many similarities with Vergil's *Aen.* 8, Propertius addresses his explanations to an anonymous *hospes* (4.1.1), thus reproducing, in a way, Evander's lectures to Aeneas.[51]

I suggest that many of the embedded narratives in the *Metamorphoses* share a number of the features of both Callimachus' antiquarian and scholarly techniques in the *Aetia* and Ovid's imitation of these in the *Fasti.* A significant

Priority to Fasti?

---

46. See Feeney, *Gods in Epic,* 185–86, on Vergil's use of Callimachus in the *Aeneid.*

47. See Wimmel, *Kallimachos in Rom,* 143; cf. Stewart, "Song of Silenus," 198, where he also lists other Alexandrian internal narrators.

48. George, *Aeneid VIII and the Aitia of Callimachus,* 7. See more fully his chapter "Speakers and Listeners," pp. 10–24. Hollis, *Callimachus Hecale,* 350, suggests that *Aeneid* 8 "has an unmistakable Hellenistic air."

49. Cairns, "Propertius and the Battle of Actium (4.6)," in *Poetry and Politics in the Age of Augustus,* ed. A.J. Woodman and D.A. West (Cambridge, 1984) 148, discusses these multiple speakers in Book 4.

50. Pages 119ff.

51. Miller, "Callimachus and the Augustan Aetiological Elegy," 383, links Propertius' use of the word *hospes* with the formula at the beginning of many Hellenistic epigrams, such as *A.P.* 6.311.1; 7.26.1; 7.416.1; cf. Callimachus fr. 392. C.W. Macleod, "Propertius 4.1," *PLLS* 1 (1976): 141, suggests that the word recalls the *hospes* in Catullus 4.1.

difference between the *Metamorphoses* and these two elegiac works is, of course, the different narrative posture of the poet. In both the *Aetia* and the *Fasti*, the status of the implied author is, in Gérard Genette's terms, "homodiegetic"; that is, "the narrator is present as a character in the story he tells."[52] The narrators in these poems report their own previous conversations. Ovid in the *Metamorphoses* is a "heterodiegetic" narrator and his embedded narratives are always those of the characters within his text, from which he is himself absent as a character.

Ovid often sets up an embedded narrative in the *Metamorphoses* by means of a question.[53] In some of these episodes the narrative is motivated by a simple request for information. The question, for example, may evince a sympathetic concern, as when Peleus and his companions ask Ceyx why he suddenly begins to weep, *moveat tantos quae causa dolores, / Peleusque comitesque rogant* (11.289–90).[54] Or, again, a question may express an avid curiosity to hear a story narrated, as when Achilles eagerly asks Nestor to tell the story of Caeneus (12.176–81) and when Macareus and Achaemenides swap adventures (14.158ff.). Some questions, however, are directed towards a specific object, about which the interrogator desires information; it is the structure of this narrative situation that is most similar to Callimachus' aetiological interrogations in the *Aetia*.[55]

M. de Cola suggested long ago that it was perhaps not a coincidence that in the *Metamorphoses* a number of stories told by internal secondary narrators in conversation with other characters seem to be indebted to Callimachus. She further suggested that Ovid constructed this similar narrative situation as a signal to his reader of his source.[56] It is this insight we will pursue in this chapter by investigating closely certain embedded narratives introduced by a question, which treat themes similar to those that interested Callimachus. I

---

52. Genette, *Narrative Discourse*, 233.

53. M.M. Avery, "The Use of Direct Speech in Ovid's *Metamorphoses*" (Ph.D. diss., University of Chicago, 1937), 7.

54. Similar to this are the motivations for the narratives of Aeacus (7.517–660), Galatea (13.738–897), and Anius (13.623–704).

55. Argus/Mercury (1.687–68), "*unus ex numero procerum*" / Perseus (4.790–93), Minerva / Urania (5.254–63), Ceres / Arethusa (5.572–73), "*nescio quis*" / "*dux*" (6.329–30), Phocus / Cephalus (7.685–86), Theseus / Achelous (8.573–76, 9.1–2), Macareus / "*una e famulis*" (14.161–65), Numa / "*e senioribus unus*" (15.9–11). Gieseking, *Die Rahmenerzählung*, places all embedded narratives (Rahmenerzählungen) within two main categories: *Aitia, exempla* (see his pages 60–61 for a chart). He recognizes that these categories frequently overlap. His list of "die direkte oder indirekte Frage nach irgendeinem interessierenden αἴτιον" adds to my list the narratives of Jupiter (1.210), Acoetes (3.579ff.), Alcithoë (4.285), Anius (13.640ff.), and Galatea (13.747ff.), but excludes that of Arethusa.

56. De Cola, *Callimaco e Ovidio*, 76.

believe de Cola was right in suspecting that the material of these embedded narratives displays affinities with Callimachus' aetiological poetry and that Ovid is drawing attention to these antecedents by constructing narrative frameworks similar to those employed by Callimachus in the *Aetia* and elsewhere. Moreover, within these inset narratives the diction and phraseology are especially reminiscent of that used by Ovid and his internal narrators in the *Fasti.*

Framed Aetiological Narratives in the *Metamorphoses*

While Ovid as primary narrator relates many aetiological stories in the course of the *Metamorphoses,* these particular embedded narratives that are introduced by a question serve to highlight his epic's associations with the Alexandrian aetiological tradition. We can chart a significant general tendency in the *Metamorphoses* to use embedded narratives as "exaggerated" examples of the numerous generic types of literature the poem is drawing on.[57] Orpheus' narrative at *Met.* 10.148–739, for example, as Knox has clearly shown,[58] encourages the reader to recognize further the elegiac features elsewhere in Ovid's epic, yet in itself it represents an example of catalog poetry whose strongly elegiac tone reflects only this one side of the *Metamorphoses,* and it should not be seen as a paradigm for the whole epic.[59] Similarly, Nestor's aggressively epic narrative in Book 12, which is highlighted through Ovid's choice of this supremely epic character-narrator and the epic setting of the narration, represents another, and equally important, aspect of the *Metamorphoses.* The Speech of Pythagoras, as we shall see, functions similarly as an example of "didactic" poetry. Although Ovid allows these other generic voices to intrude into his poem, he continues to remind us of the epic orientation of the poem as a whole. The polyphony of the *Metamorphoses* is an important aspect of Ovid's self-conscious confrontation with the generic and thematic aims and associations of his epic poem.[60]

---

57. See A. Barchiesi, "Voci e istanze narrative nelle *Metamorfosi* di Ovidio," *MD* 23 (1989): 55, on polyphony and "polyeideia"; M. Pechillo, "Ovid's Framing Technique: The Aeacus and Cephalus Epyllion (*Met.* 7.490–8.5)," *CJ* 86 (1990): 35, 43; B.R. Nagle, "Two Miniature *Carmina Perpetua* in the *Metamorphoses:* Calliope and Orpheus," *Grazer Beiträge* 15 (1988): 99; Farrell, "Dialogue of Genres."

58. Knox, *Traditions of Augustan Poetry,* 48–64.

59. So Hinds, in his review of Knox, *Traditions of Augustan Poetry,* 269. Hinds' own work, *Metamorphosis of Persephone,* on the embedded narrative of Calliope in *Met.* 5 offers a model for how to proceed.

60. See G. Rosati, "Il racconto dentro il racconto; funzioni metanarrative nelle Metamorfosi di Ovidio," *Atti del Convegno internazionale Letteratura classiche e narratologia, Selva di Fasano 1980* (Perugia, 1981), 297–309. See also Hinds, *Metamorphosis of Persephone,* xii, for his discussion of Ovid's "concern with poetic self-reference."

Perhaps the best place to start is with the appearance of the Muses them-
selves in a narrative situation in *Metamorphoses* 5 reminiscent of the aetiologi-
cal dialogues of the Muses in Callimachus' *Aetia.* The appearance of Minerva
on Helicon initiates this important and much-discussed programmatic passage,
the full importance of which we cannot discuss here, but will return to briefly in
chapter 4.[61] What we should notice at this point is that upon her arrival,
Minerva explains that the reason for her visit was to see and confirm reports
about the creation of a new spring, the Hippocrene (*fama novi fontis* 5.256).
The muse Uranie responds to Minerva with an assertion that what she has
heard is indeed true: "*vera tamen fama est: est Pegasus huius origo / fontis*"
(5.262–63). The word *origo* is a clear signal that this story may be placed in the
literary category of aetiological poetry. Not surprisingly, echoes of
Callimachus, as well as other Alexandrian poets, have been detected in this
episode, although they have been placed in a generic context that has overall as
its primary reference the norms of epic. Thus, like the poem as a whole,
Alexandrian affiliations are brought in line with epic concerns.[62] This passage,
concerned as it is with the Muses and the nature of Ovid's poetry, seems to
function as a sort of paradigm for other framed narratives in the *Meta-
morphoses* similarly constructed as learned conversations about religious
details. We should thus be encouraged to seek Alexandrian literary antecedents
in these other embedded narratives as well.

The dinner party is a popular setting for internal narratives in the *Meta-
morphoses,* and it is likely that Callimachus is an important model for Ovid in
his use of this motif.[63] In frr. 178–85 of the *Aetia* Callimachus describes the
setting of a dinner party at the house of an Athenian named Pollis in Egypt on
the occasion of the festival of the Aiora.[64] At the table, Callimachus (again, we

---

61. For full discussion see Hinds, *Metamorphosis of Persephone,* and Heinze, *Ovids elegische
Erzählung.*

62. As observed by Hinds, *Metamorphosis of Persephone,* 4–5, who shows further (pp. 4–24)
that the passage contains references to not only Callimachus (*Aet.* fr. 2.1), but also Aratus (*Phaen.*
216–24), and Nicander (A.L. 9); cf. Schmitzer, *Zeitgeschichte in Ovids Metamorphosen,* 226.

63. So Kenney, Introduction and Notes to *Ovid's Metamorphoses,* xxii–xxiii; Wilkinson, *Ovid
Recalled,* 153, compares Callimachus' questioning in fr. 178 to *Met.* 7.670–86 where Cephalus is
prompted to tell his story by the eager questioning of Phocus about the remarkable spear he is
carrying: *quaerit, / cur sit et unde datum* (7.685–86). Cf. *Met.* 4.757ff., 7.494ff., 8.565ff.,
12.152ff., 13.636ff.

64. The placement of the fragment is not established. An appealing argument has been put
forward by J.E.G. Zetzel, "On the Opening of Callimachus, *Aetia* 2," *ZPE* 42 (1981): 31–33, for
placing the fragment at the beginning of the second book of the *Aetia,* where the references to a
symposiastic setting in *Aet.* 2 fr. 43.12–17 would refer to the immediately preceding episode.
Hutchinson, *Hellenistic Poetry,* 44 n.36, however, feels that placing the fragment here would be
"imprudent."

assume) asks his neighbor Theugenes, who we are told is from the island of Icos, about the worship of Peleus on that island (fr. 178.21–30) and receives a reply. Banquets, however, were also the traditional setting for the telling of heroic tales in ancient poetry, as in *Od.* 9–12 and *Aen.* 1–3.[65] A scene in the *Metamorphoses* acknowledging the heroic-epic model is Nestor's long story about the battle of the Lapiths and Centaurs, which he relates at Achilles' request (12.146–579).

Closer to the Callimachean model of learned interrogation is the narrative situation in *Metamorphoses* 4, at the wedding banquet of Perseus and Andromeda. After the feast, the guests begin to question one another; Perseus asks about the region and is in turn himself asked to recount his adventures in capturing the head of Medusa (4.765–71). Unexpectedly, Perseus does not narrate these directly, but rather Ovid in *oratio obliqua* summarizes for us the familiar details (772–86). Ovid then adds that Perseus told many other things as well, humorously enumerating *all* of these topics we do not get to hear about:

> Addidit et longi non falsa pericula cursus,
> quae freta, quas terras sub se vidisset ab alto
> et quae iactatis tetigisset sidera pennis.
>
> (4.787–89)

Due suggests that "here the use of indirect speech reveals the conventionality of the 'hero's telling about himself at a banquet.' Ovid closely follows epic practice, but slyly makes fun of it by choosing an incongruous medium: *oratio obliqua*."[66] Someone (*unus / ex numero procerum quaerens* 4.790–91) then asks Perseus specifically for an explanation of why Medusa alone of her sisters had snakes mingled with her hair. And finally Perseus answers in direct speech, with a suggestion that this is the first really interesting question that had been asked all evening: *hospes ait "quoniam scitaris digna relatu, / accipe quaesiti causam"* (4.793–94).[67] He explains that the once beautiful Medusa had been molested by Neptune in Minerva's temple and that afterwards in punishment Minerva had turned her hair into snakes (*Gorgoneum crinem turpes mutavit in*

---

65. See G. Sandy, "Petronius and Interpolated Narrative," *TAPA* 101 (1970): 471, for a complete list of symposiastic settings for internal narratives from the *Odyssey* and Egyptian papyri to the later Greek novels. See also Gieseking, *Die Rahmenerzählung,* 67–75; E. Courtney, *A Commentary on the Satires of Juvenal* (London, 1980), *ad* 15.13.

66. Due, *Changing Forms,* 78. He adds, "it is no wonder that the audience is not satisfied and wants more (4.790: *ante exspectatum tacuit tamen*)!" Compare, however, the similar technique used by Vergil in *Ecl.* 6 to summarize the song of Silenus, esp. 41–43.

67. Cf. *Fasti* 3.541–42: *occurrit nuper (visa est mihi digna relatu) / pompa.*

hydros 4.801). Interestingly, it seems that while the other parts of the story are traditional, this *aetion* is largely Ovid's own invention. Medusa's union with Neptune is in Hesiod (*Theogony* 278–79), but not Minerva's involvement. In other accounts all three sisters had snakes entwined in their hair, and there is no evidence that these had been inflicted as a punishment.[68]

The similarity to the Callimachean aetiological framework is brought out by the nature of the question; as in Callimachus, this question elicits an explanation of a specific mythological or religious detail: *cur sola sororum / gesserit alternis inmixtos crinibus angues* (4.791–92). Most of the questions in the extant fragments of the first two books of the *Aetia* involve specific aspects of a cult. The aetiological character of Perseus' narrative is highlighted in a number of ways beyond the initial asking of a question. His response is couched in language reminiscent of the aetiological and didactic language spoken by Ovid and his interlocutors in the *Fasti*. Perseus begins with *accipe quaesiti causam* (4.794), and immediately alerts us to the aetiological focus of his narrative by the word *causam*. The phraseology, moreover, finds an almost exact parallel in the words of Ovid's first divine interlocutor in the *Fasti*, Janus, spoken in response to Ovid's questioning: *accipe, quaesitae quae causa sit altera formae* (1.115).[69] This imperative *accipe* is a typical opening for a didactic exposition and here it underlines the explanatory nature of the ensuing narrative.[70] To substantiate the rather remarkable claim that Medusa was in fact once very beautiful, and that her hair was especially outstanding, again a feature probably original to Ovid, Perseus brings forward the evidence of an eyewitness to this sight: *inveni, qui se vidisse referret* (797). In the *Fasti* the evidence of eyewitnesses is very important for asserting the veracity of the account being given and we will find below that this is also common to many of the internal narrators in the *Metamorphoses*. Here there may be a joke in this assertion of *vidisse,* since Medusa is not someone whom one could have *looked* at any time after her transformation! After Perseus has given the requested *aetion,* he adds a second *aetion,* this one anachronistic, marked by typical aetiological phraseology:

---

68. Bömer, *Met., ad* 4.791 "vor Ovid nicht bekannt." Also Kenney, Introduction and Notes to *Ovid's Metamorphoses, ad* 4.791; Niese *RE* 7.2 (1912) 1630–55 (s.v. Gorgo). Apollod. 2.4.1ff. preserves a version recounting that Medusa had been killed at Athena's command because she had dared to match herself in beauty with the goddess.

69. Also *Fasti* 5.449 *accipe causam,* 4.938 *causam percipe.* Other appearances of the imperative in aetiological contexts include *Fasti* 2.514; Prop. 4.2.2.

70. Kenney, "*Nequitiae Poeta,*" 204, includes *accipe* in his list of "words and phrases peculiarly appropriate to didactic poetry." E.g., Lucr. 1.269, 4.722; *Rem.* 292.

"nunc quoque, ut attonitos formidine terreat hostes,
pectore in adverso, quos fecit, sustinet angues."

(4.802–3)

The Gorgon's head was traditionally the centerpiece of Athena's aegis, but at
this point in the *Metamorphoses* it is still in Perseus' possession and in Book
5.177ff. he will use it in his fight with Phineus. The double *aetion* serves to
highlight Perseus' rejection of traditional heroic narrative in favor of aetiologi-
cal detail.[71] We can trace the use of similar narrative techniques when we
consider other inset narratives in the *Metamorphoses* that involve similar
aetiological themes.

A recognition of the aetiological intent of a story introduced by a question
can uncover an entirely new level of significance and elicit a further apprecia-
tion of Ovid's complex compositional technique in the *Metamorphoses*. The
story of Syrinx that Mercury narrates to Argus at *Metamorphoses* 1.682–715
has been seen mainly as a humorous and deliberately similar repetition of the
Daphne story, which preceded it in Book 1.[72] The episode is a playful depic-
tion of the use of story-telling ostensibly for the sole purpose of inducing sleep.
The story, however, should also be recognized for the learned aetiological
narrative that it is. It is clear that Ovid did not choose to have *Mercury* tell this
particular story merely because of its similarity to the Daphne episode, and
Argus' question about the pipe, which provides the immediate motivation for
the narration, supplies us with the important clue: *quaerit quoque (namque
reperta / fistula nuper erat), qua sit ratione reperta* (1.687–88). The story is in
fact an invention story (cf. *voce nova* 678, *arte nova* 709), and one that was
disputed in antiquity; in some accounts Mercury was considered the inventor
of the *syrinx,* in others Pan. Bömer notes in his commentary to this passage that
what Ovid has in fact done in this episode is to "correct" the conflicting
tradition of the invention of the reed-pipes in the previous versions.[73] The
tradition that Mercury was the inventor of the reed-pipes is found in the

---

71. Two other *aetia* are included in the Perseus episode: that for snakes in Libya at 4.614–20
(signaled by *unde* 620) and for coral at 4.740–52 (signaled by *nunc quoque* 750).

72. So critics comment on the humorous "somniferous effect" of the repeated plot: Fränkel,
Poet between Two Worlds, 85, 216 n.43; Galinsky, *Ovid's Metamorphoses,* 174; Bömer, *Met., ad*
1.689–712. Ahl, *Metaformations,* 155, observes that like Daphne, Syrinx becomes the symbol of
her would-be assailant.

73. The story of Syrinx, however, is not known before Ovid. Bömer, *Met., ad* 1.689–712,
argues that the appearance of the story in later sources (Longus 2.34.1, Achilles Tatius, Hyginus,
etc.) seems to suggest that it was not Ovid's invention.

Homeric *Hymn to Hermes* 511ff. and also in Euphorion (fr. 182 Groningen = Athen. 4.184a).[74] In Vergil's *Eclogues,* however, we find another version of its invention: *Pan primum calamos cera coniungere pluris / instituit* (2.32ff.).[75] As Bömer (*ad Met.* 1.689–712) points out, Ovid has elegantly alluded to the problem of the double tradition by letting Mercury tell about the time when *Pan* discovered the pipes, and in such a way that at first one suspects Mercury himself was the inventor. After introducing the nymph Syrinx, Mercury mentions the arrival of Pan and then almost immediately is cut off by Ovid. Ovid hastily summarizes the rest of the story, explaining the invention, presumably because the ostensible purpose of the narrative has been fulfilled: Argus is now asleep.[76] But the essential point has also been made, that it was indeed Pan who invented the pipe of reeds—and, in addition, that it can be dangerous not to listen to a story to its end.[77] Thus Ovid uses this narrating instance both to conflate and implicitly correct, in an Alexandrian fashion, the conflicting traditions of the invention of the panpipes.

We have seen that this episode corresponds to Lucretius' own version of the invention of music and are accordingly encouraged to consider what type of poetry Pan's invention may suggest. The affinities of the story of Pan and Syrinx with the Daphne and Apollo episode and the surrounding frame of the Io story, which is clearly indebted to Calvus' epyllion, function, as mentioned above, to give this part of the poem a strongly neoteric flavor. The pastoral setting of the Syrinx episode (note the geography: *Arcadiae gelidis in montibus* 1.689) further evokes Theocritean and Vergilian pastoral poetry and leads us to consider the possibility that the *sonum tenuem similemque querenti* created by the newly invented pipe (708) is meant to suggest the affinities of pastoral epic

---

74. Where we learn that the story was actually even more complicated, since Athenaeus explains that Euphorion wrote in his work on *Lyric Poets* that Hermes invented the μονοκάλαμον σύριγγα, while Silenus invented the many-reeded pipe and Marsyas the one fastened by wax.

75. Also at *Ecl.* 8.24. I.M.L. DuQuesnay, "From Polyphemus to Corydon: Virgil, *Eclogue* 2 and the *Idylls* of Theocritus," in *Creative Imitation and Latin Literature,* ed. D.A. Woodman and A.J. West (Cambridge, 1979), 35–69, notes that this version is very close to that in Longus 2.34.1 and posits a common source in Philetas of Cos. In Apollodorus 3.10.2 Hermes is the inventor.

76. B.R. Nagle, "A Trio of Love-Triangles in Ovid's *Metamorphoses,*" *Arethusa* 21 (1988): 85 n.14, remarks that "Ovid finishes up in indirect discourse what Mercury would have said, alerting the reader to the god's use of the story as strategem."

77. See D. Konstan, "The Death of Argus, or What Stories Do: Audience Response in Ancient Fiction and Theory," *Helios* 18 (1991): 15–30, for an illuminating discussion of the paradigm of audience response this scene offers; cf. also Ahl, *Metaformations,* 154; Nagle, "Two Miniature *Carmina Perpetua,*" 100.

with elegy, a relationship often explored by the bucolic poets.[78] Ovid in this section perhaps gestures towards the affiliations of his epic project with earlier experiments in the genre as represented by bucolic poetry and the epyllion. His use of this complex narrative structure of an interrupted embedded narration may reflect this tradition as well.

In the narrative structure of the series of psychologically fascinating erotic stories told by the three Minyeides in Book 4 (1–415), we see Ovid again using introductory formulae characteristic of aetiological poetry. The Minyeides' tales explain the origins of red mulberries, the frankincense bush, the heliotrope, and a fountain in Asia Minor with very strange properties. We note the appearance of numerous words listed above as aetiological, such as *causa* and *unde,* in Alcithoë's introduction to her narrative:[79]

"Unde sit infamis, quare male fortibus undis
Salmacis enervet tactosque remolliat artus,
discite. causa latet, vis est notissima fontis."

(4.285–87)

The repeated interrogatives *unde* and *quare* underline the explanatory nature of the ensuing narrative; so does the emphatic imperative *discite,* which echoes the didactic formulae often used by both Ovid and his characters to introduce *aetia* in the *Fasti,* as we find at 4.145–46 (Ovid): *discite nunc, quare Fortunae tura Virili / detis eo, gelida qui locus umet aqua.*[80] Alcithoë's story focuses primarily on the possessive passion of Salmacis. Although this story is probably an Ovidian invention, tales surrounding the miraculous properties of certain fountains and rivers were clearly widespread in Alexandrian literature, as

---

78. See Halperin, *Before Pastoral, passim;* Conte, *Rhetoric of Imitation,* 100–29. On the associations of elegy and lamentation by ancient etymology see Ov. *Am.* 3.9.1–4; Hinds, *Metamorphosis of Persephone,* 103–4; Nisbet and Hubbard *ad* Hor. *Odes* 1.33.2. Cf. also the possible elegiac note in *disparibus calamis (Met.* 1.711).

79. As observed also by Bömer, *Met., ad loc.,* and Due, *Changing Forms,* 128. Notice that the first sister (unnamed) begins similarly (4.51–52): *quae poma alba ferebat / ut nunc nigra ferat contactu sanguinis arbor.* Due's interpretation of the episode is worth noting: "what follows is a typical Alexandrian or neoteric story, showing a marked interest in the borderland between child and adult, combined with an inclination to deal with erotic phaenomena which were either abnormal or on the verge of being so" (128–29). See also N. Holzberg, "Ovid's Babyloniaka (*Met.* 4.55–166)," *WS* 101 (1988): 265–77, who suggests that the episode contains elements of parody of New Comedy and the ancient novel.

80. Frequent in the *Fasti:* (Ovid as narrator) 1.289, 2.584, 3.436, 4.140, 145, 6.639, 693; (Janus) 1.101, 133; (Mars) 3.177; (Faunus) 3.313; (Flora) 5.276. Also listed in Kenney's list of didactic vocabulary, *"Nequitiae Poeta,"* 203. Cf. *Ars* 1.50, 459; 3.298, 315, 327, 455; *Rem.* 43; *Med. Fac.* 1; *Georgics* 1.351, 2.35, 3.414.

we shall see when we examine Pythagoras' catalog of such *mirabilia fontium* (*Met.* 15.309–35),[81] where the Salmacis fountain is mentioned with a sly reference to this story in Book 4 of its origin: *cui non audita est obscenae Salmacis undae?* (15.319).

Almost all of the stories narrated or mentioned by the Minyeides are situated in the East and are unrecorded before Ovid. Bömer's suggestion (*ad* 4.1ff.) that they may all derive from a Hellenistic collection of eastern tales is appealing in light of their appearance in this aetiological narrative frame. The keynote of the cycle is obscurity and, of course, eroticism. Ovid highlights this by depicting the sisters as learned storytellers who have chosen their narratives from a great store of recondite tales at their command.[82] Thus the first sister ponders over various obscure myths before choosing which story to tell: *illa, quid e multis referat (nam plurima norat), / cogitat* (4.43–44); she makes her choice of the story of Pyramus and Thisbe precisely on the basis of its novelty: *hoc placet; haec, quoniam vulgaris fabula non est* (4.53). Alcithoë also begins with a praeteritio, *vulgatos taceo* (4.276),[83] before making her decision to tell of Salmacis based on precisely the same criterion as her sister—the obscurity of the tale: *dulcique animos novitate tenebo* (4.284). In this way, of course, Ovid reveals his own preoccupation with recherché mythological knowledge and his own careful process of the selection of stories throughout the *Metamorphoses.*[84] The elaboration of the introductions to the narratives of the Minyeides seems to serve as a further signal of the Alexandrian *doctrina* that these learned sisters display. Ovid perhaps had also hinted at their stylistic sympathies at the beginning of the episode in the introduction to the first (unnamed) sister's narration: *levi deducens pollice filum* (*Met.* 4.36) and it is possible that the Alexandrian sympathy of the sisters is also reflected in the language of their metamorphosis:

> "sustinuere tamen se perlucentibus alis
> conataeque loqui *minimam* et pro corpore *vocem*
> emittunt peraguntque *levi* stridore *querellas.*"

(4.411–13)

---

81. Pages 147–55 below.

82. Interestingly, the second sister, Leuconoë, displays no such hesitation and, in marked contrast to her sisters, narrates first a well-known story, that of Mars and Venus (*Od.* 8.266ff, narrated by Demodocus): *haec fuit in toto notissima fabula caelo* (*Met.* 4.189). Cf. for the same story *Ars* 2.561 (*fabula narratur toto notissima caelo*). Her second story concerning the loves of Leucothoe and Clytie is, however, unknown earlier.

83. Cf. Vergil *Geo.* 3.4: *omnia iam vulgata* (this appears, as noted above, page 25, in an important programmatic passage and provides an intriguing parallel).

84. Note the reappearence of this narrative enticement again at *Met.* 7.758 and 12.175–76.

A different kind of narrative structure involves the use of anonymous inter-locutors. At the beginning of Book 15 Numa sets out for Croton on a quest for knowledge of natural-philosophical subjects, *quae sit rerum natura requirit* (15.6).[85] When he arrives at Croton, however, Numa first asks who founded the city and is answered by an old man:

> Graia quis Italicis auctor posuisset in oris
> moenia, quaerenti sic e senioribus unus
> rettulit indigenis, veteris non inscius aevi.

(15.9–11)

P.E. Knox has remarked here that "the appearance of *auctor,* which in this context reproduces the Greek κτίστης, demands attention.[86] Numa asks quite explicitly for a foundation story, an archetypal theme of Greek poetry, which was revived as a suitable subject for poetry by the Alexandrians."[87] Knox is also surely right to seek for possible Callimachean references in the account,[88] but he fails to note the obvious and infinitely appropriate Callimachean frame-work of the whole narrative. Numa is represented as a seeker of antiquarian knowledge gathering information through asking questions of the inhabitants of the region, which is precisely the sort of thing we see Ovid doing in the *Fasti,* in the course of what Miller has called "his fieldwork."[89] For example, in Book 4 of the *Fasti* Ovid travels through the land of Carseoli, where he stops to visit an old native of the region, who, we learn, is an important source for the Italian material of the *Fasti: is mihi multa quidem, sed et haec narrare solebat, / unde meum praesens instrueretur opus* (4.689–90). He explains to Ovid on this occasion the reason why it is still the custom (*nunc quoque* 4.710) that a fox is burned at the festival of Ceres (4.691–712). Three other times in Books 4 and 6 of the *Fasti* Ovid reports personal encounters with Italian characters who provide him with *aetia* for various religious customs.[90] Miller points out the similarity of these encounters to that of Callimachus and Theogenes in *Aet.* fr.

---

85. The phrase is Lucretian. For a discussion of the passage see chap. 4, p. 141.

86. So also Haupt-Ehwald *ad loc.: auctor* = κτίστης. *TLL* 2.1204.66–1205.4: *urbis conditor.*

87. Knox, *Traditions of Augustan Poetry,* 67. There are three other foundation stories in the *Metamorphoses,* which Knox does not note: that of Miletus in Book 9.447–49, Caunus in Caria 9.633–34, and the more elaborate story of the foundation of Thebes by Cadmus (and the naming of Boeotia 3.13) in Book 3.1–130 (on which see P. Hardie, "Ovid's Theban History: The First Anti-*Aeneid?*" *CQ* 40 [1990]: 224–35). But none of these is as emphatically aetiological as this account.

88. Knox, *Traditions of Augustan Poetry,* 68–69.

89. Miller, "Callimachus and the Augustan Aetiological Elegy," 402.

90. *Fasti* 4.377–86, 4.905–42, 6.395–416. See on these Miller, "Callimachus and the Augustan Aetiological Elegy," 403. In *Am.* 3.13 as well, Ovid learns about local rites *in situ.*

178, but notes that Ovid in adapting the Callimachean motif has Romanized it to fit his poem. "Significantly, most of the interlocutors are old, as if to suggest that these are the *antiqui* whom Ovid elsewhere cites generally as a source."[91] Now let us turn again to *Metamorphoses* 15, and observe that Numa's interlocutor is precisely the appropriate interlocutor for an aetiological inquiry: he is old (*e senioribus unus* 15.10) and he is a native of the region (*indigenis* 15.11) and furthermore he is well-versed in its history (*veteris non inscius aevi* 15.11). Thus we can see that Ovid has chosen to present his foundation story in Book 15 in an appropriate narrative framework, incorporating a double acknowledgement of his indebtedness to Callimachus, in both his material and its treatment.

Two other episodes in which the narrator is again anonymous illustrate many of the aetiological features remarked on above. The internal narrator of the story of Aesacus, a tale already adduced as an example of an aetiological metamorphosis and as possibly indebted to Boios' earlier work,[92] is prompted to speak upon viewing the two kingfishers flying by:

> Hos aliquis senior iunctim freta lata volantes
> spectat et ad finem servatos laudat amores:
> proximus, aut idem, si fors tulit, . . . dixit.

> (11.749–51)

Ovid's careful qualification of the unnamed speaker in these lines has elicited a variety of comments.[93] We should not be surprised, however, to note the appearance of *aliquis senior* (note Ovid's interlocutor at *Fasti* 4.377–78 *quidam . . . senior*) as a narrator of an aetiological story.[94] It is humor, not doubt, that lies behind Ovid's pains to be accurate about a completely anonymous narrator. Only when we understand the scholarly aetiological tradition in which Ovid is writing do we appreciate the joke at its expense, as E.J. Kenney has noted: "Ovid gently mocks the learned poet's obsession with sources."[95]

91. Miller, "Callimachus and the Augustan Aetiological Elegy," 404; cf. Heinze, *Ovids elegische Erzählung*, 97. See *Fasti* 4.378 (*senior*), 4.687 (*hospitis antiqui*), 6.399 (*anus*) and compare Ovid's general statements acknowledging his sources, such as *ut veteres memorant, Fasti* 2.669, 3.147, etc.

92. Pages 36–37.

93. Galinsky, *Ovid's Metamorphoses*, 101, "it makes no difference who initiates the next story, so long as at least some man is around to do it." Solodow, *World of Ovid's Metamorphoses*, 66, "the narrator reveals uncertainty."

94. Observe also that he begins his narrative by pointing to the bird he is about to discuss (*ostendens spatiosum in guttura mergum* 11.753), an action similar to Ovid's interlocutors in the *Fasti*, cf. p. 90 below.

95. Kenney, Introduction and Notes to *Ovid's Metamorphoses, ad loc.*

The narrative situation at *Metamorphoses* 6.313–81 is narratologically more complex, for it involves the retelling by the internal (secondary) narrator of the story of another (tertiary) character narrator. This structural complexity, we shall see, is an important aspect of the aetiological focus of this embedded narrative. We have here one of the most elaborate of Ovid's internal narrative frames.[96] An anonymous Lydian cowherd[97] renarrates a story he had heard from his Lycian guide when the two of them in their journey through Lycia had come across an ancient altar set in a lake. The cowherd had asked about the altar, and the guide responded with the aetiological story of Latona and the peasants. The Lydian renarrates his story to a group of his countrymen, who have been struck with fear by Latona's punishment of Niobe (6.313–15) and have gathered to tell stories of other examples of divine wrath. Ovid suggests that this is the sort of occasion upon which tales of the gods' powers might be narrated: *utque fit, a facto propiore priora renarrant. / e quibus unus ait* (6.316–17).[98] The narrator begins by stating the obscurity of his story: *res obscura quidem est ignobilitate virorum, / mira tamen* (6.319–20). Again, we sense Ovid slyly advertising the great store of recherché stories he has collected.[99] The word *mira* certifies that the story is worthy of inclusion in the poem full of tales evoking this response from character narrators and audiences. The narrator then claims to have seen the location where the action of the story transpired: *vidi praesens stagnumque locumque / prodigio notum* (6.320–21). This appeal to the reliability of an eyewitness, which we have met already in the episode of Perseus (4.797), and the invocation of personal experience are common features of aetiological poetry. Callimachus uses authenticating detail of this type, as when in fr. 384.48–49 (Σωσιβίου Νίκη) he tells of a dedication at the outermost branch of the Nile that he had seen with his own eyes: κεῖνό γε μὴν ἴδον αὐτός, ὅ πὰρ ποδὶ κάτθετο Νείλου / νειατίῳ.[100] In Ovid's *Fasti* it is a feature, often humorous, of his scholarly persona to prove that he has done his research. Thus at *Fasti* 6.423, where he

---

96. The most complex internal narrative framework in the poem is that in Book 5.250–678, where an unidentified Muse (internal secondary narrator) renarrates Calliope's (tertiary narrator) story of the rape of Persephone within which Calliope includes Arethusa's (fourth level internal narrator) own story of her transformation.

97. There is some confusion as to the location of the narration; the preceding story of Niobe takes place in Thebes, but ends in Lydia; Bömer, *Met., ad loc.*, rightly points out that this episode must also take place in Lydia.

98. His anonymity is again mentioned at 6.382–83: *Sic ubi nescio quis Lycia de gente virorum / rettulit exitium.*

99. Kenney, Introduction and Notes to *Ovid's Metamorphoses, ad loc.*

100. Cf. fr. 384.47: τοῦτο μὲν ἐξ ἄλλων ἔκλυον ἱρὸν ἐγώ, fr. 178.27–29: εἰδότες ὡς ἐνέπου [σιν / κείνην ἥ περὶ σὴν [/ οὔθ᾽ἑτέρην ἔγνωκα τ[.

tells of the first appearance of the Palladium, he claims to have traveled to Troy to view the site of the occurrence: *cura videre fuit, vidi templumque locum-que.*[101] It is the practice of the didactic persona, as we have seen, to underline personally and overtly the reliability of his information; so we find these kinds of assertions of veracity in poems such as the *Fasti* and the *Georgics,* not in the primary narrative of the *Aeneid* or the *Metamorphoses.*[102] Internal narrators in Ovid's epic poem, however, frequently express this concern. We need now to take a closer look at the frame of this narrative, to consider how the embedded narration is introduced and situated.

We learn first of all the circumstances that brought the rustic to the location where the event he narrates took place (6.321–24). This attention to detail is again typical of aetiological poetry. Ovid, for example, is equally careful in *Am.* 3.13.1–2 to explain how he happened to be at Falerii to learn of the rites of Juno practiced there. The herdsman explains that he had been sent to drive back some cattle for his father from another land and in his travels through Lycia he had come across a remarkable sight: an ancient blackened altar in the middle of a lake. Struck by this he had turned to the Lycian guide his father had provided and asked for information concerning it:

> "ecce lacu medio sacrorum nigra favilla
> ara vetus stabat tremulis circumdata cannis.
> restitit et pavido 'faveas mihi !' murmure dixit
> dux meus, et simili 'faveas !' ego murmure dixi.
> Naiadum Faunine foret tamen ara rogabam
> indigenaene dei, cum talia rettulit hospes. . . . "

(6.325–30)

We know from the lines immediately preceding these (6.323–24) that his guide is in fact precisely the appropriate type of interlocutor for this kind of questioning, for he too, like the old man in Book 15 above, is a native of that region, *gentis illius* (6.323). The use of the word *hospes* in line 330 may also be a reference to the sort of interlocutor we frequently find in aetiological contexts, as Ovid's old source mentioned above at *Fasti* 4.687 (*hospes antiquus*). Here, as in the *Fasti,* an internal narrator provides the *aetion* of a cult.[103] Discussions

---

101. Also *Fasti* 1.389; 2.27; 4.725–28, 936; 6.13.

102. Kenney, "*Nequitiae Poeta,*" 202, for the use of *vidi* lists Lucr. 4.577, 6.1044; *Ars* 1.721, 3.378, 487; *Rem.* 101; *Med. Fac.* 99. Thomas, *Vergil's Georgics, ad* 1.193 (*vidi equidem*), comments: "didactic, emphatically asserting the veracity of the detail which follows." Cf. *Geo.* 1.193, 197, 318; 4.125–27.

103. As Kenney observes, Introduction and Notes to *Ovid's Metamorphoses, ad* 6.319.

of religious sites (*ara vetus* 6.326) are, of course, typical both of Ovid's model for the *Fasti,* Callimachus' *Aetia,* and Nicander as well, who in fact told a story very similar to this one (A.L. 35, see below). We soon discover that this rustic internal narrator is not only situated in an aetiological framework, but that the story the guide narrated to him, which he now renarrates to us, is marked by an extreme degree of literary conflation and allusion, from exactly the sources we might now expect given this elaborate narrative frame.

The story the Lycian guide narrates in reply explains why the altar he and the Lycian peasant have run across is dedicated to Latona. He first briefly mentions how Delos alone had offered Latona a place to give birth to Apollo and Diana (6.332–36, cf. 6.186–92, 13.634–35) and then tells of Latona's arrival in Lycia immediately after their birth (*fugisse puerpera fertur* 6.337). Latona was thirsty and sought a drink of water from a nearby lake, but was prevented from drinking by a rowdy group of Lycian farmers (*rustica turba vetat* 6.348). She attempted to entreat them to allow her to drink (348–60), but when they responded to her prayers with abuse and even muddied the water, she finally in anger inflicted upon the peasants a punishment in keeping with their rude behavior: she turned them into frogs (361–81). As frogs they continue to behave like boors—which is why frogs make such constant loud noises (*nunc quoque turpes / litibus exercent linguas* 374–75) and have such an exaggerated mouth (377–79) and like to jump around in the mud (381).[104] The story ends with the metamorphosis.

Once again it is interesting to compare Ovid's story with a version attributed to Nicander. As mentioned above, Antoninus Liberalis 35 preserves a similar story under Nicander's name, but in this instance Nicander shares attribution with a local historian of the fourth century, Menecrates of Xanthus, who had included the story in his *Lykiaka* (*FGrHist* 769 F2). This version is very close to the story of Latona in *Metamorphoses* 6, and Ovid here, as elsewhere, has probably been influenced by Nicander's aetiological poem; but Ovid has also typically changed some important details. Most notably, in Antoninus' version Latona wants the water to bathe her children, not to drink. Leto arrived in Lycia to bathe her newborn children in a fountain and when she was prevented from doing so by a group of cowherds who wanted instead to water their cows (35.1), she then left the spring and continued on to the Xanthus.[105] There she

---

104. Note how their behavior as humans at 6.365 *huc illuc limum saltu movere maligno* is echoed in the characteristic behavior of frogs at 381 *limosoque novae saliunt in gurgite ranae.*

105. Papathomopoulos, *ad* 35n.7, is probably right in suggesting that Antoninus followed Nicander's account in the section of the story involving the spring, but interrupted this with the historian's *aetion* of the naming of Lycia.

accomplished her goal and then renamed the country Lycia (previously Trem-
ilis) in honor of the wolves that had led her there (35.3). She then returned to
the fountain and turned the herdsmen into frogs: οἱ δ'ἄχρι νῦν παρὰ ποταμοὺς
βοῶσι καὶ λίμνας (35.4).[106] Ovid wittily acknowledges this earlier version by
having Latona expressly say that she has *not* come to bathe:

> "non ego nostros
> abluere hic artus lassataque membra parabam,
> sed relevare sitim. . . ."

(6.352–54)

Ovid's change of Latona's motive is perhaps significant.[107] Since we have
been signaled, as I have suggested, by the narrative frame that introduces this
episode in Book 6, we should not be surprised to find that Ovid's version
contains more echoes of earlier aetiological poetry, namely, Propertius 4.9,
where the content is strikingly similar."[108]

Propertius' aetiological poem also deals with the origin of an altar: it tells
the story of Hercules' conquest of Cacus and his foundation of the Ara Max-
ima. In accordance with the Callimachean manner of this poem, by far the
greater part of it deals with the lesser-known explanation for why women are
not allowed to partake in worship at that altar. After his fight with Cacus,
Hercules had conceived a great thirst and was wandering about on the Aventine
looking for water, but the priestess of Bona Dea, in spite of Hercules' supplica-
tions, denied him a drink. In his anger he declared that women would be
banned forever from his worship (4.9.21ff.). We should consider the possibility
that Ovid has changed Latona's motive for seeking water on the model of
Propertius' aetiological poem, and that he alerts us to this by using the same
words to describe the thirsty Latona's speech of entreaty as Propertius had used
to introduce Hercules' request for water in 4.9.[109] Hercules' plea, which, as

---

106. If we compare this version with Ovid's, we can see how once again the aetiological focus
of Ovid's account expands the description of metamorphosis in such a way as to detail humorously
the reasons for specific aspects of the appearance and behavior of frogs. In Antoninus' summary of
Nicander's version we only learn that frogs live near the water.

107. All later Latin accounts of this episode follow Ovid in this detail: Probus ("aus einem
Ovidkommentar," Wellmann *RE* vii.115), Servius, and Modestus in the *Brevis Expositio ad Geo.*
1.378, *Myth. Vat.* 1.10, 2.95. For discussion of these different versions see Castiglioni, *Studi
Intorno Alle Fonti e Alle Composizione,* 353–57. The story as represented in the *Metamorphoses* is
found nowhere earlier. It is later mentioned at Probus *Geo.* 1.378. Servius *ad Geo.* 1.378 wrongly
attributes to Ovid a different version of the story involving Ceres.

108. See Anderson, *Ovid's Metamorphoses Books 6–10, ad* 6.368.

109. Bömer, *Met., ad* 6.368.

Anderson has shown, is humorously similar to an amatory paraclausithyron,[110] is introduced at line 32: *et iacit ante fores verba minora deo.* We may perhaps hear in *minora* a programmatic suggestion that the heroic Hercules has been appropriately revamped for his new elegiac context.[111] When Ovid describes Latona's speech similarly as *verba minora dea* at *Met.* 6.368, he is surely echoing Propertius' phrase and drawing our attention to the similar situation. Latona's and Hercules' thirst and weariness are also similarly emphasized: *Met.* 6.340–41 *longo dea fessa labore / sidereo siccata sitim collegit ab aestu,* Prop. 4.9.21 *sicco torquet sitis ora palato; (fessus* 4.9.4, 34, [42], 66).[112] The allusions to Propertius' aetiological poem 4.9 in Ovid's episode in *Metamorphoses* 6 suggest that we recall the similar context of the model[113] and understand that Ovid intends his allusions to function as an acknowledgment of and an identification with the Callimachean poetic themes and methods embodied in Propertius' Fourth Book—probably the first poetic collection of Roman *aetia* in the Callimachean tradition and an important model for Ovid's two most ambitious experiments with Callimachean poetics, the *Metamorphoses* and the *Fasti.*[114]

The Callimachean poetics of Propertius 4.9 are underpinned by numerous Callimachean allusions. Propertius' humorous treatment of the thirsty Hercules, as H.E. Pillinger and Heinze before him remarked, is indebted to Alexandrian characterizations of the gluttonous hero.[115] Close precedents may be

110. W.S. Anderson, "*Hercules Exclusus*: Propertius 4.9," *AJP* 85 (1964): 1–12.

111. The adjective is similarly programmatically charged at *Ars Amatoria* 3.26: *conveniunt cumbae vela minora meae,* cf. Prop. 2.34.83. For discussion of the generic concerns involved in the conversion of this epic scene to elegy see Heinze, *Ovids elegische Erzählung,* 81ff., Anderson, "*Hercules Exclusus*: Propertius 4.9," J. DeBrohun, "Hercules Belabored: Propertius 4.9 and the Discourses of Elegy" (Ph.D. diss., University of Michigan at Ann Arbor, 1992).

112. Other possible verbal echoes of 4.9 in this episode in *Met.* 6 include mention of the hostility of *Iuno noverca* (4.9.43–44, *Met.* 6.336–37), and the similarity of the description of the god's anger: *Met.* 6.366 *distulit ira sitim,* Prop. 4.9.62 *nec tulit iratam ianua clausa sitim.*

113. According to R.F. Thomas, "Vergil's *Georgics* and the Art of Reference," *HSCP* 90 (1986): 177, in his typology of allusions, or references, this reference would be classified as a "single reference": "he intends that the reader recall the context of the model and apply that context to the new situation."

114. Conte, *The Rhetoric of Imitation,* 37, describes one motivation for an author's use of allusion as "a desire to pay tribute to the methods of a poetic he values and wishes to be identified with." Cf. G. Pasquali, "Arte Allusiva," in *Pagine stravaganti* (Florence, 1968), 278: "complimento." See pp. 118–24 below for a discussion of *Met.* 14.623–771, where Ovid engages in a similarly close intertextual dialogue with Propertius 4.2.

115. Heinze, *Ovids elegische Erzählung,* 83; H.E. Pillinger, "Some Callimachean Influences on Propertius, Book Four," *HSCP* 73 (1969): 186, remarks that "the parallel with Propertius' own explanation of the Ara Maxima rites on the basis of Hercules' instatiable thirst is perhaps more than accidental." See also P. Pinotti, "Propert. 4.9: Alessandrinismo e Arte Allusiva," *GIF* 29 n.s. 8 (1977): 70.

found in two of Callimachus' stories in the *Aetia* frr. 22–23 and frr. 24–25 (Lindian Sacrifice and Theiodamas), both of which portray a thirsty and hungry Hercules.[116] The Callimachean references are further reinforced in 4.9 when the priestess of Bona Dea, in order to discourage Hercules, adduces a warning example of the similarly thirsty Tiresias' punishment by Athena (4.9.57–58), an episode described in Callimachus' only elegiac hymn, *Hymn* 5.57–130 (*Bath of Pallas*). Editors have long defended the reading *magno* in 4.9.57 with reference to the similar phrasing of a distich from Athena's speech in this hymn (*magno* 4.9.57, Call. *Hy.* 5.101–2). To this nexus of Callimachean references surrounding these two episodes, we can add Callimachus' *Hymn to Zeus,* which tells of Rhea's search for water in which to bathe her newborn son Zeus (*Hy.* 1.15–16). As a final remark, we should note that Propertius has chosen to place the *aetion* of the worship of Hercules in the mouth of the hero himself.

It is impossible to tell how many of these antecedents Ovid may have had in mind when composing his narrative in Book 6. It would, however, be a typical mark of Ovid's humor to attribute to this rustic narrator such a complexly allusive tale, and then to highlight the aetiological models for the story by embedding it in a narrative framework typical of these poems.[117] Ovid has thus associated this story of Latona and the Lycian peasants with Callimachean poetics through both the form and content of his narrative.

In the light of J.J. Clauss' convincing arguments for a programmatic subtext in the tale of the Lycians in *Metamorphoses* 6, it is interesting to consider the contextual affinity of Ovid's story to Propertius 4.9, a poem with obvious programmatic connotations.[118] In both poems the themes of thirst and the dispute over a water source are suggestive of poetic implications.[119] Propertius' poem, by its elegiac refashioning of the story of Hercules and Cacus, explores the same sort of generic tensions between epic themes and Callimachean poetics as are found throughout the *Metamorphoses,* only reversed. We may

---

116. Cf. also Callimachus *Hy.* 3.142–61. Apollonius Rhodius also included a very similar story of the thirst Hercules acquired after killing the serpent Ladon (4.1432ff.).

117. Interestingly, Bömer, *Met., ad* 6.318, comments on numerous words and features which seem to be markedly prosaic or colloquial and thus characterize the character narrator as a rustic. As examples of "Umgangssprache" he notes the litotes *non inpune* (318), the repetition of *praesens* in conjunction with *vidi* (320), and the rare poetic words *ignobilitate* (319), *erratica* (333), and *interdixit* (333); and on *fruticosa* (344) he suggests "Ovid lässt den Fachmann sprechen." The hapax *Chimaeriferae* (339) adds a humorously incongruous and showy touch to the rustic's speech.

118. J.J. Clauss, "The Episode of the Lycian Farmers in Ovid's *Metamorphoses,*" HSCP 92 (1989): 297–314.

119. On water imagery and poetry, see Wimmel, *Kallimachos in Rom,* 222—33; Kambylis, *Die Dichterweihe und ihre Symbolik,* 23–30, 66–68, 98ff., 183–88.

note the similarity of Ovid's strategy in Book 6 with Propertius' in 4.9, in which the epic Hercules and Cacus episode is bypassed in favor of an *aetion* for an altar. In *Metamorphoses* 6, a Callimachean internal narrator passes over the better-known story of Latona's search and request for a place to give birth, an epic theme treated in the Homeric Hymns as well as by Callimachus in his *Hymn to Delos*,[120] and instead tells an obscure story of the goddess' encounter with a group of Lycian rustics, which provides another *aetion* for an altar. This manner of presentation which consists of giving an original, and deliberately "un-heroic," slant to traditional mythological stories originates in such Callimachean scenes as Hercules at the hut of Molorchus in the *Victoria Berenices* of the *Aetia* (*SH* 254–69) and Theseus' visit to Hecale in the *Hecale* (frr. 27–66 Hollis, *SH* 280–91). In 4.9, Propertius showed how an epic theme could be converted into Callimachean elegy; in this episode in *Metamorphoses* 6, as well as throughout the poem, Ovid shows how epic themes can also be accommodated to hexameters that adhere to Callimachean poetic ideals. The numerous Vergilian echoes scattered throughout the narrative of the Lycian guide seem to refer back to Propertius' original epic model in *Aeneid* 8, and to realign by association the epic orientation of the *Metamorphoses* episode.[121]

After their metamorphosis by Latona, the frogs swell their *inflata colla* (377), thus providing, perhaps, a humorous postscript to this tale embodying the poetic principles expressed by the *non inflati somnia Callimachi* (Prop. 2.34.32). Like the Pierides in Book 5, who are defeated by the Muses in a poetic contest,[122] the frogs, animals used in other poetic contexts in a similarly programmatic manner (cf. especially Theocritus *Id.* 7.37–41),[123] seem to be

---

120. We might consider that Latona's plea for *tenues undas* (6.351) in a sense repeats her famous search and requests for an *exiguam sedem* (Met. 6.187) on which to give birth to Apollo and Diana, an episode mentioned both by Niobe earlier in Book 6 (184–91) and by the Lycian guide (331–42); cf. Forbes Irving, *Metamorphosis in Greek Myths*, 313.

121. Bömer, *Met., ad* 6.321, comments on "die ungewöhnliche Häufung von Vergilreminiszenen am Anfang." He lists as Vergilian or epic 322–23 *genitor, lectos . . . boves,* 329–30 *Naiadum Faunine . . . / indigenaene dei* (cf. *Aen.* 8.314), 332 *regia coniunx,* 335–36 *incumbens, edidit.*

122. Clauss, " Episode of the Lycian Farmers," 302, suggests that the description of the metamorphosed frogs is "in tune with ancient literary polemics in general," and points out (307) that both groups are *rauca* (5.678, 6.377). The similarities, however, do not stop there. Both groups are described as a *turba* (5.305, 6.348), the loquacity of both is emphasized (5.677–78, 6.375, 378), and, like the frogs at 6.377 (*tumescunt*), the Pierides are also said at 5.305 to "swell up" (*intumuit numero*).

123. Cf. (Moschus) 3.106, *Dirae* 74. We also might recall the frogs of Aristophanes' *Frogs,* an extremely important source for the literary critical vocabulary of the Alexandrians; see Wimmel, *Kallimachos in Rom,* 115 n.1; Hopkinson, *Hellenistic Anthology,* 89–90. It is also tempting to see in the description of the frogs in line 380, *spina viret, venter, pars maxima corporis, albet,* a

characterized in programmatic terms as bad poets in language suggestive of Callimachean criticisms of undiscriminating and pompous poetry.[124] Ovid perhaps humorously implies that his own adaptation of this episode here, which is based on both elegiac and epic sources, manages to avoid these shortcomings.

Similar generic tensions are evident in the final example of this type of narrative frame we will consider. A. Crabbe has pointed out that all of the stories narrated by internal narrators at the impromptu banquet in the cave of Achelous at *Metamorphoses* 8.573–9.89 seem to have Callimachean associations.[125] The aetiological framework of this cycle of stories, like the others we have considered, can be shown once again to be appropriate to the stories' Callimachean literary antecedents. We will recognize in this episode many of the narrative conventions typical of aetiological poetry. For example, the conversation opens at the banquet[126] with Theseus pointing to a group of islands (*digitoque ostendit* 8.575) and asking the river god Achelous for an explanation of its name (8.574–76). In the *Fasti* Ovid incorporates the same attention to visual detail in his dialogues with informants, as with Janus in Book 1: *"et" clavem ostendens "haec" ait "arma gero"* (254, cf. 4.691).[127] Achelous responds with the stories of the metamorphoses of the Echinades and of Perimele (8.577–610). Stories about the origins of islands were a favorite Hellenistic topic, and the story of Perimele, as Crabbe argues, is similar to that of Asterie in Callimachus' *Hy.* 4.36–38, 191ff.[128] Achelous' two other narratives similarly share Callimachean antecedents. The story of Erysichthon narrated by

---

reference to the criticism of bad poets as γαστέρες found in Hesiod *Theog.* 26–28, and elsewhere (on which see P. Pucci, *Odysseus Polutropos* [Ithaca, 1987], 181ff.).

124. Less likely is Clauss' suggestion, "Episode of the Lycian Farmers," 302, that the frogs represent "stodgy Callimacheans." The programmatic significance of the description of the Pierides has been discussed by Hinds, *Metamorphosis of Persephone*, 129–31, and Hofman, "*Carmen Perpetuum, Carmen Deductum*," 228–30. For criticism of prolixity, cf. Call. *Aetia* fr. 1, *Hy.* 2.105–13, and of pomposity, cf. Cat. 95,10 *tumido . . . Antimacho*, Hor. *A.P.* 27.

125. A. Crabbe, "Structure and Content in Ovid's *Metamorphoses*," *ANRW* 2.31.4 (1981): 2288–90; Hutchinson, *Hellenistic Poetry*, 345–52. Note that the strongly Alexandrian tone of this episode is set off by the strong epic color of the preceding Calydonian Boar Hunt; cf. Hollis, *Ovid Metamorphoses VIII*, 77: "of all the sections in the *Metamorphoses*, this one is the most strictly formal piece of epic writing."

126. Hollis, *Ovid Metamorphoses VIII*, ad 8.574ff., notes the Callimachean precedent at *Aet.* fr. 178.

127. Note the similar action of the anonymous narrator at *Met.* 11.753: *ostendens spatiosum in guttura mergum*.

128. Crabbe, "Structure and Content in Ovid's *Metamorphoses*," 2289. She notes also that the Echinades are mentioned in Call. *Hy.* 4.155. Hellenistic works include Callimachus' Κτίσεις νήσων καὶ πόλεων καὶ μετονομασίαι (*Suda*, Call. Test. 1) and Philostephanus of Cyrene's Περὶ Νήσων (*FHG* III, pp. 30ff.).

Achelous at 8.725–878 is based on Callimachus' sixth *Hymn,* and the tale of his struggle with Hercules over Deianira related at 9.1–88, which is prompted by an aetiological question (*Quae . . . /causa rogat* 9.1–2), explains the origin of the cornucopia and finds, as Hollis suggests, an interesting parallel in Theseus' crushing of one of the horns of the Marathonian Bull in Callimachus' *Hecale* (fr. 69.1 Pf. = *SH* 288).[129] The unique wit of Ovid is to be found in his choice of Achelous as the internal narrator of these Callimachean stories, for he is described at the beginning of the episode in non-Callimachean terms as *imbre tumens* (8.550, cf. 583–87, 9.94–96). As S.E. Hinds has suggested, Ovid's choice of a swollen river to narrate Callimachean tales operates as "a self-referential comment" on his recasting of these tales in the manner of grand epic, as similarly in his choice of Calliope as narrator in Book 5.[130] Critics have remarked on the bombastic and even Ennian ring of Achelous' language and on the epic expansion of the tale of Erysichthon.[131] Ovid comes dangerously close to identifying his own narrative with the inflated frogs and Pierides and perhaps hints at the stylistic dangers involved in his large-scale epic project.

Lelex's intervening story of Baucis and Philemon, as has long been recognized, is indebted to the inspiration of Callimachus' *Hecale.*[132] The motivation for Lelex's narrative is not a question, but rather a challenge to the power of the gods stated by Pirithous (8.611–15). Lelex's goal in telling this story is to convince his audience of the gods' power: *quoque minus dubites* (8.620). So it is not surprising that he uses all the rhetorical techniques available to him to prove the "veracity" of his narrative. His own character as that of an older man (*raris iam sparsus tempora canis* 8.568, *ante omnesque Lelex animo maturus et aevo* 8.617) marks him out as someone especially qualified to narrate this sort of aetiological story. He begins by anticipating the end of his story; he

129. Hollis, *Ovid Metamorphoses VIII, ad* 8.881–82, *idem, Callimachus' Hecale, ad* fr. 69. Cf. Crabbe, "Structure and Content in Ovid's *Metamorphoses,*" 2289–90. A reference to Achelous appears in a very important and textually disputed passage in Prop. 2.34.33–34, *nam rursus licet Aetoli referas Acheloi / fluxerit ut magno f(r)actus amore liquor.* These lines form part of a passage in which the addressee Lynceus is advised of either topics to write on or to avoid (Camps reads *non rursus* [*Scaliger*]; *nam* [*codd.*]). The opening of the list at least suggests Hellenistic love stories, and its following directly upon the exortation to imitate Philetas and Callimachus (2.34.31–32) implies an Alexandrian association.

130. See Hinds, "Generalizing about Ovid," 19, and Barchiesi, "Voci e istanze narrative," 57–64.

131. Hollis, *Metamorphoses VIII, ad* 549ff., 550, 551, 603; Bömer, *Met., ad locc.;* Galinsky, *Ovid's Metamorphoses,* 5–14; Hutchinson, *Hellenistic Poetry,* 348–52.

132. See Hollis, *Ovid Metamorphoses VIII, ad loc.,* and *Callimachus Hecale,* 33, 350, *ad* frr. 29ff.

describes a pair of sacred trees in Phrygia surrounded by a wall, which he claims to have seen himself during a visit to Phrygia: *ipse locum vidi* (8.622). We note how Lelex is careful to give us the reason for his being in the region in which he sees the trees (8.622–23). He then relates the mythological story of the visit by Jupiter and Mercury to the humble house of Baucis and Philemon (8.624–724), replete with the minute details of rustic life reminiscent of Callimachus' *Hecale* (frr. 27–39 Hollis) and of the Molorchus episode in *Aet.* 3 frr. 54–59 (+ 177 Pf.; *SH* 56–68) from the *Victoria Berenices* (*SH* 254–69), both aetiological episodes.[133] E.J. Kenney points out that Theseus' presence in the audience of the tale of Baucis and Philemon "was a sly reminder that Ovid's model for much of the detail of the episode was Callimachus' epyllion *Hecale.* . . . Hence the point of the comment *Thesea praecipue* (8.726)."[134]

At the end of the tale, after describing the metamorphosis of Baucis and Philemon into trees, Lelex again takes care to underline the truth of his narrative:

". . . ostendit adhuc Thyneius illic
incola de gemino vicinos corpore truncos.
haec mihi non vani (neque erat, cur fallere vellent)
narravere senes; equidem pendentia vidi
serta super ramos ponensque recentia dixi
'cura deum di sint, et, qui coluere, colantur.' "

(8.719–24)

We recognize in these lines the familiar aetiological ending that points out the continuation of the landmark up to the present time (*adhuc*).[135] Both Hollis

---

133. This rustic setting seems to have become especially associated with aetiology after Callimachus; see Hollis, *Callimachus Hecale,* 341–54, on the "Hospitality Theme." Examples include Eratosthenes' aetiological *Erigone* (frr. 22–27 Powell, pp. 64–65). Hollis, *Ovid Metamorphoses VIII,* 107, notes that Silius Italicus' aetiological account of the beginning of the Falernian vineyards (7.166–211) is particularly close to Ovid's Baucis and Philemon episode as well as the *Erigone.* Ovid includes in the *Fasti* another aetiological episode in a rustic setting, the humorously scatological story of the origin of the constellation of Orion (5.493–544). K.W. Gransden, ed., *Virgil, Aeneid Book VIII,* 26, observes that "Evander's hospitality to Aeneas is in the tradition of the theoxeny, the reception of a god or hero into a simple dwelling," and George, *Aeneid VIII and the Aitia of Callimachus,* 25–42, has discussed the appropriateness of this setting to the aetiological nature of the dialogue between Evander and Aeneas.

134. Kenney, Introduction and Notes to *Ovid's Metamorphoses,* xxviii; Hinds, "Generalizing about Ovid," 19. Crabbe, "Structure and Content in Ovid's *Metamorphoses,*" 2288–90, also comments on the similarity of the narrative settings.

135. Crabbe, "Structure and Content in Ovid's *Metamorphoses,*" 2288 n.90, compares the final metamorphosis and cult of Baucis and Philemon with the honors Theseus paid to Hecale after her death.

and Bömer *ad loc.* observe the added appeal to local authorities characteristic of aetiological poetry (e.g., Nicander in A.L. 30.4: Καλεῖται δὲ καὶ τὸ ῥέον ἐκ τῆς πέτρας ἐκείνης ἄχρι νῦν παρὰ τοῖς ἐπιχωρίοις δάκρυον Βυβλίδος). We observe in addition that Lelex's informants were old men (*senes* 722), who, he further emphasizes, had no reason not to tell him the truth (721). This final qualification of Lelex's has occasioned a great deal of comment from scholars seeking passages in which Ovid reveals his desire to undermine the belief in myth.[136] The issue of belief is brought up in Perithous' challenge of the veracity of Achelous' tale of supernatural metamorphosis: *ficta refers* (614). Lelex's story is designed as a response to Perithous and he thus employs traditional formulae to authenticate his narrative such as we find in the *Fasti* (e.g., 5.601 *tum mihi non dubiis auctoribus incipit aestas*).

Ovid here self-consciously uncovers the use of an *aetion* as a stratagem for verification by reference to external reality. He makes explicit the mechanisms by which narrative authenticates its fictions, by providing in the framed narrative a possible audience-response to his own stories. But as an epic poet Ovid has no interest in rejecting his own mythological stories, which are necessarily defined as *falsum* or *fabula* according to rhetorical theory.[137] Rather than revealing his skepticism about his own mythological stories, these reminders of the issues of veracity and disbelief scattered throughout the poem are a component of Ovid's self-conscious—and frequently ludic—engagement with the authoritative claims of epic poetry and the mythological content of his poem. As Feeney suggests in his discussion of this episode, Ovid's technique is much more complex: "Ovid is not interested in irrevocably exploding our ability to give the necessary credence to his fictions, nor is he interested in letting us forget that fictions are indeed his subject."[138] By reminding us of the fictional status of his poetry, Ovid draws our attention to the skill with which he has created these convincing illusions that have drawn us in.

The influence of Callimachus, and other Hellenistic poets, is, of course, pervasive in the *Metamorphoses*. By no means all of the episodes that we suspect have Callimachean literary associations are narrated by internal narrators. "Ovid," for example, tells the story of Callisto at *Met.* 2.401–530 and of Actaeon and Teresias at *Met.* 3.138–338. However, in his reworking of the aetiological story of the crow from Callimachus' *Hecale* (frr. 70–74 Hollis) at

---

136. M.K. Gamel, "Baucis and Philemon: Paradigm or Paradox," *Helios* 11 (1984): 129: "a disturbing detail." Solodow, *World of Ovid's Metamorphoses,* 65. Contra, see Bömer, *Met., ad* 8.721.

137. See Stinton's similar arguments against the view of Vergil or Euripides as skeptical narrators, in "Expressions of Disbelief," 65–89.

138. Feeney, *Gods in Epic,* 230.

Met. 2.531–632 Ovid reproduces the narrative framework of the original.[139] We have found, however, that the literary background of those stories Ovid chose to embed in "aetiological frames" share features typical of aetiological narrative and are elucidated only through a careful consideration of the circumstances of the narration and of the identity of the internal narrator. These embedded stories seem to have in common a distinctively Alexandrian character, and a number share perhaps a specifically Callimachean literary genealogy. The majority of them offer an *aetion* for a specific mythological or religious detail, and for the most part no longer explain natural phenomena. Instead, they involve such subjects as the origin of Medusa's snakes, miraculous fountains, a foundation story, a pair of sacred trees, an altar, islands, and the reed-pipe, *aetia* typical of Callimachean and Hellenistic aetiological poetry in general.

As he approaches the themes of ancient Italian legend in the later books of the *Metamorphoses,* Ovid's metamorphosis stories involve still less the explanation of natural phenomena such as animals or plants and are more consistently of an Alexandrian religious-aetiological nature.[140] D. Porte has appealingly suggested that the natural metamorphoses in the poem that account for animals and plants decrease in the last three books of the poem because the cosmogonic process they represent, "l'organisation des éléments, la solidification de la terre,"[141] slows down as the chronology of the poem reaches the historical period. It is in these final books that the material of the *Metamorphoses* overlaps with the Italian religious-antiquarian subject matter of the *Fasti.* We will find that Ovid seems even more interested in drawing our attention to the associations between the narratives of his two aetiological poems. We will have to decide why Ovid's handling of this material is so emphatically Callimachean and what ramifications this may have for our understanding of Ovid's reasons for including Italian religious themes in the *Metamorphoses,* where they have sometimes been seen to reside rather uncomfortably among the preceding mythological stories.

---

139. See Keith, *Play of Fictions.*

140. This has led some critics to overlook the earlier aetiological stories and to claim that the content of *Met.* 15 is markedly different from the earlier books; see Knox, *Traditions of Augustan Poetry,* 73; Graf, "Les *Métamorphoses* et la Véracité du Mythe," 61.

141. Porte, "L'idée romaine et la métamorphose," 184.

Chapter 3

Metamorphoses 14–15: Italy and Aetiological Metamorphosis

*omne
humanum genus est avidum nimis auricularum*
—Lucretius 4.593–94

When Ovid approaches Italian themes—the mythological territory of the *Fasti*—his manner of presentation becomes even more overtly aetiological. This new Italian section of the *Metamorphoses* opens with the so-called "*Aeneid*" portion, beginning at 13.623. The stories in the final two books do not become exclusively Roman, but alternate for the most part between Greek and Italian themes.[1] It should not be surprising that as Ovid broached the themes of ancient Italian legend, he continued to innovate. Ovid in this part of his epic seems, in fact, to have been especially interested in including typically Alexandrian subjects and narrative techniques, such as inset narratives, ecphrases, metamorphoses, and erotic and aetiological stories. No fewer than five of the metamorphosis stories included in the "*Aeneid*" section were also treated by Nicander or Boios.[2] The stories from Book 14 until the end of the poem now noticeably center around religious aetiologies, mostly Italian, but some Greek as well. Included also are geographical and topographical *aetia*, the latter involving sites in Rome with religious associations. There are also numerous inset narratives in Books 13–15, and two of these in particular in Book 14 are clearly of the type we have been considering, the stories of Picus and Canens and of Vertumnus and Pomona, which we will consider in detail.

For the aetiological treatment of Italian themes in both the *Metamorphoses* and the *Fasti* Ovid had, of course, many precedents in both the poets and the antiquarians and historians of Rome, who endeavored, as T.P. Wiseman has written of Cornelius Nepos' *Chronica,* to bring "the events of the Roman

---

1. See Lafaye, *Les Métamorphoses d'Ovide,* 255 (Appendix J).
2. A.L. 25 (Nicander), *Met.* 13.685–701; A.L. 4 (Nicander), *Met.* 13.714–15; A.L. 14 (Boios?), *Met.* 13.716–18; A.L. 37 (Nicander), *Met.* 14. 483–511; A.L. 31 (Nicander), *Met.* 14.513–26.

tradition into the mainstream of 'world history' as created by the Greeks."[3] The Greek historians had already for some time been fashioning an appropriately Greek mythical history for the Romans.[4] The Romans went about tracing the roots of their culture and customs in the same way as the Greeks had before them, using the techniques of aetiology and etymology "as weapons in the reconstruction of the past."[5] When Cicero praises the works of that amazingly prolific antiquarian scholar Varro for acquainting the Romans with the history of Rome's institutions and monuments (*Acad. Post.* 1.3) he stresses aetiological themes: *tu omnium divinarum humanarumque rerum nomina, genera, officia, causas aperuisti.*[6] Varro's many antiquarian and etymological researches were used by later historians and poets alike.[7] He seems to have used Callimachus, who included Italian stories in both his *Aetia* and *Paradoxa.*[8] Greek scholars in Rome such as Gaius Julius Hyginus (*HRR* 2, 72–77, frr. 5–17, *GRF* Funaioli, pp. 526–37) and Alexander Polyhistor (*On Rome, FGrHist* 273 F 20, 70, 109–11) also wrote on Roman themes, largely geographical and etymological, as did Butas (*Aetia Romana, SH* 234–35[+236?]), Simylos (*SH* 724 Tarpeia [+725?]), and Castor of Rhodes (*FGrHist* 250 F 5, 15).[9] In verse,

---

3. Wiseman, *Clio's Cosmetics,* 157.

4. Wiseman, *Clio's Cosmetics,* 156. On early Greek versions of Rome's foundation see Dionysius of Halicarnasus *Ant. Rom.* 1.6.1, and 1.72–73; T.J. Cornell, "Aeneas and the Twins: The Development of the Roman Foundation Legend," *PCPS* n.s. 21 (1975): 1–32. See also L. Pearson, "Myth and Archaeologia in Italy and Sicily: Timaeus and His Predecessors," *YCS* 24 (1975): 171–95, and E.J. Bickerman, *"Origines Gentium," CP* 42 (1952): 65–81.

5. E. Rawson, "The First Latin Annalists," *Latomus* 35 (1976): 698, on Cassius Hemina. See A.S. Gratwick, "The Early Republic," in *The Cambridge History of Classical Literature,* vol. 2, ed. E.J. Kenney and W.V. Clausen (Cambridge, 1982), 150, on Cato's *Origines* (*HRR* cxxvii–clxiv, 55–97; see now the Budé edition of M. Chassignet [1986]). Cf. E. Badian, "The Early Historians," in *Latin Historians,* ed. T.A. Dorey (New York, 1966), 8; Kraus, "Ovidius Naso," 126.

6. Cf. Propertius 4.10.1: *Nunc Iovis incipiam causas aperire Feretri.* See Rawson, *Intellectual Life in the Late Roman Republic,* 236, and *eadem,* "Cicero the Historian and Cicero the Antiquarian," *JRS* 62 (1972): 35.

7. *Antiquitatum Rerum Humanarum et Divinarum* (see B. Cardauns' useful edition with commentary in Akademie der Wissenschaften unde der Literatur Mainz [Wiesbaden, 1976]), *De Gente Populi Romani* (*HRR* 2.9–25), *De Origine Linguae Latinae, De Lingua Latina, De Familiis Troianis.* See A. Momigliano, "Ancient History and the Antiquarian," in *Studies in Historiography* (New York and Evanston, 1966), 5.

8. Servius *ad Aen.* 1.408 (Call. fr. 189 Pf.). Cf. Call. *Aet.* frr. 93, 96, 106, 190, *Paradoxa* fr. 407.VI, XII, etc. See Fraser, *Ptolemaic Alexandria,* 763–69, on possible sources, esp. Timaeus. Rawson, *Intellectual Life in the Late Roman Republic,* 233 n.2, raises the question whether Varro's *Aetia* might have followed Callimachus also in being verse.

9. Rawson, *Intellectual Life in the Late Roman Republic,* 253 n.2, thinks Butas may be Cato's freedman (Plut. *Cat. min.* 70.2). For Simylos and Butas see also M. Hubbard, *Propertius* (New York, 1975), 119–21, J.N. Bremmer and N.M. Horsfall, *Roman Myth and Mythography,* University of London Bulletin Supplement 52 (London, 1987), 68, and F.E. Brenk, "Tarpeia among the

Ennius in his *Annales* undertook the task of narrating the history of Rome and its institutions from the arrival of the Trojans.[10] We also have a fragment of hexameter verse attributed to Accius' *Annales* (fr. 3, p. 34 Morel; p. 47 Buechner *ex incertis libris*) which explains the origin of the Roman Saturnalia as an imitation of the Athenian Kronia and constitutes our first Latin verse *aetion*.[11]

In Augustan poetry Greek mythological themes and metamorphoses appear less frequently than before, but the Augustan poets reveal a profound interest in aetiological investigation.[12] An aetiological approach to the increasingly prominent national themes allowed for the articulation of a relationship between Rome's past and its present, and simultaneously served as a way to associate poetry with the Alexandrian tradition, especially Callimachus' *Aetia*. The *Aeneid* abounds in *aetia,* for which Vergil had important epic precedents in Apollonius' *Argonautica* and Ennius' *Annales*.[13] Vergil's use of aetiology in his epic is intimately related to the poem's national theme and his interest in creating narrative authority.[14] Yet Vergil also recognized that the strategy of the aetiological approach allowed a poet to broach national themes obliquely through a representation of the mythical past instead of the present. Vergil's presentation of the site of Rome in Book 8 serves as a paradigm for the way in which aetiology can "scale down" an encomiastic theme.[15] The *Aeneid* was a significant model for the Roman aetiology of Propertius Book 4. In this book of

Celts: Watery Romance from Simylos to Propertius," *Collections Latomus* 164 (Brussels, 1979), 166–74.

10. In his first three books covering the founding of the city, Ennius seems to have included a good deal about the early development of Rome's religious and social institutions. *Annales* 1 fr. 51 Sk. deals with the institution by Romulus of a festival for Jupiter Feretrius, a theme later treated in Propertius 4.10. Book 2 of the *Annales* would have included many of Numa's religious institutions. See Skutsch, *Annals of Q. Ennius,* 263, H.D. Jocelyn, "The Poems of Quintus Ennius," *ANRW* 1.2 (1972): 1007.

11. I thank E. Courtney for pointing this out to me; cf. Courtney, *Fragmentary Latin Poets,* 57–58.

12. For the development of Roman aetiological elegy we now have the valuable study by Miller, "Callimachus and the Augustan Aetiological Elegy."

13. For a classification of *aetia* in the *Aeneid* see now Binder, "Aitiologische Erzählung und Augusteisches Programm"; see also T.P. Wiseman, "Legendary Genealogies in Late-Republican Rome," *Greece and Rome* 21 (1974): 153–64; Horsfall, "Virgil and the Poetry of Explanations." For aetiology in *Aeneid* 8 see especially George, *Aeneid VIII and the Aitia of Callimachus, passim;* Gransden's commentary on *Aeneid* 8, esp. p. 26; Norden, *Aeneis Buch VI,* 197–98, 229–31; Heinze, *Virgil's Epische Technik,* 56–57, 104, 373. For general Hellenistic influence on the *Aeneid* see W.V. Clausen, *Virgil's Aeneid and the Tradition of Hellenistic Poetry* (Berkeley, 1987), W.W. Briggs, Jr., "Vergil and the Hellenistic Epic," *ANRW* 2.31.2 (1983): 948–84, and A.S. Hollis, Hellenistic Colouring in Virgil's *Aeneid,*" *HSCP* 94 (1992): 269–85.

14. Feeney, *Gods in Epic,* 185–86.

15. On this technique, see Wimmel, *'Hirtenkrieg' und arkadisches Rom,* 104.

poems Propertius' claim to be the *Romanus Callimachus* (4.1.64) clearly refers to his aetiological treatment of Roman national themes and their accommodation to elegiacs. Included in the fourth book as we have it are five aetiological poems, all involving topography in the city of Rome and religious themes: 4.2 (the metamorphosing statue of Vertumnus), 4.4 (Tarpeian hill), 4.6 (Apollo's temple on the Palatine), 4.9 (Ara Maxima, and rites), 4.10 (temple of Jupiter Feretrius).[16] Tibullus also wrote two poems on Roman antiquarian themes: 2.1, a description of the rustic Roman festival of the Ambarvalia, and 2.5.23ff., which exhibits a great similarity to the nostalgic scenes of ancient Rome in Vergil's *Aeneid,* Book 8, and Propertius 4.1.[17]

In his *Amores* 3.13 and *Ars Amatoria,* Ovid first experimented with Italian aetiological themes. In *Ars* 1.101ff. Ovid inserted an irreverent *aetion* explaining that Romulus, by instigating the rape of the Sabine women, was the originator of the practice of hunting for dates in the theater.[18] We have already examined some of the ways in which Ovid's narrative technique in the *Metamorphoses* is similar to that of the *Fasti,* and we can now trace this connection even further in the Italian stories of the final two books. We should first of all not assume that "most of the aboriginal lore of Italy must have been a poor material for him to start with."[19] We can see from the *Fasti* alone the great store of traditional Italian and Roman material Ovid had to work with (and to innovate upon). In the *Metamorphoses* he conspicuously passes over better-known episodes of Roman history (Tarpeia, Ilia and Mars, etc.) and episodes treated in the second half of the *Aeneid* (Cacus, Evander, Latinus, etc.) to choose more obscure stories or to invent new ones.

The Framework of the *Aeneid* (*Met.* 13.623–14.608)

The fall of Troy at *Metamorphoses* 13.623 is usually taken to signal the commencement of the "*Aeneid*" framework and the deification of Aeneas at

---

16. On Propertius Book 4 see Miller, "Callimachus and the Augustan Aetiological Elegy," 380–98, and Pillinger, "Some Callimachean Influences on Propertius."

17. See Cairns, *Tibullus,* 64–86, on 2.5, 126–34 on 2.1; Ross, *Backgrounds to Augustan Poetry,* 153–58 on 2.5.

18. See the discussions of Miller, "Callimachus and the Augustan Aetiological Elegy," 397–98; idem, "Callimachus and the *Ars Amatoria*"; Hollis, *Ovid Ars Amatoria 1, ad loc.*; Wilkinson, *Ovid Recalled,* 123.

19. Fränkel, *Poet between Two Worlds,* 104. This negative judgment of Roman mythology, as T.P. Wiseman, "Roman Legend and Oral Tradition," review of *Roman Myth and Mythography,* by J.N. Bremmer and N.M. Horsfall, *JRS* 79 (1989): 129, explains, has proven to be progressively more difficult to sustain in the light of new archaeological discoveries. See now also Porte, "L'idée romaine et la métamorphose," 191–92.

14.608 to mark its end.[20] In his own characteristic manner Ovid appropriates the Aeneas myth into the mythological scheme of his poem. It is clear that for a poet with Callimachean sympathies the challenge of treating such a familiar theme in an original manner had great appeal. Ovid does not "retell" the *Aeneid.* Rather he uses Aeneas' travel itinerary from Troy to Italy in *Aeneid* 3– 6 as a framework for his own series of metamorphic narratives.[21] The manner of Ovid's treatment of Aeneas' voyage is similar to Hellenistic geographical periegeses, in which a geographical route was followed and the customs, etymologies, and local marvels of each city and region were recorded.[22] Many of the highlights of the *Aeneid* are briefly summarized and then passed over for an episode of Ovid's own invention. Included also are events from the *Odyssey.* In the course of this narrative Ovid scrupulously picks up almost all of the metamorphoses from these two epics.[23] Most of Ovid's stories take their starting point from a suggestion in the *Aeneid,* and many involve Vergilian characters depicted in new settings. Many of these new episodes, such as those of Anius at 13.632–704, Scylla and Galatea at 13.730–14.74, and the Sibyl at 14.101–55, are love stories and, interestingly, most involve internal narrators. In fact, the metamorphosis stories included in this section of the poem have notoriously little to do with the concerns of the *Aeneid.* Augustan themes and *aetia* are noticeably avoided.

We pick up Aeneas' story after his escape from burning Troy (*Met.* 13.623– 27). Ovid, briefly mentioning landmarks passed, traces Aeneas' route from

---

20. Haupt-Ehwald, *ad loc.,* Bömer, *Met., ad loc.,* Galinsky, *Ovid's Metamorphoses,* 217.

21. For a close analysis of the parallels between this section and Vergil's *Aeneid* see M. Stitz, *Ovid und Vergils Aeneis: Interpretation Met. 13.623–14.608* (Freiburg, 1962), and R. Lammacchia, "Precisazioni su alcuni aspetti dell'epica Ovidiana," *Atene e Roma* 14 (1969): 1–20. For different views on Ovid's intentions in this section see F. Bömer, "Ovid und Die Sprache Vergils," in *Ovid,* ed. M. von Albrecht and E. Zinn (Darmstadt, 1968), 173–202; C.P. Segal, "Myth and Philosophy in the *Metamorphoses:* Ovid's Augustanism and the Augustan Conclusion of Book 15," *AJP* 90 (1969): 258; Otis, *Ovid as an Epic Poet,* 278ff. (parody); Galinsky, *Ovid's Metamorphoses,* 247–48; Solodow, *World of Ovid's Metamorphoses,* 136ff.; Tissol, "Narrative Style in Ovid's *Metamorphoses,*" chap. 4.

22. F.J. Miller, "Some Features of Ovid's Style: III. Ovid's Methods of Ordering and Transition in the *Metamorphoses,*" *CJ* 16 (1920–21): 466–67, classifies this under the category of the "geographical or itinerary method"; cf. Stitz, *Ovid und Vergils Aeneis,* 116. Haupt-Ehwald *ad* 13.623ff. suggest that this series of stories could have been derived from an Alexandrian συν- αγωγή. We may compare Ovid's treatment of Medea's geographically far-reaching journey in *Met.* 7.350–90. See Pearson, "Timaeus and His Predecessors," on Timaeus, and "Apollonius of Rhodes and the Old Geographers," on Hecateus as the originator of the genre, also Fraser, *Ptolemaic Alexandria,* 522ff., 762ff.

23. *Aeneid:* Ships turned into nymphs (9.69ff.), Diomedes' men (11.271–78); *Odyssey:* Phaeacians' ship (13.146ff.), Circe (10.238ff.); the metamorphosis of Cycnus is also mentioned at *Aen.* 10.185–93.

Troy to Italy as told in Book 3 of the *Aeneid*.[24] When the Trojans reach Delos and meet king Anius, Ovid replaces the prophecies of the *Aeneid* passage (*Aen.* 3.90–120) with his own tale of metamorphosis. This episode is typical of Ovid's treatment of his framework, in that he has followed the route of the *Aeneid* until it drops him off at a convenient point to narrate one of his own metamorphosis stories, instead of repeating an episode already treated by his predecessor. The only stories he repeats involve metamorphosis: that of Diomedes' men (*Met.* 14.464–511, *Aen.* 11.271–74), and that of the Trojan ships into nymphs (*Met.* 14.530–65, *Aen.* 9.69–122). The story Anius himself narrates at *Met.* 13.644–74, the metamorphosis of his daughters into doves during the Trojan War, seems to have been a story popular with the Alexandrians. Versions are attributed to Callimachus, Euphorion, and Lycophron.[25] In addition, Ovid includes in the episode a characteristically Alexandrian ecphrasis: a description of the decoration on a drinking cup Anius gives Aeneas as a gift.[26] Depicted on the cup is the story of the death and deification of Orion's daughters (13.685–701), which provides an *aetion* for a cult in Boeotia and is similar to a story attributed to Nicander in A.L. 25. Thematically, the two stories of maidenly courage in this episode (*demisso per fortia pectora telo / pro populo cecidisse* 13.694–95) seem relevant to the intimations of self-sacrifice frequently detected in the *Aeneid,* and stylistically, this first scene sets the tone for the following narratives.

After this episode, the framework of the *Aeneid* is again picked up and followed until the Trojans reach Scylla. Along the route are very brief references to longer episodes in Vergil's poem,[27] and the non-Vergilian metamorphosis stories associated with Ambracia (13.713–15) and Chaonia (13.717–18), two stories also mentioned by Antoninus Liberalis. The story of Cragaleus' ἀπολίθωσις at Ambracia is recounted in A.L. 4 (Nicander) and King Molossus' sons' transformations into birds is found in A.L. 14 (Boios?). At this point in the narrative of the *Aeneid,* upon reaching Sicily, the Trojans

---

24. *Met.* 13.628–29, *Aen.* 3.13–68: Antandros, Thrace, Polydorus' mound.

25. Callimachus (fr. 188 *Aet. inc. lib,* cf., however, Pfeiffer's skepticism *ad loc.* "*Neque metamorphosis filiarum Anii in Call. fuisse . . . videtur*"); Euphorion fr. 4 Groningen, Lycophron *Alex.* 580. See Bömer's commentary *ad Met.* 13.632–704.

26. Kenney, Introduction and Notes to *Ovid's Metamorphoses,* ad 13.684, remarks that "Ovid goes out of his way to underline the Hellenistic flavour of the passage by calling the artist Alcon, which was the name of a real designer" (Athen. 11.469A, *Culex* 66–67 *pocula . . . Alconis,* Pliny *Nat.* 34.141).

27. Delos *Aen.* 3.96, *Met.* 13.678–79; Crete *Aen.* 3.121–91, *Met.* 13.705–8; Storm *Aen.* 3.192–208, *Met.* 13.709; Strophades and the Harpies *Aen.* 3.209–67, *Met.* 13.709–10 (Ovid mentions the harpy Aello, instead of the Vergilian Celaeno); Dulchium, Samos, Ithaca, Ambracia passed *Aen.* 3.270–77, *Met.* 13.711–18; Helenus in Epirus *Aen.* 3.276–505, *Met.* 13.719–23.

meet up with Achaemenides, the deserted companion of Ulysses, who tells of the encounter with Polyphemus (*Aen.* 3.570–691). In the *Metamorphoses* this episode is delayed until Book 14 and the love story that takes its place here (13.738–897), the first of the three "love-triangles" within this section,[28] substitutes a Theocritean version for the Homeric Cyclops, telling of events before even the *Odyssey.* The story, narrated by Galatea herself, is a masterpiece of Alexandrian allusiveness, combining the earlier versions of Theocritus and Vergil. In this episode, Ovid humorously reinflates to Homeric epic dimensions motifs pastoral had deflated in order to meet its own generic demands.[29] The story of Glaucus of Anthedon (who again narrates his own metamorphosis), Scylla, and Circe that follows seems also to have been particularly associated with Alexandrian aesthetics, as evidenced by the popularity of Glaucus and Scylla in Hellenistic literature and Roman neoteric epyllia.[30] Scylla's final transformation into an Italian landmark (*in scopulum qui nunc quoque saxeus exstat, / transformata . . . : scopulum quoque navita vitat* 14.73–74) gives the narrative the feel of an aetiological itinerary.[31] The introduction of the erotic element into the Vergilian frame at this point seems to correspond thematically with *Aeneid* 4, which Ovid's narrative reaches immediately after these two stories and summarizes in four compact lines (14.78–81). That both the stories involve women who rebuff unwanted suitors is again interesting in the light of events in the *Aeneid.* The inclusion of the tales of Polyphemus and Scylla also

---

28. See on these Nagle, "A Trio of Love-Triangles."

29. For a discussion of the generic features of this episode see Farrell, "Dialogue of Genres." Kenney, Introduction and Notes to *Ovid's Metamorphoses, ad* 750–899, uses the term "hyperpastoral"; cf. G. Tissol, "Polyphemus and His Audiences: Narrative and Power in Ovid's *Metamorphoses,*" *Syllecta Classica* 2 (1990): 45–58; H. Dörrie, "Der verliebte Kyklop. Interpretation von Ovid, *Met.* 13. 750–897," *AU* 12 (1969): 75–100. Of related interest is I.M.L. DuQuesnay, "From Polyphemus to Corydon."

30. Scylla, as noted above, is the only story attributed to Parthenius' *Metamorphoses:* (*SH* 637), also Call. *Aet.* fr. 113, *Hecale* fr. 90 Hollis. See Lyne, *Ciris,* 6–14; Hollis, *Ovid Metamorphoses VIII,* 32–34. See pp. 22–24 for the poems attributed to Callimachus, Cicero, and Cornificius on Glaucus. We do not know if Scylla was involved in these versions. The earliest version known that included Scylla (cited at Athen. 7.297B with other versions) is a poem by the early third-century poetess Hedyle called *Scylla (SH* 456; for her date see A.S.F. Gow and D.L. Page, eds., *The Greek Anthology: Hellenistic Epigrams II* [Cambridge, 1965], 289); otherwise cf. only Serv. *ad Ecl.* 6.74, *ad Aen.* 3.420, and Hyg. *Fab.* 199. Circe's involvement may well be Ovid's innovation. Glaucus appears also in, among others, Alexander Aetolus (fr. 1 Powell, pp. 121–22), Hedylus (*SH* 457), Euanthes (*SH* 409), Nicander (*Aetolica* fr. 2 G-S = *FGrHist* 271–72 F1, *Europia* fr. 25 G-S = *FGrHist* F19).

31. Haupt-Ehwald, *ad* 14.72 "Lokalsage." Cf. Sall. *Hist.* fr. 4.27 Mauren. Observe the similar wording at 8.591 "*Perimelen navita dicit,*" where Hollis, *Ovid Metamorphoses VIII, ad loc.* remarks: "the reference to passing sailors is a slightly Alexandrian touch (cf. *Met.* 9.228–29, Call. *Hy.* 4.41–43, Nicander *Ther.* 230)."

serves to recall Vergil's two earlier works in which these figures are evoked (*Ecl.* 2, *Geo.* 1.404–9). Ovid hereby tones down the epic and ideological weight of his model by interruptions characterized by magical metamorphoses, eros, and Alexandrian antecedents, as well as by references to Vergil's own earlier neoteric efforts.

Four of the other metamorphosis episodes included within the *Aeneid* framework share more than these Alexandrian and neoteric associations: they all involve the motif of speech. The first story explains the name of the island of Pithecusae by the metamorphosis of its inhabitants, the Cercopians, into apes (14.90–100). We know of this story only from Xenagoras, a first-century B.C.E. historian, in his Περὶ Νήσων (*FGrHist* 240 F28), but thematically it seems Hellenistic.[32] The description of the metamorphosis of the Cercopians is reminiscent of the literary critical language of the transformations of the Pierides and the Lycian peasants, which suggests that we should perhaps understand programmatic intent here as well.[33] The theme of language is continued in the next metamorphosis, that of the Sibyl, who narrates her own story to Aeneas at Cumae (14.120–55). Instead of the future, Aeneas learns of the Sibyl's past. The story of Apollo's love for the Sibyl, repeated only by Servius *ad Aen.* 6.321, is similar to that of Tithonus, a tale long associated with poetics and later perhaps particularly with Callimachean aesthetics.[34] In contrast to the preceding transformed apes, the Sibyl suffers her punishment by being forced to retain her voice forever, even when the rest of her has disappeared: *vocem mihi fata relinquent* (14.153). The metamorphosis of Diomedes' men as punishment for insulting Venus, narrated by Diomedes (*Met.* 14.464–511, as in the *Aeneid* 11.271–74), was also a widely recorded story, commonly included in paradoxographical collections and appearing in Antoninus (A.L. 37, probably Nicander).[35] Interestingly, Ovid omits the two *aetia* always associated with this story, as summarized by Servius (*ad Aen.* 11.271): the naming of the birds (observe his humorous circumlocutions in lines 508–9) and of the island after Diomedes, as well as their remarkably friendly behavior towards Greeks. Ovid's omission suggests these *aetia* were so well known as to need no

32. Bömer, *Met.*, *ad* 14.91–93. Pliny *Nat.* 3.82 offers a different etymology: *Pithecusa, non a simiarum multitudine (ut aliqui existimavere) sed a figlinis doliorum.*

33. *Rauco stridore* 14.100, *rauca* 5.678, 6.377, *periuria linguae* 14.99, *maledicta* 5.666, *litibus exercent linguas* 6.375.

34. Call. *Aet.* fr. 1.29ff., cf. Theocr. *Id.* 7.139; on the motif see G. Crane, "Tithonus and the Prologue to Callimachus' *Aetia*," *ZPE* 66 (1986): 269–78, H. King, "Tithonos and the Tettix," *Arethusa* 19 (1986): 15–35 (21–23 on the similarity with the Sibyl).

35. As Papathomopoulos argues *ad* A.L. 37 n.1. Call. fr. 407.163–68 (Lykos *FGrHist* 570 F 6) = Ant. Car. *Hist. Mirab.* 172; [Arist.] *mir. ausc.* 79 p.836a 7ff. Also Lycophr. 594ff.; Varro *De Gent. Pop. Rom.* fr. 17P; Pliny *Nat.* 10.126–27 (Iuba *FGrHist* 275 F60); Aelian *N.A.* 1.1.

repetition.[36] The short aetiological episode of the Apulian shepherd who mocked the nymphs and was turned into a wild olive tree (14.512–26), which follows this, is similar to one preserved by Antoninus Liberalis (31, Nicander).[37] In this story again the motif of the punishment meted out to improper speech is central.

Taken into consideration together these episodes suggest that the use of speech is a theme Ovid considered relevant to the original context of the *Aeneid*. This fits within a pattern of a concern with language and storytelling that has been detected throughout the *Metamorphoses* and seems especially relevant here as Italian myths are first being broached and Augustan themes are poised to follow.[38] The cumulative effect of these metamorphosis stories set within the *Aeneid* frame of the *Metamorphoses* is to diffuse the Augustan implications of Vergil's poem, and to uncover instead issues that have been attributed to the "other voices" of the *Aeneid:* the problems of the freedom of the individual with respect to the state.[39] The inclusion of many stories in Books 13 and 14 especially associated with Alexandrian and erotic literature at the same time serves to challenge the surrounding generic framework of Homeric and Vergilian epics. Ovid's use of multiple generic sources brings to the fore the issue of imitation, again relevant to a context in which Ovid is directly dealing with the legend recently treated in the most famous poem of the time. Ovid's *Aeneid* section represents in part, perhaps, his response to Vergil's own poetic mixture of epic and non-epic sources in the *Aeneid.* His aetiological treatment of the Italian material is also an acknowledgment of the similar

---

36. Critics have noted, however, that in his description of the metamorphoses of the Trojan ships (14.559–65), which follows the Diomedean episode, Ovid has slyly alluded to the omitted *aetion* of the birds' behavior by attributing the exact opposite behavior to the new sea nymphs: *cladis adhuc Phrygiae memores odere Pelasgos* (14.562). See Haupt-Ehwald, *ad* 14.561ff.; Bömer, *Met., ad* 14.559–61.

37. Papathomopoulos *ad* A.L. 37 n.1 observes that Ovid juxtaposes two stories probably both derived from Nicander. Note again verbal echoes of the earlier metamorphoses of the Pierides and frogs: *obscenis convicia rustica dictis* 14.522, *convicia* 5.676, 6.378. An oleaster sacred to Faunus also appears prominently in *Aen.* 12.766ff.

38. Fredericks [Nagle], "Divine Wit vs. Divine Folly," 244. Cf. Charles Altieri, "Ovid and the New Mythologists," *Novel* 7 (1973): 35; Keith, *Play of Fictions,* esp. 99–115, 135–36; Leach, "Ekphrasis and the Theme of Artistic Failure," 104–6; Rosati, "Il racconto dentro il racconto"; Lateiner, "Mythic and Non-Mythic Artists." Schmitzer, *Zeitgeschichte in Ovids Metamorphosen,* 187–238, argues that the Persephone episode in Book 5, in which the speech motif is prominent, serves as Ovid's meta-literary paradigm for the interdependence of poetry and politics.

39. E.g., A. Parry, "The Two Voices of Virgil's *Aeneid,*" *Arion* 2 (1963): 66–80, R.O.A.M. Lyne, *Further Voices in Vergil's Aeneid* (Oxford, 1987). Feeney, *Gods in Epic,* 219, in a discussion of Book 15, suggests that "Ovid enforces a rereading of the *Aeneid,* and makes one realize just how finely balanced that poem is between the private and communal."

approach used by Vergil in the *Aeneid*. The similarity of treatment only serves to highlight the different content and import of the *aetia* of the two authors.

relig. — But we have yet to consider the longest of these "interruptions," the story of Picus and Canens, the first purely Italian story, and a framed aetiological *aetiology* narrative in which the tendencies outlined above are fully elaborated. When Aeneas reaches the shores of Italy, they are described with hyperchronological accuracy as *litora adit nondum nutricis habentia nomen* (14.157), thus correcting Vergil, who mentions the name of the shore at *Aen.* 6.900, before Caieta's burial, and then gives the *aetion* at the beginning of *Aen.* 7.1–5.[40] Ovid's *Metamorphoses* has now truly reached the "Italian" half of the *Aeneid*.

"Statue Tales": Picus and Canens (*Met.* 14.308–434)

In Italy the Trojans meet a character named Macareus, *comes experientis Ulixis* (*Met.* 14.159), who seems to be a purely Ovidian invention. He is addressed by Achaemenides, who had appeared in *Aen.* 3.570–691.[41] The echo of Vergil's description of Achaemenides at *Aen.* 3.691 as *comes infelicis Ulixi* suggests that Ovid is humorously proclaiming his own innovation with Macareus, while simultaneously acknowledging the Vergilian precedent in inventing Achaemenides.[42] Ovid "in response to Vergil's response to Homer"[43] duplicates the narration of Odyssean episodes. In the *Metamorphoses,* Achaemenides tells the story of the Cyclops, as in the *Aeneid* (3.613–91), but then Macareus, the second narrator, continues even further the narration of the events of *Odyssey* 9 and 10.[44] It is striking that at the very moment of the Trojans' arrival in Italy, a story from the earlier Homeric Odyssean journey is told. After he finishes, Achaemenides asks Macareus to recount his adventures, as he has just recalled his own, *tu quoque pande tuos, comitum gratissime, casus* (14.221).[45]

---

40. Kenney, Introduction and Notes to *Ovid's Metamorphoses*, ad *Met.* 14.157. Ovid includes Caieta's burial at *Met.* 14.442–44—now the place really can be called Caieta.

41. In the *Aeneid* Achaemenides is picked up at the foot of Aetna on the shores of Sicily; at *Met.* 14.161ff. this episode is in the past and Ovid highlights this by explicitly contrasting Achaemenides' appearance in his poem with his earlier appearance in the *Aeneid*: *iam non hirsutus amictu, / iam suus et spinis conserto tegmine nullis* (*Met.* 14.165–66), cf. *Aen.* 3.590–95: *ignoti nova forma viri miserandaque cultu* (591) *immissaque barba, / consertum tegimen spinis* (593–94). See Due, *Changing Forms,* 84; Otis, *Ovid as an Epic Poet,* 73–74.

42. R.D. Williams, ed., *P. Vergili Maronis Aenidos Liber Tertius* (Oxford, 1962), ad *Aen.* 3.588–654.

43. Nagle, "A Trio of Love-Triangles," 96.

44. On Ovid's integration of events from the *Odyssey* into his "*Aeneid*" section, see J.D. Ellsworth, "Ovid's 'Odyssey': *Met.*13.623–14.608," *Mnem.* 41 (1988): 333–40.

45. Other places where this mode of transition is used: 11.289 (Peleus to Ceyx), 13.750 (Scylla to Galatea).

Macareus' narrative picks up at the exact point in the *Odyssey* where Achaemenides has left off; at *Odyssey* 9.105–566 Odysseus tells of the Cyclops and then of his arrival at the Aeolian islands (10.1–79), the Laestrygonians (10.80–132), and finally of his adventures in Circe's realms (10.133–574). Ovid's narrative follows this framework exactly (14.223–307).[46] In the *Aeneid* the Trojans avoid Circe's realms, and Vergil thus avoids narrating the fantastic stories of the transformations of Ulysses' men and only hints at Circe's frightening powers (7.10–24).[47] But Ovid presents the whole episode in glorious Technicolor. Macareus' personal perspective allows him to tell the story of Circe's powers much more vividly than Odysseus could in the *Odyssey*, since Macareus actually experienced metamorphosis, and he thus presents us with a rare description of the process of his own metamorphosis from a man to a pig and back again (14.242–307).

After finishing this story, Macareus volunteers to relate one of the amazing things he learned of while lingering in Circe's realm for a year:

"annua nos illic tenuit mora, multaque praesens
tempore tam longo vidi, multa auribus hausi
hoc quoque cum multis, quod clam mihi rettulit una
quattuor e famulis ad talia sacra paratis."

(14.308–11)

He describes the situation in which Circe's *famula* had narrated to him at his request the story of Picus, Canens, and Circe. This attendant had pointed out to him a statue of a youth with a woodpecker on its head set in a sacred shrine, and Macareus had asked for an explanation for this strange cult artifact:

"cum duce namque meo Circe dum sola moratur,
illa mihi niveo factum de marmore signum
ostendit iuvenale gerens in vertice picum,
aede sacra positum multisque insigne coronis.
quis foret et quare sacra coleretur in aede,
cur hanc ferret avem, quaerenti et scire volenti

---

46. While the narrative is most obviously here following that of the *Odyssey*, Circe is, of course, also mentioned briefly at the beginning of *Aen.* 7 and this is where the Ovidian "*Aeneid*" has actually reached at this point in the narrative.

47. Achaemenides in the *Aeneid* had warned the Trojans away from Circe (*Aen.* 3.639–40), a maneuver that signals, as Stephen Hinds has suggested to me, Vergil's avoidance of this metamorphic scene.

> 'accipe' ait, 'Macareu, dominaeque potentia quae sit
> hinc quoque disce meae; tu dictis adice mentem!"

(14.312–19)

In the description of this narrative situation, we note immediately many sim-
ilarities with the aetiological frames discussed in the previous chapter. The
maidservant is called a *dux* (312), which reminds us of the guide in Book 6,
who was similarly asked to describe an altar (*dux meus* 6.328).[48] She is an
appropriately knowledgeable authority on local Italian tradition. The statue is a
cult statue (315): it is covered with garlands and placed in a shrine. Ovid
depicts Macareus as the same sort of eager questioner about the cult statue of
Picus as we saw in Callimachus' persona in the *Aetia* and Ovid's in the *Fasti*.
Moreover, Macareus' questions about the strange attributes of this statue seem
especially interesting, in light of the prominence of statues' descriptions in
Callimachus' *Aetia*. Many of the *aetia* in Callimachus' poem concern the
unusual attributes of certain cult statues, as at *Aet.* 1 fr. 31b-e Pf. (Add., vol. II,
pp. 108ff.), where an explanation is given of why a particular statue of Artemis
in Leukas has a mortar on its head.[49] There was, furthermore, discussion of the
statues of the Graces on Paros at the beginning of the poem (*Aet.* 1 fr. 7.11–
12),[50] a statue of Athena with a wound in her thigh (*SH* 276 + fr. 667 Pf.),[51] a
bronze statue of Euthycles, the Olympic victor from Locri (*Aet.* 3 frr. 84–85),
two statues of Hera at *Aet.* 4 frr. 100 and 101, and a speaking statue of Delian
Apollo at *Aet.* fr. 114.4–17.[52] The *Fasti* also contain frequent discussion of the
attributes of certain cult statues, such as those of Janus (1.133ff. *causam . . .
figurae*), Vediovis (3.429–44), and Cybele (4.219–20).[53]

The manner of Circe's servant's reply to Macareus' questioning also under-
lines the aetiological nature of the inset narrative. The imperatives she opens
with, *accipe, disce,* and *tu dictis adice mentem,* are, as we have seen, regular
features of the didactic language Ovid uses in the *Fasti*. We might compare her

---

48. In the *Fasti* also, when he is questioning Erato as to the rites of Cybele, Ovid addresses her
as *dux operis* (4.247).

49. The lemma provided by the *Diegeseis* for this *aetion* seems to show that here again
Callimachus is questioning one of the Muses: *Aet.* fr. 31b.1.

50. Pfeiffer thinks that *Aet.* 1 fr. 7.8 might refer to the Graces at Cyrene.

51. A.S. Hollis, "Teuthis and Callimachus, *Aetia* Book 1," *CQ* 76 n.s. 32 (1982): 117–20, has
argued convincingly that this fragment should be placed in *Aetia* 1, perhaps after the similar *aetion*
of Leukadian Diana (fr. 31, b-e).

52. *Aet.* fr. 114.1–3 may refer to another statue of Apollo; the statue of Delian Apollo will be
discussed in detail below, p. 120. The *Iambi* also contain statue *aetia;* see *Iamb.* 7, fr. 197 (Hermes
Perpheraios), *Iamb.* 9, fr. 199 (Ithyphallic Herm).

53. Other statues in the *Fasti* include the Lares 5.129–42, the statues in the Temple of Mars
Ultor 5.551–68, and a strangely shrouded statue standing in Servius Tullius' Temple to Fortuna at
6.569–624.

command to pay attention with Janus' similar injunction to Ovid in the *Fasti: voces percipe mente meas* (1.102, cf. Lucr. 2.1080: *inice mentem*). J.F. Miller has noted that Calliope's response to Callimachus at *Aet.* fr. 7.24 may have provided a model for Ovid: "π]ρῶτ[ον ἐνὶ μ]νήμῃ κάτθεο."[54] The imperative *accipe* with this association also occurs in two other places in the *Metamorphoses,* both of which have been discussed as framed aetiological narratives: at 4.794, where Perseus explains the reason for Medusa's snakes (*accipe quaesiti causam*); and at 7.758, where Cephalus, again in answer to a direct question, begins to explain the origin of his miraculous spear (*accipe mirandum*). All three of these scenes draw attention to the affiliations of the epic with Callimachean aetiological narrative by means of setting up a narrative situation typical of such a work.

The story that Circe's maidservant tells Macareus involves two aetiological metamorphoses, those of Picus and of Canens. The narrative has now in a sense returned to the *Aeneid* framework. From the introduction of Picus at 14.320–21 (*Picus in Ausoniis, proles Saturnia, terris / rex fuit*) to the list of Italian rivers at 14.328–32, Ovid is careful to mention the local Italian setting of this episode.[55] The story of Picus' transformation is briefly touched upon by Vergil at *Aeneid* 7.189–91:[56]

Picus, equum domitor, quem capta cupidine coniunx
aurea percussum virga versumque venenis
fecit avem Circe sparsitque coloribus alas.

In the *Aeneid* Circe is in fact the grandmother of Latinus, Picus' wife (*coniunx* 7.189).[57] The idea of a statue of Picus seems also to have been suggested by the wooden statue Vergil describes here as standing amidst the other statues of Latinus' ancestors (*veterum effigies ex ordine avorum / antiqua e cedro* 7.177–

54. Miller, "Callimachus and the Augustan Aetiological Elegy," 413 n.158. Cf. *Fasti* 3.177–78 (Mars): "*disce, . . . / et memori pectore dicta nota.*"

55. Fränkel, *Poet between Two Worlds,* 103.

56. T. S. MacKay, "Three Poets Observe Picus," *AJP* 96 (1975): 274–75, points out that Picus is turned into "no woodpecker Ovid ever saw in the oaks of Italy, or anywhere else in his world," and suggests that the coloring and markings (14. 393–96) may have been inspired by the augural *trabea* (Servius *ad Aen.* 7.612 *augurale de purpura et cocco*).

57. Servius *ad Aen.* 7.190 claimed that *coniunx* here meant *non quae erat sed quae esse cupiebat.* C.J. Fordyce, ed., *P. Vergili Maronis Aeneidos Libri VII–VIII* (Oxford, 1977), *ad loc.,* argues that there is no occurrence of this meaning of "intending bride." The problems are discussed by R. Morton, "The Genealogy of Latinus in Vergil's *Aeneid,*" *TAPA* 118 (1988): 253–59. Most later versions also call Circe Picus' wife: Val. Flacc. 7.232 (*coniunx*), Plut. *Q.R.* 21.268F (Sil. Ital. 8.439 mentions only Picus' metamorphosis).

78) in the forecourt of the ancient palace of Laurentine Picus; there is no mention of a bird on his head:[58]

> ipse Quirinali lituo parvaque sedebat
> succinctus trabea laevaque ancile gerebat.

(*Aen.* 7.187–88)

The triangular love story in *Metamorphoses* 14 between Circe, Picus, and Canens seems to be an Ovidian innovation; Canens, like Macareus, is not attested before Ovid. Indeed, at Servius *ad Aen.* 7.190 we find the surprising claim that Pomona was Picus' wife: *Fabula autem talis est. Picum amavit Pomona, pomorum dea, et eius volentis est sortita coniugium. postea Circe, cum eum amaret et sperneretur, irata eum in avem, picum Martium, convertit.* Pomona will figure importantly in the next love story of *Met.* 14, and it is interesting to consider that Ovid has perhaps there devised for her a novel setting and here invented a character to replace her. We should note that Aemilius Macer in his *Ornithogonia* mentioned Picus' transformation (*et nunc agrestis inter Picumnus habetur,* fr. 1, p. 107 Morel; p. 138 Buechner), but we know nothing about his version. Thematically this episode is clearly linked to the two preceding love triangles of Galatea-Acis-Polyphemus and Scylla-Glaucus-Circe in Books 13 and 14, where, again, the third party angle seems to have been added by Ovid.

Ovid's new character, Canens, deserves attention. Circe's attendant obligingly provides the etymological explanation for her name:

> "rara quidem facie, sed rarior arte canendi,
> unde Canens dicta est: silvas et saxa movere
> et mulcere feras et flumina longa morari
> ore suo volucresque vagas retinere solebat."

(14.337–40)

---

58. Bömer, *Met.*, *ad* 14.313, suggests that Ovid's statue may have as its model a statue of M. Valerius Corvus (cos. 301) set up by Augustus in the porticus of the temple of Mars Ultor: *in eius statuae capite corvi simulacrum est* (Gell. 9.11.10). Haupt-Ehwald, *ad* 313, however, are probably wrong in suggesting that the statues of the temple of Mars Ultor may explain why Ovid's statue is anachronistically made of marble, whereas primitive Italian statues were traditionally, as in the *Aeneid* above, made of wood (cf. *Met.* 10.694, Tib.1.10.19–20, 2.5.28, Prop. 4.2.59–60). According-ing to Platner-Ashby (s.v. *Forum Augustum*) all ancient sources record that the statues were made of bronze, not marble, with the exception only of *Hist.Aug.Alex.Sev.* 28.6. Commentators such as Fordyce, *ad Aen.* 7.170ff., are probably right to see a connection between the statues in Picus' Palace and those of kings and heroes (Appian *B.C.* 1.16, Pliny *Nat.* 34.22–23, Suet. *Cal.* 34) set up in the Capitoline Temple (Platner-Ashby, s.v. *Area Capitolina*). There were also at least two stories told of the landing of a woodpecker on the head of a Roman statesman: P. Aelius Paetus in Varro *De Vita Pop. Rom.* (Non. p. 518M) and Aelius Tubero in Pliny *Nat.* 10.41.

She is also provided with a proper Italian genealogy, *ille colit nymphen, quam quondam in colle Palati / dicitur ancipiti peperisse Venilia Iano* (14.333–34).[59] The nymph's abilities of song are really quite remarkable, being those usually reserved for famous bards such as Orpheus (*Met.* 11.1ff.) and Arion (*Fasti* 2.84ff.). Why is this invented figure endowed with such great power? On the one hand, her magical poetic abilities parallel the malevolent powers of Circe's magic, and indeed prove to be more effective in love than magic, which in Circe's case had proven twice to be ineffective.[60] On the other hand, we suspect that her powers suggest, as does the etymological blatancy of her name, that Canens is an aetiological invention. We learn at the end of the story what Ovid intended by his introduction of this name. Circe's attendant ends her story with Canens' metamorphosis into water, accompanied by an aetion:[61]

"luctibus extremum tenues liquefacta medullas
tabuit inque leves paulatim evanuit auras,
fama tamen signata loco est, quem rite Canentem
nomine de nymphae veteres dixere Camenae."

(432–34)

She provides an *aetion* for a place called Canens after the nymph, but we have no evidence of such an actual place in Italy. The words *fama* and *veteres*, traditional auctorial signals for the authenticity or antiquity of a story, are here humorously used to "validate" Ovid's own invented story.[62] However, the

---

59. The text here is disputed. I have adopted that of Goold. Bömer and Anderson print *Ionio* (FNPh edd. pler.) for *ancipiti* (EN²UWp Lafaye) admitting that other suggestions are understandable. The etymology is, of course, not beyond Ovid's wit, but in the *Fasti* there is no mention of the god's Greek origin (*Fasti* 1.90: *nam tibi par nullum Graecia numen habet*) and at *Fasti* 1.95 we read *ancipiti mirandus imagine Janus*. Bömer admits that Janus' Greek origin seems to be a tradition only attested later (Plut. *Q.R.* 22 [*Mor.* 269A], where Plutarch's Greek bias clearly influences his description of Janus as the Greek civilizer of the rustic Italians). In the *Aeneid* 10.76, Venilia is the mother of Turnus and in Varro *L.L.* 5.72 she is mentioned in connection with Neptune (also Serv. Auct. *ad Aen.* 10.76) and seems to be a water nymph. Janus is also associated with water as the father of Fons and Tiberinus; see Porte, *L'Étiologie Religieuse dans les Fastes,* 172. Schmitzer, *Zeitgeschichte in Ovids Metamorphosen,* 108–33, discusses Canens' genealogy in the light of his political interpretation of this episode.

60. Fränkel, *Poet between Two Worlds,* 104, considers this passage in relation to Ovid's amatory works: "In his theory of love, the poet had emphatically declared that magic has no place in love, and that no witchcraft can force the beloved to return the affection, (*Ars* 2.99–104)." Cf. *Am.* 3.7.27ff.; *Her.* 12.165ff.; 6.93–94.

61. Haupt-Ehwald, *ad* 14.434: "ganz in alexandrinischer Weise."

62. Also *dicitur* above at 14.334. See Stinton, "Expressions of Disbelief," 63, for similar examples.

presence of the ancient Latin Muses, *veteres Camenae,*[63] suggests that the place referred to is actually the sacred grove and spring Numa is said to have dedicated to the Camenae near the Porta Capena.[64] The Camenae were originally water nymphs, and their fountain was clearly the most important feature of their grove in Rome.[65] It seems not too bold to suggest that Canens herself may be meant to provide the *aetion* for this very spring[66] and, by association, for the Camenae themselves.[67]

Varro connected the verb *canere* with the name Camena (Varro *L.L.* 6.75: *canere, accanit et succanit ut canto et cantatio ex Camena permutato pro M N*).[68] Not only does Canens share her etymology and watery nature with the Camenae, but the description of her amazing powers in song suggests that we are to make the association.[69] We should consider, as well, her singularly poetic liquefaction:

> "illic cum lacrimis ipso modulata dolore
> verba sono tenui maerens fundebat, ut olim
> carmina iam moriens canit exequalia cycnus."

$$(14.428-30)$$

The association of the poet with a swan is a traditional one,[70] and when Canens dies, like the swan, singing (*modulata,* cf. 341), her literary association with

---

63. Here again the text is disputed and instead of *Camenae* (M), Anderson prints *coloni* (*c(oloni in ras.)* N². Bömer and Haupt-Ehwald both print *Camenae* and offer no comment.

64. Livy 1.21.3, Plut. *Numa* 13. For the location of the spring and grove see Platner-Ashby (s.v. *Camenae*). The poet Lucius Accius set up a tall statue of himself *in Camenarum aede* (Pliny *Nat.* 34.19).

65. *RE* 3.1 (1897): 1427–28 Aust; Roscher s.v. Camenae (Wissowa); Radke, *Die Götter Altitaliens,* 78–79. For the fountain: Plut. *Numa* 4; Frontin. 1.4; Vitruv. 8.3.1.

66. Otis, *Ovid as an Epic Poet,* 289.

67. This must be by suggestion only, for the derivation of the name of the Camenae from a so-called spring is not attested in ancient sources. See below for the etymology. It is only in the light of Canens' connections with the Camenae that we might possibly want to admit for her a dual Latin and Greek heritage (cf. *Fasti* 4.245: *talibus Aoniae facunda voce Camenae*).

68. Also *L.L.* 7.26 and 7.27, see W. Pfaffel, *Quartus gradus etymologiae: Untersuchungen zur Etymologie Varros in De Lingua Latina* (Königstein, 1981), 151–54. Cf. Serv. *Ecl.* 3.59 (*Camenae musae, quibus a cantu nomen est inditum*) and Festus p. 38 Lindsay. Actually, the name of the Camenae was probably Etruscan, since the goddesses were Etruscan in origin.

69. So Bömer, *Met., ad* 14.433–34.

70. For references see Nisbet and Hubbard, *ad* Hor. *Odes* 2.20 (pp. 333–34); *TLL* 4.1585.16ff. *cycnus; TLL* 9.2.572.15ff. *olor;* D.W. Thompson, *A Glossary of Greek Birds* (London, 1936), s.v. *kuknos.* Cf. Isidor. 12.7.18: *Cygnus autem a canendo est appellatus, eo quod carminis dulcedinem modulatis vocibus fundit.* For further discussion of swans and poetry in Ovid see Hinds, *Metamorphosis of Persephone,* 44–48, and Keith, *Play of Fictions,* 137–46.

the Italian Muses of poetry seems to be implied.[71] Nymphs are prominent in the final two books of the *Metamorphoses* and serve as programmatic introductions to Ovid's new Italian material.[72]

The connection of Canens with the ancient Italian Muses seems very appropriate here in the context of the first story of the poem set in the ancient Italian past.[73] Adopted by the earliest Latin poets, Livius Andronicus and Naevius, the Camenae had become the counterparts of the Greek Muses, but had then been exiled by the Alexandrian Ennius, who preferred the Greek *Musae*.[74] They became, however, important figures in Augustan poetry. The Camenae reappear in Vergil *Ecl.* 3.59 (the only place Vergil mentions them), but it is in Horace's *Odes* that their former importance is reasserted.[75] D.O. Ross, who offers the most sensitive discussion of this "significant new stage" of their importance, especially to Horace, explains this development in a way that seems relevant to Ovid's poetry as well:

> The Camenae made their triumphant return to Rome precisely because they alone could represent for Horace the confluence of the various sources and purposes of his poetry. They are natively Italian and go back to the beginnings of Latin poetry . . . they could, as well, represent the Hellenization of the old Roman traditions by the simple assumption of a slight change of costume—or (what is almost but not quite the same thing) they could represent the Hellenistic tradition made Italian.[76]

Ovid mentions the Camenae in the *Metamorphoses* and the *Fasti,* preferring the Greek Muses in his amatory poetry.[77] In the *Metamorphoses* they are only mentioned in Books 14 and 15, both times in association with their grove, here

---

71. Keith, *Play of Fictions,* 137, concludes that an "examination of the occurrences of the swan's song in the Ovidian corpus suggests in each case the subtle evocation of song of a literary nature." Note that the description of Canens' voice, *sono tenui* (14.429), echoes the earlier metamorphosis of Cycnus in Book 2 (*vox est tenuata* 2.373)—one might be tempted to conjecture that Canens is to be understood as a poet with Alexandrian sympathies.

72. As E. Fantham observes, "Nymphas . . . *E Navibus Esse:* Decorum and Poetic Fiction in *Aen.* 9.77–122 and 10.215–59," *CP* 85 (1990): 116–17. Italian nymphs (14.512–26), Trojan ships turn into nymphs (14.530–65), Pomona (14.623–771), nymphs at Janus' shrine (14.785–99), Egeria (15.482–551).

73. Nagle, "A Trio of Love-Triangles," 89.

74. Ennius *Ann.* 1 Sk., on which see O. Skutsch, *Studia Enniana* (London, 1968), 18ff.

75. The Camenae appear significantly once in each book of *Odes* 1–3: 1.12.39, 2.16.38, 3.4.21, and 4.6.27, 4.9.8. Ross, *Backgrounds to Augustan Poetry,* 147 n.2, notes that between Ennius and Vergil's *Ecl.* 3.59 the Camenae are mentioned only by Lucilius (1028 Marx).

76. Ross, *Backgrounds to Augustan Poetry,* 149.

77. The Muses appear in the *Metamorphoses* and the *Fasti* as well: *Met.* 5.294, 5.337, 10.148, 15.622; *Fasti* 1.660, 2.359, 4.83, (also Pierides, *Fasti* 2.269, 6.798, 799).

and at 15.482.[78] Ovid hereby underlines the arrival of his poem in Italy by adumbrating the *aetion* for the Italian Muses, and he acknowledges as well the affiliations of his poem with earlier Latin poets who treated these Italian themes.

It is a statue of Picus—not, say, a woodpecker—which motivates the narration of the story of Picus, Canens, and Circe. Thus Macareus' question concerning this cult object has the effect of underlining the aetiological focus of the story, since it sets up a narrative situation similar to those in the *Aetia* and the *Fasti,* in which inset narrators frequently explain the features of statues. Macareus' story of Picus and Canens involves two Italian *aetia,* both of them religious: for the statue of Picus (and indirectly for the minor Italian deity Picus Martius) and for the *locus Canens,* an unknown place meant perhaps to evoke the *aetion* for the Camenae and their sacred spring and grove in Rome. Picus was honored in Italy as an ancient king and in the form of a woodpecker.[79] Plutarch in his *Quaestiones Romanae* 268 E-269 A explains that the Latins revered the woodpecker because it was traditionally thought to give oracles and prophecies,[80] and because it played a role in aiding Romulus and Remus, and was therefore sacred to Mars.[81] In the *Fasti* Ovid tells a story of Picus' and Faunus' (*Romani numen utrumque soli* 3.292, *di . . . agrestes* 3.315) involvement with Numa in the reception of the *ancilia* from Jupiter Elicius (3.259–392, cf. Plut. *Num.* 15). In the *Metamorphoses* there is no mention of Picus' augural abilities or of the significance of the woodpecker.

Macareus ends with the *aetion* of Canens (14.434) and with a reminder that he has been retelling the story as narrated to him by Circe's *famula: Talia multa mihi longum narrata per annum / visaque sunt* (14.435–36). This episode is characterized, as are many of the other stories within the *Aeneid* framework, by a complex allusiveness to non-epic and Alexandrian models, which contrasts stylistically with the first Homeric tale narrated by Macareus. With this first Italian episode, Ovid programmatically marks the tone and themes for the

---

78. The Camenae also appear only twice in the *Fasti:* at 3.275 (associated with Egeria as at *Met.* 15.482) and at 4.245 where the muse Erato is intriguingly called Camena: *talibus Aoniae facunda voce Camenae.* Cf. *Pont.* 4.13.33.

79. For more on this deity see G. Radke, *Die Götter Altitaliens* (Münster, 1965), 255; A.H. Krappe, "Picus Who is Also Zeus," *Mnemosyne* 9 (1941): 241–57; Courtney, *Fragmentary Latin Poets,* 293. J.G. Frazer, ed., *The Fasti of Ovid III* (London, 1929), 10, offers interesting suggestions about the possible development of the story.

80. For the role of the woodpecker in augury see Pliny *Nat.* 10.40–41; Dion. Hal. *Ant. Rom.* 1.14.5; Serv. *Aen.* 7.190. On Aemilius Macer's version, Dahlmann, *Über Aemilius Macer,* 7, remarks that it is likely that the connection of Picus with augury was featured.

81. Thus Picus Martius, Serv. *Aen.* 7.190, Non. p. 518M = Fabius Pictor *Rerum Gest.* 1; Pliny *Nat.* 10.40; Plut. *Rom.* 4.

following Italian stories. For we find in Books 14 and 15 of the *Metamorphoses* that almost all of the ensuing Italian stories involve *aetia* of a religious nature, either of deities or of sacred sites.

The primary narrative returns to the events of the *Aeneid* 7 at *Met.* 14.441. It will not take more than the next 131 lines to encompass the events covered by the second half of the *Aeneid,* and the apotheosis of Aeneas concludes the section (*Met.* 14.581–608). The narrative then embarks into the mainstream of ancient Roman legendary history with the traditional list of Alban kings (609–22).[82] The list is interrupted at the reign of Proca (14.623), and, with the story of Vertumnus and Pomona, the narrative returns to the more obscure realm of Italian myth. The transition to the story in the middle of the list of kings is amusingly abrupt: *iamque Palatinae summam Proca gentis habebat / rege sub hoc Pomona fuit* (14.622–23).[83] The tale of Pomona and Vertumnus, the next main Italian metamorphosis story in this book, offers many obvious parallels to the story of Picus and Canens. Both episodes treat native Italian deities paired in novel amatory contexts, both episodes explain the origins of a statue and of a sacred grove, and both involve internal narrators. This latter episode follows immediately the conclusion of the "*Aeneid*" section of the *Metamorphoses* and provides a link with this section of the poem in its similarity to the amatory and aetiological episodes inserted there.

Pomona and Vertumnus (*Met.* 14.623–771)

The story of Pomona and Vertumnus is the last of the many amatory episodes of the *Metamorphoses.* Poised as it is immediately after the section of the poem that deals with the events of Vergil's *Aeneid* and before the reintroduction of cosmogonic themes of Pythagoras' speech in Book 15, the tale invites com-

---

82. Ovid gives essentially the same list at *Fasti* 4.39–56. (Cf. Dion. Hal. *Ant. Rom.* 1.70ff., *Aen.* 6.756ff., Livy 1.3.1ff., Diod. 7.5.1ff., Dio fr. 4, Appian 1.1.2). Interestingly, the differences between Ovid's two lists, Capetus (*Met.* 14.613) = Calpetus (*Fasti* 4.46) and Acrota (*Met.* 14.617) = Agrippa (*Fasti* 4.49), seem to suggest that in the *Metamorphoses* Ovid has chosen the older and more obscure version. Acrota is attested only here (Bömer, *Met., ad loc.,* notes that the reading is supported by *Mythogr. Vat.* 1.204.20). Ogilvie, *Commentary on Livy Books I–V, ad* Livy 1.3.9, argues that Acrota is likely to have been the original name, which was then rationalized to Agrippa (perhaps out of compliment to Augustus' general). Capetus occurs only in Livy and Appian, and Calpetus probably was a later change, as Ogilvie remarks, "to provide a pedigree for the Calpurnii." Thus it seems that in keeping with the national character of the *Fasti,* Ovid has chosen to include there a more "patriotic" king list than the one here in the *Metamorphoses* (note also the change of Ascanius [*Met.* 14.610] to Iulus in *Fasti* 4.39–40). See Ogilvie, *Commentary on Livy Books I–V,* 43–45 and Frazer, *The Fasti of Ovid III,* 172ff.

83. We know very little about Proca. While he may have simply liked the alliteration in these lines, Ovid may also have chosen this king precisely because he was so obscure.

parison with the episode of Daphne and Apollo in Book 1, which first intro-
duced erotic and Alexandrian themes into the poem after the initial cosmogony.
The story of Vertumnus and Pomona not only inverts the amatory norms
established by the first love story but contains a number of parallels and echoes
of this story that suggest it performs a similarly programmatic function in
highlighting themes that are important in the remainder of the poem: Italian
and Roman religious and topographical *aetia*.[84]

Vertumnus and Pomona are both associated with the distant Italian mythical
past.[85] They are paired nowhere else, but their similar rustic associations make
them an ideal couple. Their love story here once again seems original to Ovid
and is made more complex by the inclusion of a Greek aetiological inset
narrative. About Pomona we know very little, and as we can see from Varro,
(quoted below), it seems little was known about her even in Ovid's time.[86] We
can, unfortunately, do little with the intriguing statement of Servius (mentioned
above at p. 108),[87] which makes her the wife of Picus, since no other source
reflects this tradition. She is introduced, as was Canens, with an etymological
explanation for her name:[88]

> Rege sub hoc Pomona fuit, qua nulla Latinas
> inter hamadryadas coluit sollertius hortos
> nec fuit arborei studiosior altera fetus;
> unde tenet nomen: non silvas illa nec amnes,
> rus amat et ramos felicia poma ferentes.

> (14.623–27)

Varro (*L.L.* 7.45) quotes three lines from Ennius' *Annales* (116–18 Sk.) listing
six of the lesser-known *flamines* instituted by Numa, *sunt in quibus flaminum
cognominibus latent origines, ut in his qui sunt versibus plerique . . . quae
o⟨b⟩scura sunt,* among which is listed the *Pomonalis.* Varro explains that the
origo for this name is Pomona, but he tells us nothing else. Besides having her
own Flamen, the goddess Pomona seems to have had her own sanctuary (Fest.

---

84. Davis, *Death of Procris,* 67: "[a] carefully constructed narrative (whose purpose is retro-
spective and summational as that of Apollo-Daphne is prospective)." See K.S. Myers, "*Ultimus
Ardor*: Pomona and Vertumnus in Ovid's *Met.* 14.623–771," *CJ* (1994): 225–50, for a more ex-
tensive discussion of this episode and its relation to the first amatory episode of Daphne and Apollo.

85. On the episode see, C. Fantazzi, "The Revindication of Roman Myth in the Pomona-
Vertumnus Tale," in *Acta Ovidianum,* ed. N. Barbu, E. Dobroiu, M. Nasta (Bucharest, 1976), 288.

86. See for Pomona *RE* 21.2 (1952), *s.v. Pomona* (W. Ehlers), 1876–78; Radke, *Die Götter
Altitaliens,* 257–58; K. Latte, *Römische Religionsgeschichte* (Munich, 1960), 74.

87. We are of course also in the dark as to Aemilius Macer's version.

88. Cf. Serv. *Aen.* 7.190 *pomorum dea,* Fest. p. 144, 13 L. *praesidet pomis.*

p. 296, 15ff. L. *in agro Solonio via Ostiensi ad duodecimum lapidem deverticulo a miliario octavo),* which most agree was probably a grove, and a festival that was not included in the calendar because it was a wandering one.[89] Her association with a sacred grove is suggested by Ovid's description of her walled-in garden.[90] Although scholars have suggested that the popularity of the goddess revived under Augustus, there is no real evidence for this,[91] despite her suitability to Augustan propaganda promoting "The Imagery of Fertility and Abundance."[92] Besides the intriguing mention in Ennius, Ovid's passage is her earliest appearance in any sources.[93] It seems likely that Ovid discovered this old Italian goddess in his researches into ancient Italian legend for the *Fasti.*[94]

Pomona, like Canens and so many other heroines in the *Metamorphoses,* is a nymph, *hamadryas* (624),[95] but she is Latin (623). The juxtaposition of the two terms, *hamadryas* and *Latina,* is amusingly contradictory; like Ovid's poetry, Pomona is a blend of the Greek and Roman. Hamadryads are rare in Latin poetry, and their appearance has been observed to be confined to passages that seem to refer to the amatory poetry of Gallus: Vergil *Ecl.* 10.62, Prop. 1.20.32, 2.32.37, 2.34.76, and *Culex* 95.[96] Their literary genealogy, as I have suggested elsewhere, may be traced ultimately back to the poetry of

89. For *Feriae Conceptivae,* see Bömer, *Fasti I,* 37 (cf. *Fasti* 1.657–704, 2.512–532).

90. See Ahl's appealing suggestion, *Metaformations,* 316, that in line 635, *pomaria claudit,* "Ovid is obviously punning here on the Roman term for city limit" (cf. Varro *L.L.* 5.143 *Pomerium*).

91. Ehlers, *RE* 21.2, 1877; Radke, *Die Götter Altitaliens,* 257. There is an inscription from Dalmatia (*CIL* 3 Suppl. 12732) mentioning a *flamen Pomaonalis* in association with the name C. Iulius Silvanus Melanio, *procurator Augusti,* but the date is uncertain (see *RE* 10.1 (1917) 823.34–48 Stein). There is also an inscription (*CIL* 10 531 = Dessau 3593) from the first century C.E., which mentions a male god Pomo, and a Puemonus is mentioned in the Iguvine Tablets III–IV (see *RE* XXIII.1948–49, Suppl. IX.1814 [Radke]), who is connected by Radke, 268, with Pomona (as perhaps part of a male / female deity pair), and by W.W. Fowler, *The Roman Festivals of the Period of the Republic* (London, 1908), 201 n.8, with Vertumnus.

92. As outlined by P. Zanker, *The Power of Images in the Age of Augustus* (Ann Arbor, 1988), chap. 5, 172–79.

93. She is found later in Calpurnius Siculus 2.33, Martial 1.49.8, and Pliny *Nat.* 23.1ff. (on which see T. Köves-Zulauf, "Plinius und die Römische Religion," *ANRW* 2.16.1 [1978]: 249).

94. In Ennius' list of flamines in *Annales* 116–18 Sk. the Floralis is mentioned along with the Pomonalis, and in *Fasti* 5.183–378 Ovid included Flora's festival, the Floralia.

95. *TLL* 6.2520.73 *proprie i.q. nympha arboris, fere i. q. "dryas."* Serv. *Ecl.* 10.62: *nymphae, quae cum arboribus et nascuntur et pereunt.*

96. D.F. Kennedy, "Gallus and the *Culex,*" *CQ* n.s. 32 (1982): 377–82, suggests that hamadryads be seen as Gallus' surrogate Muses of rural and amatory poetry; while Ross argued earlier, *Backgrounds to Augustan Poetry,* 95 n.4, that they may "stand for scientific or abstract mythological poetry" as written by Gallus.

Callimachus and Catullus.[97] The tradition evoked is an Alexandrian and neo-teric one associated with nonheroic poetry, ranging from erotic lyric and elegy, to pastoral epic, and learned aetiological poetry. It is worth observing that the only other appearance of *hamadryas* in the *Metamorphoses* is to describe Syrinx at *Met.* 1.690, in a passage that, as we have seen, is suggestive of poetics and the pastoral tradition.[98] The poetic associations of hamadryads may be relevant to Pomona's name and her erotic and orchard setting. Especially so if Propertius' description of the pastoral landscape in 1.20.33–38, with its men-tion of apple trees, is meant to recall Gallus' Grynean grove, with whose *aetion* Gallus is associated in Vergil's sixth *Eclogue*.[99] We observe that Pomona's garden is emphatically *cultus* (624–25, 656), and the technical language of her gardening skills (*nec fuit arborei studiosior altera fetus* 625) playfully suggests that she perhaps has read the *Georgics*.[100]

The usual nymph of this sort, however, was not associated with a garden but rather with the woods (Serv. *Ecl.* 10.62). G. Davis has pointed out that Pomona's occupation is described in contrast with hunting: *non silvas illa nec amnes, / rus amat et ramos felicia poma ferentes / nec iaculo gravis est, sed adunca dextera falce*(14.626–28).[101] This is a clue, as Davis has shown, that she will not follow the pattern of the huntress-determined-virgin type (such as Daphne or Syrinx) whom she seems at first to resemble in her rejection of amatory advances:

---

97. See Myers, "Ultimus Ardor," 230–33. The passages are Hesiod *Th.* 187, Callimachus *Hymn to Delos* 79–85, Apollonius *Argon.* 2.477, Catullus 61.23.

98. See pages 77–79. *Fasti* 2.155 is Ovid's only other use of the term *hamadryad,* here used to describe Callisto, another Callimachean nymph. We might also keep in mind Daphne's association with her tree.

99. Ross, *Backgrounds to Augustan Poetry,* 79–80. Recall in this connection that there was a version of the story in which Apollo raped the Amazon Gryne in this grove (Serv. Auct. *ad Aen.* 4.345). A reference to Gallus finds a parallel in the earlier tale of Daphne and Apollo, where the appearance of the *medicina* motif (*Met.* 1.521–24) has been convincingly seen to function as an allusion to Gallus' love poetry; see H. Tränkle, *Die Sprachkunst des Properz und die Tradition der lateinischen Dichtersprache,* Hermes Einzelschriften 15 (Wiesbaden, 1960), 22–23; Knox, *Traditions of Augustan Poetry,* 15–17.

100. See Bömer, *ad locc.,* for detailed linguistic correspondences between the *Georgics* and this episode. For similar associations of the term *cultus* with georgic imagery see *Med. Fac.* 1ff. and *Ars* 3.101–2. Other gardens in the *Metamorphoses* called *cultus* are that of the Lyceum at *Met.* 2.710, and the garden from which Persephone is abducted at *Met.* 5.535. The verbatim reminis-cence from Vergil's *Aeneid* 11.739 at line 634: *hic amor, hoc studium,* at first strikes a discordant note until we recall that the context of this expression in the *Aeneid* is amatory as well: the Etruscan leader Tarchon urges on his men by chiding them for being too fond of *nocturna bella.*

101. Davis, *Death of Procris,* 68. Compare Ovid's description of Diana: *silvarum latebris captivarumque ferarum / exuviis gaudens innuptaeque aemula Phoebes* (*Met.* 1.475–76).

hic amor, hoc studium, Veneris quoque nulla cupido est;
vim tamen agrestum metuens pomaria claudit
intus et accessus prohibet refugitque viriles.

(14.634–36)

The association of the garden as a sexual term, (κῆπος or *hortus* = *culus*)
contributes to the erotic coloring of the landscape.[102] The sexual innuendoes of
this georgic imagery will become more explicit when Vertumnus enters the
scene.[103] Pomona's garden is, we discover, surrounded by the potential sexual
violence (635 *vim agrestum*) always present in the landscape of the *Meta-
morphoses*. She is beset by a wild and unsuitable group of suitors, Pan, Satyrs,
Silvanus, and Priapus (cf. 1.692–93), but will prove susceptible finally to
Vertumnus, her male counterpart.

Vertumnus was an Italian deity who seems to have been well-known in
Rome mainly because of a bronze statue of him that stood behind the temple of
Castor in the Vicus Tuscus.[104] The frequent references to this statue in Latin
literature show it was a landmark of sorts in the city.[105] Varro (*L.L.* 5.46)
explains that Vertumnus' statue stood in the Vicus Tuscus because *is deus
Etruriae princeps.*[106] Vertumnus also had a temple on the Aventine (Fest. 228

---

102. J.N. Adams, *The Latin Sexual Vocabulary* (London, 1982), 84. We find gardens used in
this way frequently in the *Priapea*, e.g., *Priap.* 5.3–4, for garden and orchard settings (*pomaria*),
e.g., 15, 38, 71, 72. C.P. Segal, *Landscape in Ovid's Metamorphoses* (Wiesbaden, 1969), 68–69,
discusses the garden as a symbol of both virginity and the sensual realm. H. Parry, "Ovid's
Metamorphoses: Violence in a Pastoral Landscape," *TAPA* 95 (1964): 276, has shown that virginal
settings in the *Metamorphoses* often "portend and prefigure" deeds of violence.

103. Cf., e.g., 14.657 *pomaque mirata est,* 688 *primus habet laetaque tenet tua munera dextra.*
For similar use of gardening and georgic imagery for courtship and sex, see *Ars* 1.757ff., 2.320ff.,
513, 649–52 (grafting), 3.576 (*poma*); *Her.* 4.29–30 (*pomaria*).

104. A pedestal possibly still *in situ* when it was discovered near the spot in 1549 (but since
lost) bore the inscription (*CIL* 6.1.804 = Dessau 3588): *Vortumnus temporibus Diocletiani et
Maximiani.* This statue was probably a restoration. See Platner-Ashby, s.v. *Signum Vortumni;*
Eisenhut *RE* 2.6.1669–88. M.C.J. Putnam, "The Shrine of Vortumnus," *AJA* 71 (1967): 177–79,
reviews the literary and epigraphical evidence for the placement of the statue and supports Platner-
Ashby in situating it at the borderline between the edge of the Forum Romanum and the Velabrum.

105. The Vicus Tuscus entered the Sacra Via between the Temple of Castor and the Basilica
Julia. It connected the Forum Romanum with the Forum Boarium and must have been one of
Rome's busiest streets. Cf. Livy 44.16.10, Cic. *Verr.* 2.1.54 (with ps. Ascon. comm.), Hor. *Epist.*
1.20.1 (with Porph. comm.).

106. On Vertumnus in general see Eisenhut *RE* 2.6. 1669–88; Radke, *Die Götter Altitaliens,*
317–20; D.P. Harmon, "Religion in the Latin Elegists," *ANRW* 2.16.3 (1986): 1959–65; E. Simon,
Die Götter der Römer (Munich, 1990), 111–12. On his Etruscan origins, see E.C. Marquis,
"Vertumnus in Propertius 4.2," *Hermes* 102 (1974): 491–500, and L.R. Taylor, *Local Cults in
Etruria,* Papers and Monographs of the American Academy in Rome 2 (Rome, 1923), 152–53.

L.)[107] and a state cult associated with the date 13 August.[108] Propertius in the fourth book of his elegies devoted a whole poem to this statue (4.2), in which the best exposition of the origins and nature of Vertumnus is given by the statue itself:

> Quid mirare meas tot in uno corpore formas ?
> accipe Vertumni signa paterna dei.
> Tuscus ego ⟨et⟩ Tuscis orior, nec paenitet inter
> proelia Volsinios deseruisse focos.

> (Prop. 4.2.1–4)

Vertumnus' statue explains that three etymologies[109] have been suggested for his name: (1) from his turning back of the flood waters of the Tiber (4.2.10 *Vertumnus* verso *dicor ab* amne *deus*), (2) from the offerings of the first-fruits of the "turning" year (4.2.11 *quia* vertentis *fructum praecepimus* anni), and (3) from his ability to turn himself into many forms (4.2.47–48 *at mihi, quod formas* unus vertebar *in* omnes / *nomen ab eventu patria lingua dedit*). The god insists the last etymology is correct: *de se narranti tu modo crede deo* (4.2.20).[110]

At *Fasti* 6.395–416 Ovid recalls meeting and talking to an old woman in the Velabrum, who points to Vertumnus' statue and gives the etymology Vertumnus himself rejected in Propertius 4.2: *nondum conveniens diversis iste figuris / nomen ab averso ceperat amne deus* (409–10). Her reliability as an informant on scholarly matters of Roman religion is perhaps hereby brought into question.[111] In the *Metamorphoses,* not surprisingly, it is the god's ability

---

107. In the Vicus Loreti Maioris, containing within a painting of M. Fulvius Flaccus celebrating his triumph over the Volsinians in 264 B.C.E. (Fest. 228L); Platner-Ashby s.v. *Vortumnus, Aedes.*

108. Fasti Amiternini (*CIL* 1² p. 324, Degrassi XIII, 25); Allifani (*CIL* 1² p. 299, Degrassi XIII, 24; Vallenses (*CIL* 1² p. 320, Degrassi XIII,18) *ad* Id. Aug. (13th, Id. Sext.).

109. L. Richardson, Jr., ed., *Propertius Elegies 1–4* (Oklahoma, 1977), *ad* 4.2.11–12, notes that there may have been a fourth etymology between lines 10 and 11 containing the derivation of the name from the exchange of goods in the adjacent *fora* (*ex mercibus vertendis*); cf. ps. Ascon. *Verr.* 2 (p. 199 Orr, Colum. *Rust.* 10.308ff., Porph. *ad* Hor. *Epist.* 1.20.1. G.P. Goold, "*Noctes Propertianae,*" *HSCP* 71 (1966): 95, is inclined to accept Paley's emendation in line 10 of *Vertumnus* to *Vertamnus* and in line 12 *Vertumni* to *Vertanni,* thereby making the etymologies explicit.

110. On the god as the best authority on himself see Call. *Aet.* fr. 114.5 Apollo "ναὶ, μὰ τὸν αὐτὸν ἐμέ," and *Fasti* 5.191–92 hominum sententia fallax / optima tu proprii nominis auctor eris, cf. 5.449–50 *accipe causam / nominis: ex ipso est cognita causa deo.*

111. Newlands, "Ovid's Narrator in the *Fasti,*" 40–41, discusses the old woman's questionable etymology.

to change his form that is exploited. While in Propertius' poem Vertumnus, in his humorously garrulous fashion, describes seventeen of the various forms he has taken, in Ovid Vertumnus changes only eight times.[112] Ovid has contrived the perfect motivation for Vertumnus' transformations, that is, to gain access to Pomona:

> denique per multas aditum sibi saepe figuras
> repperit, ut caperet spectatae gaudia formae.
>
> (14.652–53)

Vertumnus adopts four of the guises described in Propertius' poem: a reaper (*messor* 14.643–44 = 4.2.28), a mower (14.645–46 = 4.2.25–26), a soldier (*miles* 14.651 = 4.2.27), and a fisherman (*piscator* 14.651 = 4.2.37). Later, while pleading his own case in the guise of an old woman, he will also opportunistically point out that he is, in fact, very similar to Pomona (cf. Prop. 4.2.41–46, 11–18):

> "quid, quod amatis idem, quod, quae tibi poma coluntur,
> primus habet laetaque tenet tua munera dextra."
>
> (14.687–88)

Ovid recalls Propertius' poem through numerous echoes in the lines describing Vertumnus' transformations (14.643–55).[113] These allusions to Propertius 4.2 function in such a way as to suggest that we compare the two poems intertextually.

Propertius 4.2 occupies in the fourth book of elegies a privileged position as the first poem after the ambiguously programmatic introductory poem 4.1, where Propertius first announces his intentions to apply the technique of Callimachean aetiology to Roman themes, only to seemingly reject them later in the same poem. Propertius 4.2 thoroughly fulfills the expectations of Italian aetiological narrative announced by the newly declared Callimachus Romanus in 4.1.64–69 and seems to function as a second program for the content of the

---

112. Two other passages suggest that Vertumnus was associated with these character changes: (Tibullus) 3.8.13, Hor. *Sat.* 2.7.14.

113. Prop. 4.2.28 *corbis in imposito pondere messor eram, Met.*14.644 *corbe tulit veriqué fuit messoris imago* (Bömer, *Met., ad loc.,* points out that *corbis* occurs only in these two passages in classical Latin poetry; otherwise, Varro *R.R.* 1.22.1, 1.50.2, *L.L.* 5.135; Cato *Agr.* 136); 4.2.25–26 *da falcem et torto frontem mihi comprime faeno: / iurabis nostra gramina secta manu,* 14.645–46 *tempora saepe gerens faeno religata recenti / desectum poterat gramen versasse videri;* 4.2.26 *iurabis* = 14.648 *iurares;* 4.2.25 *da falcem* = 14.649 *falce data;* cf. also 4.2.21–22, 47 and 14.684–85.

fourth book.[114] A number of scholars have discussed the clear relationship of Propertius 4.2 to the unplaced Callimachean fragment 114 from the *Aetia,* where a statue of Delian Apollo explains his appearance and attributes to a questioning interlocutor.[115] Pfeiffer remarks that: "From the point of literary history we have to notice that we have for the first time the Greek model followed by Ovid in his *Fasti.*"[116] In the *Fasti* a number of deities answer questions about their own representations and attributes in statue form (e.g., Janus 1.133f *causam . . . figurae,* Vediovis 3.429–44, and Cybele 4.219–20), as Apollo does in the *Aetia.* It has also been pointed out that Propertius' poem resembles a common situation in the short poems concerned with the god Priapus, in which a statue of the god converses with a passerby, usually explaining its own attributes. This is not the only way in which Vertumnus shares Priapic associations.[117]

There is no question, I believe, but that Ovid means us to recall this earlier appearance of Vertumnus as both a statue and an aetiological internal narrator in Propertius' poem. It is thus very interesting to consider that in Ovid's episode Vertumnus, in order to win over Pomona, chooses to tell her an admonitory tale, the obscure Cypriot story of Iphis and the hard-hearted Salaminian princess Anaxarete, which provides the *aetion* for a cult statue of Aphrodite in Salamis (14.698–764). Ovid means us to recognize the appropriateness of the appearance of this particular character, a statue in Propertius' aetiological

---

114. For convincing arguments for viewing 4.2 as programmatic see M. Wyke, "The Elegiac Woman at Rome," *PCPS* 33 (1987): 153–78, and C. Shea, "The Vertumnus Elegy and Propertius Book IV," *ICS* 13 (1988): 63–71.

115. R. Pfeiffer, "The Image of Delian Apollo and Apolline Ethics," *JWI* 25 (1952): 20–32; Pillinger, "Some Callimachean Influences on Propertius," 178–81; Miller, "Callimachus and the Augustan Aetiological Elegy," 389–92. See also P. Pinotti, "Properzio e Vertumno: Anticonformismo e Restaurazione Augustea," in *Colloquium Propertianum (Tertium),* ed. S. Vivona (Assisi, 1983), 75–96. See further, on speaking statues in poetry, R. Kassel, "Dialogue mit Statuen," *ZPE* 51 (1983): 1–12. For various speaking monuments or dialogue epigrams of the sepulchral or dedicatory type see *A.P.* 6 (dedicatory epigrams, e.g., 49, 113, 114, 127, 159, 224, 245, etc.), *A.P.* 7 (sepulchral epigrams, e.g., 37, 62, 64, 79, 161, 163–65, etc.); Call. *Ep.* 5, 13, 21, 24. On some of the conventional epigrammatic motifs in Propertius 4.2, see T.A. Suits, "The Vertumnus Elegy of Propertius," *TAPA* 100 (1969): 475–86.

116. Pfeiffer, "Delian Apollo and Apolline Ethics," 27.

117. Suits, "The Vertumnus Elegy of Propertius," 477, with further parallels; also Richardson, *Propertius Elegies, ad* 4.2.59. In *Iamb.* 7 a Herm explains how he earned the cult title Hermes Perpheraios and includes mention of the artist who made him (as does Vertumnus 4.2.59–64). *Iamb.* 9 opens with a question in which a Herm is asked the reason for his ithyphallic condition. Tibullus 1.4 and Hor. *Sat.* 1.8 also contain speaking statues of Priapus. On the similarities between Vertumnus and Priapus, see [Vergil] *Cat.* 1–3, *Priap.* 16, 21, 42, 53; Roscher *Lex.* 6 (1965) 220 (Wissowa). Both Pomona (14.628) and Vertumnus (14.649, Prop. 4.2.25) have a *falx,* a common attribute of Priapus, e.g., *Priap.* 6.2, 11.2, Tib. 1.4.8, Vergil *Geo.* 4.109–11.

elegy 4.2, as a narrator in the *Metamorphoses* of an aetiological tale about a statue. To this end also he includes the battle between Romulus and Titus Tatius at *Met.*14.799–804 as related at Propertius 4.2.51–52. The allusions should be understood as a further acknowledgment of the importance of Propertius' Fourth Book as a model for Ovid's own treatment of the Italian themes. By recalling the literary genealogy of Vertumnus, Ovid again places his poem firmly within the Callimachean aetiological tradition.

Vertumnus, disguised as an old woman,[118] and amusingly referring to himself throughout the speech in the third person,[119] tries to convince Pomona of the advantages of a union with himself and brings forward the admonitory example of Iphis and Anaxarete to illustrate what happens to women who do not submit to love:

"ultoresque deos et pectora dura perosam
Idalien memoremque time Rhamnusidis iram !
quoque magis timeas, (etenim mihi multa vetustas
scire dedit) referam tota notissima Cypro
facta, quibus flecti facile et mitescere possis."

(14.693–97)

The Vergilian echo in *memorem . . . Rhamnusidis iram* (694) bestows upon Vertumnus' introduction a solemn tone, which soon gives way to a stylistic register closer to amatory poetry.[120] We should recall the similarly Vergilian motivation of the erotic story of Daphne and Apollo: *saeva Cupidinis ira* (1.453). Like Apollo in Book 1, Vertumnus plays the role of elegiac suitor in a dramatic situation resembling an amatory paraclausithyron (*pomaria claudit* 14.635). His embedded narrative will be an explicit paraclausithyron. We note in the passage above that Vertumnus exploits the age and authority of his old woman disguise (*vetustas*) to strengthen the authoritative narrative force of his *exemplum*. His insistence on the notoriety of the story about to be told (*notissima*) functions similarly, although the story seems to be anything but

---

118. Hints of Vertumnus' transvestism appear already in Propertius 4.2.23: *indue me Cois, fiam non dura puella.* See Harmon,"Religion in the Latin Elegists," 1961–63, on the possibility that, like Pomona, there were both male and female (or bisexual?) versions of this divinity.

119. See Doblhofer, "Ovidius Urbanus," 89–90 (Ichspaltung); von Albrecht, *Die Parenthese,* 418. Examples include Acoetes, 3.572ff., Jupiter 2.428–30, Neptune 2.575–76.

120. The passage, as in many amatory episodes in the poem, contains many erotic and elegiac words. The simile at 663–65 is reminiscent of Catullus' epithalamia 61.102–6 and 62.49–55. Note also the nuptial language of *socia* (662), *caelebs* (663), *nupta* (666, this word [Heinsius] is not accepted by Anderson, who prints *iuncta* [A]).

common.[121] Ovid alerts us to Vertumnus' use of narrative as stratagem.[122] The contrast between this rustic Italian narrator and his obscure and learned Cypriot narrative is as humorous here as in the similarly religious-aetiological episode of the Lydian cowherd in Book 6 (which, like this episode in Book 14, recalls a poem from Propertius Book 4).

We find a version of the story Vertumnus tells in Antoninus Liberalis 39, which is attributed to Hermesianax's *Leontion* Book Two (fr. 4 Powell, pp. 96–97), where, surprisingly, the religious *aetion* for the statue is missing.[123] As Antoninus retells it, Hermesianax's story was set within an historical framework and told of the love of the young man Arkeophon for Arsinoe, the daughter of King Nicocreon, who succeeded to the throne of Salamis in 332/1 B.C.E. (Diod. Sic. 19.79.5). In Vertumnus' story the "heroine," Anaxarete (Arsinoe) is also specified as being of the royal Salaminian family: *a veteris generosam sanguine Teucri* (14.698). In Hermesianax, Arkeophon is carefully described as being of humble birth, but nevertheless wealthy (39.1). Vertumnus, however, only wants to emphasize Iphis' lowly state in contrast to that of the princess, *humili de stirpe creatus* (14.699). A.L. 39 makes it clear from the outset that Hermesianax's story had a social bias; Arkeophon falls in love with Arsinoe but is further incited to marriage with her because of her impressive lineage (39.2). Arsinoe's father, however, does not approve of the marriage because Arkeophon's family hailed originally from Phoenicia (39.2). Vertumnus is not concerned with such details. He is interested only in representing this as a love story and in manipulating his narrative in such a way as to gain as much sympathy as possible for the unlucky lover Iphis (and for himself).

The short description in A.L. 39 of Arkeophon's vigil at Arsinoe's door and his imprecations to her nurse (39.3) are elaborated by Vertumnus into a full

---

121. Cf. other internal narrators' attempts to gain credibility: *Met.* 2.570 (the crow is speaking) *nota loquor,* 2.591 *res est notissima; Met.* 6.26–44 (Athena, also disguised as an old woman, is speaking to Arachne) *seris venit usus ab annis* (6.29).

122. See Ahl, *Metaformations,* 202–4, on the importance of considering the intentions of Ovid's internal narrators.

123. Papathomopoulos *ad* A.L. 39n.3 (p. 159) remarks that both the *aetion* and a reference to Nicander as a source were perhaps omitted by Antoninus. Most of the summaries, however, do contain such *aetia.* He conjectures, *ad* A.L. 39 n.13, that a Hellenistic love story had been invented to explain this statue; see also Forbes Irving, *Metamorphosis in Greek Myths,* 285. Haupt-Ehwald, *ad* 14.698ff., note that the aetiological character of the tale suggests a possible source in Philostephanus Cyrenaeus, a student of Callimachus (Athen. 331D). A section of his geographical work entitled Περὶ Νήσων (*FHG* 3 pp. 30ff.) dealt with stories about Cyprus (*FHG* 3 frr. 10–14). For Philostephanus see Fraser, *Ptolemaic Alexandria,* 522–24, 778, and Gisenger *RE* 20.1.104–18. Fraser (523) suggests that Philostephanus may have derived much of his material from Callimachus' Κτίσεις νήσων καὶ πόλεων καὶ μετονομασίαι (*Suda*).

scale description of the paraclausithyron that forms the bulk of his narrative. Most of the elements of this traditional amatory genre are present:[124] the suppliant (*supplex ad limina venit* 702), the nurse (*et modo nutrici miserum confessus amorem* 703), the tablets, the tear-bedewed garlands, and the sleeping on the hard threshold:

> "saepe ferenda dedit blandis sua verba tabellis,
> interdum madidas lacrimarum rore coronas
> postibus intendit posuitque in limine duro
> molle latus tristisque serae convicia fecit."

$$(14.707-10)$$

Anaxarete is depicted in the role of the *puella dura* of Roman elegy (e.g., Tib. 1.1.64, Prop. 1.7.6, Ovid *Am.* 1.9.19), and Vertumnus takes great care to underline the appropriateness of her transformation into stone: *paulatimque occupat artus, / quod fuit in duro iam pridem pectore, saxum* (14.757–58). In none of the many other love stories of the *Metamorphoses* does the unrelenting heroine meet with such a grim punishment; metamorphosis is usually "granted" as a means of escape (e.g., Daphne 1.452–567, Syrinx 1.689–712, Arethusa 5.572–641). Vertumnus underlines the moral lesson of this metamorphosis, a maneuver unusual in the rest of the *Metamorphoses,* in order to gain his desired effect of frightening Pomona with the prospect of the vengeance of Venus: *quoque magis timeas* (14.693–95).[125] Iphis finally despairs of his vigil, and, unlike Arkeophon in Hermesianax who starves himself to death (39.5), he hangs himself in the traditional lovers' manner of suicide.[126]

Vertumnus finally ends his narrative with the new and thematically important *aetion* for the statue of *Venus Prospiciens:*

> "neve ea ficta putes, dominae sub imagine signum
> servat adhuc Salamis, Veneris quoque nomine templum

---

124. See the classic study by F.O. Copley, *Exclusus Amator: A Study in Latin Love Poetry,* APA Monographs no. 17 (Madison, 1956).

125. The transformation of the Propoetides, the first prostitutes, into stone is described in a similarly moralizing manner in Orpheus' biased narration: *in rigidum parvo silicem discrimine versae* (*Met.* 10.242). See B.R. Nagle, "Byblis and Myrrha: Two Incest Narratives in the *Metamorphoses,*" *CJ* 78 (1983): 301–15, for an illuminating comparison of a primary narrative tale with a similar secondary (embedded) narrative.

126. On this motif see G. Lucke, *P. Ovidius Naso Remedia Amoris, Kommentar zu Vers 397–814* (Bonn, 1982), *ad* 603ff.; Bömer, *Met., ad* 14.735–36. Cf. Myrrha *Met.* 10.378ff.; Byblis *Ars* 1.284, Parthenius 11. Pseudo-Theocr. *Idyll* 23 also contains interesting parallels with our passaage, on which see Copley, *Exclusus Amator,* 138–39.

Prospicientis habet.—quorum memor, o mea, lentos
pone, precor, fastus et amanti iungere, nymphe."

(14.759–62)

In Antoninus, Aphrodite merely turns Arsinoe into stone (A.L. 39.6). The
statue referred to in Ovid seems to be that of a well-known Cypriot cult-
representation of Venus, called the Ἀφροδίτη Παρακύπτουσα.[127] While the
dramatic motivation for the *aetion* is Vertumnus' concern to prove the truth of
his story in order to frighten Pomona—*neve ea ficta putes* (759); we observe
again the utilization of an *aetion* as a strategy of narrative verification—at the
same time Ovid's insertion of a statue *aetion* in the narrative functions as a
clear allusion to Propertius' poem 4.2, another aetiological poem about a
statue—that of Vertumnus himself.

Although Vertumnus' tale has no effect on his listener, Pomona (14.765
nequiquam),[128] in a surprising reversal of expectations, just as Vertumnus
prepares to resort to rape (cf. *Met.* 5.288 *vimque parat*) Pomona succumbs to
his desires when he finally sheds the last of his disguises:

vimque parat: sed vi non est opus, inque figura
capta dei nympha est et mutua vulnera sensit.

(14.770–71)

The earlier hints of Pomona's difference from other determined virgins in the
poem seem confirmed and the final love story of the poem is ended on this

---

127. W. Fauth in his monograph on this representation of Venus, *Aphrodite Parakyptusa:
Untersuchungen zum Erscheinungsbild der vorderasiatischen Dea Prospiciens,* Abhandlungen
der Geistes und Sozial wissenschaftlichen Klasse Nr. 6 (Mainz. Wiesbaden, 1966), attempts to
reconcile the literary sources (which are only Ovid, A.L. 39, and Plut. *Amat.* 21[*Mor.* 766C-D])
with the archaeological evidence. He concludes that the only cultic-religious facts we can assume
are that (a) in Salamis on Cyprus there was a sanctuary to Aphrodite Παρακύπτουσα (Venus
Prospiciens) up to the time of the Caesars, and (b) that the cultic epithet must indicate a unique
characteristic of the Salaminian Aphrodite (338–39). See also A. Borghini, "Riflessioni An-
thropologiche sopra Mito di Probizione: La ragazza alla finestra (Ovidio *Met.* 14.795–861 e
Antonio Liberale *Met.* 39)" *MD* 2 (1979): 137–61.

128. From the earlier examples of warning narratives in the *Metamorphoses*, we might suspect
that Vertumnus' tale will not have the desired effect. We can compare Polyphemus' song at *Met.*
13.789–870 (with Galatea's withering comment: *Talia nequiquam questus* 13.870) and Apollo in
Book 1; cf. cornix 2.550ff., Neptune 2.574–76, Acoetes 3.564–672, Venus 10.552ff.. For the
theme of the failure of love poetry see Tib. 2.4.13, 2.5.11–112; Prop. 2.1.1–16, 2.30.40; Ovid *Am.*
1.3.19, 2.17.33, 3.12.15; Mart. 8.73.3. See also J. Fabre, "L'Etre et les Figures: Une réflexion sur le
récit dans le récit chez Ovide (*Met.* 14.622–771)," *LALIES* 6 (1987): 167–73, on this episode and
Fredericks [Nagle], "Divine Wit vs. Divine Folly," on Apollo.

theme of mutual attraction. Vertumnus, the god whose name is a sort of ety-mological play on the subject of the poem as a whole, only wins his love when he casts off his disguises and stands as himself. His special ability of self-transformation is no more aid to him in his amatory suit than was Circe's magic in hers.[129] Before resting too comfortably with a seemingly happy ending to this episode,[130] we should note that the description of Vertumnus in lines 765–71 is very similar to that of Sol in Book 4, where Sol, also after having disguised himself as an old woman,[131] enters Leucothoe's apartments and reveals his true form to the girl who, out of terror, endures his assault and is, as a result, later killed: *in veram rediit speciem solitumque nitorem; / at virgo quamvis inopino territa visu / victa nitore dei posita vim passa querella est* (4.231–33). The comparison of Vertumnus with the sun (14.765–69) encourages us to remember the earlier story.[132]

The first amatory tale in the *Metamorphoses*, that of Apollo and Daphne (*primus amor* 1.452) programmatically introduced the erotic as a major theme in the poem. The story of Vertumnus and Pomona, the final erotic tale in the poem (14.682–83 *tu primus et ultimus illi / ardor eris*) reverses with its "happy" ending the amatory norm introduced by the first amatory episode. Along with its secondary narrative, the scene functions in a summational manner to reaffirm the affiliation of the *Metamorphoses* with poetry in the amatory neoteric tradition as the poem turns to the weightier national and cosmogonic themes in the final book. The association of Vertumnus, and perhaps Pomona, with actual religious landmarks in the city of Rome also, however, effects a transition from the themes of early Latin legend to Rome. Programatically the story prepares for Ovid's predominantly Callimachean treatment of Roman themes in the final books of the poem, where the stories

---

129. No other transformers in the *Metamorphoses* reap any benefits from their abilities: see Mestra (8.725–884), Achelous (9.1–97), Thetis (11.221–65), Periclymene (12.536–79), Anius' daughters (13.632–74).

130. A. Richlin, "Reading Ovid's Rapes," in *Pornography and Representation in Greece and Rome,* ed. A. Richlin (New York, 1992), 169, notes that in Ovid's scenes of transvestism, "gender revelation equals penetration." Among other critics who have detected uncomfortable undertones in this ending, see Parry, "Violence in a Pastoral Landscape," 275 n.10. L.C. Curran, "Rape and Rape Victims in the *Metamorphoses,*" in *Women in the Ancient World,* ed. J. Peradotto and J.P. Sullivan (Albany, 1984), 278, wrongly warns against imputing to Ovid "that favorite modern [?] male fantasy, the reluctant virgin who learns during or after rape that she actually enjoys it in spite of herself," but cf. *Ars* 1.673ff.: *vim licet appeles: grata est vis ista puellis* (673).

131. This amatory ploy is also used by Jove, 2.425–33, and Phoebus, 11.310. Compare especially the threatening kisses of both Vertumnus (14.658–59) and Jove (2.430–32).

132. Parry, "Violence in a Pastoral Landscape," 277, comments on the fact that in the *Metamorphoses* "the sun frequently is suggestive of danger."

from Italian legend Ovid chooses to present are almost all of a religious-aetiological nature.[133]

Although the ending of the episode of Vertumnus and Pomona has been seen to herald the generally upward tendency of Ovid's Italian metamorphoses, which consist mostly of apotheoses from the end of Book 14 until the end of the poem,[134] the evocation of the world of elegy, defined so often by contrast with conventional Roman *mores,* militates against this interpretation, as does the tragic nature of the embedded tale of Iphis and Anaxarete. Setting aside the disputed question of Propertius' Augustan sympathies in his Roman elegies, it is difficult to believe that the motivation for the choice of the obscure Vertumnus in either Propertius or Ovid will have been to accommodate Augustan concerns.[135] Not only his obscurity but his rather improper Priapic associations would seem to exclude Vertumnus. Thus, it does seem significant that this irreverent amatory tale in Book 14 about minor Italian deities (and a Cypriot cult) should be so emphatically placed between the apotheoses of Aeneas (14.581–608) and Romulus and Hersilia (805–51) and right before the series of apotheoses that follow in the next book. Franz Bömer (*ad loc.*) is, for example, troubled by the fact that the Vertumnus tale occupies 150 lines, making it one of the longer episodes in the poem, in contrast to the following story of Romulus with only 80 lines. Thematically and generically, the Vertumnus-Pomona story, with its erotic content, relegates the surrounding apotheoses in Books 14 to a nonhierarchical position in the poem and does not allow the patriotic Augustan themes to overwhelm the narrative.[136] It is understandable that Ovid, as he approached the Augustan conclusion of the *Metamorphoses,* would be especially concerned to display his freedom to treat his mythological material in a wholly original manner. It might, in fact, be argued that one of Ovid's goals in this poem was to show that Greek and Roman

---

133. Lafaye, *Les Métamorphoses d'Ovide,* 234–35. See also M.G. Di Geronimo, *Ovidio tra Pitagorismo. Aition ed Encomio* (Naples and Florence, 1972), and Knox, *Traditions of Augustan Poetry,* 65–83.

134. D. Porte, "L'idée romaine et la métamorphose," in *Journées Ovidiennes de Parméne: Actes du Colloque sur Ovide,* ed. J.M. Frécault and D. Porte (Brussels, 1985), 188, 190; see also Barkan, *The Gods Made Flesh,* 81–82; Fantham, "Decorum and Poetic Fiction," 118.

135. See H.P. Stahl, *Propertius: Love and War. Individual and State Under Augustus* (Berkeley, 1985), 248–305, for an illuminating discussion of Propertius Book 4 and a summary of earlier scholarship. Pinotti, "Properzio e Vertumno," interprets Propertius 4.2 as part of an Augustan program of restoration and religious and political conciliation.

136. D.A. Little, "The Non-Augustanism of Ovid's *Metamorphoses,*" *Mnemosyne* 25 (1972): 399.

mythology were still fields fully open to innovation and invention even after Vergil's codification of the Roman myth in the *Aeneid*.[137]

When Ovid approaches Italian themes in the *Metamorphoses* he is, of course, entering the poetic territory of the *Fasti*. It is interesting that his manner of presentation becomes even more overtly aetiological in this part of his epic than elsewhere and that internal narrators, an integral part of the narrative structure of the *Fasti*, proliferate.[138] In light of this interpretation of the Vertumnus and Pomona episode as summational and programmatic, it is worth considering briefly a number of congruences in subject matter between the beginnings and endings of the *Fasti* and *Metamorphoses*.[139] We have seen that Vertumnus puts in an oblique appearance in *Fasti* 6.395–416 in a markedly Callimachean scene, and Aesculapius and Virbius also appear in *Metamorphoses* 15.497–546 and *Fasti* 6.733–62, where there are a number of very close verbal echoes.[140] Interestingly, the amatory episode of Janus and Carna (6.101–68) is connected with the lifetime of the otherwise completely obscure king Proca, as is that of Vertumnus and Pomona.

Janus' programmatic importance in the *Fasti* is established in Book 1 where he appears as Ovid's first interlocutor (*inque meo primum carmine Ianus adest* 64) in a manner very similar to that of Vertumnus in Propertius 4.2 and their common model in Callimachus fr. 114.[141] Connections between Janus and

---

137. Lateiner, "Mythic and Non-Mythic Artists," 3, speaks of Ovid's "attempt to rescue myth from the bear-hug of Augustus."

138. Observe that of the roughly thirty-five embedded narratives in the *Metamorphoses* spoken by internal narrators, twelve occur in the two final books.

139. A. Barchiesi, "Discordant Muses," *PCPS* 37 (1991): 6, 19 n.12, suggests that closural signals be sought in *Fasti* 6, while E. Fantham, "The Role of Evander in the *Fasti*," *Arethusa* 25 (1992): 155–70, has offered convincing evidence of Ovid's remodeling of *Fasti* 1 and 6; cf. E. Courtney, "Ovidian and non-Ovidian *Heroides*," *BICS* 12 (1965): 63–66.

140. Compare *Met.* 15.506 (*curru Troezena petebam*) and *Fasti* 6.739 (*iuvenis Troezena petebat*), 15.524 (*excutior curru, lorisque tenentibus artus*) and 6.743 (*exciderat curru lorisque morantibus artus*). Observe that mention is made of Galatea, an important character in *Met.* 13.738–899, at the beginning of the *Fasti* version at 6.733–34. There may be a witty programmatic cross-reference in Virbius' words to Egeria at *Met.* 15.497 to the *Fasti* version: *fando aliquem Hippolytum vestras si contigit aures.* For other such references between the two poems, see *Fasti* 4.418 *plura recognosces* (the two Rapes of Persephone; see Hinds, *Metamorphosis of Persephone,* 40); *Met.* 9.346: *ut referunt tardi nunc denique agrestes* (Lotis, cf. *Fasti* 1.415–40); *Fasti* 3.723–24: *ecce libet subitos pisces Tyrrhenaque monstra / dicere, sed non est carminis huius opus* (cf. *Met.* 3.597–691); and see Barchiesi, "Discordant Muses," 6, on the appearance of *tempora* in *Met.* 1.4 and *Fasti* 1.1. Other parallels between *Met.* 14–15 and the *Fasti* include Picus, Numa, Virbius, and Egeria (*Fasti* 3.259–60), and the apotheosis of Romulus (*Fasti* 2.481–512). See Heinze's discussion, *Ovids elegische Erzählung,* 35–41.

141. On Janus see Miller, "Ovid's Divine Interlocutors in the *Fasti*," 164–74, and P. Hardie, "The Janus Episode in Ovid's *Fasti*," *MD* 26 (1991): 47–64.

Vertumnus include their mutable natures (*Fasti* 1.65, 89, 95) and their involvement with the changing of the year (*Fasti* 1.65).[142] Horace in his *Epistles* 1.20.1 mentions Vertumnus and Janus together as inhibitors of the rather disreputable booksellers district. Janus also explains his origins, biform nature, and the attributes of his statue representation. He narrates the story of Tarpeia and the war with the Sabines, along with the flooding of the gates of Janus (*Fasti* 1.257–76), events also appearing immediately after the episode of Pomona and Vertumnus in *Metamorphoses* 14.775–804. At the end of Janus' disquisition we learn, as A. Barchiesi has pointed out, that on the first day of the official calendar the establishment of the cult of Aesculapius at Rome was celebrated (*Fasti* 1.289–94), while the *aetion* of this cult is explained at *Met.* 15.626–744.[143] Janus typically faces in both directions. His cosmogony (*Fasti* 1.103ff.) is "an outline in miniature of the plan of the epic, *prima . . . ab origine mundi / ad mea . . . tempora*," and thus looks forward to the opening and closing of *Metamorphoses*.[144] The connections between Janus and Vertumnus suggest again that Vertumnus stands poised at an important point at which Ovid wished once again to underline the connections between his two aetiological efforts, the *Metamorphoses* and the *Fasti*.

Metamorphoses 14 ends with an unusual degree of finality in the catasterism of Hersilia, prefiguring the similar fate of Julius Caesar at the end of Book 15.[145] In this final book the apotheoses continue with those of Hippolytus/Virbius, Aesculapius, and, of course, the Caesars. The stories of Egeria and Virbius in *Met.* 15 obviously follow in this religious-aetiological pattern. Egeria, like Canens, provides the *aetion* for a sacred stream (*rivus*), hers in the famous grove of Diana Nemorensis in Aricia (*Met.* 15.547–51).[146] Egeria, originally a fountain nymph, was elsewhere connected with the worship of the Camenae at their fountain near the Porta Capena.[147] The story of Virbius is

---

142. As Barchiesi, "Discordant Muses," 16, observes.

143. Barchiesi, "Discordant Muses," 6, where he also points out that *tempora* is the first word of the *Fasti;* cf. Hardie, *Epic Successors,* 13. For more parallels between *Met.* 15 and *Fasti* 1, see Bömer, "Über das zeitliche Verhältnis zwischen den Fasten und den Metamorphosen," 218–19.

144. Hardie, "The Janus Episode," 52.

145. Knox, *Traditions of Augustan Poetry,* 76, observes that Ovid's lines describing Caesar's deification contain a clear verbal echo of Catullus' translation of Callimachus' *Coma Berenices* (66. 64: *sidus . . . novum*) and Ovid's use of the word *comans* (15.749) recalls the catasterism of the lock in the *Aetia* as well. Hersilia's deification may recall the same model, *Met.* 14.848: *Hersilie crinis cum sidere cessit in auras,* cf. Catullus 66.39: *tuo de vertice cessi.*

146. *Fasti* 3.261ff; Strab. 5.240; for the connection with Aricia, cf. Vergil *Aen.* 7.763ff.

147. *Fasti* 3.275: *dea grata Camenis*; Dion. Hal. *Ant. Rom.* 2.60: τῶν Μουσῶν μίαν. (The Camenae were *not* traditionally associated with the cult at Aricia, *pace* Knox, *Traditions of Augustan Poetry,* 74.) See also Platner-Ashby, sv. *Camenae (vallis Egeriae)*; Juv. 3.17. For the

found first in Vergil (*Aen.* 7.761–82), where Servius (*ad* 7.778) comments: *exponit* τὸ αἴτιον. *nam Callimachus scripsit* Αἴτια, *in quibus etiam hoc commemorat* (fr. 190 Pf).[148] It is uncertain whether, as Knox suggests, "the association would be recognized, as Servius' note indicates, as a Callimachean touch."[149] The story was clearly invented at some point to explain the exclusion of horses from Diana's grove at Aricia, *hic latet Hippolytus loris direptus equorum / unde nemus nullis illud aditur equis* (*Fasti* 3.265–66), and hinges on Virbius' etymologically suggestive name.[150]

Two miraculous stories serve to introduce the next main episode, that of Cipus. The strange story of Tages, briefly related at *Met.*15.552–59, explains the remarkable birth from the earth of the first Etruscan *vates: indigenae dixere Tagen, qui primus Etruscam / edocuit gentem casus aperire futuros* (15.558–59).[151] As the founder of this Etruscan practice of divination, Tages has an obvious place in this series of religious aetiologies and inventors. Next, the origin of a cornel tree on the Palatine, which was sacred to Romulus and was still extant in Ovid's day, is explained at 15.560–64.[152] The longer and more complex episode of Cipus follows these at 15.565–621. This story involves an aetiological explanation for the presence of two horns depicted on the Porta Raudusculana, a gate in the wall of Servius Tullius at the eastern part of the

tradition that Numa consulted Egeria and the Muses at their fountain by the Porta Capena, see Livy 1.21.3, Juv. 3.11ff., "Sulpicia" *Sat.* 67–68, Plut. *Numa* 13.2. Skutsch, *Annals of Q. Ennius, ad Ann.* 113 (the opening of *Annales* 2), suggests that here Egeria spoke with Numa at the Roman site.

148. Pfeiffer, *ad loc.,* comments: *veri non dissimile est.* Cf. Schol. (G) Ov. *Ib.* 279: *tangit fabulam de Hippolyto: unde Callimachus.* Ovid also relates Virbius' story in the *Fasti* 6.741–56. The story is otherwise mentioned only in Hor. *Odes* 4.7.25–26; Stat. *Silv.* 3.1.55–57. See also Hollis, "Hellenistic Colouring in Virgil's *Aeneid,*" 276.

149. Knox, *Traditions of Augustan Poetry,* 74. Fraser, *Ptolemaic Alexandria,* 768, expresses uncertainty, but raises the possibility that Timaeus might have been Callimachus' source. Varro's antiquarian studies, as Bömer has suggested, *Met., ad* 15.492–546, are a likely source for both Vergil and Ovid. Varro, as we have seen (Call. fr. 189), made use of Callimachus.

150. Porte, *L'Étiologie Religieuse dans les Fastes,* 403: "C'est le besoin étiologique qui a créé la légende. . . . A pu jouer également une bizarrerie étymologique, l'analyse du nom Virbius comme condensant un *vir bis vivus* à tous égards remarquable, entraînant le rapprochement explicatif de cet 'homme deux fois rendu à la vie' avec le héros Hippolyte, ressucité par Artémis." Cf. Haupt-Ehwald, *ad* 542: "Der μετονομασία scheint eine griechische Namensform für Virbius zugrunde zu liegen (cf. Cassiod. *Gr.L.* 7.181 K). Aus dieser etymologischen Spielerei ('Ἱππό-λυτος, Ἡρώ-βιος) wie sie die alexandrinische Poesie liebte, erklärt sich die, durch mythologische Beziehung nicht begründete, Gleichsetzung." See also Radke *RE* IXA.1 (1961) 178–82, and *idem, Die Götter Altitaliens,* s.v. *Virbius.*

151. Lucan 1.636–37 *conditor artis . . . Tages.* The story is also related by Cicero at *Div.* 2.50 and emphatically rejected as absurd at *Div.* 2.51.

152. Plut. *Rom.* 20.4–6 tells us that the tree was located by the *casa Romuli,* near the descent into the Circus Maximus from the Palatine, and that it was walled in and worshiped up to the time of Gaius Caesar, at which time it was inadvertently destroyed.

Aventine in Rome: *cornuaque aeratis miram referentia formam / postibus insculpunt, longum mansura per aevum* (15.620–21).[153]

The Cipus episode and that of Aesculapius that follows are relevant to the political interpretation of Book 15 and of the *Metamorphoses* as a whole.[154] The story of Aesculapius (15.622–744), describing the god's arrival in Rome from Epidaurus and the establishment of his temple and cult on the Tiber island, is introduced in a familiar aetiological manner: *unde Coroniden circumflua Thybridis alti / insula Romuleae sacris adiecerit urbis* (15.624–25). The episode also recalls the statue themes of the previous book by means of a dream scene in which Aesculapius, *qualis in aede / esse solet* (15.654–55), speaks to a Roman envoy. Aesculapius' acceptance at Rome is directly connected by Ovid with the deification of Caesar: *Hic tamen accessit delubris advena nostris: / Caesar in urbe sua deus est* (15.745–46).[155] This episode and that of Cipus are the only two stories from the period of the Roman Republic. While there is no room in this study to deal in any depth with the question of the political interpretation of the *Metamorphoses* in its Augustan context, this question cannot be brushed off with claims that Ovid was indifferent to or unaware of the political situation of his time or that myth by Ovid's day, or at least to Ovid, no longer had any religious or political meaning.[156] It is worth

---

153. Platner-Ashby, s.v. *Porta Raudusculana*. Aside from a brief mention in Pliny *Nat.* 11.123 (*fabulosos reor*), Valerius Maximus alone preserves a similar version of this story (5.6.3); Bömer, *Met., ad* 565–621, thinks Ovid may have been his source. See Bömer, *ad loc.*, and Porte, *L'Étiologie Religieuse dans les Fastes*, 194, for discussions of the various theories proposed to explain Cipus' name.

154. G.K. Galinsky, "The Cipus Episode in Ovid's *Metamorphoses*," *TAPA* 98 (1968): 183. Fränkel, *Poet between Two Worlds*, 226 n.104, tentatively suggested a connection between Julius Caesar and Cipus. W. Marg, review of *Ovid: A Poet Between Two Worlds*, by H. Fränkel, *Gnomon* 21 (1949): 56, argued that a connection with Augustus is more plausible. Galinsky (181–91) agrees with Marg. Davis, "Problem of Closure in a *Carmen Perpetuum*," 129–32, also discusses the importance of the theme of "the acceptance versus the rejection of a *numen*." Schmitzer, *Zeitgeschichte in Ovids Metamorphosen*, 271–72, connects Cipus and the symbol of the Capricorn in Augustan ideology and program.

155. On this episode see the important discussion of Feeney, *Gods in Epic*, 208ff.

156. For views of both the *Metamorphoses* and the *Fasti* as apolitical see Little, "Non-Augustanism of Ovid's *Metamorphoses*"; Due, *Changing Forms*, 66–89; McKeown, "Ovid's *Fasti* and Augustan Politics"; Knox, *Traditions of Augustan Poetry*, 77–80; Solodow, *World of Ovid's Metamorphoses*, 75. For anti-Augustan interpretations see Segal, "Myth and Philosophy in the *Metamorphoses*," and *idem*, "Orpheus and Augustan Ideology," *TAPA* 103 (1972): 473–94; A.W.J. Holleman, "Ovidii Metamorphoseon liber xv.622–870: (*Carmen et Error*)," *Latomus* 28 (1969): 42–60; R. Coleman, "Structure and Intention in the *Metamorphoses*," *CQ* 21 (1971): 461–77; L.C. Curran, "Transformation and Anti-Augustanism in Ovid's *Metamorphoses*," *Arethusa* 5 (1972): 71–91; Otis, *Ovid as an Epic Poet*; Schmitzer, *Zeitgeschichte in Ovids Metamorphosen*; Lateiner, "Mythic and Non-Mythic Artists."

taking seriously recently renewed arguments for a politically aware Ovid who was very much interested in the development of state cult and religious ideology under Augustus.[157] It is unlikely that any poet under Augustus could have remained unpolitical.[158] Paul Zanker has explored the dynamics of the constant struggle that went on in Rome between poets, artists, and Princeps over the appropriation and articulation of the language and images of power largely through the exploitation and manipulation of mythological symbols.[159]

It remains to ask briefly what it entails to have these Italian religious stories included at all within this collection of metamorphoses. E. Fantham calls our attention to the extreme discomfort expressed by ancient and modern critics in reaction to Vergil's inclusion of metamorphosis in the *Aeneid*.[160] We cannot help but wonder whether Ovid's decision to treat Roman national legends and Caesar's and Augustus' deifications on the same basis as the long series of fantastic Greek myths "does not *ipso facto* constitute a diminution of the former."[161] The aetiological focus of the Italian stories further problematizes this issue, for, as discussed earlier, *aetia* themselves stand as truth markers and signs of authentication in a narrative. The ironic contrast between the "truth" of the *aetia* and the inherent fictionality of his mythological narrative is a tension we have seen Ovid exploit to humorous effect in the previous books of the *Metamorphoses*. When the poem moves on to Roman themes, especially religious ones, however, this tension is different in nature, and a tension with which Vergil had already had to grapple. Religious aetiology occupies potentially dangerous ground between fiction and reality.[162] The ancient critics traditionally distinguished between gods who were figures of mythological literature and the gods who were the objects of official worship.[163] Religious

---

157. Feeney, *Gods in Epic*, 207–8, 218, and *idem*, "*Si licet fas est:* Ovid's *Fasti* and the Problem of Free Speech under the Principate," in *Roman Poetry and Propaganda in the Age of Augustus*, ed. A. Powell (London, 1992), 1–25; C.R. Philips, "Rethinking Augustan Poetry," *Latomus* 42 (1983): esp. 806–17; E. Fantham, "Ceres, Liber, and Flora: Georgic and anti-Georgic Elements in Ovid's *Fasti*," *PCPS* 38 (1992): 39–56. Hinds' arguments concerning the figure of Numa in the *Fasti, "Arma* in Ovid's *Fasti:* Parts I and II," seem especially relevant to *Met.* 14–15.

158. See A. Wallace-Hadrill, "Time for Augustus: Ovid, Augustus and the *Fasti,"* in *Homo Viator: Classical Essays for John Bramble*, ed. M. Whitby, P. Hardie, and M. Whitby (Bristol and Oak Park. Ill., 1987), 223. Cf. J. Griffin, "Augustus and the Poets: *Caesar Qui Cogere Posset,"* in *Caesar Augustus: Seven Aspects*, ed. F. Millar and E. Segal (Oxford, 1984), 189–218.

159. Zanker, *The Power of Images;* cf. N. Hannestad, *Roman Art and Imperial Policy* (Aarhus, 1986).

160. Fantham, "Decorum and Poetic Fiction," 102–3.

161. Galinsky, *Ovid's Metamorphoses*, 218, who, however, concludes that "we should be careful not to read ideological criticism into the *Metamorphoses*."

162. Graf, "Les Métamorphoses et la Véracité du Mythe," 68.

163. For the theory of the three ancient theologies, for the poet, philosopher, and statesman,

aetia in a mythological poem participate uncomfortably in both *theologia mythice* and *theologia politice.* Ovid's self-consciously ambiguous authorial position vis-à-vis his mythical material may be in part a reaction to Vergil's reassertion, largely effected through religious aetiology, of the validating power of mythological narrative to explain Roman realities.[164]

Ovid seems instead interested in the *Metamorphoses* to exploit the paradox involved in this friction between fact and fiction. He does not wish to undermine his narrative authority by casting doubt on his fictions, but, as we have seen, he uses his narrative presence in the poem in order to call attention to the arbitrariness of his authority, of his absolute freedom and power "to command or suspend our credence in his fictions."[165] We have seen that when Ovid exploits traditional narrative modes of authentication, he does so in such a way as to destabilize his narrative authority by calling attention to the way in which fiction creates credibility. The return to cosmogonic epic themes in Pythagoras' discourse in *Metamorphoses* 15 functions as a reassertion of the authoritative claims of the epic narrator and an introduction to the following political themes. Yet within this narrative itself, Ovid will characteristically challenge his own pretensions in this epic by juxtaposing mythological and philosophical modes of narrative, and thereby ultimately equating the two and denying to both the power to validate or to explain fully *rerum causas.*

---

see Varro *(Ant. Div.* fr. 7ff. Cardauns): *Mythicon appellant, quo maxime utuntur poetae; physicon, quo philosophi; civile, quo populi* (see Cardauns' commentary *ad loc.*). In general on the *"theologia tripertita,"* see G. Lieberg, "Die *'theologia tripertita'* in Forschung und Bezeugung," *ANRW* 1.4 (1973): 63–115. Cf. Feeney, *Gods in Epic,* 6ff.

164. Graf, "Les Métamorphoses et la Véracité du Mythe," 68.

165. Feeney, *Gods in Epic,* 225.

Chapter 4

Pythagoras, Philosophy, and Paradoxography

veraque constituunt quae belle tangere possunt
auris et lepido quae sunt fucata sonore
—Lucretius 1.643–44

In Books 1 through 14 of the *Metamorphoses* Ovid explains how various phenomena in the world, both natural and cultural, came about. The discourse of his internal narrator, the philosopher "Pythagoras," in Book 15 purports to deal with natural-philosophical explanations—*rerum causas et, quid natura, docebat* (15.68)—and thus parallels and recapitulates Ovid's claims in Book 1 to be writing a sort of cosmic history. We have seen that he does this throughout the poem by treating mythology and metamorphosis aetiologically, albeit on a humorously humble scale. Aetiology provides actual proofs throughout the world of the fictions that Ovid has been telling us. The affinity between philosophy and mythology lies in their universal claims to account for the origins of the cosmos, and of the objects and persons within it.[1] In his long disquisition Pythagoras frequently mentions examples from the natural world that are included as metamorphoses earlier in the poem. These echoes reinforce the similarities between Pythagoras' *causae* and the mythological aetiological metamorphoses we have been considering in the rest of the *Metamorphoses*. Recent critics have rightly emphasized the formal importance of the Pythagoras episode to the structure of the *Metamorphoses* as a whole. The speech reviews the entire sequence of the poem by recapitulating themes from earlier passages of the poem, especially Book 1,[2] as well as foreshadowing the Augustan conclusion of the poem. Far from being a digression, the discourse of

---

1. See Hardie, *Cosmos and Imperium,* 68.
2. Golden Age 1.89ff., 15.96ff., 259ff.; four elements 1.15ff., 15.237ff.; thunder 1.54–56, 15.69–70; generation from slime 1.416ff., 15.375ff. See Davis, "Problem of Closure in a *Carmen Perpetuum,*" 124. R.A. Swanson, "Ovid's Pythagorean Essay," *CJ* 54 (1968): 21, points out that the arrangement of themes in Book 15 is the reverse of that of Book 1: Book 1 four elements, evolution, time / four ages ; Book 15 time / ages, living forms, elements.

Pythagoras assembles many of the themes of this long poem, and while it does not tie them together, it brings together and highlights many of the important interpretative issues we have already discussed.

We should be careful, however, to qualify what we consider the unifying effect of this passage to be. Many critics have held that Pythagoras' speech is meant to provide the philosophical vindication for or explanation of the mythical metamorphoses in the rest of the poem.[3] Clearly, the metamorphic fictional world of the bulk of the poem does not allow for or require such a philosophical underpinning.[4] Others maintain instead Pythagoras' philosophy is meant to undermine Ovid's myths. Thus Fränkel argued that the speech "is conceived throughout in a rationalizing spirit, and thus it contradicts rather than clarifies the purport of the stories."[5] Upon close consideration of Pythagoras' discourse, however, we discover that this philosopher by no means treats his material in a "scientific" manner and therefore cannot be understood either to provide a coherent philosophic basis for Ovid's metamorphic myths or to repudiate them. The Pythagorean theory of metempsychosis, the cyclical process of the immortal soul's migration into random living bodies (15.166 *quoslibet occupat artus*), uses language that clearly resembles that of metamorphosis (15.172 *in varias . . . figuras*), and yet describes a process completely different from Ovidian metamorphosis. Many of Ovid's mythological transformations, as we have seen, have an aetiological intent that suggests a permanence, while others

---

3. E. Zinn, "Die Dichter des alten Rom und die Anfänge des Weltgedichts," *Ant. Ab.* 5 (1956): 20: "didaktische Offenbarung des Prinzips der Metamorphose als des waltenden Lebensprinzips in Natur und Menschenwelt"; Alfonsi, "L'Inquadramento Filosofico," 265–66: "Ovidio ha sentito il bisogno di interpretare, in base ai grandi principi speculativi, la realtà che a lui si configurava in transformazione: non bastava il mito accettato in se, gli è occorso il principio metafisico"; R. Crahay and J. Hubaux, "Sous le Masque de Pythagore," in *Ovidiana,* ed. N.I. Herescu (Paris, 1958), 287: "un fondement . . . à toutes les Métamorphoses"; R. Segl, *Die Pythagorasrede im 15. Buch von Ovids Metamorphosen* (Diss. Salzburg, 1970), 70: "philosophischen Untermauerung des Metamorphosen Gedankens." Two different and rather idiosyncratic interpretations have been offered by Stephens, *Function of Religious and Philosophical Ideas,* who argues for the pervasiveness of Orphic and Stoic ideas throughout the poem, and M.M. Colavito, *The Pythagorean Intertext in Ovid's Metamorphoses* (Lewiston, Lampeter, and Queenston, 1989), who presents us with an Ovid who is a devoted Pythagorean.

4. Cf. Otis, *Ovid as an Epic Poet,* 302, "What we cannot do—what is in fact the cardinal sin so far at least as the morality of literary criticism goes—is to force a coherent symbolism on the whole poem solely on the basis of those two philosophical digressions. Ovid's attitude toward myth is to be discovered in his treatment of myth, not elsewhere."

5. Fränkel, *Poet between Two Worlds,* 110. For the same view see Otis, *Ovid as an Epic Poet,* 358, 361, D.A. Little, "The Speech of Pythagoras in *Metamorphoses* 15 and the Structure of the *Metamorphoses*," *Hermes* 98 (1970): 345, and Coleman, "Structure and Intention."

represent merely a temporary state or disguise.[6] Closer to metempsychosis are the numerous apotheoses that surround the Pythagoras episode, especially that of Hippolytus/Virbius immediately following it in Book 15. The recent trend towards a purely formal and literary interpretation of Pythagoras' essay is in large part a response to this earlier criticism. It would, however, be equally mistaken to disregard completely the philosophical content of this embedded speech. Clearly Pythagoras' theory at least superficially has much in common with the processes we have seen throughout the poem.

Instead of setting up a dichotomy between the mythical metamorphoses of the poem and natural philosophy, his speech emphasizes their similarity.[7] Pythagoras does this by combining in his discourse scientific and mythological explanations and by highlighting the marvelous in nature, thus drawing our attention to the similarity of natural phenomena and mythical metamorphoses: they are both *mirabilia*. Many of Ovid's stories in the *Metamorphoses* are, in fact, found in ancient paradoxographical collections. Pythagoras' character narrative invites us to compare his "philosophical" approach with that of the primary narrator throughout the epic, "Ovid." Ovid continues with this inset narrative his humorous "inversion"[8] of philosophical physics. Ovid's Pythagoras delights in deviating from and misrepresenting the expected "scientific" approach to natural phenomena, as exemplified especially by Lucretius. The whole narrative should not, however, be reduced to the status of a joke.[9] The speech of Pythagoras intensifies a process in evidence throughout the *Metamorphoses:* the juxtaposition of "scientific" and mythical accounts of the origins of natural phenomena. In chapter 1 we looked at passages in which Ovid describes mythical transformations in language suggestive of physical and physiological scientific theory. Ovid continually reminds us that there have been two ways to account for the physical world: aetiological mythology and

---

6. Swanson, "Ovid's Pythagorean Essay," 22, points out the many transformations in the poem into inanimate objects; Coleman, "Structure and Intention," 462 n.4, remarks on the randomness of metempsychosis.

7. Similarly Haege, *Terminologie und Typologie der Verwandlungsvorgangs,* 269ff.

8. Hardie, "Lucretius and the Delusions of Narcissus," 72, uses this term to describe Ovid's use of Lucretian themes in *Met.* 3.

9. Segal, "Myth and Philosophy in the *Metamorphoses,*" 281–82; Solodow, *World of Ovid's Metamorphoses,* 167; R. McKim, "Myth Against Philosophy in Ovid's Account of Creation," *CJ* 80 (1985): 97–108. Galinsky, *Ovid's Metamorphoses,* 104–6, suggests that Pythagoras' speech is "intentionally monotonous, dreary, and long-winded" in order to serve as a "foil" to Ovid's own narrative. Little seems to recant his earlier view of the episode, "Speech of Pythagoras," 360, "the poet did not take it very seriously, and neither should we," in a later article, "Non-Parody in *Metamorphoses* 15," *Prudentia* 6 (1974): 17–21.

natural philosophy.[10] It is not so much that Ovid wished to "expose philosophy as inferior to myth in its understanding of man and his world,"[11] but that he wished to expose the difficulty of trying to make sense at all of his world through either of these traditional means. Barkan has described well the paradox of metamorphosis: "it proves the natural world magical and the magical world natural."[12] Philosophy is, however, ultimately subsumed into Ovid's "remythologization" of cosmogony. Pythagoras' speech is closer to the *fabulae* of poets than the *res prudentes* of science. The philosopher is made more a poet than the poet a philosopher.

"Pythagoras" as Philosopher

Over four-hundred lines of *Metamorphoses* 15 are taken up with the narrative of Pythagoras (15.60–478). It is not surprising that this episode has received more attention than any other in the poem. How does his discourse fit into the sequence of Italian religious-aetiological stories we have just examined? into the poem as a whole? The figure of Numa provides the connection between this episode and the aetiological stories preceding and following it, those of Croton and Egeria. Numa sets out at the beginning of Book 15 for the Italian city of Croton in order to seek natural-philosophical knowledge of the workings of the cosmos: *quae sit rerum natura, requirit* (15.6). Numa was traditionally seen as the founder of many of Rome's religious institutions (*Met.* 15.483 *sacrificos docuit ritus*)[13] and according to one tradition it was from Pythagoras that he received his instruction about this.[14] Numa is thus an appropriate figure to link together this episode with the surrounding Italian religious aetiological themes. The alternation between Greek and Italian themes we have seen in Books 14 and 15 and the motif of the amalgamation of the Greek into Italy is also represented here in Numa's meeting with Pythagoras.[15] This meeting between Pythagoras and Numa was a notorious anachronism in antiquity. It was much

---

10. Hardie, *Cosmos and Imperium*, 5–32. Boillat, *Les Métamorphoses d'Ovide*, 37, slightly differently suggests "une hypothèse séduisante: notre poète n'aurait-il pas cherché à reproduire l'évolution du mythe à la philosophie telle qu'on peut se la représenter de l'orphisme au pythagorisme?"

11. McKim, "Myth Against Philosophy," 97.

12. Barkan, *The Gods Made Flesh*, 19.

13. Livy 1.18.1–1.21.5; *Fasti* 3.277–84; Plutarch *Numa*. In Ennius' *Annales* Numa is evidently responsible for establishing the *flamines minores*, among whom is listed (118 Sk.) the Pomonalis.

14. For the origin of the tradition about Numa and Pythagoras see Skutsch, *Annals of Q. Ennius*, 263. Pythagoras was also credited with establishing a constitution for the Italian Greeks at Croton (Diog. Laer. 8.3).

15. Segal, "Myth and Philosophy in the *Metamorphoses*," 288.

discussed and frequently dismissed as chronologically impossible.[16] This anachronism Ovid seems to flout by including a second one in the foundation story of Croton. For as Dionysius of Halicarnassus points out (*Ant. Rom.* 2.59), at the time when Numa was said to have begun his reign, the city of Croton did not yet exist, but was founded by Myscelus four years later in 709 B.C.E.[17] The story of Egeria's assistance to Numa (*Fasti* 3.276 *illa Numae coniunx consiliumque fuit*) was also usually rejected by historians, such as Livy (1.19.5), on the grounds of implausibility.[18] Ovid, however, is no historian and it is striking that his philosophical discourse is emphatically and ironically framed by these poetic fictions.

The prominence of the theme of vegetarianism in Pythagoras' speech has engendered much discussion, and many critics have pointed out that it was precisely this aspect of Pythagoras' teaching that invited the most ridicule.[19] While it is clear that Ovid enjoyed humorously exaggerating the dramatic language of Pythagoras' exordium, the presence here of vegetarianism does not reduce the whole of Pythagoras' speech to the status of parody. The theme has rightly been understood as part of the *ethopoeia* of the narrator Pythagoras[20] and it leads directly to the theory of metempsychosis. Ovid furthermore presents it in such a way as to fit within the general scheme of religious aetiology in the concluding Italian section of his poem. Pythagoras is introduced as the first advocate of vegetarianism and this becomes the main theme of the following section:

. . . *primusque* animalia mensis
arguit imponi, *primus* quoque talibus ora
docta quidem solvit, sed non et credita, verbis.

(15.72–74)

---

16. Numa's reign was set in the second half of the eighth century, while Pythagoras was said to have lived in the late sixth. Skutsch, *Annals of Q. Ennius,* 263, argues that Ennius "can hardly have told the old tale that Numa was a pupil of Pythagoras." Jocelyn, "Poems of Quintus Ennius," 1011, suggests otherwise. For the argument against their meeting, see Cic. *Rep.* 2.29, *Tusc.* 4.1.3; Livy 1.18.2.

17. Dionysius of Halicarnassus *Ant. Rom.* 2.59–61 points out both anachronisms and also argues that Numa invented the story concerning Egeria. Knox, *Traditions of Augustan Poetry,* 66, rightly remarks that the second anachronism has often been overlooked.

18. Cf. Plut. *Numa* 4, 8.6, 15. In Ennius' *Annales* Numa did perhaps appear in converse with Egeria (113 Sk.).

19. Segal, "Myth and Philosophy in the *Metamorphoses,*" 281; Knox, *Traditions of Augustan Poetry,* 82 nn.36, 37. Pythagorean alimentary strictures had a long history of literary ridicule, especially among the poets of Middle Comedy (the quotations are conveniently collected in Athen. 4.161; Diog. Laer. 8.37–38); also Callimachus fr. 191 and Mime, Laberius fr. 17 R. In Roman literature, see Hor. *Sat.* 2.4.3, 2.6.63; *Epod.* 15.21; Juv. 3.229, 15.173.

20. Otis, *Ovid as an Epic Poet,* 298.

This *primus* theme is in keeping with the aetiological coloring of this part of the poem and is continued in the passages that follow. Again, these lines seem to be a humorous echo of Lucretius' claims that Epicurus was the first to conquer the fears of superstition:

> *primum* Graius homo mortalis tollere contra
> est oculos ausus *primusque* obsistere contra.

(DRN 1.66-67)

Pythagoras' plea for vegetarianism incorporates an explanation of the origins of the practice of eating meat, which he suggests brought an end to the Golden Age:

> postquam non utilis *auctor*
> victibus invidit, quisquis fuit ille, leonum[21]
> corporeasque dapes avidam demersit in alvum,
> fecit iter sceleri, *primoque* e caede ferarum
> incaluisse potest maculatum sanguine ferrum . . .

(15.103–7)

This use of the *topos* of the *malus auctor* seems a humorous version of a common theme in the legend of the Golden Age; namely, the idea, largely promulgated by the Cynics and Stoics, that the downfall of man was brought about to some extent by his own inventions.[22] The discovery of sea-faring is frequently cited among the evil inventions absent during the Golden Age, and this is what we read in Book 1 of the *Metamorphoses* (1.89–112).[23] Here in Book 15 Pythagoras locates carnivorism as the "original sin which causes the decline."[24]

---

21. I adopt Goold's text. Anderson prints *deorum* (*suspectum, sed tolerabile*), for *leonum.*

22. See B. Gatz, *Weltalter, goldene Zeit und sinnverwandte Vorstellungen* (Hildesheim, 1967), esp. pp. 144–65 (Die Kulturentstehungslehren); also K.J. Reckford, "Some Appearances of the Golden Age," *CJ* 54 (1958): 79–87; K.F. Smith, *Tibullus the Elegies* (New York, Cincinnati, and Chicago, 1913), *ad* Tibullus 1.3.37–40.

23. For references to sea-faring passages see Smith, *Tibullus the Elegies, ad* Tibullus 1.3.37–40, A.S. Pease in his commentary, *M. Tulli Ciceronis De Natura Deorum* (Cambridge, 1955), *ad N.D.* 2.89, and Nisbet-Hubbard *ad* Hor. *Odes* 1.3.

24. W.R. Johnson, "The Problem of the Counter-Classical Sensibility and its Critics," *CSCA* 3 (1970): 141. On connections between the Golden Age and vegetarianism see Gatz, *Weltalter, goldene Zeit und sinnverwandte Vorstellungen,* 165–71, Plato *Politicus* 271Cff., *Fasti* 4.393–416; Plut. *Mor.* 998Bff. also associates the beginning of carnivorism with the origin of war.

Pythagoras explains how the practice of animal sacrifice developed out of this first atrocity: *longius inde nefas abiit* (15.111). In the first book of the *Fasti* (337–456) Ovid includes a very similar, but much longer, account of the origins of various animal sacrifices.[25] The two accounts share many verbal echoes[26] and confirm once again that themes shared between the two poems may serve to highlight a religious-aetiological feature in the *Metamorphoses*. Moreover, the topic is not without importance to the earlier part of the *Metamorphoses*, where, as critics have observed, many of Ovid's stories frequently involve the exploration of the transgressions of forbidden boundaries and sometimes involve alimentary norms.[27] In the first story in the poem, that of Lycaon, for example, the race of humans is brought to ruin because of Lycaon's cannibalism.[28] This is but one of the many ways in which the material of Pythagoras' speech is intimately related to the concerns of the rest of the epic.

By including this embedded speech, Ovid incorporates yet another type of narrative into his "encyclopedic" poem: didactic natural philosophy. As we have seen, collections of metamorphoses most likely first appeared as didactic poems. Ovid invites us to compare his own presentation of these scientific themes at the beginning of the *Metamorphoses* with that of his internal narrator Pythagoras. The repetition of the verb *docere* (*docebat* 68, *doceo* 172, *docebo* 238; *discenda dabat* 66) underlines the didactic nature of Pythagoras' speech. The language and style are close to Lucretius' didactic epos. We thus find the vivid imperatives (*parcite* 15.75, *scite et sentite* 142), the addresses to the reader to consider the evidence of the senses (*cernis* 15.186, *adspicis* 200, *si quaeris* 293, *nonne vides* 362, 382),[29] and the appeal for belief and attention typical of didactic narrative (*mihi credite* 15.254, *monitis animos advertite nostris* 140, *animos adhibete* 238).[30] We should note also Pythagoras' concern

---

25. Varro explains the origins of the sacrifice of the pig (*R.R.* 2.4.9 *Ab suillo enim pecore immolandi initium primum sumptum videtur*) and the goat (*R.R.* 1.2.18–19).

26. Pythagoras' lament at the conclusion of the explanation of the punishments of the sow and goat (*Met.* 15.115–21) is very similar to Ovid's own shorter interjection after the same two examples in the *Fasti* (1.361–62).

27. Feeney, *Gods in Epic*, 195; Haege, *Terminologie und Typologie der Verwandlungsvorgangs*, 276 n.779, lists, e.g., 2.623ff., 7.348, 8.688, 13.768, 14.208ff., contra Little, "Speech of Pythagoras," 343: "this part of the Pythagorean digression . . . has no essential connection with the main body of the *Metamorphoses*."

28. See Barkan, *The Gods Made Flesh*, 27, with his discussion (n.65) of the applicability of structuralist approaches to myth.

29. On this last phrase, which seems particularly Lucretian, see A. Schiesaro, "*Nonne vides* in Lucrezio," *MD* 13 (1984): 143–57. In *De Rerum Natura* Lucretius uses it fifteen times.

30. Kenney, "*Nequitiae Poeta,*" 202–3, in his list of didactic imitations in Ovid's *Ars Amatoria* lists as Lucretian echoes *vidi, credo, animum advertite, quaero, disco, adspicio*.

with evidence revealed in his frequent appeal to his own experience (*vidi ego
. . . vidi* 15.262–63) or the authority of others (*adhuc ostendere nautae* 15.294,
veteres habuere coloni 15.289, *quod indigenae memorant* 15.325, *dixere pri-
ores* 15.332, *res observata colonis* 15.373). We may recall how in chapter 2 we
discovered these same appeals to authority, as well as other didactic linguistic
features (e.g., *discite*), in the framed aetiological narratives considered there.
These sorts of expressions, along with the concentrated use of the familiar
qualifications such as *fama est* (15.356) and *narratur* (15.312), which "invoke
the authority of tradition,"[31] serve to enhance the properly objective tone of
Pythagoras' "scientific" discourse.

Another didactic feature of Pythagoras' discourse is the statement of multi-
ple causes. Pythagoras in discussing the cause of the volcanic activity of Aetna
gives a choice of three causes (15.340–55): *sive est animal tellus* (342) . . . *sive
leves imis venti cohibentur in antris* (346) . . . *sive bitumineae rapiunt incendia
vires* (350). This is an imitation of Lucretius' technique throughout *De Rerum
Natura* and is the result of a specifically stated Epicurean belief that thorough-
ness of investigation demanded the statement of alternative causes: *Sunt ali-
quot quoque res quarum unam dicere causam / non satis est, verum pluris,
unde una tamen sit* (*DRN* 6.703–4).[32] So we find Lucretius at 5.517-25 offer-
ing three explanations for why stars move, or again at 5.1241–49 suggesting
four accounts of how metals were first discovered.[33] Other didactic poets, such
as Vergil at *Georgics* 1.86–91,[34] Manilius at 1.118–144 (*sive . . . seu . . . sive
. . . sive . . . aut*), and the poet of the *Aetna* at 110–16 also make use of this
Lucretian multiple causation device.[35] We find an example of this phraseology
in the *Metamorphoses* precisely where we might expect to, in the cosmogony
in Book 1.78ff., where Ovid offers two accounts for the origin of humankind.[36]

---

31. Stinton, "Expressions of Disbelief," 65. Also *ferunt* (15.278), *dicitur* (15.291), *memoran-
tur* (15.360), *ut memorant* (15.414).

32. Cf. *DRN* 5.526–33 *plurisque sequor disponere causas* (529), . . . *sed quae sit earum /
praecipere haudquaquamst pedetemptim progredientis* (532–33); Epicurus *Ep. ad Hdt.* 79–80, *Ep.
ad Pyth.* 86–87. But observe that Lucretius *does* give a single explanation for the activity of Aetna
at *DRN* 6.639–702 (winds in underground caverns).

33. Also 1.977–79, 5.575–76, 5.751ff. (the last a presentation of alternative theories for the
occurrence of solar eclipses, as at Epicurus *Ep. ad Pyth.* 96).

34. Where Thomas, *Vergil's Georgics,* remarks that "the style is Lucretian."

35. The frequent appearance of the statement of multiple causes in the *Fasti* (e.g., 2.81–82,
477–80, 3.153–54, 3.773–79, 4.170–78) is related to this tradition and may be compared also to
the thorough and conscientious scholarly tradition reflected in Varro's practice of offering multiple
etymologies, e.g., *L.L.* 5.25, 37, 43. See on this now Miller, "The *Fasti* and Hellenistic Didactic."

36. Due, *Changing Forms,* 99; D.E. Hill, *Ovid: Metamorphoses 1–4* (Oak Park, Ill., 1985), *ad
loc.*

Let us now look closer at the content of this narrative. Pythagoras is not introduced by name, but simply as *vir Samius* (15.60).[37] As commentators are quick to point out, this description is similar to Lucretius' introduction of Epicurus as *Graius homo* (1.66).[38] The first allusion to Lucretius' didactic poem in Book 15 occurs at the beginning of the book, when Ovid states the reason for Numa's travel to Croton: *quae sit rerum natura requirit* (15.6). This is only the first of many Lucretian echoes; Pythagoras' speech draws much not only on Lucretian language and style but on its content as well. As many have pointed out, the philosophical composition of Pythagoras' narrative is a mixed bag, like that of Ovid's opening cosmogony, due either to Ovid's lack of concern for providing a cohesive philosophical system or to the general eclecticism of the neo-Pythagoreanism of his time.[39] It is probably a little of both. Clearly, as P. DeLacy, among others, has rightly argued, Ovid will have chosen both here and in Book 1 those features of various philosophical theories that best suited his purpose in this context.[40] Ovid's description of Pythagoras' philosophical-scientific investigation of the nature of the physical universe (15.62–72) outlines many topics included in Lucretius' poem, but it does not at all, in fact, describe what Pythagoras actually goes on to talk about in Book 15:

> in medium discenda dabat coetusque silentum
> dictaque mirantum magni primordia mundi
> et rerum causas et, quid natura, docebat,
> quid deus, unde nives, quae fulminis esset origo,
> Iuppiter an venti discussa nube tonarent,
> quid quateret terras, qua sidera lege mearent,
> et quodcumque latet . . .
>
> (15.66–72)

We would expect from this that Pythagoras' discourse would provide rational scientific explanations for the natural phenomena listed above, as Lu-

---

37. Bömer, *Met., ad* 15.60ff., notes that Pythagoreans avoided naming their founder (Iambl. *Vit. Pyth.* 88) and that Vergil, Tibullus, and Propertius never mention his name; Horace, however, does (*Epod.* 15.21, *Sat.* 2.4.3, 2.6.63, *Ep.* 2.1.52). Ovid mentions him by name only at *Pont.* 3.3.44. Lucretius names Epicurus only once, at 3.1042, where Bailey, *Lucretius De Rerum Natura, ad loc.,* comments on this practice.

38. Bailey, *Lucretius De Rerum Natura, ad* 1.66, notes that this may be an echo from Ennius' *Annales* 165 Sk.: *Navos repertus homo, Graio patre, Graius homo, rex.*

39. On Pythagoreanism, see Burkert, *Lore and Science in Ancient Pythagoreanism;* on neo-Pythagoreanism in Rome, see Rawson, *Intellectual Life in the Late Roman Republic,* 291–94.

40. P. DeLacy, "Philosophical Doctrine and Poetic Technique in Ovid," *CJ* 43 (1947): 155–61; similarly E. Saint-Denis, "Le Génie d'Ovide d'Après le Livre XV des Métamorphoses," *REL* 18 (1940): 125.

cretius does,[41] but it does not. Instead the main theme of the discourse becomes that of eternal change (*cuncta fluunt* 178) and, despite verbal similarities, Pythagoras' philosophical approach to his material is very different from, and ultimately opposed to, that of Lucretius.

"Pythagoras" as *Vates*

Pythagoras introduces his theme with a proem (15.143–52), in which he claims divine inspiration and originality:

> "Et quoniam deus ora movet, sequar ora moventem
> rite deum Delphosque meos ipsumque recludam
> aethera et augustae reserabo oracula mentis:
> magna nec ingeniis investigata priorum
> quaeque diu latuere, canam . . ."

> (15.143–47)

Pythagoras was credited by his followers with mantic powers (Diog. Laer. 8.11, 20) and there was a tradition that he received his doctrines from the Delphic priestess Themistoclea (Diog. Laer. 8.8, 21 [Aristoxenus]). Diogenes Laertius tells us further that Aristippus claimed that his name was derived from these powers: Πυθαγόραν αὐτὸν ὀνομασθῆναι ὅτι τὴν ἀλήθειαν ἠγόρευεν οὐχ ἧττον τοῦ Πυθίου (8.21).[42] Prophesying and prophecies will form an important part of Pythagoras' speech and of Book 15 as a whole. Here the presence of the word *augustae* is no doubt meant to foreshadow the oracles concerning Augustus that appear later in the book (15.446–49, 807–42).[43] It is worth noting that the historical Pythagoras was associated not only with Apollo, but with the Muses as well.[44] By having Pythagoras so pointedly avow a divine inspiration, Ovid subverts the Lucretian claims for the primacy of reason in philosophical investigation.[45] Epicurus was traditionally vehemently

41. *Quid deus DRN* 2.1090ff.; *unde nives* 6.527ff.; *fulmen . . . tonare* 6.96ff., 160ff., 173f.; *quatere terras* 6.535ff.; *sidera* 5.509ff. Pythagoras does obliquely allude to theories about earthquakes at *Met.* 15.296–306, 340–54.

42. Bömer, *Met., ad loc.* finds a reference to this etymology at *Met.* 15.143–44 unlikely. For more on the association between Apollo and Pythagoras see Burkert, *Lore and Science in Ancient Pythagoreanism,* 140ff.

43. Bömer, *Met., ad loc.*

44. Iambl. *Vit. Pyth.* 9. See P. Boyancé, *Le Culte des Muses chez les philosophes grecs: Études d'histoire et de psychologie religieuses.* Bibl. des Écoles françaises d'Athènes et de Rome, fasc. 141 (Paris, 1937), 241.

45. *DRN* (praise of Epicurus) 1.72 *vivida vis animi pervicit,* 3.14–15 *ratio tua coepit vociferari ⁄ naturam rerum,* 5.9 *qui princeps vitae rationem invenit.*

opposed to the practice of divination,[46] and Lucretius contrasts both his own philosophic knowledge and that of the Pre-Socratic philosophers with the Pythian oracle, claiming that the philosophers have spoken *multo certa ratione magis quam / Pythia quae tripode a Phoebi lauroque profatur* (*DRN* 1.738–39, 5.111–12).[47] Yet it was claimed even of Epicurus that he had oracular powers[48] and Lucretius' own attitude towards divine inspiration is notoriously ambiguous in the light of his dual posture as poet and philosopher. Lucretius' similar supernatural claims for Epicurus (e.g., 3.15 *divina mente;* 5.8 *deus ille fuit, deus*) and himself (1.921ff.) are however most likely to be understood as his exploitation of literary convention for the purpose of emphasizing the *truth* of Epicureanism.[49]

Pythagoras' prophetic powers align him with the vatic tradition of poetry, which Lucretius had attacked as perpetuating religious fear of the gods (*vatum / terriloquis . . . dictis* 1.102–3), whether as promulgated by priests or by the mythology of the poets. He attacks specifically Ennius' depiction of the Underworld and his claim to supernatural revelation by "Homer" (1.117–26).[50] Lucretius, as we have already discussed, was a crucial figure in the evolution of the "*vates*-concept" in Latin poetry. He provided an important model of the poet qualified to reveal important truths about the cosmos because of his knowledge of the inner workings of nature.[51] However, the association of this philosophic ideal with prophetic or divine authority, as developed by Vergil and Ovid, would not have sat well with Lucretius, who was so deeply concerned to contrast natural-philosophical truth with religious falseness. Far from misunderstanding the *vates* concept in Augustan poetry,[52] Ovid plays with the dual, and to Lucretius antithetical, associations of the *vates,* as, on the one hand, a figure of supernatural, even sacerdotal, authority, and, on the other hand, as a scientific investigator of and knowledgeable authority on philosoph-

46. Diog. Laer. 10.135; Cic. *Div.* 1.5; H. Usener, *Epicurea* (Lipsiae, 1887), 261–62.

47. So Bailey, *Lucretius De Rerum Natura, ad* 5.111–12.

48. Diog. Laer. 10.12 (an epigram for Epicurus); *Sent. Vat.* 29, Bömer, *Met., ad* 15.143–44. Pease's observations on the description of philosophic knowledge as oracular at Cic. *N.D.* 1.66 are instructive. Cf. Cicero's comments at *Tusc.* 1.21.48: *soleo saepe mirari non nullorum insolentiam philosophorum, qui naturae cognitionem admirantur eiusque inventori et principi gratias exsultantes agunt eumque venerantur ut deum.*

49. Schrijvers, *Horror ac divina voluptas,* 255; cf. Kenney, "*Doctus Lucretius,*" 373–80; Hardie, *Cosmos and Imperium,* 18–21. Ackermann, *Lukrez und der Mythos,* 173–79, suggests that the tradition of Euhemerism is also activated (Lucr. 5.13–54).

50. Kenney, "*Doctus Lucretius,*" 377–78.

51. Hardie, *Cosmos and Imperium,* esp. 17–22. For Ovid Lucretius was a *vates* (*Tr.* 2.425–26): *explicat ut causas rapidi Lucretius ignis, / casurumque triplex* vaticinatur *opus.*

52. *Pace* J.K. Newman, *The Concept of Vates in Augustan Poetry* (Brussels, 1967), 108.

ical truths. This incongruity between prophetic authority and scientific or empirical method is similarly highlighted at the beginning of the *Ars Amatoria,* where Ovid's repudiation of divine inspiration for the primacy of empirical investigation (*usus*) conflicts with his claim to be a *vates peritus* (*Ars* 1.27–30).[53]

Ovid's inversion of Lucretian aims continues in Pythagoras' proem with a passage drawing liberally on Lucretius' praises of the power of philosophy to conquer the fear of death (15.147–52). In the genuine spirit and language of Lucretius,[54] Pythagoras decries the lies and myths poets (among them Ovid in this poem, 5.341ff., 10.11ff., 14.104ff.) have told about the existence of an underworld. These lies have been the cause of unnecessary fear:

> "O genus attonitum gelidae formidine mortis,
> quid Styga, quid tenebras et nomina vana timetis,
> materiem vatum, falsique pericula mundi ?"

> (15.153–55)

As has been seen, of course, Pythagoras is using this Lucretian language to make a point that turns out to be completely the opposite of Lucretius' basic tenet, *fateare necessest / mortalem esse animam* (*DRN* 3.766–67):[55]

> "morte carent animae semperque priore relicta
> sede novis domibus vivunt habitantque receptae."

> (15.158–59)

Lucretius, like other philosophers, deplores the fabrications of the poets and repeatedly inveighs against the dangers of their fictions. He is especially concerned to denounce precisely these stories about the existence of an underworld and afterlife and does so frequently.[56] The refutation of the fictions of poets was, as we have seen, a *topos* of philosophical writing from its earliest period: παλαιὰ μέν τις διαφορὰ φιλοσοφίᾳ τε καὶ ποιητικῇ (Plato *Rep.*

---

53. Kenney, "*Doctus Lucretius*," 379; see also C. Ahern, "Ovid as *Vates* in the Proem to the *Ars Amatoria*," *CP* 85 (1990): 44–48.

54. *DRN* 5.1194: *O genus infelix hominum;* cf. 2.14.

55. See the whole discussion of the mortal nature of the *anima* and *animus* in *DRN* 3.136ff. Lucretius argues against the Pythagorean doctrine (and others who held a similar view) at 3.670–783 (*quod si immortalis foret et mutare soleret / corpora, permixtis animantes moribus essent* 3.748–49).

56. Esp. *DRN* 1.112ff., 3.978–1024. Bailey, *Lucretius De Rerum Natura, ad* 3.978, points out that this was a commonplace of philosophical thought in Lucretius' time.

10.607b5–6).[57] The philosophic critique of myth, so powerfully inaugurated by Plato, involves primarily the perceived danger of the anthropomorphized depiction of the gods. Didactic scientific poets regularly reject myth in favor of *ratio*, or, as we have also seen, take pains to explain how scientific wisdom may lurk under traditional mythology. Manilius at the beginning of Book 2 of the *Astronomica*, before announcing his own new theme, reviews and critiques the mythological stories of previous poets: *quorum carminibus nihil est nisi fabula caelum* (2.37).[58] The poet of the *Aetna*, in his concern to convince his reader of the truth of his own theories, adopts a strong polemical tone as he argues step by step against the stories told by poets (*impia fabula* 42) to explain Aetna's activity: *principio ne quem capiat fallacia vatum* (29, the story of Typhoeus) *. . . discrepat a prima facies haec altera vatum . . . turpe et sine pignore carmen* (36, 40, the Cyclopes), etc. He sums up in a hostile manner the traditional definition of the essentially autonomous nature of poetry, *haec est mendosae vulgata licentia famae* (74ff.). After reviewing various themes, he concludes by explaining the difference between the nature of this poetry and his own didactic poetry: *debita carminibus libertas ista; sed omnis / in vero mihi cura* (91–92).[59]

Thus Lucretius also sets out to prove that the many wonderful tales that have been promulgated by poets provide dangerously false supernatural explanations for natural phenomena, which are perfectly comprehensible through an understanding of Epicurean materialist physics. These myths were all to be included later by Ovid in the *Metamorphoses*. Lucretius pointedly argues against the possibility of the existence of mythical monsters (*portenta*) such as the Centaurs or Scylla (*DRN* 2.700ff., 4.732–45, 5.878–924), both of which monsters are, of course, included in the *Metamorphoses*. Lucretius even denies in passing the possibility of metamorphoses into trees, such as those of Daphne (*Met.* 1.452–567) or the sisters of Phaethon (*Met.* 2.340–66): *Nec tamen omnimodis conecti posse putandum est / omnia; nam vulgo fieri portenta videres, . . . / altos / interdum ramos egigni corpore vivo . . . / quorum nil fieri manifestum est* (*DRN* 2.700–703, 707). The mythological stories of Cybele

---

57. Kroll, *Studien zum Verständnis,* 56: "Der Kontrast der πλάσματα alten stiles mit der modernen Naturkenntnis musste schliesslich die Philosophen in Harnisch bringen." (e.g., Xenophanes fr. 21 B1.22 DK, πλάσματα τῶν προτέρων); cf. the παροιμία attributed to Solon (fr. 29 West): πολλὰ ψεύδονται ἀοιδοί.

58. Manilius does, however, include the myth of Phaethon in his list of six possible causes for the Milky Way in Book 1.735–49: *fama etiam antiquis ad nos descendit ab annis* (1.735).

59. Recall the completely different tone of Ovid's own claims for the freedom of creativity in poetry at *Am.* 3.12.41–42: *exit in inmensum fecunda licentia vatum / obligat historica nec sua verba fide.*

and Phaethon, although allegorized, are both criticized as poetic and religious fictions popularized by *veteres Graium poetae* (*DRN* 2.600, 5.405) and rejected as false (*longe sunt tamen a vera ratione repulsa* 2.645, 5.406) and as dangerously promoting *religio*. At *De Rerum Natura* 4.580–93 Lucretius gives a rational scientific reason (*ratio DRN* 4.572) for the existence of an echo in certain places (*DRN* 4.572ff.), while explaining how fabulous stories have arisen to account for the phenomenon:

> Haec loca capripedes satyros nymphasque tenere
> finitimi fingunt, et faunos esse loquuntur.
>
> (*DRN* 4.580–81)

This is only one of the many places in which Lucretius consciously demythologizes a mythological account of the origin (*aetion*) of a natural phenomenon. We have already considered in chapter 1 how Ovid's story of Echo and Narcissus remythologizes this same thing. Interestingly, Lucretius here pauses to consider the reason why such tales have arisen:

> cetera de genere hoc monstra ac portenta loquuntur,
> ne loca deserta ab divis quoque forte putentur
> sola tenere. ideo iactant miracula dictis
> aut aliqua ratione alia ducuntur, ut omne
> humanum genus est avidum nimis auricularum.
>
> (*DRN* 4.590–94)

As we shall see, while Lucretius' goal was to explain away the miraculous in the world (*non est mirandum* 4.595) in order to prove that the world is governed by its own constant and fixed natural laws, the whole purport of Pythagoras' discourse seems to be to inspire a feeling of wonder at the miracles of nature. This goal is closer to that of Ovid in the *Metamorphoses* as a whole than to that of philosophers like Lucretius.

Pythagoras' approach can best be illustrated by a close examination of the long and remarkable catalog of natural marvels he introduces in order to prove the truth of his more general theme of eternal change in the natural world (*nihil est toto, quod perstet, in orbe* 15.177), which also has obvious similarities with the main theme of the poem as a whole: *Nec species sua cuique manet, rerumque novatrix / ex aliis alias reparat natura figuras* (15.252–53). The effect of this catalog of *mirabilia naturae* is not to undermine the mythological stories of the previous fourteen books of the *Metamorphoses*, but rather to blur the distinction between mythical and scientific modes of narrative. Ovid hereby also reveals another literary tradition, paradoxography, which shares many of the features of his collection of metamorphoses and suggests a new reading of the poem as a thaumastic work.

Mirabilia: Paradoxography vs. Philosophy

In this collection of natural marvels, Pythagoras often alludes to metamorphoses that have appeared earlier in the *Metamorphoses* and thus invites the reader to compare his accounts with those of the primary narrator. The parallels also serve as another aspect of the recapitulation of themes from earlier in the poem. So, for instance, Pythagoras' first example of the mutability of the natural world involves the change from land to sea and recalls unmistakably the flood of Book 1 (15.262–312). He next speaks of fountains and rivers that suddenly spring forth and again are swallowed up by the earth (15.270–86). The rivers of Lycus and Erasinus (15.273–76) reemerge after underground passages in a manner similar to Arethusa (5.635-41). Is the similarity of this natural philosophical account in Book 15 (*terreno . . . hiatu* 15.273) meant either to explain or to discredit the divine mythical account earlier in the poem (*Delia rupit humum* 5.639)? The continuous coexistence in Pythagoras' speech of the mythical and the scientific suggests that we are intended to do neither of these things, but rather to consider that both types of narrative provide equally valid accounts (*causae*) for the same phenomena.

This collection of natural marvels deserves attention. While we shall never know precisely what source or sources Ovid drew this list from,[60] it is clear that most of these natural phenomena were originally assembled in paradoxographical works. Almost all of them appear in the collections of marvels that are still extant, both Greek and Latin.[61] Paradoxography is an interesting and

---

60. Lafaye, *Les Métamorphoses d'Ovide*, 203ff., has argued for the importance of Posidonius (cited frequently by Strabo as a source), with Varro's paradoxographical work (see n.66 below) as the intermediary. Haupt-Ehwald, *ad* 259ff., Bömer, *Met., ad* 15.274, and Segl, *Die Pythagorasrede*, also mention Posidonius as a source, but Bömer adds: "*Sed num quis vel quis inter Posidonium et Ovidium intercesserit, ignoramus.*" Sotion, the Stoic teacher of Seneca to whom a paradoxographical work has doubtfully been ascribed (*Paradox. Gr.* Westermann, pp. 183–91), has also been put forward as a model. Four of his *paradoxa* (11, 20, 24, 44) are found in Pythagoras' list.

61. For a collection of the Greek paradoxographers see Westermann, *Scriptores Rerum Mirabilium Graeci* (= *Paradoxographoi Graeci*) (Amsterdam, 1963), to which I refer. See also the edition of A. Giannini, *Paradoxographorum Graecorum Reliquiae* (Milan, 1965). Strabo and Aelian also reflect this tradition. The best discussions of the Greek paradoxographical tradition are Fraser, *Ptolemaic Alexandria*, 454ff., 522ff., 761ff., and the articles by Giannini, "Studi Sulla

[handwritten margin note: = Diodorus Siculus ed. A. Burton]

much-neglected genre, related to the historical, geographical, and aetiological traditions, ultimately deriving from the early accounts of Hecataeus and Herodotus, but first pursued as a separate genre in the Alexandrian period.[62] Callimachus himself produced perhaps the first *Collection of Wonders* (frr. 407–11 Pf.), which seem to have been mostly of the natural variety.[63] These collections of marvels or curiosities included natural phenomena as well as historical and mythological events. They were written in both poetry (Philostephanus Cyrenaeus *SH* 691, Archelaus of Chersonesus *Epigrammata de mirabilibus SH* 125–29) and prose, and were arranged either geographically (as Callimachus' *Paradoxa* fr. 407 Pf.) or according to subject matter (as Antigonus of Carystus' *Historia Mirabilium* Westermann pp. 61–102). Though the literary form first developed as a type of semiscientific writing similar to collections of *aetia* and metamorphoses, meant both to amaze and to acquaint readers with various obscure mythological stories and local folktales,[64] it seems that in the Roman period the collections were taken up mainly by the natural philosophers and used to provide examples of the ability of the laws of natural philosophy to explain even the most remarkable in nature. This is how we find Lucretius, Pliny, Seneca, and Strabo using lists of *mirabilia* very similar to Ovid's in Book 15.[65] We also have evidence that Varro and Cicero both wrote paradoxographical collections, and, although we know essentially nothing about the nature and content of these, we might

Paradossografia Greca I and II." Collections of *mirabilia* in Latin are found in Lucretius, Pliny, Seneca, and Vitruvius, on which see more below. Aulus Gellius (9.4) has a wonderful passage describing his discovery of some old and decaying volumes of Greek paradoxography at a book stall in Brundisium.

62. See the diverse sources listed in Callimachus' *Paradoxa* (fr. 407 Pf.), as cited by Antigonus of Carystus, among which are Eudoxus (I), Theophrastus (II), Lycus (V), Timaeus (VI), Pindar (XII), Theopompus (XIII), Aristotle (XVI), Ctesias (XVII), etc. For the thaumastic tradition in Herodotus and Hecataeus, see Pearson, "Apollonius of Rhodes and the Old Geographers," and Murray, "Herodotus and Hellenistic Culture."

63. Fraser, *Ptolemaic Alexandria,* 772; Pfeiffer, *History of Classical Scholarship,* 135; Westermann (1839) x–xi. Pfeiffer gives the title (among others) from the *Suda:* ΘΑΥΜΑΤΩΝ ΤΩΝ ΕΙΣ ΑΠΑΣΑΝ ΤΗΝ ΓΗΝ ΚΑΤΑ ΤΟΠΟΥΣ ΟΝΤΩΝ ΣΥΝΑΓΩΓΗ.

64. See Ziegler *RE* 18.3 (1949) 1137–66, s.v. *Paradoxographoi:* "in der Regel, ohne ein Urteil über die Wahrheit oder Unglaubwürdigkeit des Berichteten" (1140). Despite the natural-philosophic content of Callimachus' collection, it is doubtful that it had any scientific intent; see Pfeiffer, *History of Classical Scholarship,* 135. Dickie, "Talos Bewitched," 291 n.54, and Giannini, "Studi Sulla Paradossografia Greca II," 108, 119, argue for a scientific element.

65. Lafaye, *Les Métamorphoses d'Ovide,* 251–54, provides extremely useful appendices (D–H) of the correspondences between Ovid's *mirabilia* and other paradoxographical and natural philosophical works. See also Bömer, *Met.,* and Haupt-Ehwald, *ad loc.* Fraser, *Ptolemaic Alexandria,* 454–55, has remarked that "it is a regular feature of surviving paradoxographical texts, the production of which continued for almost fifteen hundred years, that they largely use the same sources (both independently and at second-hand) and repeat the same stories and fantasies."

conjecture that they were indebted to Callimachus' earlier work in content and allegiance.[66]

We know that quite a few of Ovid's metamorphoses that are connected with geographical features would have been found in such collections. The formation of the islands of the Echinades, the mythological account of which is narrated by Achelous in Book 8 of the *Metamorphoses,* is explained by Pliny (*Nat.* 2.201),[67] as is the golden stream of Pactolus (*Nat.* 33.66), the *aetion* for which is explained in the *Metamorphoses* by the story of Midas (11.136–45). The spring of Arethusa, who tells her own story in *Met.* 5.572–641, is also found explained in Pliny (*Nat.* 2.225), Seneca (*N.Q.* 3.26.5–6), and Strabo (6.2.4, pp. 270–71),[68] and was included in Callimachus' *Paradoxa* (fr. 407.XII).[69] The transformation of Diomedes' men into birds (*Met.* 14.464ff.) was, as we have seen, also a standard marvel in paradoxographical collections,[70] as was the story of crows' strange avoidance of the Acropolis (*Met.* 2.531–632).[71] Even marvelous stories concerning the figure of Pythagoras are found in these works (Apollon. *Hist. Mirab.* 6). By comparing Ovid's Pythagorean discourse with other natural philosophical treatises that include these same marvelous natural phenomena, we can see how Ovid represents Pythagoras' approach as decidedly "unscientific."

A traditional feature of ancient philosophy is the expression of wonderment at the "cosmic show"; the next step being to account rationally for these marvelous natural phenomena with scientific explanations.[72] Aristotle had in fact pinpointed the origin of philosophy in the human desire to explain logically and naturally τὸ θαυμάζειν (*Metaph.* 982b 11–28). Lucretius thus introduces natural marvels precisely in order to heighten and then to quell through a rational, scientific explanation, the reader's wonder at seemingly supernatural events in nature; *miratio* gives way to *ratio.*[73] In *DRN* 6.608ff. Lucretius introduces a long list of famous remarkable terrestrial phenomena (e.g., Aetna, Lake Avernus, the Nile floods, crows' avoidance of the Acropolis) for which he

---

66. Varro *Gallus De Admirandis* (Riese *Logistorici* pp. 253–54); Macr. *Sat.* 3.15.8 *sed dicam quid M. Varro in libro qui inscribitur Gallus de admirandis dixerat his verbis;* Cicero *Admiranda* (cited twice in Plin. *Nat.* 31.12, 51), see *RE* 7A.1.1271 (Büchner).

67. Explained as being created by the silting of the river; also in Strabo 1.3.18, p. 59.

68. Strabo tells the mythological story and concludes: παντάπασιν ἀμήχανόν ἐστιν (6.2.4, p. 271).

69. Where Antigonus lists the source as Timaeus.

70. See p. 102.

71. Antig. *Hist. Mir.* 12 (pp. 63–64 Westermann), Apollon. *Hist. Mirab.* 8 (p. 107 Westermann), Aelian *NA* 5.8, Plin. *Nat.* 10.30.

72. Hardie, *Cosmos and Imperium,* 171; Schrijvers, *Horror ac Divina Voluptas,* 273 n.49.

73. Schrijvers, *Horror ac Divina Voluptas,* 262–66.

provides scientific causes according to Epicurean laws of physical causation, thus replacing the traditional mythological explanations and demonstrating that *omnia quae naturali ratione geruntur / et quibus e fiant causis apparet origo* (6.760–61).[74] Strabo also introduces a similar series of *mirabilia naturae* with the express purpose of making them understandable: Πρὸς δὲ τὴν ἀθαυμαστίαν τῶν τοιούτων μεταβολῶν, οἵας ἔφαμεν αἰτίας εἶναι . . . ἄξιον παραθεῖναι καὶ ἄλλα πλείω τῶν ἐν ἑτέροις τόποις ὄντων . . . ἀθρόα γὰρ τὰ τοιαῦτα παραδείγματα πρὸ ὀφθαλμῶν τεθέντα παύσει τὴν ἔκπληξιν (1.3.16, p. 57, cf. 1.3.21, p. 61). Whereas, rather than the rational, it is precisely the miraculous aspect of the contents of his narrative that Pythagoras repeatedly emphasizes.

The natural phenomena listed by Pythagoras at 15.259–306, disappearing and reappearing rivers and streams, and the changes from islands to mainland and vice-versa, were explained by almost all of the natural philosophers as the results of vacant spaces underground and the underground air activity that takes place in these caves, that is, earthquakes.[75] This is the theory articulated by Lucretius in his explanations for earthquakes and volcanoes at *DRN* 6.535–607, 639–702. So Seneca quotes *Met.* 15.273–76 (the Lycus and Erasinus) and explains that the peculiar behavior of these rivers is due to underground caves: *Causa manifesta est: sub terra vacat locus; omnis autem natura umor ad inferius et ad inane defertur* (*N.Q.* 3.26.3), and ascribes the sudden appearance of islands to earthquakes at *N.Q.* 6.21. Pliny explains the birth of new lands in the same way: *Eadem nascentium causa terrarum est, cum idem ille spiritus adtollendo potens solo non valuit erumpere* (*Nat.* 2.201), and mentions Antissa and Sicily (*Nat.* 2.204). Strabo lists Pharos, Tyre, Antissa, and the disappearance of Bura and Helice, all as results of earthquakes (1.3.17–19, pp. 58–60, cf. Lucr. 6.585–87).

Ovid's Pythagoras, on the other hand, merely lists these phenomena, with a brief adumbration of a cause at 15.271 (*tremoribus orbis*). Moreover, he even inserts a wholly mythical explanation for the noxious waters of the Anigrus at 15.281–84: *illic lavere bimembres / vulnera, clavigeri quae fecerat Herculis arcus* (283–84). Strabo, by contrast, in his account of the river provides the missing rationalization. He explains that this story arose because the river Anigrus flowed slowly and formed a marsh and that the muddiness of the

---

74. Bailey, *Lucretius De Rerum Natura III*, 1646. Cf. *DRN* 6.608 *mirantur,* 654 *mirari multa relinquas,* 850 *admirantur,* 910 *mirantur* (introducing Lucretius' extraordinarily long account of the effects of the magnet 6.906–1064), 1056 *mirari mitte.*

75. Cf. Plin *Nat.* 2.191–200: *ventos in causa esse non dubium reor;* Sen. *N.Q.* 6.12–18, 24–26; *Aetna* 210ff.; Strab. 1.3.18, p. 59.

region emitted a stench and rendered fish inedible (8.3.19 p. 346). Pausanias, on the other hand, is convinced that the odor is due to the earth through which the water passes: τῷ δὲ ᾿Ανίγρῳ τὸ ἄτοπον εἶναι τῆς ὀσμῆς ἀπὸ τῆς γῆς πείθομαι δι᾿ῆς ἄνεισι τὸ ὕδωρ (5.5.9). We should have expected that Pythagoras would also have provided such rational explanations, but he does not. At the end of this first catalog of *mirabilia* Pythagoras includes the scientific account we have been missing, containing many Lucretian echoes (see *DRN* 6.577ff.): the construction of the hill of Pittheus due to the natural underground forces of wind trapped beneath the earth and seeking a way out (15.296–306). The insertion of this scientific-sounding passage, surrounded, as we shall see, by many marvelous unexplained phenomena, and introduced with an inappropriately dramatic rhetorical flourish, *res horrenda relatu* (298), does little to mitigate the general unscientific tone of Pythagoras' discourse. Moreover, as we have seen, Ovid has already alluded to this scientific wind theory earlier in the mythological story of Boreas at *Met.* 6.697–99. Mythological and philosophical explanation coexist and create the tension characteristic of the poem as a whole.

At 15.307 Pythagoras introduces a long catalog of *mirabilia fontium* and the echoes from the proem of the *Metamorphoses* are clear:

"Plurima cum subeant audita et cognita nobis,
pauca super referam. quid? non et lympha *figuras*
datque capitque *novas?*"

(15.307–9)

The similarity between Ovid's list of marvelous waters in Book 15 and those of Vitruvius, Pliny, and Seneca, even the order in which they are listed,[76] shows that they were all probably drawing from paradoxographical collections.[77] Such aquatic collections were popular, as Pliny suggests, because it was believed that *in nulla parte naturae maiora esse miracula* (*Nat.* 31.21). Commentators have noted that within the two categories of Pythagoras' *mirabilia fon-*

---

76. Esp. Pliny *Nat.* 2.224–34 (*Mirabilia Fontium et Fluminum*, where he lists among his sources Marcus Varro, Titus Livius, Cornelius Nepos, Pythagorici, and Timaeus), also 31.2–30 (*aquarum mirabilia*); Seneca *N.Q.* 3.20.3ff. (where he is quoting Ovid's verses from Pythagoras' speech); Vitruvius 8.3. On such lists see L. Callebat, "Science et Irrationnel: *Les Mirabilia Aquarum*," *Euphrosyne* n.s. 16 (1988): 155–67.

77. Many of these *mirabilia* are recorded in Callimachus' paradoxographical work, as cited in the collection (*Historia Mirabilium*) of Antigonus of Carystus (Call. fr. 407 Pf. = *Parad. Gr.* frr. 129ff., pp. 61–102 Westermann): fr. 407 VI (Crathis), XII (Arethusa), XVI (Ammon), XVII (Aethiopes lacus), XX (Athamas), XXX (Pheneus), XXXVI (Lyncestius amnis), XLIII (Diomedes' men).

tium, those that change the body and those that affect the mind (15.317–18), the springs are arranged alphabetically, except for the fountain of Salmacis, whose strange property, as we have seen, one of the Minyeides explained in a story in Book 4.[78] We note again that Pythagoras does not challenge Ovid's earlier mythical account of the fountain's properties, whereas Vitruvius (*De Arch.* 2.8.12) and Strabo (14.2.16, p. 656) both argue that there is no truth to the story that the fountain causes effeminacy, but that it is rather the inhabitants' luxurious way of life that made them that way. The appearance of the fountain of Salmacis so prominently in Pythagoras' speech seems to be a sly acknowledgment (*cui non audita* 15.319) by Ovid of the affinity of this thaumastic genre with his own stories.

In order to illuminate further the differences between the Ovidian Pythagoras' presentation of these natural marvels and that of the Roman natural philosophers, let us now examine some specific examples.[79] Pythagoras begins his collection with an example of a wonder first recorded by Herodotus (4.181) and included in most paradoxographical collections, the stream at Ammon, which is cold in the daytime and hot at night:

> "medio tua, corniger Ammon,
> unda die gelida est, ortuque obituque calescit,
> admotis Athamanas aquis accendere lignum
> narratur, minimos cum luna recessit in orbes."

(15.309–12)

In his own list of natural marvels, Lucretius discusses the miraculous properties of this spring at 6.848–78, beginning with the complaint *hunc homines fontem nimis admirantur* (6.850). Lucretius then proceeds to give the rationalistic atomic explanation of this phenomenon: *multaque sunt ignis prope semina corpus aquai* (6.863). Although, like Lucretius (*fertur* 6.849), Pythagoras includes a qualification of his evidence for this account (*narratur* 15.312), he merely states the phenomenon and moves on to the next example, offering no scientific explanation of it. This method is much closer to the original form of paradoxographical collections in Greek, as we find in

---

78. Pages 79–80.

79. It should always be kept in mind, of course, that not all natural historians were equally scrupulous. Pliny's *Naturalis Historia* can at times sound very much like Ovid's *Metamorphoses*. Although he claims in his preface to exclude the marvellous (*neque admittunt excessus aut orationes sermonesve aut casus mirabiles vel eventus varios* Praef. 12–13), Pliny includes plenty of incredible stories and numerous lists of phenomena specifically introduced as *mirabilia* (see *Nat.* 1 for the list of contents). Thus Ziegler includes Pliny under Paradoxographers (*RE* XVIII.3, 1165–66); see also Callebat, "Science et Irrationnel: *Les Mirabilia Aquarum,*" esp. 159–61.

Callimachus or Antigonus, than to works of serious scientific purpose such as Lucretius. Seneca, on the other hand, when he quotes from Pythagoras' list of *mirabilia fontium* in the *Metamorphoses* does so precisely in order to explain the causes of their properties: *Quaeramus ergo de terrestribus aquis et investigemus qua ratione fiant* (*N.Q.* 3.1.1). At *N.Q.* 3.20.1–2 Seneca explains that these properties come about *propter quattuor causas* and embarks on a list of *mirabilia fontium* in order to elucidate them individually. Thus he quotes the example following that of Ammon at *Met.* 15.313–14—*Flumen habent Ciones quod potum saxea reddit / viscera, quod tactis inducit marmora rebus*—and explains that the river has this effect because of the adulterated mud (*medicatum . . . limum*) through which its water passes (*N.Q.* 3.20.3). His theory of the *venae aquarum* through which all waters pass and through which they receive their properties is that described by Vitruvius (8.3.26) and Pliny (*Nat.* 2.166) as well, but Ovid's Pythagoras offers no such physical explanation.

At 15.322–28 Pythagoras does examine the cause of the strange sobering effect of the waters of Clitor's spring and gives two possible reasons for this property, one vaguely "scientific" and the other wholly mythical:

"seu vis est in aqua calido contraria vino,
sive, quod indigenae memorant, Amythaone natus,
Proetidas attonitas postquam per carmen et herbas
eripuit furiis, purgamina mentis in illas
misit aquas, odiumque meri permansit in undis."

(15.324–28).

Can we really call Pythagoras' tone in this passage "cool and dispassionate, the doubt that of an honest, inquiring scientist"?[80] Surely this is no choice Lucretius would ever have condoned. Consider how extremely odd it is that Pythagoras at all offers this second wildly fantastic mythical explanation for the properties of the waters, instead of the scientific explanation we might expect from a natural philosopher.[81] We should rather compare this with Ovid's own methods in Book 1 of the *Metamorphoses*, where he first gives both a "philosophical" and a mythical explanation for the origin of mankind (*sive hunc divino semine fecit / ille opifex rerum . . . /sive . . . satus Iapeto*

---

80. Solodow, *World of Ovid's Metamorphoses*, 66.
81. Interestingly the latter mythical story is specifically noted as the local version: *quod indigenae memorant* (15.325), a qualification that does not undermine the account, but rather once again highlights the local nature of these sorts of stories, while providing eyewitness authorities for the story. We learn from Vitruvius 8.3.21 that there was an inscription at the spring recording this mythological *aetion*.

1.78–88) without making a choice between them, and then offers two more
accounts that also involve a vague mixture of philosophical theory and mythol-
ogy (151–62 *Terra,* 395–415 *saxa*).[82] Like Ovid's account in Book 1,
Pythagoras' speech juxtaposes mythical and philosophical explanations for the
same phenomena, but privileges neither.

The long "scientific" account of the volcano of Aetna that follows is framed
by two pairs of marvels that seem designed to create an amusing contrast with
this intervening rational explanation. Preceding it are two examples of moving
lands, Ortygia and the Symplegades, which are both mentioned uncritically
with the mythological stories associated with them (15.336–39),[83] and follow-
ing are two especially miraculous stories, the first one being that of the Hyper-
boreans, which reminds us of the many ornithological metamorphoses in the
poem:

> "Esse viros fama est in Hyperborea Pallene,
> qui soleant levibus velari corpora plumis,
> cum Tritoniacam noviens subiere paludem."

> (15.356–58)

Pythagoras then adds that certain Scythian witches are said to have a similar
power, but inserts a qualification of the veracity of this account that reads very
humorously after the equally remarkable wonders preceding and following it
in his catalog, which have been presented without any comment whatsoever:

> "haut equidem credo: sparsae quoque membra venenis
> exercere artes Scythides memorantur easdem."

> (15.359–60)

Aetna was traditionally included among lists of *mirabilia,* and for this
reason its volcanic nature is carefully explained by Lucretius (6.639–702) and
Seneca (*N.Q.* 2.30). Pythagoras here gives not one, but three, different

---

82. Commentators have read this passage differently. Many see here a sudden and abrupt
switch from philosophy to myth that reveals the "antithesis" between cosmogony and meta-
morphosis; so Coleman, "Structure and Intention," 473 n.1; McKim, "Myth Against Philosophy,"
101; Little, "Speech of Pythagoras," 349. But others have rightly, I believe, argued that Ovid
refuses here, as elsewhere, to make a clear distinction, e.g., Wilkinson, *Ovid Recalled,* 214. Later at
Met. 7.392–93 he offers yet another, surely humorous, *aetion: hic aevo veteres mortalia primo /
corpora vulgarunt pluvialibus edita fungis.*

83. The story of Latona, Delos, and the birth of Apollo is referred to at *Met.* 1.694, 6.108, 187;
the Symplegades are mentioned at *Met.* 7.62–63.

rationalistic accounts for the phenomenon of its activity, as we have noted above. The style is Lucretian, and conspicuously "scientific," although Lucretius himself gave only one cause for Aetna's eruptions. The mythological explanation for the cause of Aetna's activity was the punishment of Typhoeus, a story related at *Met.* 5.346–55: *degravat Aetna caput, sub qua resupinus harenas / eiectat flammamque ferox vomit ore Typhoeus* (5.352–53).[84] But unlike the poet of the *Aetna,* Pythagoras indulges in no polemic against the mythical versions.

When Pythagoras next turns to the world of animal nature, with a series of *miracula animalium* (15.361ff.), the parallels with the mythical metamorphoses of the poem continue. Critics have wrongly claimed that Pythagoras' list of *mira generationum* contains instances "of what Ovid and others believed to be recorded natural phenomena."[85] It is clear that despite Pythagoras' strong appeals to experience, *siqua fides rebus tamen est addenda probatis* (15.361), *cognita res usu* (15.365), and *res observata colonis* (15.373), most of these examples are merely more *miracula.* The spontaneous generation of bees from the carcasses of bulls (15.364–67), for example, appears in Vergil's *Georgics* at 4.281ff.,[86] where the *bugonia* is clearly presented as an eastern marvel (309 *modis . . . miris* and 554–55 *mirabile monstrum*).[87] It can scarcely have been a common practice and is found more often in fiction than in technical writings. Varro, significantly mentions it only briefly in a speech by "Vaccius" along with Jupiter's metamorphosis into a bull to abduct Europa, and a Latin-speaking ox (*R.R.* 2.5.5). Varro tells us furthermore at *R.R.* 3.16.4 that the birth of bees from dead cows and of wasps from horses were included in Archelaus' verse paradoxa (*SH* 127-28), and these same examples are recorded in Antigonus' *Hist. Mir.* (XIX [23], p. 66 Westermann). The generation of snakes from the backbones of corpses was also included in both Archelaus' (*SH* 129) and Antigonus' (*Hist. Mir.* LXXXIX [96], p. 83 Westermann) paradoxographical collections. We find as well that while Pliny does indeed include most of these phenomena in his *Historia Naturalis,* even

---

84. Also referred to at *Met.* 14.1: *iamque Giganteis iniectam faucibus Aetnen.*

85. Little, "Speech of Pythagoras," 357. Lucretius' belief in the generation of life from decayed matter (worms, *DRN* 2.871ff., 898f., 928ff.; 3.719ff.; 5.797–98) is different from these examples. Bailey, *Lucretius De Rerum Natura, ad* 2.871, explains that his theory is close to the idea of the generation of life from primeval slime.

86. S.E. Hinds has suggested, in conversation, that Ovid in 15.365 (*cognita res usu*) archly footnotes Vergil's *bugonia,* thus showing that he knows about this from Vergilian literary "practice" rather than from so-called agricultural practice.

87. So Thomas, *Vergil's Georgics, ad* 4.281–314.

he frequently qualifies his belief in their veracity.[88] The contextual affinities of this section of Pythagoras' discourse with the *bugonia* in *Georgics* 4 are perhaps suggestive. Vergil is playing there with the same tensions between truth and fiction, between the different claims of philosophical poetry and mythological poetry.[89]

As noted above, one of the most interesting aspects of this long list of *mirabilia animalium* is that many of these examples of natural phenomena relate to stories that appeared earlier in the *Metamorphoses*. Thus Pythagoras, for example, mentions that frogs are born from slime (15.375–78 *limus*). This account is surely not meant to contradict, but rather to recall, the story of Latona and the Lycian peasants who are turned into frogs in *Met.* 6.316–81 (note the mention of slime at 6.381: *limosoque novae saliunt in gurgite ranae*) and the "scientific" account of the evolution of animal life from slime given at *Met.* 1.416–37. The birds Pythagoras lists are all associated with deities and all have been mentioned earlier in the poem: *Iunonis volucrem, quae cauda sidera portat, / armigerumque Iovis Cythereiadasque columbas* (15.385–86).[90] Cadmus and his wife were turned into snakes at *Met.* 4.563–603, which here are mentioned in connection with a theory that snakes evolve from backbones of the dead (15.389–90). Again, Pythagoras stresses the fact that hyenas can change their sex (15.408–10), as could Caeneus at *Met.* 12.169ff. and Iphis at *Met.* 9.666ff. We hear as well of lynxes whose urine turns into stone (15.413–15; cf. Pliny *Nat.* 37.53 *ego falsum id totum arbitror*), and at *Met.* 5.650–61 we had seen King Lyncus turned into a lynx. And finally, the mention of coral at 15.416–17 recalls the story of Perseus and Andromeda in Book 4, where Medusa's severed head provides the *aetion* for coral (4.740–52).

The Phoenix (15.391–407), truly a *miraculum naturae,* is Ovid's philosopher's pièce de resistance. The remarkable behavior of this bird is first recorded by Herodotus (2.73), who is not at all inclined to believe those who have told him the story: ἐμοὶ οὐ πιστὰ λέγοντες. Pliny (*Nat.* 10.3–5) provides an account of the phoenix, which is very similar to that in the *Metamorphoses,* with a similar disclaimer: *haut scio an fabulose.*[91] With the choice of this

---

88. *Bugonia: Nat.* 11.69–70 (*sunt qui mortuas . . . putent revivescere . . . sed horum omnium coitus cernuntur, et tamen in fetu eadem prope natura quae apibus*); crab and scorpion: *Nat.* 9.99 (*narratur*); snake from backbone: *Nat.* 10.188 (*accepimus a multis*); hyena: *Nat.* 8.105 (*vulgus credit, Aristoteles negat*).

89. See the interesting discussion of these issues in Perkell, *The Poet's Truth,* 139–90, where she suggests that the *bugonia* in *Georgics* 4 "undermines the values of the 'real,' thus using the form of the genre to challenge its own values" (141).

90. Peacock 1.722–23; eagle 4.362–63, 10.155ff., 12.560ff.; doves 13.670–74.

91. Pliny's source is a senator named Manilius (*RE* XIV.1.1115.26–46 [Münzer]). Pliny says that it is recorded (*actis testatum est*) that a phoenix was once displayed in the Comitium and adds: *sed quem falsum esse nemo dubitaret.*

particularly exotic and outlandish example, Pythagoras seems to challenge Lucretius' arguments against the possibility of there existing any unique living being (*DRN* 2.1077ff.: *in summa res nulla sit una*), in addition to the central doctrine of Epicureanism concerning the impossibility of the reincarnation of the spirit.[92]

Pythagoras does occasionally insert in his narrative traditional denunciations of the fictions of poets about the Underworld: *materiem vatum* 155, *nisi vatibus omnis / eripienda fides* 282–83. Such statements as these have again prompted critics to claim broadly that through Pythagoras, Ovid "presents the whole metier of poets as suspect."[93] Pythagoras' expressions of mere uncertainty are, however, different from the strong denunciations of the didactic poets reviewed above, and the few places where he does question his material stand in humorous contrast to the many miraculous phenomena he narrates without pausing to question or even rationally explain them. As Stinton points out, expressions of disbelief frequently can serve rhetorically to "encourage the reader's belief in what has gone before."[94] Although Pythagoras represents the traditional position of the philosopher antithetical to the fictions of poets, unlike the primary narrator "Ovid," his expressions convey no more than the sort of rhetorical expressions of doubt found throughout the *Metamorphoses,* which serve both "to heighten the discourse"[95] and self-consciously to call attention to the "fictional" content of the narrative.

Pythagoras' narrative is thus by no means characterized as a "rational scientific" discourse, *physica,* but rather is closer to thaumastic literature in the tradition of the Alexandrian paradoxographical collections of natural wonders,[96] or to mythological poetry such as the *Metamorphoses.* Neither is it merely a parody of natural philosophy, for rather than merely "make a mockery"[97] of the pretensions of philosophy, it assimilates such physical speculation to the mythical world of the poem, thus mirroring Ovid's own practice in

92. Crahay and Hubaux, "Sous le Masque de Pythagore," 290, suggest that this example may have relevance to Ovid's own claims for immortality in the epilogue to his poem (15.871–79).

93. Galinsky, *Ovid's Métamorphoses,* 175.

94. Stinton, "Expressions of Disbelief," 61.

95. Stinton, "Expressions of Disbelief," 60. R.F. Thomas, *Lands and Peoples in Roman Poetry: The Ethnographical Tradition* (Cambridge, 1982), 17, comments on the appearance of these phrases in association with thaumastic as well as ethnographic material. See also N. Horsfall, "Virgil and the Illusory Footnote," *PLLS* 6 (1990): 49–63, on the complexity of these sorts of expressions of disbelief and authority in Vergil.

96. Lafaye, *Les Métamorphoses d'Ovide,* 203: "un ouvrage où des faits merveilleux, relatifs à divers règnes de la nature, avaient été condensés, soit par pure curiosité, soit dans une intention philosophique."

97. McKim, "Myth against Philosophy," 106.

the rest of the poem of juxtaposing, but not thereby necessarily opposing, science and myth. Ovid's collocation of natural philosophy and mythology neither implicitly refutes myth nor indicates that mythology has a scientific basis. The pretensions of philosophy to explain rationally the world and (wo)man's place in it are exposed as equal to the claims of myth, but myth fares no better. Natural and supernatural causation exist side by side throughout the poem, like the multiple versions of some of Ovid's metamorphoses. The three different versions in the poem of Cycnus' transformation (*Met.* 2.367–80, 7.371–79, 12.72–145) stand as a sort of leitmotif for Ovid's treatment of this mythical material for which no "true" version ever was considered to exist. Similarly in the *Fasti* Ovid refuses to choose authoritatively between the multiple explanations he offers.[98] Ovid plays throughout the *Metamorphoses* with the use of aetiology as a component of the authoritative knowledge required of the epic poet. We have seen that he ultimately is more interested in drawing attention to the narrative strategies traditionally employed to create authentication and verisimilitude than in maintaining his own authority. Ovid does not reject philosophy, but appropriates and assimilates it, as he does every genre, to his mythical-metamorphic world. In the end, the cosmos, like Pythagoras' speech, is shown not to be rational, but rather a chaos, and thus both philosophic and poetic narrative are stripped of the power adequately to explain the world in all its arbitrariness.[99]

Although Pythagoras is introduced at the beginning of *Met.* 15 as a "Lucretius," since his speech is ostensibly an answer to Numa's request *quae sit rerum natura* (15.6),[100] his speech represents in the end a complete reversal of Lucretius' endeavors in his *De Rerum Natura.* Just as earnestly as Lucretius had implored his reader throughout his poem *not* to wonder at the workings of nature,[101] Pythagoras actively encourages amazement at the marvelous in nature: *quodque magis mirum est* (15.317, cf. also *Met.* 15.321, 408, 410). Ovid, moreover, tells us in his introduction to the narrative, in which he describes the reaction of the internal audience, that Pythagoras is successful in

---

98. On this aspect of Ovid's persona in the *Fasti* see Newlands, "Ovid's Narrator in the *Fasti,*" and Miller, "The *Fasti* and Hellenistic Didactic."

99. See McKim, "Myth against Philosophy," 99, where he notes how the description of chaos in *Met.* 1.17 (*nulli sua forma manebat*) accurately describes the metamorphic world of the poem.

100. As Otis, *Ovid as an Epic Poet,* 298, observes.

101. A search quickly reveals Lucretius' insistent negations of the miraculous, e.g., *neque enim mirum* (2.87, 338), *non est mirabile* (2.308, 898), *minime mirabile* (2.465, 4.259), *non est mirandum* (4.595, 5.592). When used to describe an event or phenomenon, the term has an implication that is clearly negative. Thus *simulacra,* because their distortions frequently cause unnecessary fear (*quae nos horrifice languentis saepe sopore / excierunt* 4.40–41 [36–37]), are frequently associated with such "miraculous" terms, e.g., 1.123, 4.39 [35].

this aim: *coetusque silentum / dictaque mirantum* (15.66–67).[102] Yet as scientific didactic poetry, which is meant to teach and convince by the force of the truth of its assertions, Pythagoras' speech fails: *ora / docta quidem solvit, sed non et credita* (15.73–74).[103] Commentators have pointed out that Pythagoras' aims are closer to that of the poets, to please, rather than to teach.[104]

Pythagoras' approach is in fact the same as that of the primary narrator, "Ovid," who throughout the *Metamorphoses* continually invites this reaction of wonder to his metamorphosis stories. As Anderson has demonstrated, "Ovid regularly associates with his descriptions of metamorphosis dramatic directions, by which he represents the amazement caused by the change in the individual and/or his companions, or through which he announces a story of change."[105] The promise of or the desire for the miraculous or novel is also a frequent motivation for Ovid's inset narratives; thus Cephalus begins his narrative: *accipe mirandum: novitate movebere facti!* (*Met.* 7.758).[106] The reactions of the internal audiences to the inset narratives of the poem provide paradigms for appropriate responses to the epic as a whole. We are invited to marvel throughout the poem at the skill with which Ovid presents his material in wholly original and unexpected ways. Ovid's profoundly antinaturalistic aesthetic self-consciously displays its own artistry and asks for admiration, not complete credence. In paradoxography the *factum mirabile* may equally be a *fictum* (cf. *Met.* 8.611 15).

Carmen Perpetuum et Deductum

By calling his philosophical internal narrator a *vates*, Ovid forges a connection between Pythagoras and his own role as primary narrator, and this obviously involves generic associations important to the conclusion of his epic. The literary background of Pythagoras' speech, an aspect that has received much attention, is highly suggestive. Many recent commentators have observed that the passage recalls the *somnia Pythagorea* (Hor. *Epist.* 2.1.52) at the beginning

---

102. Bömer, *Met., ad loc.,* points out that traditional reactions to the real Pythagoras' teachings included secrecy (silence, Iambl. *Vit. Pyth.* 31) and enthusiasm (Diog. Laert. *Pyth.* 15).

103. Barchiesi, "Voci e istanze narrative," 82, points out the similar response to Pythagoras' speech in Callimachus' first *Iamb.,* fr. 191.63 Pf.

104. Bömer, *Met., ad* 15.60ff. (p. 271), Saint-Denis, "Le Génie d'Ovide d'Après le Livre XV," 124.

105. Anderson, "Multiple Change," 4. Anderson provides here a useful list of the key terms of the "vocabulary of surprise" in the *Metamorphoses*.

106. Cf. also Alcithoë in *Met.* 4.284, *dulcique animos novitate tenebo* (see my earlier discussion at p. 80); 8.727–28; 9.327, 394; 10.552–53; 12.175–76, 15.499.

of Ennius' *Annales*.[107] In the proem of the *Annales* Homer appeared to Ennius and evidently explained the Pythagorean theory of metempsychosis and perhaps also embarked on broader cosmological themes. The question of the extent to which we are to understand Lucretius' claims that Homer spoke about *rerum natura* has recently been reopened:[108]

> unde sibi exortam semper florentis Homeri
> commemorat speciem lacrimas effundere salsas
> coepisse et *rerum naturam* expandere dictis

(DRN 1.124–26)

Skutsch suggested that the lines following these (*DRN* 1.127ff.), a summary of the themes to be discussed in the *De Rerum Natura*, may provide us with some idea of how Ennius' Homer proceeded.[109] Hardie conjectures that the speech began with cosmogony and moved on to the nature of the soul.[110] In this way Ennius, through the speech of Homer, provided for the Roman poets "a substantial model for natural-philosophical didactic, on the subject, precisely, of *rerum natura*."[111] Clearly Ovid's Pythagorean discourse offers obvious parallels with the Ennian model.[112] Pythagoras' comment at *Met.* 15.160–61, *ipse ego (nam memini) Troiani tempore belli / Panthoides Euphorbus eram*, with its echo of *Ann.* 11 Sk., *memini me fiere pavom*, may imply an "intertextual" memory of the whole Ennian Pythagorean passage.[113]

107. See especially Hofmann, "*Carmen Perpetuum, Carmen Deductum*"; Hardie, *Cosmos and Imperium*, 83 n.121; Knox, *Traditions of Augustan Poetry*, 69–74.

108. Hardie, *Cosmos and Imperium*, 76–83; also Farrell, *Traditions of Ancient Epic*, 307 n.85. The issue was first broached by Skutsch, *Studia Enniana*, 105ff. See also Skutsch, *Annals of Q. Ennius*, *ad Ann.* 5, *desunt rivos camposque remanant*, a passage that he argues "seems to prove that Homer's exposition of the *natura rerum* was not restricted to matter closely connected with the migration of souls."

109. Skutsch, *Studia Enniana*, 109.

110. Hardie, *Cosmos and Imperium*, 80. Hardie also points out that this is also the sequence of the Speech of Anchises in Vergil's *Aen.* 6, and offers an important discussion of Ennius' significance to Vergil (pp. 69–83). For more on Pythagoreanism in the *Annales*, see the two articles by U. Todini, "La Cosmologia Pitagorica e Le Muse Enniane," *RCCM* 13 (1971): 21–38, "*Pedibus Pulsare*: Postilla e Non," *RCCM* 16 (1974): 301–9.

111. Hardie, *Cosmos and Imperium*, 80. Worth considering also are the associations of Pythagorean teaching with the earliest allegorical interpretation of Homer, as discussed by Lamberton, *Homer the Theologian*, 31–43; cf. M. Detienne, *Homère, Hésiode et Pythagore: Poésie et philosophie dans le pythagorisme ancien* (Brussels and Berchem, 1962).

112. As both Skutsch, *Studia Enniana*, 109, and Hardie, *Cosmos and Imperium*, 83 n.121, suggest.

113. Barchiesi, "Voci e istanze narrative," 85; similarly Knox, *Traditions of Augustan Poetry*, 72. Note further that the Ennian quotation at *Met.* 14.814 (below) is also introduced with a similar formula: *nam memoro memorique animo pia verba notavi* (14.813).

Echoes of Ennius' *Annales* appear elsewhere in the final books of the *Metamorphoses*. The first three books of Ennius' *Annales,* which dealt with early Roman legend from the foundation period, must have been an important model for the final books of the *Metamorphoses.*[114] Commentators have noted how the transition from the end of Book 14 with the deification of Romulus to the opening of Book 15 with Numa and Pythagoras reflects the similar structure of the end of *Annales* Book 1, the deification of Romulus,[115] and the beginning of Book 2, the meeting of Numa and Egeria (*Ann.* 113 Sk.).[116] This thematic and structural correspondence is highlighted by the verbatim quotation of a line from the *Annales* at *Met.* 14.814: *unus erit, quem tu tolles in caerula caeli* (= *Ann.* 54 Sk.).[117]

What then is the significance of these Ennian allusions at the end of the *Metamorphoses*? It seems that with the reminiscences of Ennius, and the reintroduction of cosmic themes in language redolent of Lucretius at the end of the *Metamorphoses,* Ovid has reemphasized the cosmogonic "epic" affiliations of his poem and prepared the way for the political conclusion of the poem.[118] As Hardie has proposed, "the Ovidian Pythagoras provides a kind of retrospective 'cosmic' setting for the whole theme of metamorphosis; natural philosophy also acts as a prelude to the historical 'metamorphosis' that leads to Roman empire."[119] Parallels with Vergil's similarly philosophic and historical *Aeneid* 6 and Pythagoras' recollection of Helenus' prophesies from *Aeneid* 3.374–462 at *Metamorphoses* 15.435–52 underpin these generic associations. Yet at the same time, it is well known that Ennius' Pythagorean vision at the beginning of the *Annales* clearly owes much to the Callimachean dream at the beginning of

---

114. As Knox notes, *Traditions of Augustan Poetry,* 69.

115. The argument of Skutsch, *Annals of Q. Ennius,* 245, against the inclusion of the deification of Hersilia in the *Annales* ("it is a little difficult to credit Ennius with the Ovidian metamorphosis which turns Hersilia into Hora [14.829–51], and to imagine that he deified Hersilia at the same moment as Romulus") seems generally persuasive, although it is not universally accepted. Cf. *Annales* 100 Sk.: *Quirine pater veneror Horamque Quirini* (*Met.* 14.851: *Horamque* with a short o, which Skutsch, *Annals of Q. Ennius, ad* 99, argues is "undoubtedly correct").

116. Ludwig, *Struktur und Einheit,* 71; Hofmann, "*Carmen Perpetuum, Carmen Deductum,*" 225.

117. Also quoted at *Fasti* 2.485. See Conte's illuminating discussion of these passages, *Rhetoric of Imitation,* 57-63.

118. Knox, *Traditions of Augustan Poetry,* 72, argues differently that "the exposition of Pythagorean doctrine [i.e., in Ennius] amounts to the equivalent of the divine sanction that Callimachus received from the Muses. And it is this exposition of Pythagoreanism that forms the basis for Ovid's Pythagoras in Book Fifteen of the *Metamorphoses.*"

119. Hardie, *Cosmos and Imperium,* 83 n.121. Knox makes a similar point, *Traditions of Augustan Poetry,* 73: "the rational exposition of Pythagoras establishes the basis for Ovid's own transition to the world of history."

his *Aetia.*[120] Less discussed is the significant fact that Callimachus in his programmatic first *Iambus* (fr. 191 Pf.) had introduced the reborn Hipponax, his literary model for the *Iambi,* along with Pythagoras in his reincarnation as Euphorbus (fr. 191.59ff.).[121] This important scene of literary initiation was parodied by Herodas in his *Mimiambus* 8 and Apollonius also seems to acknowledge it at *Argon.* 1.640–52 with his mention of Aethalides, another of Pythagoras' incarnations, in conjunction with an apparent reference to Callimachus' earlier treatment: ἀλλὰ τί μύθους / Αἰθαλίδεω χρειώ με διηνεκέως ἀγορεύειν (648–49).[122] Ennius' scene of poetic initiation is therefore perhaps doubly indebted to Callimachus.[123] Although Ovid and his contemporaries typically characterized Ennius as a non-Callimachean literary model, mainly because of his lack of polish,[124] his achievement in fusing Callimachean poetics with Roman historical epic containing elements of both cosmology and aetiology was surely not unnoticed by the later Roman poets.[125] We are returned, rather, through the allusions to both Pythagoras and Ennius to a mixed poetic tradition involving both cosmogonic epic themes and Callimachean aesthetics.

The passages cited above suggest that Pythagoras should perhaps be understood as representing as much a literary as a philosophical figure. Pythagoras' speech provides another example of the way in which Ovid uses internal narratives self-referentially to highlight and comment upon the generic and interpretive tensions of the epic as a whole. Most commentators now agree that we cannot seek for the model of the *Metamorphoses* in any one of these internal narratives. It is only in juxtaposition that the many different narratives

---

120. See Skutsch, *Studia Enniana,* 1–29, 119–29, *Annals of Q. Ennius,* 147–53. (Differently Jocelyn, "Poems of Quintus Ennius," 1015.) See also Kambylis, *Die Dichterweihe und ihre Symbolik,* 191–201; J.K. Newman, *Augustus and the New Poetry* (Brussels, 1967), 64–77; G. Sheets, "*Ennius Lyricus,*" *ICS* 8 (1983): 22–32.

121. See Pfeiffer, *ad loc.,* and M. Puelma-Piwonka, *Lucilius und Kallimachos: Zur Geschichte einer Gattung der hellenistisch-römischen Poesie* (Frankfurt, 1949), 345ff. For an illuminating discussion of Ennius and of the whole theme of the "*poeta redivivus*" see W. Suerbaum, *Untersuchungen zur Selbstdarstellung älterer römischer Dichter* (Hildesheim, 1968), 82–113.

122. See Dickie, "Talos Bewitched," 280–81; A. Ardizzioni, "Echi Pitagorici in Apollonio Rodio e Callimaco," *RIFC* 93 (1965): 257–67.

123. Hardie, *Cosmos and Imperium,* 81–82, calls attention to Ennius' similar literary dream of initiation in his *Epicharmus.*

124. The passages in which Ovid and other Roman poets discuss Ennius are collected and discussed by J.F. Miller, "Ennius and the Elegists," *ICS* 8 (1983): 277–95; see also Hofmann, "*Carmen Perpetuum, Carmen Deductum,*" 226, 237 n.7. Ovid mentions Ennius at *Am.* 1.15, *Ars* 3.405–12, *Tr.* 2.259–60, 2.424.

125. Farrell, *Traditions of Ancient Epic,* 297, rightly complains that "we have been asked to believe that this ambitious transformation made no lasting impression on Roman poetry."

create a balanced reflection on the epic as whole as both a *carmen perpetuum* and a *carmen deductum*.[126] It has been observed that three of the longest internal narratives appear significantly marking each of the pentads of the poem and share important features: Book 5 containing the song of Calliope, Book 10 that of Orpheus, and Book 15 that of Pythagoras.[127] These narratives clearly participate in a self-reflexive dialogue about the nature of the poem as a whole, in terms of both its genre and its themes, and ultimately, its reception. The figure of Calliope, Orpheus, and Pythagoras all appear in earlier poetry as important literary figures of inspiration. Their embedded narratives in the *Metamorphoses* function as authenticators of the "truth" and inspiration of the poem as whole, analogous to invocations of the Muses, which are famously and conspicuously absent from the poem until Book 15.622–25. In fact, it has been observed that the Muses appear prominently only in Books 5 (250–678), 10 (148–49), and 15 (622–25).[128] Callimachus' conversations with the Muses in the *Aetia* and Ovid's divine interlocutors in the *Fasti* function similarly. All three of these embedded narratives explicitly bring up issues of truth and fiction, and the presence of an internal audience for each narrative provides a paradigm for possible audience responses.

The narrative of Calliope in the Contest of the Muses at 5.346–661 has long been recognized as an important programmatic passage in the *Metamorphoses*. As S.E. Hinds has shown, the episode shares the same dual generic associations as the epic. Hinds has argued that the embedded narrative is involved in two exercises in poetic contrast, each of which bring out different aspects of the narrative. Calliope's song, in opposition with the parallel version of the story in the *Fasti* 4.417ff., exhibits "marked epic tendencies which are in contrast with elegiac tendencies in [the] parallel treatment of the same theme in the *Fasti*."[129] In competition with the rival effort of the Pierids in the poetry contest of *Metamorphoses* 5, however, Calliope's narrative seems to represent

---

126. See Leach, "Ekphrasis and the Theme of Artistic Failure," 117, Lausberg, "Zur Bildbeschreibung bei Ovid," 115–16. For warnings against interpreting any *one* internal narrative in the poem, as a paradigm of the *Metamorphoses* as a whole, see Hinds' review of P.E. Knox's *Traditions of Augustan Poetry,* 269; Otis, *Ovid as an Epic Poet,* 58.

127. R. Rieks, "Zum Aufbau Ovids Metamorphosen," *WJA* 6b (1980): 85–103. The "primary narrator's" cosmogony in Book 1 and the episode at the cave of Achelous in Book 8, which marks the center of the poem, share similar generic tensions and may also form a part of this programmatic pattern.

128. See Rieks, "Zum Aufbau Ovids Metamorphosen," 97; M. von Albrecht, "Les Dieux et la Religion dans les *Métamorphoses* d'Ovide," in *Hommages à Henri Le Bonniec: Res Sacrae,* ed. D. Porte and J.-P. Néraudau, Collections Latomus 201 (Brussels, 1988), 1. The invocation of the Muses at *Met.* 10.48–49 is part of Orpheus' embedded narrative.

129. Hinds, *Metamorphosis of Persephone,* 127.

a properly neoteric type of epic narrative, *doctos . . . cantus* (5.662), in contrast with the "extreme of epic represented by the Pierid Gigantomachy."[130] Calliope's epic program is underlined by her own status as the Muse frequently associated with elevated poetry (*maxima* 5.662).[131] As a narrator of meta-morphosis stories similar to those in the rest of the poem, Calliope clearly functions in some way to authorize those tales Ovid has narrated *in propria persona*. Aetiology and the issue of narrative reliability opened the episode in Minerva's arrival on Helicon to determine whether the rumor she had heard about the origin of a new fountain was true (5.256–65). But the reliability of Calliope's tale is already questioned by her own son Orpheus at the beginning of Book 10: *famaque si veteris non est mentita rapinae, / vos quoque iunxit Amor* (28–29).[132] As we have seen, Ovid continually destabilizes his own narrative authority and challenges our response to his fictions.[133]

Orpheus uses this sly dig at an earlier tale in the poem to strengthen his own claims to be speaking truthfully: *si licet et falsi positis ambagibus oris / vera loqui sinitis* (10.19–20). Orpheus exhibits further concerns with narrative au-thority and reliability when he later invites his audience either to believe or disbelieve his tale of Myrrha:

> "dira canam; procul hinc natae, procul este parentes
> aut, mea si vestras mulcebunt carmina mentes,
> desit in hac mihi parte fides, nec credite factum,
> vel, si credetis, facti quoque credite poenam."

(10.300–303)

Once again, "Ovid reveals the complicity between poet and audience which underpins his enterprise."[134] In generic terms, Orpheus' narrative at 10.148–739 clearly forms somewhat of a contrast with that of Calliope, since it is explicitly introduced with a *recusatio* as being of a lighter strain of poetry: *cecini plectro graviore Gigantas / sparsaque Phlegraeis victricia fulmina*

---

130. Hinds, *Metamorphosis of Persephone,* 131; cf. Hoffman, "*Carmen Perpetuum, Carmen Deductum,*" 227–30, who argues that Calliope's song is represented as a *carmen deductum* in contrast to the Pierides' *carmen perpetuum*. Anderson, review of *Ovid as an Epic Poet,* 2d ed., by B. Otis, *AJP* 89 (1968): 103, Rosati, "Il racconto dentro il racconto," 303, and Nagle, "Two Miniature *Carmina Perpetua,*" 121, all remark on the similarity of the structure of Calliope's song and the *Metamorphoses* as a whole.

131. Hinds, *Metamorphosis of Persephone,* 125–26.

132. Hinds, *Metamorphosis of Persephone,* 135.

133. Newlands, "Ovid's Narrator in the *Fasti,*" shows how in the *Fasti* Ovid similarly inverts the use of divine interlocutors as authenticators by depicting them frequently as unreliable narra-tors.

134. Feeney, *Gods in Epic,* 229.

campis, / nunc opus est leviore lyra (150–52). P.E. Knox has elucidated the strong elegiac cast of Orpheus' narrative.[135] However, Orpheus is emphatically also a *vates* (10.12, 82, 89, 143; 11.2, 8, 19, 27) and he tells us that he has in fact already composed a Gigantomachy, as did "Ovid" in Book 1.151–56 and the Pierids in Book 5.319–20. We are perhaps asked to recall Orpheus' earlier cosmogonic song in Apollonius 1.492–511,[136] in addition to the philosophical associations of traditional Orphic poetry. Orpheus, like Calliope with her stories of Etna and the Underworld, is both a cosmogonic and Callimachean narrator. Through his internal narrators Ovid affirms both the universal cosmogonical scope of his epic and its affinities with Callimachean aesthetic ideals.[137]

The discourse of Pythagoras shares in the themes and programmatic tensions of these earlier narratives while introducing the new historical themes of the poem's conclusion.[138] His narrative participates in the Alexandrian themes of aetiology and paradoxography prominent especially in the final books, while it reasserts the affiliations of the poem with the tradition of "scientific" cosmogonic epic. Allusions to Lucretius and Ennius are combined with references to important Callimachean scenes of poetic inspiration. That these seemingly conflicting generic associations should again appear in the final book of a poem that has from its opening lines made its genre an issue is not surprising. Ovid does not resolve these tensions, but continues to exploit them.

Epilogue

All three of these programmatic episodes in Books 5, 10, and 15 also share the themes of death and immortality.[139] Pythagoras' discourse with its thesis of transmigration revives these concerns at a crucial juncture in the poem as Ovid

---

135. Knox, *Traditions of Augustan Poetry*, 48–64.

136. Knox, *Traditions of Augustan Poetry*, 51.

137. Similarly Ovid's other prominent internal artists have cosmogonic powers: on Vulcan see Brown, "The Palace of the Sun," 219; on Arachne see M. von Albrecht, "L'episode d'Arachne dans les *Mét.* d'Ovide," *REL* 57 (1979): 270, Anderson, *Ovid's Metamorphoses Books 6–10, ad loc.,* Feeney, *Gods in Epic,* 191, who points to Ovid's description of Arachne's activities in *Met.* 6.19–23 as containing language suggestive of cosmogony (esp. 6.19 *rudem primos lanam glomerabat in orbes,* cf. *Met.* 1.7, 35); on Daedalus (*opifex* 8.201, cf. 1.19, *naturamque novat* 8.189) see Lateiner, "Mythic and Non-Mythic Artists," 17; cf. Pygmalion (10.248 *formamque dedit,* 281ff. *mollescit* 283, 285).

138. Rieks, "Zum Aufbau Ovids Metamorphosen," 100, points out that Calliope's narrative programmatically recapitulates the divine themes of the opening books, while Orpheus' song deals with themes of the "heroic" period; cf. Otis, *Ovid as an Epic Poet,* 371.

139. Rieks, "Zum Aufbau Ovids Metamorphosen," 103; Nagle, "Two Miniature *Carmina Perpetua,*" 124, on Calliope and Orpheus.

nears the conclusion of his epic. Prophecies also figure prominently in Book 15. The speech of Pythagoras includes an important and already-fulfilled prophecy concerning the growth of Rome, as well as a veiled hint about its future decline (15.431–52). Prophecies from earlier parts of the *Metamorphoses* are also fulfilled. The restoration of Hippolytus/Virbius as well as the deification of Aesculapius, which occur in Book 15, were prophesied by Ocyroe in Book 2.[140] Finally, at the end of the poem, the apotheoses of both Julius Caesar and Augustus are prophesied to Venus by Jupiter (15.807–42) before their enactment. Not only does Ovid in this way create another aspect of unity in his poem, but by underlining the truth of these prophecies in his poem, he supports his own claims to immortality expressed in the epilogue to the poem; that is, he has effectively quelled any doubt expressed in the last line of the *Metamorphoses: siquid habent veri vatum praesagia, vivam* (15.879).

140. *Met.*. 2.640–45, 15.531–34; 2.645–48, 15.742–44. See Keith, *Play of Fictions*, chap. 3, and her detailed discussion of the correspondences between these passages, where she notes further that Ocyroe's prophecies concerning Aesculapius are fulfilled in the *Fasti* (6.753–60).

Selected Bibliography

Ackermann, E. *Lukrez und der Mythos.* Wiesbaden, 1979.

Adams, J.N. *The Latin Sexual Vocabulary.* London, 1982.

Ahern, C. "Ovid as *Vates* in the Proem to the *Ars Amatoria.*" *CP* 85 (1990): 44–48.

Ahl, F. "The Art of Safe Criticism in Greece and Rome." *AJP* 105 (1984): 174–208.

———. *Metaformations: Soundplay and Wordplay in Ovid and Other Classical Poets.* Ithaca, 1985.

Alfonsi, L. "L'Inquadramento Filosofico delle Metamorfosi Ovidiane." In *Ovidiana: Recherches sur Ovide publiées à l'occasion du bimillénaire de la naissance du poète,* edited by N.I. Herescu, 265–72. Paris, 1958.

Alter, R. *Partial Magic: The Novel as a Self-conscious Genre.* Berkeley, 1975.

Altieri, Charles. "Ovid and the New Mythologists." *Novel* 7 (1973): 31–40.

Anderson, W.S. "Multiple Change in the *Metamorphoses.*" *TAPA* 94 (1963): 1–27.

———. "*Hercules Exclusus:* Propertius 4.9." *AJP* 85 (1964): 1–12.

———. Review of *Ovid as an Epic Poet,* 2d ed., by B. Otis. *AJP* 89 (1968): 93–104.

———. Review of *Ovid's Metamorphoses and the Traditions of Augustan Poetry,* by P.E. Knox. *AJP* 109 (1988): 457–61.

———, ed. *Ovid's Metamorphoses Books 6–10.* Oklahoma, 1972.

Ardizzioni, A. "Echi Pitagorici in Apollonio Rodio e Callimaco." *RIFC* 93 (1965): 257–67.

Austin, R.G., ed. *P. Vergilius Maronis: Aeneidos Liber Sextus.* Oxford, 1977.

Avery, M.M. "The Use of Direct Speech in Ovid's *Metamorphoses.*" Ph.D. dissertation, University of Chicago, 1937.

Bailey, C., ed. *Lucretius De Rerum Natura.* 3 vols. Oxford, 1947.

Bakhtin, M.M. *The Dialogic Imagination: Four Essays.* Translated by C. Emerson and M. Holquist. Austin, 1981.

———. *Rabelais and His World.* Translated by H. Iswolsky. Indiana, 1984.

Bal, Mieke. *Introduction to the Theory of Narrative.* Translated by C. van Boheeman. Toronto, 1985.

Baldo, Gianluigi. "Il codice epico nelle *Metamorfosi* di Ovidio." *MD* 16 (1986): 109–31.

Barchiesi, A. "Voci e istanze narrative nelle *Metamorfosi* di Ovidio." *MD* 23 (1989): 55–97.

———. "Discordant Muses." *PCPS* 37 (1991): 1–21.

Bardon, H. *La Littérature Latine Inconnue I.* Paris, 1952.

———. "Ovide et la métamorphose." *Latomus* 20 (1961): 485–500.

Barkan, L. *The Gods Made Flesh: Metamorphosis and the Pursuit of Paganism.* New Haven, 1986.

Barsby, J.A. *Ovid.* Greece and Rome New Surveys in the Classics 12. Oxford, 1978.

Barthes, R. *S/Z.* Translated by R. Miller. New York, 1974.

Bernbeck, E.J. *Beobachtungen zur Darstellungsart in Ovids Metamorphosen.* Zetemata 43. Munich, 1967.

Binder, G. "Aitiologische Erzählung und Augusteisches Programm in Vergils *Aeneis.*" In *Saeculum Augustum II,* edited by G. Binder, 255–87. Darmstadt, 1988.

Bing, P. *The Well-Read Muse: Present and Past in Callimachus and the Hellenistic Poets.* Hypomnemata 90. Göttingen, 1988.

Binns, J.W., ed. *Ovid.* Greek and Latin Studies: Classical Literature and its Influence. London, 1973.

Boillat, M. *Les Métamorphoses d'Ovide: Themes majeurs et problemes de composition.* Berne and Frankfurt, 1976.

———. "*Mutatas dicere formas.* Intentions et réalité." In *Journées Ovidiennes de Parménie,* edited by J.-M. Frécaut and D. Porte, 43–56. Brussels, 1985.

Bömer, F. "Ovid und Die Sprache Vergils." In *Ovid,* edited by M. von Albrecht and E. Zinn, 173–202. Darmstadt, 1968.

———. "Aeneas landet bei Cumae: Zu Verg. *Aen.* 6.2 und Ov. *Met.* 14.102ff." *Gymnasium* 93 (1986): 97–101.

———. "Über das zeitliche Verhältnis zwischen den Fasten und den Metamorphosen Ovids." *Gymnasium* 95 (1988): 207–21.

Boyancé, P. *Le Culte des Muses chez les philosophes grecs: Études d'histoire et de psychologie religieuses.* Bibl. des Écoles françaises d'Athènes et de Rome. Fasc. 141. Paris, 1937.

Bremmer, J.N., and N.M. Horsfall. *Roman Myth and Mythography.* University of London Institute of Classical Studies Bulletin Supplement 52. London, 1987.

Brenk, F.E. "Tarpeia among the Celts: Watery Romance from Simylos to Propertius." *Collections Latomus* 164, 166–74. Brussels, 1979.

Briggs, W.W., Jr. "Vergil and the Hellenistic Epic." *ANRW* 2.31.2 (1983): 948–84.

Brink, C.O., ed. *Horace on Poetry: The 'Ars Poetica.'* Cambridge, 1971.

Brown, R.D. "Lucretius and Callimachus." *ICS* 7 (1982): 77–97.

———. "The Palace of the Sun in Ovid's *Métamorphoses.*" In *Homo Viator: Classical Essays for John Bramble,* edited by M. Whitby, P. Hardie, and M. Whitby, 211–20. Bristol and Oak Park, Ill., 1987.

———. "The Structural Function of the Song of Iopas." *HSCP* 93 (1990): 315–34.

Brunel, P. *Le Mythe de La Métamorphose.* Paris, 1974.

Brunner, T.F. "Deinon vs. Eleeinon: Heinze Revisited." *AJP* 92 (1971): 275–84.

Bubbe, G. *De Metamorphosibus Graecorum Capita Selecta.* Academia Fridericiana Halensi cum Vitebergensi Consociata, 1913.

Buffière, F. *Les Mythes d'Homère et la Pensée Grecque.* Paris, 1956.

Bulloch, A.W. "Hellenistic Poetry." In *The Cambridge History of Classical Literature,* vol. 1, edited by P.E. Easterling and B.M.W. Knox, 541–621. Cambridge, 1985.

Burkert, W. *Lore and Science in Ancient Pythagoreanism.* Translated by E.L. Minar, Jr. Cambridge, Mass., 1972.

Cairns, F. *Tibullus: A Hellenistic Poet at Rome.* Cambridge, 1979.

———. "Propertius and the Battle of Actium (4.6)." In *Poetry and Politics in the Age of Augustus,* edited by A.J. Woodman and D.A. West, 129–68. Cambridge, 1984.

Callebat, L. "Science et Irrationnel: *Les Mirabilia Aquarum.*" *Euphrosyne* n.s. 16 (1988): 155–67.

Cameron, A. "Genre and Style in Callimachus." *TAPA* 122 (1992): 305–12.

Cardauns, B., ed. *M. Terentius Varro Antiquitates Rerum Divinarum.* Akademie der Wissenschaften unde der Literatur Mainz. Wiesbaden, 1976.

Castiglioni, L. *Studi Intorno alle Fonti e alle Composizione delle Metamorfosi di Ovidio.* Rome, 1906.

Celoria, F., ed. *The Metamorphoses of Antoninus Liberalis.* London, 1992.

Chatman, Seymour. *Story and Discourse: Narrative Structure in Fiction and Film.* Ithaca, 1978.

Classen, C.J. "Poetry and Rhetoric in Lucretius." *TAPA* 99 (1968): 77–118.

Clausen, W.V. "Callimachus and Latin Poetry." *GRBS* 5 (1964): 181–96.

———. *Virgil's Aeneid and the Tradition of Hellenistic Poetry.* Berkeley and Los Angeles, 1987.

Clauss, J.J. "The Episode of the Lycian Farmers in Ovid's *Metamorphoses.*" *HSCP* 92 (1989): 297–314.

Clayman, D.L. *Callimachus' Iambi.* Mnemosyne Supplement 59. Leiden, 1980.

Codrignani, G. "L'Aition nella poesia greca prima di Callimaco." *Convivium* 26 (1958): 527–45.

Colavito, M.M. *The Pythagorean Intertext in Ovid's Metamorphoses.* Studies in Comparative Literature, vol. 5. Lewiston, Lampeter, and Queenston, 1989.

Coleman, R. "Structure and Intention in the *Metamorphoses.*" *CQ* 21 (1971): 461–77.

———, ed. *Vergil: Eclogues.* Cambridge Greek and Latin Classics. Cambridge, 1977.

Conte, Gian Biagio. *The Rhetoric of Imitation: Genre and Poetic Memory in Virgil and Other Latin Poets.* Edited by C.P. Segal. Ithaca, 1986.

———. "Love without Elegy: The *Remedia amoris* and the Logic of a Genre." *Poetics Today* 10.3 (1989): 441–69.

———. *Generi e Lettori: Lucrezio, l'elegia d'amore, l'enciclopedia di Plinio.* Milan, 1991.

Copley, F.O. *Exclusus Amator: A Study in Latin Love Poetry.* APA Monographs no. 17. Madison, 1956.

Courtney, E. "Three Poems of Propertius." *BICS* 16 (1969): 70–87.

———. *A Commentary on the Satires of Juvenal.* London, 1980.

———. "Vergil's Sixth *Eclogue.*" *Quaderni Urbinati* 34 (1990): 99–112.

———, ed. *The Fragmentary Latin Poets.* Oxford, 1993.

Crabbe, Anna. "Structure and Content in Ovid's *Metamorphoses.*" *ANRW* 2.31.4 (1981): 2274–2327.

Crahay, R., and J. Hubaux. "Sous le Masque de Pythagore." In *Ovidiana: Recherches sur Ovide publiées à l'occasion du bimillénaire de la naissance du poète,* edited by N.I. Herescu, 283–300. Paris, 1958.

Crowther, N.B. "Parthenius and Roman Poetry." *Mnemosyne* 29 (1976): 65–71.

Crump, M. *The Epyllion from Theocritus to Ovid.* Oxford, 1931.

Curran, L. C. "Transformation and Anti-Augustanism in Ovid's *Metamorphoses.*" *Arethusa* 5 (1972): 71–91.

———. "Rape and Rape Victims in the *Metamorphoses.*" In *Women in the Ancient World,* edited by J. Peradotto and J.P. Sullivan, 263–86. Albany, 1984.

Dahlmann, H. *Über Aemilius Macer.* Abhandlungen der Geistes und Sozial wissenschaftlichen Klasse Nr. 6. Akademie der Wissenschaften und der Literatur Mainz. Wiesbaden, 1981.

Davis, G. "The Problem of Closure in a *Carmen Perpetuum* : Aspects of Thematic Recapitulation in Ovid's *Metamorphoses* 15." *Grazer Beiträge* 9 (1980): 123–32.

———. *The Death of Procris.* Rome, 1983.

Dawson, D. *Allegorical Readers and Cultural Revision in Ancient Alexandria.* Berkeley and Los Angeles, 1992.

De Cola, Maria. *Callimaco e Ovidio.* Palermo, 1937.

De Jong, Irene. *Narrators and Focalizers: The Presentation of the Story in the Iliad.* Amsterdam, 1987.

De Saint-Denis, E. "Le Génie D'Ovide d'après le livre xv des *Métamorphoses.*" *REL* 18 (1940): 111–40.

Dee, J.H. "Propertius 4.2 : *Callimachus Romanus* at Work." *AJP* 95 (1974): 43–55.

DeLacy, P. "Philosophical Doctrine and Poetic Technique in Ovid." *CJ* 43 (1947): 153–61.

———. "Lucretius and the History of Epicureanism." *TAPA* 79 (1948): 12–23.

Della Corte, F. "Gli Empedoclea e Ovidio." *Maia* 37 (1985): 3–12.

Deremetz, A. "L'Élegie de Vertumne: L'Oevre Trompeuse." *REL* 64 (1986): 116–49.

———. "Le *carmen deductum* ou le fil du poème: À propos de Virgile *Buc.* 6." *Latomus* 46 (1987): 762–77.

Di Geronimo, M.G. *Ovidio tra Pitagorismo: Aition ed Encomio.* Naples and Florence, 1972.

Dickie, M.W. "Talos Bewitched: Magic, Atomic Theory and Paradoxography in Apollonius *Argonautica* 4.1638–88." *PLLS* 6 (1990): 267–96.

Doblhofer, E. "*Ovidius Urbanus:* Eine Studie zum Humor in Ovids Metamorphosen." *Philologus* 103–4 (1959–60): 63–91, 223–35.

Döpp, S. *Virgilischer Einfluss in Werk Ovids.* Munich, 1968.

Döscher, T. *Ovidius Narrans: Studien zur Erzählkunst Ovids in den Metamorphosen.* Inaugural Dissertation Doktorwürde, Heidelberg, 1971.

Due, O.S. *Changing Forms: Studies in the Metamorphoses of Ovid.* Copenhagen, 1974.

DuQuesnay, I.M.L. "From Polyphemus to Corydon: Virgil, *Eclogue* 2 and the *Idylls* of Theocritus." In *Creative Imitation and Latin Literature,* edited by D.A. Woodman and A.J. West, 35–69. Cambridge, 1979.

Duret, L. "Dans l'ombre des plus grands: 1. Poètes et Prosateurs mal connus de l'époque augustéenne." *ANRW* 2.30.3 (1983): 1447–1560.

Effe, B. *Dichtung und Lehre.* Munich, 1977.

———. "Epische Objektivität und auktoriales Erzählen: Zur Entfaltung emotionaler Subjektivität in Vergils *Aeneis.*" *Gymnasium* 90 (1983): 171–86.

Eisenhut, W. "*Deducere Carmen:* Ein Beitrag zum Problem der literarischen

Beziehungen zwischen Horaz und Properz." In *Properz,* edited by W. Eisenhut, 247–63. Wege der Forschung 237. Darmstadt, 1975.

Elder, J.P. *"Non iniussa cano:* Virgil's Sixth *Eclogue." HSCP* 65 (1961): 109–25.

Ellsworth, J.D. "Ovid's *Iliad (Met.* 12.1–13.622)." *Prudentia* 12 (1980): 23–29.

———. "Ovid's *'Aeneid'* Reconsidered (*Met.* 13.623–14.608)." *Vergilius* 32 (1986): 27–32.

———. "Ovid's *'Odyssey': Met.* 13.623–14.608." *Mnem.* 41 (1988): 333–40.

Fabre, J. "L'Etre et les Figures: Une réflexion sur le récit dans le récit chez Ovide (*Met.* 14.622–771)." *LALIES* 6 (1987): 167–73.

Fantazzi, C. "The Revindication of Roman Myth in the Pomona-Vertumnus Tale." In *Acta Ovidianum,* edited by N. Barbu, E. Dobroiu, and M. Nasta, 283–93. Bucharest, 1976.

———. "Roman Ovid," In *Filologia e Forme Letterarie: Studi Offerti a Francesco della Corte III,* 173–87. Università degli Studi di Urbino. Urbino, 1987.

Fantham, E. "Ovid's Ceyx and Alcyone." *Phoenix* 33 (1979): 330–45.

———. "Sexual Comedy in Ovid's *Fasti:* Sources and Motivation." *HSCP* 87 (1983): 185–216.

———. "Ovid, Germanicus, and the Composition of the *Fasti." PLLS* 5 (1985): 243–81.

———. "Nymphas . . . *E Navibus Esse:* Decorum and Poetic Fiction in *Aen.* 9.77–122 and 10.215–59." *CP* 85 (1990): 102–19.

———. Review of *Virgil: Georgics,* vols. 1–2, edited by R.F. Thomas. *CP* 86 (1991): 163–67.

———. "Ceres, Liber, and Flora: Georgic and anti-Georgic Elements in Ovid's *Fasti." PCPS* 38 (1992): 39–56.

Fantuzzi, M. "La Contaminazione dei generi letterari nella letturatura greca ellenistica: Rifiuto del sistema o evoluzione di un sistema?" *Lingua e Stile* 15 (1980): 433–50.

Farrell, J. *Vergil's Georgics and the Traditions of Ancient Epic: The Art of Allusion in Literary History.* New York, 1991.

———. "Dialogue of Genres in Ovid's Lovesong of Polyphemus (*Met.*13.719–897)." *AJP* 113 (1992): 235–68.

Fauth, W. *Aphrodite Parakyptusa: Untersuchungen zum Erscheinungsbild der vorderasiatischen Dea Prospiciens.* Abhandlungen der Geistes und Sozial wissenschaftlichen Klasse Nr. 6. Akademie der Wissenschaften und der Literatur aMainz. Wiesbaden, 1966.

———. "Zur Typologie Mythischen Metamorphosen in der Homerischen Dichtung." *Poetica* 7 (1975): 235–68.

Fedeli, P., ed. *Properzio Elegie Libro IV, Testo Critico e Commento.* Bari, 1965.

Feeney, D.C. "Epic Hero and Epic Fable." *Comp. Lit.* 38 (1986): 137–58.

———. "The Paradoxical Country." Review of *Virgil's Elements,* by D.O. Ross. *TLS* 4.439, April 29–May 5 (1988): 476.

———. *The Gods in Epic.* Oxford, 1991.

———. *"Si licet et fas est:* Ovid's *Fasti* and the Problem of Free Speech under the Principate." In *Roman Poetry and Propaganda in the Age of Augustus,* edited by A. Powell, 1–25. London, 1992.

Fishwick, D. "Ovid and Divus Augustus." *CP* 86 (1991): 36–41.

Forbes Irving, P.M.C. *Metamorphosis in Greek Myths.* Oxford, 1990.

Fordyce, C.J., ed. *P. Vergili Maronis Aeneidos Libri VII–VIII.* Oxford, 1977.

Fornara, C.W. *The Nature of History in Ancient Greece and Rome.* Berkeley and Los Angeles, 1983.

Fowler, W.W. *The Roman Festivals of the Period of the Republic.* London, 1908.

Fränkel, H. *Ovid: A Poet between Two Worlds.* Berkeley, 1945.

———. *Noten zu den Argonautika des Apollonius.* Munich, 1968.

———. *Early Greek Poetry and Philosophy.* Translated by M. Hadas and J. Willis. Oxford, 1975.

Fraser, P.M. *Ptolemaic Alexandria.* 3 vols. Oxford, 1972.

Frazer, J.G., ed. *The Fasti of Ovid.* 5 vols. London, 1929.

Frécaut, J.-M. "Les Transitions dans les *Mét.* d'Ovide." *REL* 46 (1968): 261–63.

———. *L'Esprit et l'Humour chez Ovide.* Grenoble, 1972.

Fredericks [Nagle], B.R. "Divine Wit vs. Divine Folly: Mercury and Apollo in *Met.* 1–2." *CJ* 72 (1977): 244–49.

Furley, D. "Variations on Themes from Empedocles in Lucretius' Proem." *BICS* 17 (1970): 55–64.

Fusillo, M. *Il tempo delle Argonautiche.* Rome, 1985.

Galinsky, G.K. "The Cipus Episode in Ovid's *Metamorphoses.*" *TAPA* 98 (1968): 181–91.

———. *Ovid's Metamorphoses: An Introduction to the Basic Aspects.* Berkeley and Los Angeles, 1975.

Gamel, Mary-Kay. "Baucis and Philemon: Paradigm or Paradox." *Helios* 11 (1984): 117–31.

Gatz, B. *Weltalter, goldene Zeit und sinnverwandte Vorstellungen.* Spudasmata 16. Hildesheim, 1967.

Genette, Gérard. *Narrative Discourse.* Translated by J.E. Lewin. Oxford, 1980.

———. *Narrative Discourse Revisited.* Translated by J.E. Lewin. Ithaca, 1988.

George, E.V. *Aeneid VIII and the Aitia of Callimachus.* Mnemosyne Suppl. 27. Leiden, 1974.

Giannini, A. "Studi Sulla Paradossografia Greca I. Da Omero a Callimaco: Motivi e Forme del Meraviglioso." *Ist. Lomb.* 97 (1963): 247–66.

———. "Studi Sulla Paradossografia Greca II. Da Callimaco all'Eta' Imperiale: La Letteratura Paradossografia." *Acme* 17 (1964): 99–140.

———. *Paradoxographorum Graecorum Reliquiae.* Milan, 1965.

Gieseking, K. *Die Rahmenerzählung in Ovids Metamorphosen.* Dissertation, Tübingen, 1965.

Gilbert, C.D. "Ovid *Met.* 1.4." *CQ* 26 (1976): 111–12.

Ginsberg, W. "Ovid's *Metamorphoses* and the Politics of Interpretation." *CJ* 84 (1989): 222–31.

Goldhill, S. "Framing and Polyphony: Readings in Hellenistic Poetry." *PCPS* 212 n.s. 32 (1986): 25–52.

———. *The Poet's Voice.* Cambridge, 1991.

Goold, G.P. "*Noctes Propertianae.*" *HSCP* 71 (1966): 59–106.

Gow, A.S.F., and A.F. Scholfield, eds. *Nicander, the Poems and Poetical Fragments.* Cambridge, 1953.

Graf, F. "Ovide, Les Métamorphoses et la Véracité du Mythe." In *Métamorphoses du Mythe en Grèce Antique,* edited by C. Calame, 57–70. Religions en Perspectives 4. Geneva, 1988.

Granarolo, J. "L'époque néotérique ou la poésie romaine d'avant garde au dernier siècle de la République (Catulle excepté)." *ANRW* 1.3 (1973): 278–360.

Gransden, K.W., ed. *Virgil, Aeneid Book VIII.* Cambridge, 1976.

———. *Virgil's Iliad: An Essay on Epic Narrative.* Cambridge, 1984.

Gratwick, A.S. "The Early Republic." In *The Cambridge History of Classical Literature,* vol. 2, edited by E.J. Kenney and W.V. Clausen, 53–174. Cambridge, 1982.

Haege, H. *Terminologie und Typologie der Verwandlungsvorgangs in den Metamorphosen Ovids.* Göppingen, 1976.

Hainsworth, J.B. *The Idea of Epic.* Berkeley and Los Angeles, 1991.

Halperin, D. *Before Pastoral: Theocritus and the Ancient Tradition of Bucolic Poetry.* New Haven, 1983.

Hannestad, N. *Roman Art and Imperial Policy.* Aarhus, 1986.

Hardie, P.R. "Cosmological Patterns in the *Aeneid.*" *PLLS* 5 (1985): 85–97.

———. *Vergil's Aeneid: Cosmos and Imperium.* Oxford, 1986.

———. "Lucretius and the Delusions of Narcissus." *MD* 20–21 (1988): 71–89.

———. "Ovid's Theban History: The First Anti-Aeneid?" *CQ* 40 (1990): 224–35.

———. "The Janus Episode in Ovid's *Fasti.*" *MD* 26 (1991): 47–64.

———. *The Epic Successors of Virgil: A Study in the Dynamics of a Tradition.* Cambridge, 1993.

Harmon, D.P. "Religion in the Latin Elegists." *ANRW* 2.16.3 (1986): 1909–73.

Harries, B. "Causation and the Authority of the Poet in Ovid's *Fasti.*" *CQ* n.s. 39 (1989): 164–85.

———. "The Spinner and the Poet: Arachne in Ovid's *Metamorphoses.*" *PCPS* 36 (1990): 64–82.

Haüssler, R. *Das Historische Epos der Griechen und Römer bis Vergil: Studien zum historischen Epos der Antike. I. Teil: Von Homer zu Vergil.* Heidelberg, 1976.

Heath, J. "Diana's Understanding of Ovid's *Metamorphoses.*" *CJ* 86 (1991): 233–43.

Heinze, R. *Ovids elegische Erzählung.* Berichte der Sächsischen Akademie zu Leipzig. Philologische-historische Klasse. 71.7. Leipzig, 1919.

———. *Virgils Epische Technik.* Stuttgart, 1957.

Henderson, A.A.R., ed. *A Commentary on Ovid's Metamorphoses III.* Bristol, 1979.

Herescu, N.I., ed. *Ovidiana, recherches sur Ovid publiées à l'occasion du bimillénaire de la naissance du poète.* Paris, 1958.

Herter, H. "Ovid's Kunstprinzip in den Metamorphosen." In *Ovid,* edited by M. von Albrecht and E. Zinn, 340–61. Darmstadt, 1968.

———. "Verwandlung und Persönlichkeit in Ovids *Metamorphosen.*" In *Kulturwissenschaften. Festgabe für Wilhelm Perpeet zum 65. Geburtstag,* 185–228. Bonn, 1980.

Hill, D.E., ed. *Ovid: Metamorphoses 1–4.* Oak Park, Ill., 1985.

Hinds, S. E. "Generalizing about Ovid." In *The Imperial Muse.* Ramus Essays on

Roman Literature of the Empire (= *Ramus* 16), edited by A.J. Boyle, 4–31. Victoria, 1987.

———. *The Metamorphosis of Persephone: Ovid and the Self-Conscious Muse.* Cambridge, 1987.

———. Review of *Ovid's Metamorphoses and the Traditions of Augustan Poetry,* by P.E. Knox. *CP* 84 (1989): 266–71.

———. "*Arma* in Ovid's *Fasti* Part 1: Genre and Mannerism." *Arethusa* 25 (1992): 81–112.

———. "*Arma* in Ovid's *Fasti* Part 2: Genre, Romulean Rome and Augustan Ideology." *Arethusa* 25 (1992): 113–53.

Hofmann, H. "Ovid's *Metamorphoses: Carmen Perpetuum, Carmen Deductum.*" *PLLS* 5 (1985): 223–41.

Holleman, A.W.J. "Ovidii Metamorphoseon liber xv.622–870: (*Carmen et Error?*)." *Latomus* 28 (1969): 42–60

Hollis, A.S., ed. *Ovid Metamorphoses VIII.* Oxford, 1970.

———. *Ovid Ars Amatoria 1.* Oxford, 1977.

———. *Callimachus Hecale.* Oxford, 1990.

———. "Hellenistic Colouring in Virgil's *Aeneid.*" *HSCP* 94 (1992): 269–85.

Hopkinson, N., ed. *A Hellenistic Anthology.* Cambridge Greek and Latin Classics. Cambridge, 1988.

Horsfall, N. "Epic Burlesque in Ovid *Metamorphoses* 8.260ff." *CJ* 74 (1979): 319–332.

———. "Virgil and the Illusory Footnote." *PLLS* 6 (1990): 49–63.

———. "Virgil and the Poetry of Explanations." *GR* 38 (1991): 203–11.

Hubbard, M. "The Capture of Silenus." *PCPS* 21 (1975): 53–62.

———. *Propertius.* New York, 1975.

Huebner, W. "Manilius als Astrologe und Dichter." *ANRW* 2.32.1 (1984): 126–320.

Hunter, R.L., ed. *Apollonius of Rhodes Argonautica Book 3.* Cambridge, 1989.

Hutchinson, G.O. *Hellenistic Poetry.* Oxford, 1988.

Innes, D.C. "Gigantomachy and Natural Philosophy." *CQ* 29 (1979): 165–71.

Istituto della Enciclopedia Italiana. *Enciclopedia Virgiliana.* Vol. 1. Rome, 1984.

Jannaccone, Silvia. *La Letteratura Greco-Latina delle Metamorfosi.* Messina-Florence, 1953.

Jocelyn, H.D. "The Poems of Quintus Ennius." *ANRW* 1.2 (1972): 987–1026.

———. "Romulus and the *di genitales* (Ennius, *Annales* 110–11 Sk.)." In *Studies in Latin Literature and its Tradition in Honour of C.O. Brink,* edited by J. Diggle, J.B. Hall, and H.D. Jocelyn, 39–65. Cambridge, 1989.

Johnson, P., and M. Malamud. "Ovid's *Musomachia.*" *PCP* 23 (1988) 30–38.

Johnson, W.R. "The Problem of the Counter-Classical Sensibility and Its Critics." *CSCA* 3 (1970): 123–51.

Kambylis, A . *Die Dichterweihe und ihre Symbolik.* Heidelberg, 1965.

Keith, A.M. *The Play of Fictions: Studies in Ovid's Metamorphoses Book 2.* Ann Arbor, 1992.

Kennedy, D.F. Review of *Ovid's Metamorphoses and the Traditions of Augustan Poetry,* by P.E. Knox, and *The Metamorphosis of Persephone: Ovid and the Self-conscious Muse,* by S.E. Hinds. *JRS* 79 (1989): 209–10.

Kenney, E.J. *"Nequitiae Poeta."* In *Ovidiana: Recherches sur Ovide publiées à l'occasion du bimillénaire de la naissance du poète,* edited by N.I. Herescu, 201–9. Paris, 1958.

———. *"Discordia Semina Rerum."* Review of *L'image et la Pensée dans les Métamorphoses d'Ovide,* by S. Viarre. *CR* 17 (1967): 51–52.

———. *"Doctus Lucretius."* *Mnemosyne* 23 (1970): 366–92.

———. "The Style of the *Metamorphoses."* In *Ovid,* edited by J.W. Binns, 116–53. London, 1973.

———. *"Ovidius Prooemians."* *PCPS* 22 (1976): 46–53.

———. "Ovid." In *The Cambridge History of Classical Literature,* vol. 2, edited by E.J. Kenney and W.V. Clausen, 420–57. Cambridge, 1982.

———. Introduction and Notes to Ovid's *Metamorphoses.* Translated by A.D. Melville. Oxford, 1987.

———. Review of *P. Ovidius Naso, Metamorphosen Kommentar XIV–XV,* by F. Bömer. *CR* n.s. 38 (1988): 247–49.

Kidd, I.G. "Philosophy and Science in Posidonius." *Antike und Abendland* 24 (1978): 7–15.

Kirk, G.S. *Myth: Its Meaning and Functions in Ancient and Other Cultures.* Berkeley and Los Angeles, 1970.

———. "Aetiology, Ritual, Charter: Three Equivocal Terms in the Study of Myths." *YCS* 22 (1972): 83–102.

Klein, T.M. "The Role of Callimachus in the Development of the Concept of the Countergenre." *Latomus* 33 (1974): 217–31.

Knauer, G. N. *Die Aeneis und Homer: Studien zur poetischen Technik Vergils mit Listen der Homerzitate in der Aeneis.* Hypomnemata 7. Göttingen, 1964.

Knox, P.E. *Ovid's Metamorphoses and the Traditions of Augustan Poetry.* Cambridge Philological Society Supplementary vol. 11. Cambridge, 1986.

Konstan, D. "The Death of Argus, or What Stories Do: Audience Response in Ancient Fiction and Theory." *Helios* 18 (1991): 15–30.

Koster, S. *Antike Epostheorien.* Wiesbaden, 1970.

Kovacs, D. "Ovid *Metamorphoses* 1.2." *CQ* n.s. 37 (1987): 458–65.

Kraus, W. "Ovidius Naso." In *Ovid,* edited by M. von Albrecht and E. Zinn, 67–166. Darmstadt, 1968.

Kroll, W. *Studien zum Verständnis der römischen Literatur.* Stuttgart, 1924.

Lafaye, G. *Les Métamorphoses d'Ovide et leurs modèles grecques.* Paris, 1904.

Lamberton, R. *Homer the Theologian. Neoplatonist Allegorical Reading and the Growth of the Epic Tradition.* Berkeley, 1986.

Lammacchia, R. "Precisazioni su alcuni aspetti dell'epica Ovidiana." *Atene e Roma* 14 (1969): 1–20

Lämmli, F. *Vom Chaos Zum Cosmos: Zur Geschichte einer Idee.* Basel, 1962.

Latacz, Joachim. "Ovids *Metamorphosen* als Spiel mit der Tradition." *WJA* 5 (1979): 133–55.

Lateiner, D. "Mythic and Non-Mythic Artists in Ovid's *Metamorphoses."* *Ramus* 13 (1984): 1–30.

Latte, K. *Römische Religionsgeschichte.* Munich, 1960.

Lausberg, M. "Αρχέτυπον τῆς ἰδίας ποιήσεως: Zur Bildbeschreibung bei Ovid." *Boreas* 5 (1982): 112–23.

Leach, E.W. "Ekphrasis and the Theme of Artistic Failure in Ovid's *Metamorphoses.*" *Ramus* 3 (1974): 102–42.

Lee, A.G., ed. *Metamorphoses, Book 1.* Cambridge, 1953.

Lieberg, G. "Die '*theologia tripertita*' in Forschung und Bezeugung." *ANRW* 1.4 (1973): 63–115.

———. *Poeta Creator: Studien Zu Einer Figur der Antiken Dichtung.* Amsterdam, 1982.

———. "*Poeta Creator:* Some 'Religious' Aspects." *PLLS* 5 (1985): 23–32.

Little, D.A. "Richard Heinze: Ovids elegische Erzählung." In *Ovids Ars Amatoria und Remedia Amoris: Untersuchungen zum Aufbau,* edited by E. Zinn, 64–105. Stuttgart, 1970.

———. "The Speech of Pythagoras in *Metamorphoses* 15 and the Structure of the *Metamorphoses.*" *Hermes* 98 (1970): 340–60.

———. "The Non-Augustanism of Ovid's *Metamorphoses.*" *Mnemosyne* 25 (1972): 389–401.

———. "Non-Parody in *Metamorphoses* 15." *Prudentia* 6 (1974): 17-21.

Long, A.A. "Early Greek Philosophy." In *The Cambridge History of Classical Literature,* vol. 1, edited by P.E. Easterling and B.M.W. Knox, 245–57. Cambridge, 1985.

———. "Stoic Readings of Homer." In *Homer's Ancient Readers,* edited by R. Lamberton and J. J. Keaney, 41–66. Princeton, 1992.

Lonie, I.M. *The Hippocratic Treatises.* Berlin and New York, 1981.

Ludwig, W. *Struktur und Einheit der Metamorphosen Ovids.* Berlin, 1965.

Lundstrom, S. *Ovids Metamorphosen und die Politik des Kaisers.* Acta Universitatis Upsaliensis 12. Uppsala, 1980.

Lyne, R.O.A.M., ed. *Ciris: A Poem Attributed to Vergil.* Cambridge Classical Texts and Commentaries 20. Cambridge, 1978.

———. "The Neoteric Poets." *CQ* 28 (1978): 167–87.

———. "Ovid's *Metamorphoses,* Callimachus, and l'art pour l'art." *MD* 12 (1984): 9–34.

McKeown, J.C. "Ovid *Amores* 3.12." *PLLS* 2 (1979): 163–77.

———. "*Fabula proposito nulla tegenda meo:* Ovid's *Fasti* and Augustan Politics." In *Poetry and Politics in the Age of Augustus,* edited by A.J. Woodman and D.A. West, 169–87. Cambridge, 1984.

———, ed. *Ovid: Amores Volume I. Text and Prolegomena.* Liverpool, 1987.

———, ed. *Ovid: Amores Volume II. A Commentary on Book One.* Leeds, 1989.

McKim, R. "Myth against Philosophy in Ovid's Account of Creation." *CJ* 80 (1985): 97–108.

Macleod, C.W. "Propertius 4.1." *PLLS* 1 (1976): 141–53.

Maltby, R. *A Lexicon of Ancient Latin Etymologies.* Leeds, 1991.

Marg, W. Review of *Ovid: A Poet Between Two Worlds,* by H. Fränkel. *Gnomon* 21 (1949): 44–57.

Marquis, E.C. "Vertumnus in Propertius 4.2." *Hermes* 102 (1974): 491–500.

Martindale, C., ed. *Ovid Renewed: Ovidian Influence on Literature and Art from the Middle Ages to the Twentieth Century.* Cambridge, 1988.

Martini, E. *Einleitung zu Ovid.* Darmstadt, 1970. (Repr. of Schriften der Philosophischen Fakultät der Deutschen Universität in Prag, vol 12. Brünn, Prague, Leipzig, and Vienna, 1933.)

Maurach, G. "Ovids Kosmogonie: Quellenbenutzung und Traditionsstiftung." *Gymnasium* 86 (1979): 131–48.

Melville, A.D., trans. *Ovid's Metamorphoses.* Oxford, 1987.

Miller, F.J. "Some Features of Ovid's Style: III. Ovid's Methods of Ordering and Transition in the *Metamorphoses.*" *CJ* 16 (1920–21): 464–76.

Miller, J.F. "Ritual Directions in Ovid's *Fasti*: Dramatic Hymns and Didactic Poetry." *CJ* 75 (1980): 204–14.

———. "Callimachus and the Augustan Aetiological Elegy." *ANRW* 2.30.1 (1982): 371–417.

———. "Callimachus and the *Ars Amatoria.*" *CP* 78 (1983): 26–34.

———. "Ennius and the Elegists." *ICS* 8 (1983): 277–95.

———. "Disclaiming Divine Inspiration: A Programmatic Pattern." *WS* 20 (1986): 151–64.

———. "Ovid's Divine Interlocutors in the *Fasti.*" In *Studies in Latin Literature,* edited by C. Deroux, 156–92. Collections Latomus 180. Brussels, 1983.

———. *Ovid's Elegiac Festivals: Studies in the Fasti.* Studien zur Klassischen Philologie, vol 55. Frankfurt am Main, 1991.

———. "The *Fasti* and Hellenistic Didactic: Ovid's Variant Aetiologies." *Arethusa* 25 (1992): 11–31.

Momigliano, A. "Ancient History and the Antiquarian." In *Studies in Historiography,* 1–39. New York and Evanston, 1966.

Murphy, G.M.H., ed. *Ovid's Metamorphoses XI.* Bristol, 1979.

Murray, O. "Herodotus and Hellenistic Culture." *CQ* 22 (1972): 200–213.

Murrin, M. *The Allegorical Epic: Essays in its Rise and Decline.* Chicago, 1980.

Myers, K.S. "The Lizard and the Owl: An Etymological Pair in Ovid, *Metamorphoses,* Book 5." *AJP* 113 (1992): 63–68.

———. '*Ultimus Ardor:* Pomona and Vertumnus in Ovid's *Met.* 14.623–771." *CJ* 89 (1994): 225–50.

Nagle, B.R. "Byblis and Myrrha: Two Incest Narratives in the *Metamorphoses.*" *CJ* 78 (1983): 301–15.

———. "A Trio of Love-Triangles in Ovid's *Metamorphoses.*" *Arethusa* 21 (1988): 75–98.

———. "Two Miniature *Carmina Perpetua* in the *Metamorphoses:* Calliope and Orpheus." *Grazer Beiträge* 15 (1988): 99–125.

———. "Ovid's *Metamorphoses:* A Narratological Catalogue." *Syllecta Classica* 1 (1989): 97–138.

Néraudau, J.-P. "Aemilius Macer, ou la gloire du second rang." *ANRW* 2.30.3 (1983): 1708–17.

Newlands, C. "Ovid's Ravenous Raven." *CJ* 86 (1991): 244–55.

———. "Ovid's Narrator in the *Fasti.*" *Arethusa* 25 (1992): 33–54.

Newman, J.K. *Augustus and the New Poetry.* Collections Latomus 88. Brussels, 1967.

———. *The Concept of Vates in Augustan Poetry.* Collections Latomus 89. Brussels, 1967.

―――. *The Classical Epic Tradition.* Madison, 1986.

Nicoll, W.S.M. "Cupid, Apollo, and Daphne (Ovid, *Metamorphoses* 1.452ff.)." *CQ* n.s. 30 (1980): 174–82.

Nisbet, R.G.M., and M. Hubbard, eds. *A Commentary on Horace, Odes Book I.* Oxford, 1970.

―――. *A Commentary on Horace, Odes Book II.* Oxford, 1978.

Norden, E., ed. *P. Vergilius Maro, Aeneis Buch VI.* 3d ed. Leipzig and Berlin, 1926.

Notopoulos, J. "Silenus the Scientist." *CJ* 62 (1967): 308–9.

Ogilvie, R.M. *A Commentary on Livy Books I–V.* Repr. with addenda. Oxford, 1970.

Otis, Brooks. *Virgil: A Study in Civilized Poetry.* Oxford, 1963.

―――. *Ovid as an Epic Poet.* 2d ed. Cambridge, 1970.

Papathomopoulos, M., ed. *Antoninus Liberalis: Les Métamorphoses.* Paris, 1968.

Parker, W.H. *Priapea: Poems for a Phallic God.* London and Sydney, 1988.

Parry, H. "Ovid's *Metamorphoses:* Violence in a Pastoral Landscape." *TAPA* 95 (1964): 268–82.

Pasquali, G. "Arte Allusiva." In *Pagine stravaganti,* 275–83. Florence, 1968.

Pearson, L. "Apollonius of Rhodes and the Old Geographers." *AJP* 59 (1938): 443–59.

―――. "Myth and Archaeologia in Italy and Sicily: Timaeus and His Predecessors." *YCS* 24 (1975): 171–95.

Pease, A.S., ed. *M. Tulli Ciceronis De Divinatione.* 2 vols. Urbana, 1920.

―――, ed. *M. Tulli Ciceronis De Natura Deorum.* 2 vols. Cambridge, 1955.

Pechillo, M. "Ovid's Framing Technique: The Aeacus and Cephalus Epyllion (*Met.* 7.490–8.5)." *CJ* 86 (1990): 35–44.

Perkell, C.G. *The Poet's Truth: A Study of the Poet in Virgil's Georgics.* Berkeley and Los Angeles, 1989.

Pfaffel, W. *Quartus gradus etymologiae: Untersuchungen zur Etymologie Varros in De Lingua Latina.* Beiträge zur Klassischen Philologie, part 131. Königstein, 1981.

Pfeiffer, R., ed. *Callimachus.* 2 vols. Oxford, 1949–53.

―――. "The Image of Delian Apollo and Apolline Ethics." *JWI* 25 (1952): 20–32.

―――. *History of Classical Scholarship from the Beginnings to the End of the Hellenistic Age.* Oxford, 1968.

Philips, C.R. "Rethinking Augustan Poetry." *Latomus* 42 (1983): 780–817.

Pillinger, H.E. "Some Callimachean Influences on Propertius, Book Four." *HSCP* 73 (1969): 171–99.

Pinotti, P. "Propert. 4.9: Alessandrinismo e Arte Allusiva." *GIF* 29 n.s. 8 (1977): 50–71.

―――. "Properzio e Vertumno: Anticonformismo e Restaurazione Augustea." In *Colloquium Propertianum (Tertium),* edited by S. Vivona, 75–96. Assisi, 1983.

Pöhlmann, E. "Charakteristika des Römischen Lehrgedichts." *ANRW* 1.3 (1973): 813–901.

Porte, D. *L'Étiologie Religieuse Dans Les Fastes D'Ovide.* Paris, 1985.

―――. "L'idée romaine et la métamorphose." In *Journées Ovidiennes de Parméne: Actes du Colloque sur Ovide,* edited by J.-M. Frécault and D. Porte, 175–98. Collections Latomus 189. Brussels, 1985.

Primmer, A. "Mythos and Natur in Ovids 'Apollo und Daphne.'" *WS* 10 (1976): 210–20.

Puelma Piwonka, M. *Lucilius und Kallimachos: Zur Geschichte einer Gattung der hellenistisch-römischen Poesie.* Frankfurt, 1949.

Radke, G. *Die Götter Altitaliens.* Fontes et Commentationes, Universität Münster, Heft 3. Münster, 1965.

Rawson, E. "Cicero the Historian and Cicero the Antiquarian." *JRS* 62 (1972): 33–45.

———. "The First Latin Annalists." *Latomus* 35 (1976): 689–717.

———. *Intellectual Life in the Late Roman Republic.* Baltimore, 1985.

Reitzenstein, E. "Zur Stiltheorie des Kallimachos." In *Festschrift Richard Reitzenstein,* 23–69. Leipzig and Berlin, 1931.

Rheinsch-Werner, H. *Callimachus Hesiodicus: Die Rezeption der hesiodischen Dichtung durch Kallimachos von Kyrene.* Berlin, 1976.

Rhorer, C.C. "Ideology, Tripartition, and Ovid's *Metamorphoses.*" *Arethusa* 13 (1980): 299–313.

Richardson, L., Jr., ed. *Propertius Elegies 1–4.* Oklahoma, 1977.

Richardson, N.J. "Homeric Professors in the Age of the Sophists." *PCPS* 21 (1975): 65–81.

———. "Aristotle's Reading of Homer and Its Background." In *Homer's Ancient Readers,* edited by R. Lamberton and J.J. Keaney, 30–40. Princeton, 1992.

Richlin, A. *The Garden of Priapus: Sexuality and Aggression in Roman Humor.* Revised edition. New York, 1992.

———. "Reading Ovid's Rapes." In *Pornography and Representation in Greece and Rome,* edited by A. Richlin, 158–79. New York, 1992.

Rieks, R. "Zum Aufbau Ovids Metamorphosen" *WJA* 6b (1980): 85–103.

Roberts, F.E. "The Creation Story in Ovid's *Metamorphoses* 1." *CP* (1913): 401–14.

Rosati, Gianpiero. "L'esistenza letteraria: Ovidio e l'autoscienza della poesia." *MD* 2 (1979): 101–36.

———. "Il racconto dentro il racconto; funzioni metanarrative nelle Metamorfosi di Ovidio." *Atti del Convegno internazionale Letteratura classiche e narratologia, Selva di Fasano 1980,* 297–309. Perugia, 1981.

———. *Narciso e Pigmalione: Illusione e spettacolo nelle Metamorfosi di Ovidio.* Florence, 1983.

Rosenmeyer, T.G. "Ancient Literary Genres: A Mirage?" *Yearbook of Comparative and General Literature* 34 (1985): 74–84.

Rösler, W. "Die Entdeckung der Fiktionalität in der Antike." *Poetica* 12 (1980): 283–319.

Ross, D.O. *Backgrounds to Augustan Poetry: Gallus, Elegy and Rome.* Cambridge, 1975.

———. *Virgil's Elements: Physics and Poetry in the Georgics.* Princeton, 1987.

Rossi, L.E. "I generi letterari e le loro leggi scritte nelle letterature classiche." *BICS* 18 (1971): 69–94.

Rutherford, R.B. "Virgil's Poetic Ambitions in *Eclogue* 6." *GR* 36 (1989): 42–50.

Saint-Denis, E. "Le Génie d'Ovide d'Après le Livre XV des Métamorphoses." *REL* 18 (1940): 11–40.

Sandy, G. "Petronius and Interpolated Narrative." *TAPA* 101 (1970): 463–76.

Schmidt, E.A. *Ovids Poetische Menschenwelt: Die Metamorphosen als Metapher und*

Symphonie. Sitzungsbericht der Heidelberger Akademie der Wissenschaften, Philosophisch-Historische Klasse, Bericht 2. Heidelberg, 1991.

Schmitzer, U. *Zeitgeschichte in Ovids Metamorphosen.* Stuttgart, 1990.

Schrijvers, P.H. *Horror ac Divina Voluptas: Études sur la poétique et la poésie de Lucrèce.* Amsterdam, 1970.

Schwabl, H. "Weltschöpfung." *RE* Supplement 9 (1962): 1433–1589.

Scullard, H.H. *Festivals and Ceremonies of the Roman Republic.* Aspects of Greek and Roman Life. Ithaca, 1981.

Seeck, Gustav Adolf. "Dichterische Technik in Theokrits Thalysien und das Theorie der Hirtendichtung." In *Dorema Hans Diller,* 195–209. Athens, 1975.

Segal, C.P. "Myth and Philosophy in the *Metamorphoses:* Ovid's Augustanism and the Augustan Conclusion of Book 15." *AJP* 90 (1969): 257–92.

———. *Landscape in Ovid's Metamorphoses: A Study in the Transformations of a Literary Symbol.* Hermes Supplement 23. Wiesbaden, 1969.

———. "Ovid's Cephalus and Procris: Myth and Tragedy." *Grazer Beiträge* 7 (1978): 175–205.

———. "Archaic Choral Lyric." In *The Cambridge History of Classical Literature,* vol. 1, edited by P.E. Easterling and B.M.W. Knox, 165–201. Cambridge, 1985.

Segl, R. *Die Pythagorasrede im 15. Buch von Ovids Metamorphosen.* Dissertation, Salzburg, 1970.

Shea, C. "The Vertumnus Elegy and Propertius Book IV." *ICS* 13 (1988): 63–71.

Shechter, S. "The *Aition* and Vergil's *Georgics.*" *TAPA* 105 (1975): 347–91.

Sheets, G. "*Ennius Lyricus.*" *ICS* 8 (1983): 22–32.

Simon, E. *Die Götter der Römer.* Munich, 1990.

Skulsky, H. *Metamorphosis: The Mind in Exile.* Cambridge, Mass., 1981.

Skutsch, O. "'Zu Vergil's Eklogen." *RhM* 99 (1956): 193–201.

———. *Studia Enniana.* London, 1968.

———, ed. *The Annals of Q. Ennius.* Oxford, 1985.

Smith, K.F. *Tibullus the Elegies.* New York, Cincinnati, and Chicago, 1913.

Solodow, J.B. *The World of Ovid's Metamorphoses.* Chapel Hill, 1988.

Spoerri, W. *Späthellenistische Berichte über Welt, Kultur und Götter.* Schweizerische Beiträge zur Altertumswissenschaft, part 9. Basel, 1959.

Steiner, G. "Ovid's *Carmen Perpetuum.*" *TAPA* 89 (1958): 218–36.

Stephens, W.C. "The Function of Religious and Philosophical Ideas in Ovid's *Metamorphoses.*" Ph.D. dissertation, Princeton University, 1957.

Stewart, Z. "The Song of Silenus." *HSCP* 64 (1959): 179–205.

Stinton, T.C.W. " '*Si credere dignum est':* Some Expressions of Disbelief in Euripides and Others." *PCPS* 202 n.s. 22 (1976): 60–89.

Stitz, M. *Ovid und Vergils Aeneis: Interpretation Met. 13.623–14.608.* Freiburg, 1962.

Suerbaum, W. *Untersuchungen zur Selbstdarstellung älterer römischer Dichter.* Spudasmata XIX. Hildesheim, 1968.

Suits, T. A. "The Vertumnus Elegy of Propertius." *TAPA* 100 (1969): 475–86.

Sullivan, J. P. *Propertius: A Critical Introduction.* Cambridge, 1976.

Swanson, R.A. "Ovid's Pythagorean Essay." *CJ* 54 (1968): 21–24.

Syme, R. *History in Ovid.* Oxford, 1978.

Tarrant, R.J. "Editing Ovid's *Metamorphoses:* Problems and Possibilities." *CP* 77 (1982): 342–60.

Thomas, R.F. "New Comedy, Callimachus, and Roman Poetry." *HSCP* 83 (1978): 179–206.

———. *Lands and Peoples in Roman Poetry: The Ethnographical Tradition.* Cambridge Phil. Suppl. 7. Cambridge, 1982.

———. "Callimachus, the *Victoria Berenices* and Roman Poetry." *CQ* 33 (1983): 92–113.

———. "From *Recusatio* to Commitment: The Evolution of the Vergilian Programme." *PLLS* 5 (1985): 61–73.

———. "Vergil's *Georgics* and the Art of Reference." *HSCP* 90 (1986): 171–98.

———, ed. *Vergil's Georgics.* 2 vols. Cambridge Greek and Latin Classics. Cambridge, 1988.

———. Review of *The Metamorphosis of Persephone,* by S.E. Hinds. *CP* 85 (1990): 77–80.

Thomlinson, C. *Poetry and Metamorphosis.* Cambridge, 1983.

Thompson, D.W. *A Glossary of Greek Birds.* London, 1936.

Tissol, G. "Narrative Style in Ovid's *Metamorphoses* and the Influence of Callimachus." Ph.D. dissertation, University of California at Berkeley, 1988.

———. "Polyphemus and His Audiences: Narrative and Power in Ovid's *Metamorphoses.*" *Syllecta Classica* 2 (1990): 45–58.

Todini, U. "La Cosmologia Pitagorica e Le Muse Enniane." *RCCM* 13 (1971): 21–38.

———. "*Pedibus Pulsare:* Postilla e Non." *RCCM* 16 (1974): 301–9.

Todorov, T. "The Origin of Genres." *NLH* 8 (1976/77): 159–70.

Traglia, A., ed. *Poetae Novi.* Rome, 1962.

Tränkle, H. "Elegisches in Ovids Metamorphosen." *Hermes* 91 (1963): 459–76.

Trypanis, C.A. *Callimachus Fragments.* Loeb Classical Library. Cambridge, Mass., 1968.

Usener, H. *Epicurea.* Lipsiae, 1887.

Veyne, P. *Did the Greeks Believe in Their Myths? An Essay on the Constitutive Imagination.* Translated by P. Wissing. Chicago and London, 1983.

Vian, F., and E. Delage, eds. *Apollonius de Rhodes Argonautiques I–II.* Paris, 1976.

Viarre, S. *L'Image et La Pensée dans les Métamorphoses d'Ovide.* Paris, 1964.

———. *La Survie d'Ovide dans la Littérature Scientifique des XIIe et XIIIe Siècles.* Poitiers, 1966.

von Albrecht, M. "Zum Metamorphosen-Proem Ovids." *RhM* 104 (1961): 269–78.

———. *Die Parenthese in Ovids Metamorphosen und ihre dichterische Funktion.* Spudasmata 7. Hildesheim, 1964.

———. "Ovid's Humor." In *Ovid,* edited by M. von Albrecht and E. Zinn, 405–37. Darmstadt, 1968.

———. "Les Dieux et la Religion dans les *Métamorphoses* d'Ovide." In *Hommages à Henri Le Bonniec: Res Sacrae,* edited by D. Porte and J.-P. Néraudau, 1–9. Collection Latomus 201. Brussels, 1988.

von Albrecht, M., and E. Zinn, eds. *Ovid.* Wege der Forschung 92. Darmstadt, 1968.

Wallace-Hadrill, A. "Time for Augustus: Ovid, Augustus and the *Fasti.*" In *Homo*

Viator: Classical Essays for John Bramble, edited by M. Whitby, P. Hardie, and M. Whitby, 221–30. Bristol and Oak Park, Ill., 1987.

Waszink, J.H. *Lucretius and Poetry.* Medelingen der Koninklijke Nederlandse Akademie van Wetenschappen 17.8. Amsterdam, 1954.

West, D. *The Imagery and Poetry of Lucretius.* Edinburgh, 1969.

West, M.L., ed. *Hesiod, Theogony.* Oxford, 1966.

———. *Hesiod, Works and Days.* Oxford, 1978.

———. *The Orphic Poems.* Oxford, 1983.

———. *The Hesiodic Catalogue of Women.* Oxford, 1985.

Whitman, J. *Allegory: The Dynamics of an Ancient and Medieval Technique.* Oxford, 1987.

Wilamowitz-Moellendorff, U. von. *Hellenistische Dichtung in der Zeit des Kallimachos.* 2 vols. Berlin, 1924.

Wilkinson, L.P. *Ovid Recalled.* Cambridge, 1955.

———. "The World of the *Metamorphoses.*" In *Ovidiana: Recherches sur Ovide publiées à l'occasion du bimillénaire de la naissance du poète,* edited by N.I. Herescu, 231–44. Paris, 1958.

Williams, F. "Augustus and Daphne: Ovid's *Met.* 1.560–63 and Phylarchus *FGrH* 81 F 32(b)." *PLLS* 3 (1981): 249–57.

———, ed. *Callimachus, Hymn to Apollo.* Oxford, 1978.

Williams, R.D., ed. *P. Vergili Maronis Aeneidos Liber Quintus.* Oxford, 1960.

———. *P. Vergili Maronis Aeneidos Liber Tertius.* Oxford, 1962.

Wills, J. "Callimachean Models for Ovid's Apollo-Daphne." *MD* 24 (1990): 143–56.

Wimmel, Walter. *Kallimachos in Rom.* Hermes Einzelschriften 16. Wiesbaden, 1960.

———. *'Hirtenkrieg' und arkadisches Rom. Reduktionsmedien in Vergils Aeneis.* Abh. d. Marburger Gel. Ges. Nr. 1. Munich, 1972.

Winkler, J.J. *Auctor and Actor: A Narratological Reading of Apuleius' The Golden Ass.* Berkeley and Los Angeles, 1985.

Wise, V. "Flight Myths in Ovid's *Metamorphoses:* An Interpretation of Phaethon and Daedalus." *Ramus* 6 (1977): 44–59.

Wiseman, T.P. *Catullan Questions.* Leicester, 1969.

———. *Cinna the Poet.* Leicester, 1974.

———. "Legendary Genealogies in Late-Republican Rome." *Greece and Rome* 21 (1974): 153–64.

———. *Clio's Cosmetics.* Leicester, 1979.

———. "Roman Legend and Oral Tradition." Review of *Roman Myth and Mythography,* by J.N. Bremmer and N.M. Horsfall. *JRS* 79 (1989): 129–37.

Wlosok, A. "*Gemina Doctrina:* On Allegorical Interpretation." *PLLS* 5 (1985): 75–84.

Wormell, D.E.W. "Ovid and the *Fasti.*" *Hermathena* 127 (1979): 39–50.

Wülfing-von Martitz, P. "Ennius als hellenistischer Dichter." In *Ennius.* Fond. Hardt 17, 253–83. Geneva, 1972.

Wyke, M. "The Elegiac Woman at Rome." *PCPS* 33 (1987): 153–78.

Zanker, G. *Realism in Alexandrian Poetry: A Literature and Its Audience.* London and Sydney, 1987.

Zanker, P. *The Power of Images in the Age of Augustus.* Ann Arbor, 1988.

Zetzel, J.E.G. "Gallus, Elegy, and Ross." *CP* 72 (1977): 249–60.

————. "Catullus, Ennius, and the Poetics of Allusion." *ICS* 8 (1983): 251–66.

————. "Recreating the Canon: Augustan Poetry and the Alexandrian Past." *Critical Inquiry* 10 (1983): 83–105.

Ziegler, K. "Paradoxographoi." *RE* 18.3 (1949): 1137–66.

Zingerle, A. *Ovidius und sein Verhältnis zu den Vorgängern und gleichzeitigen römischen Dichtern 1–2.* Innsbruck, 1869–71.

Zinn, E. "Die Dichter des alten Rom und die Anfänge des Weltgedichts." *Ant. Ab.* 5 (1956): 7–26.

Index of Passages and Works Discussed

Theocritus
  Id. 1: 70
    7: 70
    7.37–41: 89
    7.139: 102n.34
    11: 70
    17.1: 6n.14
Tibullus
  1.4: 120n.117
  2.1: 98
  2.5.23 ff.: 98

Valerius Cato
  Dictynna: 24n.86
Varro Atacinus
  Chorographia: 11
  Ephemeris: 11
Varro Reatinus
  Admiranda: 148, 149n.66
  De Gen. Pop. Rom. frr. 3P: 50n.84
    fr. 8: 50n.84
    17: 50n.84
  L.L. 5.13: 54n.108
    5.46: 117
    5.61: 45n.62
    5.78: 37
    6.75: 110
    7.45: 114
  R.R. 2.5.5: 155
    3.16.4: 155
Vergil
  Aen. 1.740–46: 7
    3.90–120: 100
    3.374–462: 161
    3.570–691: 101, 104
    3.590–95: 104n.41
    3.613–91: 104
    3.639–40: 105n.47
    3.691: 104
    5.602: 66
    6.234–35: 66
    6.900: 104
    7.1–5: 104
    7.177–78: 107–8

    7.187–88: 108
    7.189–91: 25n.90, 107
    7.761–82: 25n.90, 129
    7.778–80: 67n.26
    8.311–12: 71
    9.69–122: 25n.90, 100
    10.76: 109n.59
    10.189–93: 25n.90
    11.271–74: 25n.90, 100, 102
    11.739: 116n.100
    12.766 ff.: 103n.37
  Ecl. 2.32 ff.: 78
    3.59: 111
    6.3: 8
    6.5: 7–8
    6.15: 8
    6.31–40: 13, 41
    6.41–43: 75n.66
    6.64–73: 16n.57
    6.69–70: 8
    6.72: 65
    10.62: 115
  Geo. 1.86–91: 140
    2.458–3.48: 12
    3.4: 25
    4.281 ff.: 155
    4.309: 155
    4.345–47: 7, 13
    4.453–527: 70
    4.554–55: 155
[Vergil]
  Ciris 493–519: 30
  Culex 95: 115
Vitruvius
  De Arch. 1.4.8: 45
    2.8.12: 152
    8 Praef. 3: 46n.66
    8.3: 151n.76
    8.3.21: 153n.81
    8.3.26: 153

Xenagoras
  FGrHist 240 F28: 102
Xenophanes, B1.22: 145n.57

General Index

Accius, first verse *aetion*, 97
Achaemenides, 72; and Macareus, 104–13
Achelous, 90–93, 149, 163n.127
Actaeon, 93
Adonis, 47
Aeacus, 47
Aemilius Macer, 25, 31–32, 108, 114n.87
"Aeneid" framework, 95–113
Aeneas: 100, 104; as aetiological interlocutor in *Aen.* 8, 71, 92n.133; deification of, 46n.68, 98–99, 113, 126
Aesacus, 36–37, 82
Aesculapius, 127–28, 130, 166
aetiological frame narratives: viii, 15, ch. 2 *passim*; associated with Callimachus, viii, 15, 67–69, 71–76, 81–82, 106–7, 112, 120. *See also individual authors; Fasti; Metamorphoses*
aetiology: vii–ix, 1, 5, 6, 15, 16, 18–20, 23, 24, 27, 34, 37, 38, 39, 40, 63–65, 93, 98, 158, *passim*; and Alexandrianism, ix, 16–18, 21, 23–24, 65, 73, 95, 97, 116, 165; in Augustan poetry, 97; and avoidance of encomium, 18, 97; "Callimachean," defined, 15–21; Callimachean associations of, viii-ix, 5, 15–21, 85, 97; "Cosmogonic," defined, 5–15; and cosmogony, 5, 135; cultural, viii, 15, 63–64; and genre, ix; geographical, viii, 15, 27, 63, 95, 101; associated with Hesiod, 5; and history, 95–96; associated with internal narrators, 68–69; Italian, 20, 94, ch. 3 *passim*, 136–37;

in Latin literature, 23; mythical, viii, 15; and narrative authority, 18–20, 59, 97, 132, 158; natural, viii, 27, 65; and natural philosophy, viii, 58; and neoterics, 25; and paradoxography, 21, 22n.78; phraseology, 63–67, 73–74, 76, 79, 84–85, 90–93; as propaganda, 18; as pseudoscientific explanation, ix, 14, 18, 19, 27, 58; religious, viii, 15, 30, 34, 60, 62–64, 75–76, 81, 84–85, 94, ch. 3 *passim*, 136, 139; in Roman elegy, 16; and Roman nationalistic themes, 20, 97–98; as strategy of accommodation of national themes in elegy, 98; as truth markers/authentication, 18–20, 59, 93, 124, 131–33, 158. *See also* aetiological frame narratives; metamorphosis; mythology; *individual authors and works*
Aetna, 140; attack on myth/poetry, 145
Aetna, 140, 154–55
Aglaurus, 46
Alcmene, 32
Alcyone, 36, 38
Alexander Aetolus, 22
Alexandrian literature: aetiological interests of, ix, 5, 16, 21, 23, 58–59; and antiquarianism, 64; complex narrative structures in, 70; *doctrina,* 80; and epyllion, 24–25; and metamorphosis, 21, 29–30; and natural philosophy, 10, 21, 58; and paradoxography, 79, 148, 165; cataloging interests of, 21; concern with authority-belief, 17–19, 57–58, 70; didactic, 10, 21, 58; epic, views

Baucis and Philemon, 91–93

belief/disbelief, in poet's authority, 19–20, 25, 91–94, 132, 159. *See also* authentication; authority; fictionality; poetry; truth

Boios, *Ornithogonia:* 23, 25, 31, 34–37, 82, 95; and aetiological metamorphosis, 31, 34–37, 66

Boreas, and Lucretian scientific theory, 55–56, 151

bucolic epic: contrasted with "grand" epic, 8, 101, 116; and elegy, 8n.28, 78–79

Butas, *Aetia Romana*, 96

Byblis, 22, 24

Cadmus, 156

Caeneus, 28, 156

Caesar, deification of, 46, 46n.68, 128, 130, 166; and Aesculapius, 130

Callimachus: aetiological conversations in the *Aetia*, viii, 15, 67–69, 71–76, 81–82, 106–7, 120, 127, 163; Apollo, 68, 106, 120, 127; and Aratus, 23; Asterie, 90; authority, 18–19, 58, 68, 69; Calliope, 107; and *carmen perpetuum/deductum*, 2–5, 7, 14; *"Coma,"* 10n.34, 11, 25; in epic tradition, 5, 10, 12, 15, 18; and epyllion, 24; Erysichthon, 90–91; Glaucus, 22; and hamadryads, 116; *Hecale,* 3, 10n.34, 16n.56, 91–94; Hercules, 87–88; heroic/nonheroic themes of, 3, 18; and Herophilus, 59; and Hesiod, 3, 8–9, 16, 18; acknowledgment of Hesiod's Muses, 68; Hippolytus, 22; and Hipponax, 162; and Homer, 3, 29n.5; *Hymns*, 3, 62n.8, 88; *Iambi,* 68, 120n.117, 159n.103, 162; influence on Roman poets, 3, 69; Italian aetiology, 96; literary ideals, 2–5, 9, 14, and metamorphosis, 22, 100n.25, 165; Molorchus, 92; Muses, 68, 74, 106n.49, 163; Ovid's debt to, viii–ix, 2–15, ch. 2 *passim*, 99, 116, 121, 125, 165; *Paradoxa,* 21n.77, 96, 148, 153; polemical language of, 3–4; Pollis and Theugenes, 74–75, 81–82; *Prologue to the Aetia,* 2–4, 8; and Pythagoras, 159n.103, 162; religious aetiology in, 15, 16–18, 58–59, 66, 76, 85, 106; and Roman elegy, 16; scale of epic favored by, 2–5; scholarly persona, 18, 71, 106, "scientific" themes in, 14, 58–59; Theseus, 91–92;

Tithonus, 102. *See also individual authors and works*

Calliope, and the contest of the Muses: 83n.96, 163–64; and aetiology, 164; as programmatic, 163–64; as learned internal narrator, 46, 91

Callisto, 22n.79, 29, 93, 116n.98

Calvus, *Io,* 24, 78

Camenae, 109–12, 128

Canens, 46; and Picus, 38, 95, 104–13

carmen deductum, 1, 4–5, 7, 8, 14, 15, 63, 159–65

carmen perpetuum, 1–3, 5, 7, 15, 63, 159–65

Castor of Rhodes, 96

catalog poetry, 15, 73

catasterism, 22

Catullus: 16n.57, 24, 70; and Callimachus, 11, 25, 128n.145; and hamadryads, 116; and Parthenius, 24

causae, ix, 5, 25, 27, 52, 64, 65, 132, 133, 147

Cephalus, 107, 159

Cerberus, 38

Cercopians, 102

Ceyx and Alcyone, 36–37

Chaos, 43, 44

Cicero: and Hellenistic poetry; 11, 23–24, and paradoxography, 148–49

Cinna, 11, *Smyrna,* 24

Cipus, 129–30

Circe, 105, 109

Ciris: 22; and metamorphosis, 30

Cleanthes, 10

Clymene, Song of (Vergil), as cosmogony, 7, 12

Cornelius Gallus: 8, 16n.57, 24, 62, 116n.99; and hamadryads, 115–16

Cornelius Nepos, and aetiology, 95–96

Cornificius, 24

cosmic epic. *See* cosmogonic epic

"cosmogonic aetiology," definition of, 5–15

cosmogonic epic: as Callimachean, 5, 12, 162; didactic, 11, 13–14; and dual Homeric/Hesiodic tradition, 11, 12, 14; Ennius as model, 10, 12, 160, 162; as grand epic, 5, 11–13, 14; Hesiod as model, ix, 5–10, 12, 14; Homer as model, 9–11, 14; and Lucretius, ix, 6, 10, 54–55; *Metamorphoses* as, ix, 5–7, 13–15, 25, 40–41,

metamorphosis (*continued*)
93, 131. *See also individual authors and works*
Midas, 28
Minerva, 74–76
Minyeides, 34, 79–80, 152
Moschus, *Europa*, 22, 70
Muses: appeal to as authority, 19, 68, 163; and Callimachus, 68, 74, 163; and the Camenae, 111; "contest" of, 163–64; Hesiod's initiation by, 68
Myrrha, 38, 164
mythology: aetiological, vii-ix, 5, 16, 22, 27–29, 135; allegorized, 51–52, 55, contrasted with philosophy, 19–20, 25, 41, 49–54, 57; distinction between mythology and philosophy blurred, 135, 147, 158; explanatory function of, 58; juxtaposed with philosophy, 25, 29–30, 57, 132, 135, 147, 153–54, 157–58; modernized, 15; rationalized, 50, 54, 146, 150, in Vergil, 132

Naevius, and the Camenae, 111
natural philosophy: and aetiology, viii, 29; in Hellenistic literature, 58; and myth, 135; in Ovid, viii, 6, ch. 1 *passim*, 63, 81, ch. 4 *passim;* and paradoxography, 21, 148; in *recusatio*, 11, in Vergil, 8–9. *See also* cosmogony; cosmology; philosophy
neoteric poetry: ix, 4, 9, 11, 12, 13, 15, 22, 24, 25; and Callimachus, 4, 12; and epic, 9, 12; and Hesiod, 9; and Homer, 9; and metamorphosis, 23–25; and Ovid, ix, 13, 15, 60, 62–63, 78–79, 101–2, 116, 125, 164; and Parthenius, 24; "scientific" themes of, 11; and Vergil, 8, 25, 102
Nestor and Achilles, 72, 73, 75
Nicaenetus of Samos, 15
Nicander: 6, 10, 23; and aetiology, 23, 30, 32, 34, 58–59, 66, 85; as didactic, 30; Galinthias, 32–33; Hecuba, 31; Latona and the Lycians, 85–86; metamorphosis in, 31; Minyeides 34; parallels with the *Metamorphoses*, 31–34, 74n.62; 85–86, 95, 100, 101, 122n.123; science and myth combined in, 29–30
Numa, 81–82, 110, 136–37, 141, 158

Ocyroe, 166
Orion's daughters, 100

Orpheus: viii, 73, 109, 123n.125; 163–65; as catalogue poetry, 73; as cosmogonic and Callimachean narrator, 165; as elegiac 73, 165; as *vates* 165
Ovid: belief/disbelief, 20, 20n.69, 25, 93–94, 132, 159; exploits tension between poetry and philosophic authority, 19, 27, 49, 51, 56–57, 132, 156; reversal of (Lucretian) philosophical physics, 48, 55–57, 135, 142–44, 157–58; and poetic autonomy, 56–58, 93, 126, 132, 145n.59, 159; refusal of consistent authoritative voice, 14, 20, 57, 69, 93, 132, 158, 164; remythologizing, 54–57, 136; as self-conscious narrator, 58, 73, 93, 132, 159. *See individual works*

Palace of the Sun, as cosmological, 44
paraclausithyron, 121–23
paradoxography: ix, 29, 146–49, 155, 165; and aetiology, 147–48; Alexandrian, 21–22, 29, 79,148; Diomedes' men in, 102; and metamorphosis, 21, 135, 147–49; and natural philosophy, 21, and "Pythagoras," 146–49, 155, 157
Parmenides, 52
Parthenius, 24; and aetiology, 24; Cydus, 24; metamorphosis in, 24; Scylla, 24
pastoral. *See* bucolic epic
Pausanias, 151
Peleus and Ceyx, 72
Perdix, 34–36
Perimele, 90
Perseus and Andromeda, and aetiology, 75–77, 107, 156
Phaethon, as ecpyrosis, 44
Phanocles, 15, 22, 22n.80
philosophy: 25, 39, 50, 52, 53; attack on mythology/divinities in, 50n.84, 52–54, 143–46; and creation of poetic authority, 18, 21, 53, 57; debate with mythological poetry, 19–20, 25, 27, 41, 49–54, 144–45, 157–58; distinction between mythology and philosophy blurred, 135, 147, 158; truth claims of, 52, 57; use of poetry, 52; and Vergil, 9, 132. *See also* cosmology; cosmogony; mythology; natural philosophy; *individual authors and works*
Philostephanus of Cyrenaeus, 90n.128, 122n.123, 148

physiological theory of humors, 42–47, 53, 135
Picus, 32n.15, 38, 39, 40, 114; and Canens, 38, 95, 104–13
Pierides, 34, 40, 89n.122, 90n.124, 91, 102, 164–65
Plato, and the critique of myth, 145
Pliny the Elder: 28, and natural marvels, 148, 149–51, 152n.79, 153, 155–56
poetry: ancient critical theories of, 49, 50, 51, 58; autonomy of, 49–50, 56, 58, 145; and authority, 52, 59, 70; criterion of verisimilitude, 50–52, 58; defended, 52; as *"fabula,"* 50–51; and the fantastic, 50–51; lying and, 50–51, 144–45; and philosophy/ dichotomy, 49–52; poetic illusion, 58, 93; "poetic license," 50–51, 144; use of philosophy for authority, 53. *See also* authority; belief/disbelief; fictionality; truth
Polyphemus, 101
Pomona, 108; and Vertumnus, 95, 113–27, 128
Pre-Socratics, 52
Proca, 113, 127
Propertius: 16, 61n.1, 122; and aetiology, 18, 64, 65, 71, 86, 97–98; and Achelous, 91n.129; and Alexandrianism, 87–88; and Augustus, 126; and Callimachus, 16, 18, 71, 86–88, 98, 119, 120, 127; and didactic, 69n.40; generic tensions in, 88; hamadryads, 115; Hercules and Cacus, 86–90; internal narrators in, 71, 88; as model for Ovid, 86–90; nationalistic themes and aetiology, 98; and Vergil, 71, 97; Vertumnus, 71, 118–21, 124, 126, 127
prophecy, 142–43, 161, 166
Pygmalion, 28, 165n.137
Pyramus and Thisbe, as *aetion,* 80
Pythagoras, Speech of: 6, 21, 25, 27, 41, 45, 46, 51, 58, 59, 73, 80, 113, 132, ch. 4 *passim;* and aetiology, 136–38, 165; Aetna, 140, 154–55; Ammon, 152–53; animal marvels, 155–57; and Apollo, 142; attack on animal sacrifice, 139; authority, appeals to, 140, 153n.81, 155; audience response, 158–59; and belief, 139; *bugonia,* 156; Clitor, 153–54; combination of science and myth, 135, 147, 151, 153–54, 157–58; denunciation of poetic fictions/myth, 144, 150, 153, 157; didactic features of, 139–

40; dissimilar to natural philosophical treatises, 149–59; generic associations of, 159–65; Hyperboreans, 154; as internal narrator, 135, 139, 159; "inversion" of physics, 135, 142–44, 157–58; as literary figure, 162–63; and Lucretius, 139–40, 141–44, 151, 155, 157–58; natural marvels, 135, 146, 152–54; and metamorphosis, 147, 154–57; metempsychosis, 134–35, 165; and multiple causes, 140; and Muses 142; and mythological explanation, 150, 153; parallels with poem, 133–35, 139, 146, 147, 151, 155–57; and paradoxography, 135, 147–59, 165; phoenix, 156–57; and scientific theory, 151, 154–55; as unscientific, 134–36, 142, 149, 151, 157; as *vates,* 142–44, 159; and vegetarianism, 137–38
Pythian games, foundation of, 62

Quintilian, 51

recusatio, 4, 11, 12, 13, 13n.43, 63, 164
Romulus, deification of, 46n.68, 126, 129

Salmacis fountain, 152, *aetion* for, 79–80
scientific epic. *See* cosmogonic epic
scientific poetry: and Alexandrianism, 10, 12; and Hellenistic poetry, 10–11, 29; at Rome, 5, 11, 12; truth claims in, 51. *See* cosmogony; cosmology; natural philosophy; philosophy
Scylla, 22n79, 24, 38, 99; as *aetion,* 101
Seneca, 148; explanations for natural marvels, 149–51, 153–55
Sibyl, 99, 102
Silenus, Song of (Vergil): 7–8, 12, 75n.66; as internal narrator, 8, 71; mythological cosmogony in, 7–8, 12; as natural philosopher, 8
Simylos, 96
Stoics, 9, 10, 43, 138
Strabo, 148; explanations for natural marvels, 149–52
swans, and poetry, 110–11
Syrinx and Pan, 56, 63; as aetiological narrative, 77–79

Tages, 47, 129
Theocritus: 3, 8, 10, 78, 101; and internal narrative, 70; and *carmen deductum,* 8; and epic tradition, 3; and Vergil *Ecl.* 6, 8

Theodorus, 23
Theogony, 41
theologia tripertita, 131n.163, 132
Theophrastus, as source for paradoxography, 29
Theseus, 90–92
Tibullus, and Roman aetiology, 98
Tiresias, 28, 93
Tithonus, 102
Triad of narrative forms, 50
Truth claims: and fiction, 51, 58, 156; in didactic, 19, 51–53, 69, 84, 143, 159; and philosophy, 52, 57, 156. *See also* authentication; authority; belief/disbelief

Valerius Cato, 24
Varro Atacinus, 11
Varro: 110, 114; and aetiology, 96; *bugonia,* 156; and etymology, 38, 96; and paradoxography, 148–49; and philosophy, 50n.84
vates, 14, 18, 69, 129, 142–43, 159, 165
Venus, as internal narrator, 66; Prospiciens, 120, 123–24
Vergil: 2, 5–15, 49, 52, 54, 78; and allegorization of Homer, 11–12; authority, 20, 97; and Callimachus, 8; and the Camenae, 111; and cosmology, 7, 11–12, 54; and hamadryads, 115; and Lucretius, 6, 8, 54, 57; and philosophy, 6, 9, 12; and the Roman epic tradition, 2; and neotericism, 8, 25, 102; use of internal narrators for cosmogony, 7, 9, 13, 71; and valorization, 57, 97, 132
Vergil, *Aeneid*: Achaemenides, 101, 104, 105n.47; "Aeneid" framework in the *Metamorphoses,* 95–113; and aetiology, 16, 17, 20, 64, 66, 71, 97, 104, 132; aetiology as authentication, 97, 132; Aeneas as aetiological investigator, 71, 92n.133; and

Apollonius, 97; and Augustus, 103; and Callimachus, 71; Circe, 105; codification of Roman myth, 127; and cosmology, 11, 12, 14, 54; Diomedes, 100, 102; and Ennius, 97; generic polyphony of, 12, 103; Helenus, 161; as heroic epic, 5, 14; and Homer, 11–12, 104; Iopas, 12; Latinus,107; metamorphosis in, 25n.90, 100, 131; "other voices" in, 103; philosophy and history in, 161; Picus, 107–8; Polyphemus, 101; Virbius, 129
Vergil, *Eclogue* 6–8, 13, 25, 41, 75n.66, and aetiology, 8, 25; and Alexandrianism, 8, 71; and Callimachus, 8, 71; and cosmogony, 7–8, 12, 13, 41; and Gallus, 8; and grand epic, 8; and erotic themes in, 8; and Hesiodic model of scientific poetry, 8; internal narrator in, 8, 13, 71; and Lucretius, 8; metamorphosis in, 8, 25; and natural philosophy, 8–9; and neoteric poetry, 8, 25
Vergil, *Georgics*: 9, 12, 13, 14, 25, 54, 78, 80n.83, 140; and aetiology, 66; *bugonia,* 155n.86, 156; Clymene as a cosmological poet, 7, 12; combination of nationalistic and natural-philosophical themes, 12; and cosmogony, 7, 12; as cosmological epic, 9, 14; and grand epic, 12; internal narrator, 13, 70; philosophy and myth, tension between, 156; *recusatio* in, 12; Scylla, 102; and theory of four elements, 54
Vertumnus, 28; and Janus, 127–28; and Pomona, 95, 113–27; 128; and Priapus, 120, 126
Virbius, 128–29, 135, 166
Vitruvius, on marvelous waters, 151–53
Vulcan, 165n.137

Xenophanes, 52